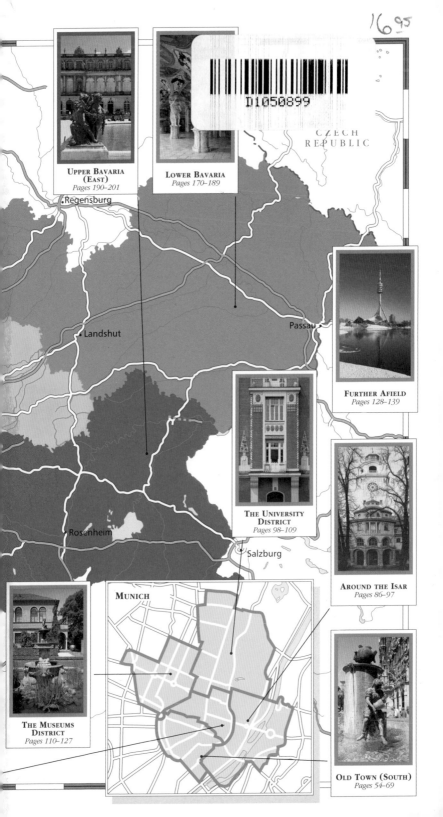

16 95

UPPER BAVARIA
(EAST)
Pages 190–201

LOWER BAVARIA
Pages 170–189

CZECH
REPUBLIC

Regensburg

Landshut

Passau

FURTHER AFIELD
Pages 128–139

THE UNIVERSITY
DISTRICT
Pages 98–109

Rosenheim

Salzburg

AROUND THE ISAR
Pages 86–97

MUNICH

THE MUSEUMS
DISTRICT
Pages 110–127

OLD TOWN (SOUTH)
Pages 54–69

EYEWITNESS *TRAVEL GUIDES*

MUNICH
& THE BAVARIAN ALPS

DK EYEWITNESS *TRAVEL GUIDES*

MUNICH
& THE BAVARIAN ALPS

IZABELLA GALICKA
KATARZYNA MICHALSKA

DK PUBLISHING, INC.
LONDON • NEW YORK • MUNICH
MELBOURNE • DELHI
www.dk.com

DK Publishing, Inc.

www.dk.com

Produced by Wydawnictwo Wiedza i Życie S.A., Warsaw

CONTRIBUTORS Izabella Galicka, Katarzyna Michalska
CONSULTANT Sergiusz Michalski
ILLUSTRATORS Lena Maminajszwili,
Bohdan Wróblewski, Piotr Zubrzycki
PHOTOGRAPHERS Dorota and Mariusz Jarymowiczowie
CARTOGRAPHERS Magdalena Polak, Dariusz Romanowski,
Kartographie Huber (Munich)
JACKET DESIGN AND GRAPHICS Paweł Kamiński
GRAPHIC DESIGNER Paweł Pasternak
EDITORS Robert G. Pasieczny, Dorota Szatańska
TECHNICAL EDITOR Anna Kożurno-Królikowska
DESIGNERS Ewa Roguska, Piotr Kiedrowski

Dorling Kindersley Limited
EDITOR Lucilla Watson
TRANSLATOR Mark Cole (Linguists for Business)

Printed and bound in Italy by Graphicom s.r.l.

First American Edition 2002
2 4 6 8 10 9 7 5 3 1
Published in the United States by Dorling Kindersley Publishing, Inc.,
95 Madison Avenue, New York, NY 10016

Library of Congress Cataloging-in-Publication Data

Galicka, Izabella.
  Munich & the Bavarian Alps / main contributors, Izabella Galicka,
Katarzyna Michalska.
    p. cm. -- (DK eyewitness travel guides)
  Includes index.
  ISBN 0-7894-8328-9 (alk. paper)
  1. Munich (Germany)--Guidebooks. 2. Alps, Bavarian (Germany)--
Guidebooks. I. Title: Munich and the Bavarian Alps. II. Michalska,
Katarzyna. III Title. IV. Eyewitness travel guides.

DD901.M76 G35 2002
914.3'3640488--dc21
                                        2001047748

> **The information in every
> Dorling Kindersley Travel Guide is checked regularly**.
> Every effort has been made to ensure that this book is as up-to-date as
> possible at the time of going to press. Some details, however, such as
> telephone numbers, opening hours, prices, gallery hanging arrangements
> and travel information are liable to change. The publishers cannot
> accept responsibility for any consequences arising from the use of this
> book, nor for any material on third party websites, and cannot guarantee
> that any website address in this book will be a suitable source of travel
> information. We value the views and suggestions of our readers very
> highly. Please write to: Publisher, DK Eyewitness Travel Guides,
> Dorling Kindersley, 80 Strand, London WC2R 0RL.

THROUGHOUT THIS BOOK, FLOORS ARE REFERRED TO IN ACCORDANCE WITH EUROPEAN
USAGE, I.E., THE "FIRST FLOOR" IS ONE FLIGHT UP.

CONTENTS

HOW TO USE
THIS GUIDE *6*

**Gothic figure of a Dancing Moor
from the Stadtmuseum, Munich**

INTRODUCING
MUNICH
AND THE
BAVARIAN ALPS

PUTTING MUNICH
& THE BAVARIAN ALPS
ON THE MAP *10*

A PORTRAIT OF THE
BAVARIAN ALPS *16*

**View of Munich, with the Neues
Rathaus in the foreground**

A verdant, flower-filled meadow near Schwangau, in the Allgäu

The Propyläen in Munich,
designed by Leo von Klenze

Weißwurst with sweet mustard
and pretzel: a Bavarian snack

The Frauenkirche,
one of Munich's most
prominent landmarks

HOW TO USE THIS GUIDE

THIS GUIDE will help you to get the most out of your stay in Munich and the Bavarian Alps. The first section, *Introducing Munich and the Bavarian Alps,* locates the city and the region geographically and gives an outline of its history and culture. The subsequent sections, *Munich Area by Area* and *The Bavarian Alps*

Area by Area, describe the main sights and attractions. Feature spreads, with maps, illustrations and drawings, focus on important sights. Information about accommodation and restaurants is given in *Travellers' Needs,* while the *Survival Guide* provides useful tips on everything you need to know, from money to getting around.

MUNICH AREA BY AREA

In this guide, Munich has been divided into five central areas and a Further Afield section. Each area is described in an individual section, giving the names of all the main sights and attractions. The sights are numbered on the area maps.

Sights at a glance lists the buildings in a particular area by category: churches, museums and art galleries, historic buildings, and streets and squares.

2 Street-by-Street Map
This gives a bird's-eye view of a particularly interesting sightseeing area described in the section.

Stars indicate the sights that no visitor should miss.

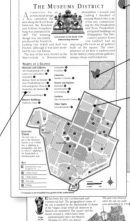

All pages relating to Munich have red thumb tabs.

A locator map shows at a glance where you are in relation to the city plan.

1 Area Map
For easy reference the sights in each area are numbered and located on an area map, as well as on the Munich Street Finder on pp144–9.

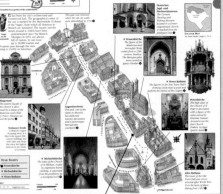

A suggested route takes in some of the most interesting streets in the area.

3 Detailed Information
All the important sights of Munich are described individually. The address, telephone number, opening hours, admission charges, how to get there and disabled access are given for each sight.

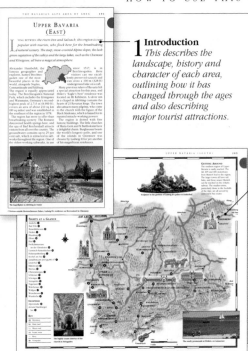

1 Introduction
This describes the landscape, history and character of each area, outlining how it has changed through the ages and also describing major tourist attractions.

THE BAVARIAN ALPS AREA BY AREA
In this guide the Bavarian Alps are divided into six areas, each of which is described in an individual chapter. The most interesting places to visit are marked on the area map.

2 Pictorial Map
The pictorial map shows the main roads and the main sights in the area. All sights are numbered, and information is given on how to get there.

Colour coding makes each area in the guidebook easy to find.

3 Detailed Information
All the important towns and other places to visit are described individually. They are listed in order, following the numbering on the pictorial map. Each entry contains detailed information on opening times and how to get there.

Stars indicate works of art and architectural features that no visitor should miss.

For all the top sights, a Visitors' Checklist provides the practical information you will need to plan your visit.

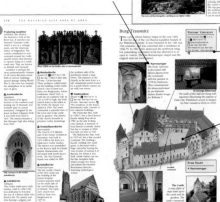

4 Major Sights
At least one page is dedicated to each major sight. Historic palaces and parks are shown in detail. Dissected views of buildings and floorplans of museums and galleries and buildings are colour-coded to show you the best ways to enjoy the exhibits.

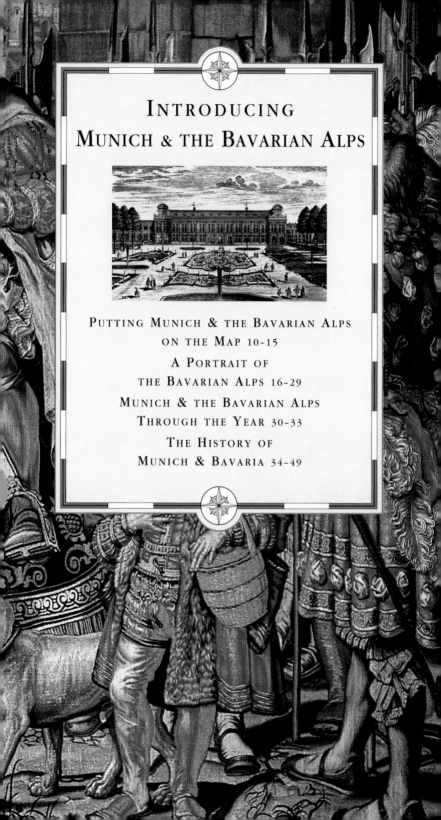

INTRODUCING
MUNICH & THE BAVARIAN ALPS

Putting Munich and the Bavarian Alps on the Map

SOUTHERN BAVARIA, the southernmost part of Germany,
consists of three administrative regions: Upper
Bavaria (Oberbayern), Swabia (Schwaben) and Lower
Bavaria (Niederbayern). The region borders the Czech
Republic, Austria and, across Lake Constance,
Switzerland. To the north it is bounded
by the Danube, and the
south by the Alps.
Munich, on the River
Isar, is the capital
(Land), with 1.3
million inhabitants.

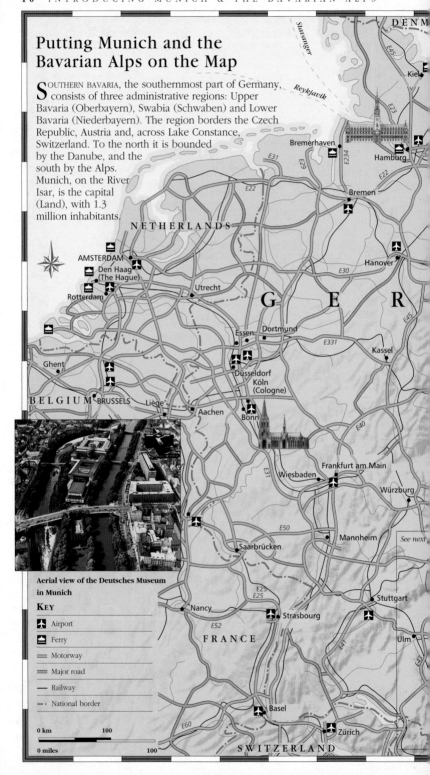

**Aerial view of the Deutsches Museum
in Munich**

KEY

✈	Airport
⛴	Ferry
▬	Motorway
▬	Major road
─	Railway
∙∙∙	National border

0 km   100

0 miles   100

See next

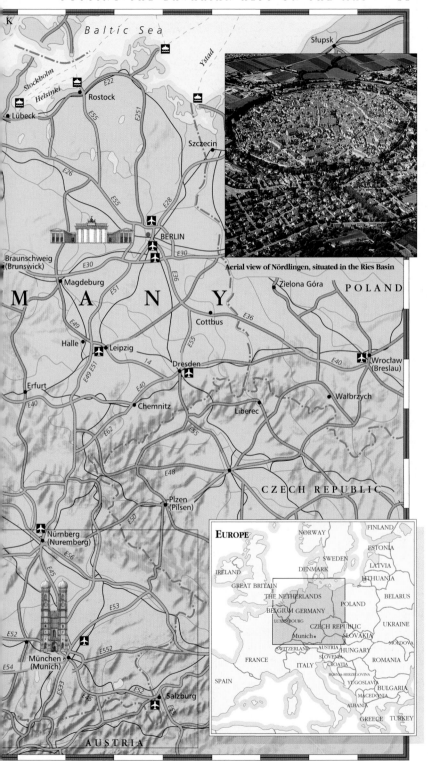

Baltic Sea

Słupsk

Stockholm
Helsinki
Ystad

Lübeck

Rostock

Szczecin

BERLIN

Braunschweig
(Brunswick)

Magdeburg

M A N Y

Zielona Góra

P O L A N D

Halle

Leipzig

Cottbus

Dresden

Erfurt

Chemnitz

Liberec

Wałbrzych

Wrocław
(Breslau)

C Z E C H   R E P U B L I C

Plzen
(Pilsen)

Nürnberg
(Nuremberg)

München
(Munich)

Salzburg

A U S T R I A

Aerial view of Nördlingen, situated in the Ries Basin

EUROPE

NORWAY   FINLAND

SWEDEN   ESTONIA

IRELAND   DENMARK   LATVIA

                                   LITHUANIA

GREAT BRITAIN

THE NETHERLANDS   POLAND   BELARUS

BELGIUM GERMANY

LUXEMBOURG   CZECH REPUBLIC   UKRAINE

Munich   SLOVAKIA

SWITZERLAND   AUSTRIA   HUNGARY   MOLDOVA

FRANCE   SLOVENIA   ROMANIA

                CROATIA

ITALY   BOSNIA-HERZEGOVINA

                YUGOSLAVIA   BULGARIA

SPAIN   MACEDONIA

                ALBANIA

                GREECE   TURKEY

Greater Munich

MUNICH, THE CAPITAL of Bavaria, is
divided into 12 districts. The Old Town
(Altstadt) is surrounded by the Altstadtring,
or ring road, while a larger area is bounded
by the Mittlerer Ring, or central ring road.
The outskirts of the city can easily be
reached by the suburban railway known as
the S-Bahn. Some 30 km (19 miles) to the
northeast of the city centre is the major
Franz-Josef-Strauß International Airport.

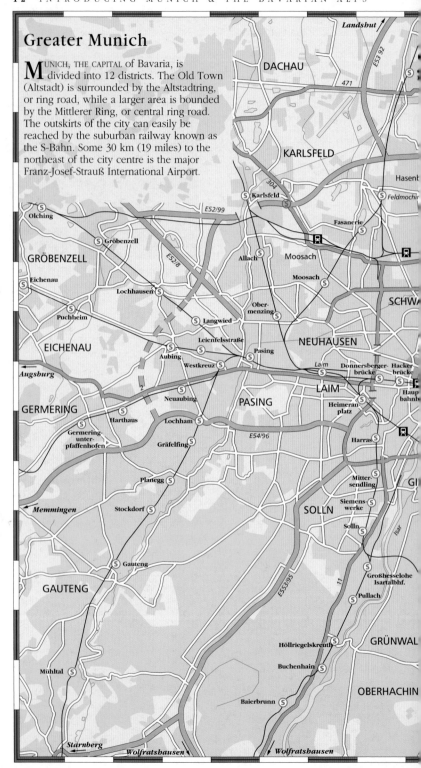

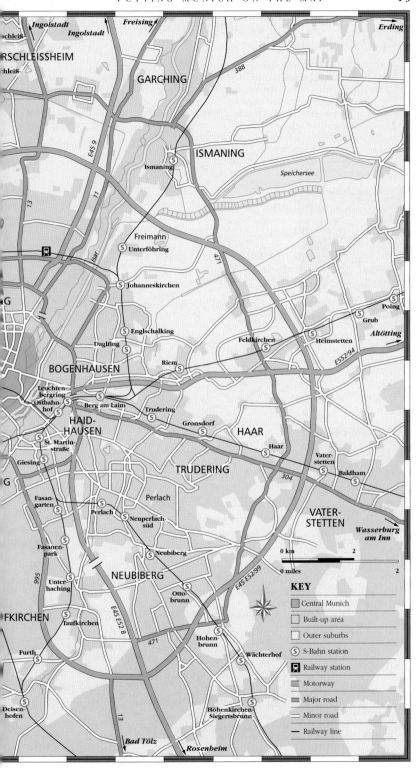

Central Munich

CENTRAL MUNICH boasts a variety of architectural styles, and each of the five areas has its own unique atmosphere. Marienplatz, and the Old Town around it, abounds in old-world architecture, and is the main tourist area. Along the River Isar, green areas are flanked by grand 19th-century urban thoroughfares. The great thoroughfare of Ludwig-straße/Leopoldstraße sets the tone for the northern quarter, which includes the picturesque Schwabing and Englischer Garten districts. The suburb of Maxvorstadt to the northeast has a wealth of museums and art galleries.

Lenbachhaus
*The home of the
19th-century portrait
painter Franz von Lenbach
is built in the style of an
Italian villa and is fronted
by a picturesque garden.*

Asamkirche
*Also known as the
Church of St Johann
Nepomuk, it is named
after the Asam brothers
who built it. The finest
work of their careers, it
is also one of the most
outstanding examples
of European Baroque
architecture.*

New Town Hall
*The coat of arms on the
New Town Hall features
the monk who
symbolizes Munich.
The city took its
name from the
legendary monks
(Munchen meaning
"monk settlement")
who settled there.*

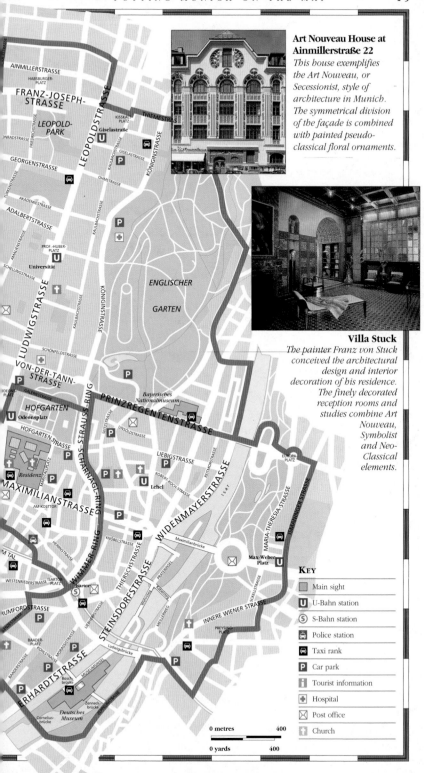

Art Nouveau House at Ainmillerstraße 22
This house exemplifies the Art Nouveau, or Secessionist, style of architecture in Munich. The symmetrical division of the façade is combined with painted pseudo-classical floral ornaments.

Villa Stuck
The painter Franz von Stuck conceived the architectural design and interior decoration of his residence. The finely decorated reception rooms and studies combine Art Nouveau, Symbolist and Neo-Classical elements.

KEY

⬜	Main sight
U	U-Bahn station
Ⓢ	S-Bahn station
🚓	Police station
🚕	Taxi rank
P	Car park
ℹ	Tourist information
✚	Hospital
⊠	Post office
✝	Church

0 metres 400

0 yards 400

A Portrait of the Bavarian Alps

THREE OUT OF *every four Germans say they would like to live in Bavaria, especially southern Bavaria. As it is one of the most picturesque and also one of the most prosperous parts of Europe, this is not so surprising. For many foreigners, Bavaria is quintessentially German; this is not, however, strictly true, as Bavaria has always nurtured its own distinct political framework and culture.*

Southern Bavaria is inhabited by three main groups of people: a branch of the Swabian tribes of Württemberg, in the western region, who are the descendants of the legendary Baiuvarii; the Upper Bavarians, in the central region, and the Lower Bavarians, centred in the eastern region.

To this day, there are still distinct regional differences in the Bavarians' dialect, folklore and cuisine and, arguably, in their mentality as well. The shared characteristics that they have are a love of tradition, a certain conservatism and a strong sense of loyalty to the Free State of Bavaria (Freistaat Bayern).

White and sky-blue, the colours of the Bavarian flag

Bavarian culture and customs were developed as much in court circles as by the peasantry. This development on two social levels has left its mark on the character of the people and their traditions. The latter include an affinity with the soil, and a tendency to a certain stubbornness and defiance coupled with warm hospitality and friendliness. These qualities are combined with tolerance and at times a fondness for absolute rulers and politicians ranging from men such as Maximilian I, Maximilian I Josef and Franz-Josef Strauss to eccentrics and dreamers such as Ludwig II.

Summer in the old quarter of Lindau

◁ **A beer hall during Oktoberfest – Munich's famed beer festival**

Peaceful sub-alpine landscape

THE LANDSCAPE OF THE BAVARIAN ALPS

When they look up at the sky, the Bavarians see the colours of their national flag – white and sky-blue. On clear days the sky takes on a Mediterranean translucence; this may be because Bavaria is the bridge between northern Europe and the Mediterranean region. Munich is in fact much closer to Venice than it is to Berlin.

Bavaria's mild climate and varied scenery combine to create an idyllic landscape. Lush green meadows populated with grey and brown Alpine cattle alternate with thick woodland, countless brooks and streams, rocky outcrops, lakes and rolling hills, against which rise majestic Alpine peaks. When the famous *Föhn* (warm Alpine wind) blows, the Alps can be clearly seen from as far as 100 km (60 miles) away.

The local architecture complements the scenery perfectly. Picture-postcard towns and villages, large monasteries, castles and palaces, and village churches with their onion domes fit together in perfect harmony. A typical feature of the region is the way in which high art is combined with kitsch. Exquisite Baroque churches and monasteries with ephemeral frescoes stand side by side with simple peasant art, while the splendid Neo-classical architecture of the Wittelsbachs contrasts with the enchanting fairy-tale castles of Ludwig II.

Bay window of a house in Garmisch-Partenkirchen

RELIGION, TRADITION AND CULTURE

Bavaria is a land of defiant, ritualised Catholicism, which once effectively blocked the march of Protestant Germany to Rome. It is no surprise then to find that Bavaria

Nativity scene on a house in Hindelang – a 20th-century example of Lüftlmalerei (the Bavarian art of façade painting)

has its own conservative ruling party, the CSU, and that in place of the ubiquitous "Guten Tag", the people here greet each other with "Gruß Gott" ("Greetings to God"). The Bavarian national anthem, which is played every day when the local television station closes for the night, begins with the words: "God be with you, land of Bavaria."

Futuristic style of the BMW works in Munich

Catholic ritual is omnipresent – during the celebration of Sunday Mass, at innumerable church fairs, and during processions and pilgrimages. However, piety expresses an affirmation of life rather than prudishness. Many stereotypes are attached to the Bavarians: among the best known are green hats with feathers in them, short *Lederhosen* and knee-socks, beer-mugs joyfully held on high.

Folk traditions have survived too: perhaps nowhere else in the world is there such a proliferation of folk festivals and music groups. Almost everywhere you can see the characteristic but regionally differentiated men's *Trachten*, which includes a short jacket with bone buttons, and the women's *Dirndl*, with their wide, low-cut dresses and a narrow waistcoat. Simplified versions of these costumes are also worn as everyday clothing, even by Bavarian politicians. More refined and lavish versions are worn when attending official functions or going to the opera.

Beer-drinking is another integral part of Bavarian folk tradition. Some 1,100 breweries work to quench beer-lovers' thirst. Bavaria has some of the oldest breweries in the world (including the Weihenstephan brewery), and it was the first place where a ducal decree (1516) banned the

Decoration for a maypole

use of any other ingredients than millet, hops and water in beer-making. The best way to drink beer is from a large, litre mug, known as a Maß, or "measure", preferably in a beer garden beneath a chestnut tree, in the cellars of a monastic brewery, or in a marquee to the strains of folk music, as during the famous Oktoberfest.

THE SOURCES OF BAVARIA'S WEALTH

For centuries farming and trade have been the main source of Bavaria's wealth . It is the largest supplier of farm produce in Germany. It also has the largest hop harvest in the world. After World War II Bavaria's economy expanded enormously, with some of Germany's largest companies based here, such as Audi, BMW and Siemens. Bavaria has chemicals, aircraft, printing, electronics and tourism industries.

The Maß – the best way to drink beer

Landscape of the Bavarian Alps

Southern Bavaria is one of Germany's most
picturesque and scenically varied regions. To the
south it is bordered by the Alps, with their breathtaking
limestone peaks and verdant slopes. To the north it is
bounded by the Danube, with its marshy flood plains.
The region's landscape consists of undulating hills and
many lakes and mountain streams, which were formed
by glaciers during the Ice Age. Much of the terrain takes
the form of pasture and fields, or is covered in forests,
while industrialization has remained unobtrusive.

*Alpine meadows are
covered in lush grass
which produces high-
quality hay and provides
rich grazing for cattle.*

*A hop plantation in Hallertau, which is
the largest hop-producing region in
Bavaria. Wooden poles overgrown with
hops are a characteristic sight.*

Mountain peaks
with breathtaking
escarpments are a
common sight.

**Local
buildings**
harmonize
with the
surrounding
landscape.

*Mountain streams have over millennia
cut their way through the Alpine rocks,
creating scenic gorges. The picturesque
Wimbachklamm is accessible to hikers.*

SOUTHERN BAVARIAN LAKES

Huge glaciers that melted
centuries ago left many
lakes in southern Bavaria.
Their limpid waters attract
watersports enthusiasts
and swimmers. This
breathtakingly beautiful
environment is ideal for
walking and many other
outdoor activities.

*This marina on Chiemsee,
also known as the Bavarian
Sea, is one of the finest spots
in southern Bavaria for
amateur yachting.*

The Zugspitze, rising to a height of 2,963 m (9,725 ft), is the highest German peak.

Forests are thick and extensive, many of them in a pristine state.

Plants and Animals of the Bavarian Alps

Southern Bavaria's varied natural scenery has remained largely unspoiled thanks to careful protection and clean air. Animals and plants occur in several bands of vegetation. While in the higher parts of the Alps only mosses and lichens grow, at altitudes of under 1,500 m (4,900 ft) there is an abundance of flora and fauna. The forests contain a wealth of plants, animals and birds, while the extensive meadows and marshes are covered in various grasses, and the clear waters of the rivers and lakes are home to many species of fish. The parks and nature reserves help to preserve endangered species.

The grey-brown Alpine cow is especially common in the Allgäu, a region known for its dairy products.

Goats are able to negotiate rough terrain and steep slopes and are a common sight on mountain hikes.

Marmots peep out from mountain screes and crevasses, emitting their characteristic whistling call.

Ravens appear in large flocks over ploughed fields, searching for worms and leftover grains of corn.

Trout is the most common species of fish to be found in Bavaria's mountain streams. They thrive in the clear, unpolluted waters.

Butterflies share the flowery Alpine meadows with bees, gadflies and grasshoppers. The most colourful of the butterflies is the peacock butterfly.

Edelweiss is an increasingly rare sight in the Alps. This protected Alpine flower is a favourite decorative motif in the Bavarian national costume.

The gentian is the "national" flower of Bavaria. It is honoured in song and is used in making the famous gentian schnapps.

Architecture of the Bavarian Alps

THE ARCHITECTURAL LANDSCAPE of southern Bavaria features a large number of churches and monasteries. These noble buildings, in perfect harmony with the surrounding landscape, are topped by onion-domed towers. Although each architectural era created a legacy of fine buildings, it was during the Baroque period (the late 16th to the early 18th century) that the region flourished architecturally. Many new churches built, and existing ones were endowed with stunning ornamentation. In southern Bavaria architectural splendours were also built in the 19th century. These include the Neo-Classical monasteries and the fairy-tale residences of Ludwig II.

Statue in Michaelskirche in Munich

***Altenstadt basilica** is one of Bavaria's many Romanesque buildings.*

GOTHIC

The Gothic style of architecture is widely represented in Bavaria, although its impact in Europe went far beyond this region. As well as in surviving town houses, the Gothic style in Bavaria is seen in fortified residences and religious buildings. A specific regional characteristic is the wide nave of Gothic churches. The oldest Gothic church was built in Laufen. The largest is the Frauenkirche in Munich, and the most resplendent is the Martinskirche in Landshut. The use of pointed arches and ribbed vaulting made it possible to create much higher, light-filled spaces. Gothic architecture reached its apogee in the mid-15th century.

***The Chapel of St Sigismund** in Blutenburg Castle is a typical example of late Gothic religious architecture.*

Entrance to the church of St Ulrich and St Afra, Augsburg

RENAISSANCE AND MANNERISM

The Renaissance reached Bavaria from Italy via Augsburg, where in 1510 the Renaissance chapel of the Fugger family was built. This set the style for the architecture of town houses (as at Landshut, Neuburg and Augsburg). At the end of the century it was overtaken by Mannerism, which departed from classical forms.

The window is set under a broken pediment.

Carvings contrast with the austere façade.

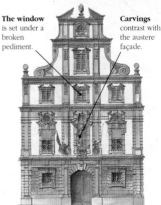

The façade of the Arsenal at Augsburg, designed by Joseph Heintz the Elder in 1607, is a fine example of Mannerism, distinguished by a flat façade and the rejection of classical proportions.

***The Archangel Michael overcoming Satan** displays dramatic poses typical of Mannerism.*

BAROQUE

No architectural style left such a strong impression on southern Bavaria as did the Baroque. Its highly decorated, almost theatrical style held a special appeal, and it was expressed in skilfully articulated spaces to which abundant ornamentation was added. The first Baroque buildings were by Italian architects, but a local school was soon producing work of the highest quality. The Bavarian Baroque reached its height with the Asam brothers *(see pp66 & 68–9).*

The vaulting of Passau Cathedral is a fine example of late Baroque forms derived directly from Italy. Despite the excessive stuccowork and elaborate fresco decorations, the main architectural elements are still discernible.

The façade of the church of Berg am Laim illustrates the typical Baroque rhythm of architectural elements, accentuated by cornices, pilasters and columns.

The windows of the Neues Schloss in Schleißheim are framed and decorated with rosettes and mock-antique masks. Doorways and windows with exuberant ornamentation were highly characteristic of Baroque architecture.

NEO-CLASSICISM

The Neo-Classical style developed in France in the 18th century. After 1806, when Bavaria proclaimed itself a kingdom, it was adapted to serve the purposes of the Napoleonic Empire Style. Neo-Classicism reached the peak of its splendour after 1816, but was confined to Munich. Ludwig I intended to rebuild the city to turn it into "Athens on Isar". To this end the court architect Leo von Klenze designed many fine buildings, with references to ancient Greece and the Italian Renaissance.

This capital of a column in the portico of the Glyptothek is decorated with typically Ionic scrolled volutes.

The Prinz Karl Palais, by the architect Karl von Fischer, is a typical example of early Neo-Classical architecture. It is fronted by an imposing portico with Ionic columns supporting a tympanum.

An akroterion is a decorative element often used in Classical architecture.

The tympanum of the Propyläen contains sculptures of Otto I and other kings of the Greeks. Otto I abdicated before the building was completed. The people mocked: "Do not glorify the day before the sun is down – the proof is the Propyläen."

Sculptures in a style evoking the glory of ancient Greece were carved by Ludwig Schwanthaler.

Monasteries and Abbeys

A SURPRISING FEATURE of the Bavarian Alps is the large number of monasteries and abbeys that are to be seen here. The first Benedictine monastery was founded in the early Middle Ages. In the 11th and 12th centuries monastic establishments were built in the foothills of the Alps. The next period at which such building activity flourished was the Baroque, when medieval abbeys were rebuilt and new ones, such as Ottobeuren and Ettal, were constructed. In the 18th century, with the spirit of the Enlightenment, fine libraries with valuable collections of books were built. The secularization of more than 160 monasteries in 1803 led to the destruction of a large part of Bavarian monastic culture.

Figure of the emperor in Kaisersaal

Altarpieces *often take the form of large statues of saints or of one of the Church Fathers. They are a prominent feature of church interiors.*

Heilig Kreuz-Kapelle
The Chapel of the Holy Cross is one of the few monastic chapels open only to monks. Such chapels were used for gatherings and for silent prayer away from the outside world. Their decoration is no less lavish than that of the rest of the monastery.

The church interior *is graced by numerous altars, and the architectural features, mouldings, paintings and furniture combine to form a unified whole.*

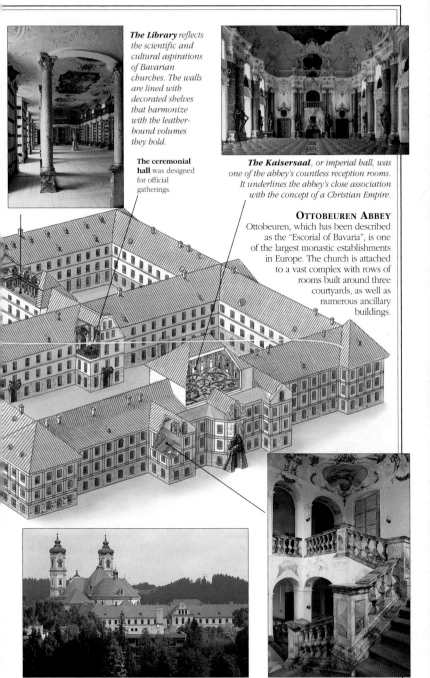

The Library *reflects the scientific and cultural aspirations of Bavarian churches. The walls are lined with decorated shelves that harmonize with the leather-bound volumes they hold.*

The ceremonial hall was designed for official gatherings.

The Kaisersaal, *or imperial hall, was one of the abbey's countless reception rooms. It underlines the abbey's close association with the concept of a Christian Empire.*

OTTOBEUREN ABBEY

Ottobeuren, which has been described as the "Escorial of Bavaria", is one of the largest monastic establishments in Europe. The church is attached to a vast complex with rows of rooms built around three courtyards, as well as numerous ancillary buildings.

Ottobeuren Abbey *blends with the sub-Alpine landscape in a way that is characteristic of many Bavarian monasteries, with their red roofs and their tall belfries. In spring and summer, the entire building stands in striking contrast to the lush greenery with which it is surrounded.*

The staircase, *a feature of conscious pomp and elegance, shows the importance that abbeys attached to the appearance of public reception areas.*

Art of the Bavarian Alps

Late Gothic miniature in Passau Museum

ART IN THE region developed in two main directions, against the background of the major trends in European art. The ecclesiastical and ducal protectorate, and later that of free cities, led to the development of important artistic centres in Munich, Augsburg, Landshut and Passau. Schools of painting, sculpture and craftsmanship developed as early as the Gothic period, and the Renaissance and Mannerism also left their mark. But it was in the Baroque period that the arts of fresco, stucco and sculpture reached their peak. Folk elements meanwhile were always a feature of Bavarian art, taking the form of votive images, roadside shrines and mural paintings on village houses.

This man with a shield is a late Gothic figure from Ottobeuern Abbey.

ROMANESQUE AND GOTHIC ART

Romanesque art is characterized by a stylization rooted in Byzantine art. As well as the crafts and sculpture, southern Bavaria has interesting examples of mural painting. The windows of Augsburg Cathedral are as important as the finest examples elsewhere in Europe. The Gothic period, which continued until about 1520, brought in a new style, primarily in the way that human figures were depicted, with flowing garments and expressive gestures. By about 1500 Gothic painting and sculpture had their greatest exponents in Jan Polack and Erasmus Grasser.

Masks are placed at the intersections between panels.

Bas-reliefs are of allegorical and Old Testament subjects.

Door handles take the shape of lions' masks.

The Moriskentänzer is one of ten expressive carvings by Erasmus Grasser of Moors in a court dance. According to custom, the men would dance in sophisticated poses, and capture the ladies' attention with elegant gestures. These sculptures are a rare example of secular subject matter in Gothic art.

The bronze doors of Augsburg Cathedral show the influence of Byzantine art. They initially consisted of four wings, with a total of 224 reliefs. Only 35 remain today.

GREAT ARTISTS

1400	1450	1500	1550
	1450–1518 Erasmus Grasser		**c.1540–99** Friedrich Sustris	
		c.1460/65–1524 Hans Holbein the Elder	**c.1500–62** Christoph Amberger	**c.1570–1634** Hans Krumper
		1516–73 Hans Mielich		
One of Erasmus Grasser's Dancing Moors	**c.1435–1519** Jan Polack	**1473–1531** Hans Burgkmair	**c.1548–1628** Peter Candid de Witte	**c.1570 164** Hans Reich
			c.1550–1620 Hubert Gerhard	

RENAISSANCE AND MANNERISM

The southern Bavarian Renaissance was influenced by Italy and the Netherlands, but it developed its own elements. The crafts flourished, and in sculpture and painting new themes, such as genre scenes, classical mythology and portraiture, appeared. The most prominent artists of the time were the Augsburg painters Hans Holbein the Elder, Hans Burgkmair and Christoph Amberger. Mannerism developed in the mid-16th century, its most outstanding exponents in southern Bavaria being Hans Krumper and Hans Reichle.

This portrait of Felicitas Seiler by Christoph Amberger is typical of Renaissance portraiture in that it shows a certain rigidity of pose combined with a care to capture the sitter's individuality and accurately depict the costume. The coloration reveals a Venetian influence.

This ornamental cup dating from 1570–80 was made in one of Augsburg's famous goldsmiths' workshops. The work of Augsburg goldsmiths graced many churches and grand houses in Europe.

BAROQUE

During the Baroque period the walls of churches, monasteries and palaces were lavishly covered with stucco mouldings and trompe-l'oeil paintings. An important centre for such art was Wessobrunn. From the 18th century the prominent Asam brothers began working in Bavaria *(see p66)*. Lüftlmalerei, paintings on the walls of houses *(see p208)*, is a typically Bavarian phenomenon. Fine Rococo sculpture was produced by Ignaz Günther and Johann Baptist Straub, while the court artist François Cuvilliés refined the art of Rococo decor to perfection.

This traditional wardrobe is from the renowned furniture-making centre in Bad Tölz. The distinctive furniture made here was covered in folk paintings. Sideboards, beds and the carts associated with the St Leonard's Day festival can be seen in the town's local history museum.

This amber sculpture from the Bürgersaal in Munich by Ignaz Günther embodies all the elements of the late Baroque: pathos, levity and dynamism.

1601–34 Georg Petel	**1692–1750** Egid Quirin Asam	
		Guardian angel by Ignaz Günther
1680–1758 Johann Baptiste Zimmermann		
1600	**1650**	**1700**
1609–82 Johann Heinrich Schönfeld	**1686–1739** Cosmas Damian Asam	**1704–84** Johann Baptist Straub
Portrait of Cosmas Damian Asam	**1695–1768** François Cuvilliés	**1725–75** Ignaz Günther
	1697–1776 George Desmarées	

Traditions of the Bavarian Alps

BAVARIA IS A land where old local traditions and folklore are cultivated and revered. Almost every town and village has its own local holiday, with folk bands, beer-drinking and general merriment in the streets. These events variously involve folk dancing and fire-work displays. The Catholic tradition is strong in the region, the countless religious feast days and church processions often coinciding with fairs. Many places also commemorate local historical events.

Landshut Wedding newly-weds

PASSION PLAYS

ONCE EVERY ten years the mountain village of Oberammergau becomes the centre of the Easter mystery plays *(Passionsspiele)* that are performed over four months from late May to early October. This tradition dates back to 1633.

At that time, so as to ward off the plague, the villagers vowed to act out scenes from the Passion of Christ. Initially these were staged outside the church, but since 1930 they have been held in a special open-air theatre with seating for 4,800. The performances, lasting from morning until late afternoon with a break in between, take place five days a week. According to tradition, the actors must be residents of Oberammergau by birth. The lavish decorations and the costumes, of which there are over 1,000, are provided by the local populace. The scenes, accompanied by a choir and music, are performed by amateur actors in a natural and expressive way. Against the backdrop of mountains they have the realism of *tableaux vivants*.

The Passion plays have gained world renown, and tickets must be booked well in advance. A similar tradition exists in certain other Bavarian villages.

THE MAYPOLE

ON 30 APRIL each year, small groups of people can be seen beside fires, drinking beer and watching over a long, barkless tree trunk. Recovering a tree trunk stolen by the inhabi-tants of the neighbouring village is rewarded by a large number of barrels (or today, cases) of the Bavarians' favourite drink. Next day the trunk is decorated and ceremonially raised in the village square.

According to tradition, the maypole, the pride of every local community, ensures a successful year. The custom of raising the maypole, the tree of life, goes back to medieval times. Usually painted in the Bavarian colours of white and blue, maypoles are decorated with the emblems of local crafts and crowned with a large wreath. Traditions include dancing round the maypole and climbing up it to reach the prizes tied to the wreath.

Residents of a small town joining forces to raise the maypole

LANDSHUT WEDDING

IN 1475, Landshut saw the wedding of Georg, son of Ludwig the Rich, and Princess Jadwiga of Poland, daughter of Casimir Jagiellon. The celebrations lasted eight days, and went down in history as one of the most sumptuous in medieval Bavaria.

Since 1903 the Landshut Wedding (Landshuter Fürstenhochzeit) has been re-enacted every three years on three weekends in June and July. About 100,000 visitors come to enjoy this historic drama. Medieval costumes are worn during the young couple's triumphal procession, which is accompanied by court dances and by tests of the skills of knights and squires.

Christ stumbling under the Cross during the Oberammergau Passion play

THE OKTOBERFEST

THIS FAMOUS beer festival, the world's largest, began in 1810, when Princess Theresa von Sachsen-Hildburghausen married Ludwig (later to become King Ludwig I), the heir to the Bavarian throne. Horse races were organized in a meadow on the edge of Munich, which was named the Theresienwiese in honour of the young lady. It was decided to make this a regular event, and gradually it became customary to organize agricultural shows, which were combined with equestrian events and shooting contests. To these were added roundabouts, beer tents and fireworks, thus giving rise to the present Oktoberfest (it was moved from October to September due to the weather).

Today the Oktoberfest attracts some 6 million visitors from all over the world. Year after year the record for amounts of beer, sausages and roast chickens consumed at the festival is broken. The Oktoberfest opens with a grand procession of waggons of the city's seven main breweries accompanied by folk bands. On the stroke of noon, the city's mayor broaches a barrel of beer to open the two-week revelry surrounding the city's fair.

Folksong and beer – the world-renowned Oktoberfest

THE CHRISTMAS FAIR

ADVENT, which comes from the Latin *adventus*, "the coming", is the period in the Christian calendar leading up to Christmas. It starts on the fourth Sunday before 24 December. In Bavaria this period is marked with a number of rituals.

Advent candles are lit in churches and in people's houses, and special biscuits known as *Plätzchen* are baked. In the larger towns and cities, market stalls are set up for the Christmas fairs, which are known as *Christkindlmarkt* or *Weihnachtsmarkt*. They begin with the ritual raising of a huge Christmas tree in the brightly illuminated market squares.

Wooden decorations, Nativity figures and all sorts of delicacies and gifts are displayed for sale round the tree. The air is filled with the delicious aroma of freshly baked gingerbread and roasted almonds. The rituals also include drinking hot wine (*Glühwein*) in the frosty air. St Nicholas and the Wicked Witch distribute apples and nuts to children, and the holiday atmosphere is heightened by the joyful singing of carollers. The best Christmas fairs in southern Bavaria are those that are held in Munich, Augsburg and Landsberg.

BAVARIAN FOLK COSTUME

TO MANY people, traditional Bavarian folk costume epitomizes Bavaria. Nowhere else in Europe is traditional costume so widely celebrated, and no other national costume has become so well known in Europe. The traditional men's *Tracht* includes: *Lederhosen*, leather shorts held up by leather braces and sometimes tied up at the knees; the *Janker*, a waistcoat of rough cloth with bone buttons; the *Gamsbart*, a hat with a goat's hair tassel, and asymmetrically tied shoes. Women wear the *Dirndl*, a blouse with puffed sleeves, a corset, a waistcoat, a crimped skirt and an apron. Jewellery and ornaments are an important element of Bavarian costume. Men's trousers are decorated with chains with pendants and their shirts have letters, medallions, coats of arms and embroidery. The women wear intricate necklaces and richly decorated chokers.

Illuminated tree, the focal point of a Christmas market

Bavarian in national costume

MUNICH & THE BAVARIAN ALPS THROUGH THE YEAR

THE BAVARIAN CALENDAR is filled with picturesque rituals, historical spectacles, festivals and trade fairs. The type of event depends on the season, and in Bavaria they are varied indeed. The snowy winter is the season for skiers and toboggan-ists, while hikers enjoy walking along the scenic and well-marked trails. From springtime

Turnfest mascot

onwards, colourful paragliders can be spotted as they soar over mountain peaks, and the appear-ance of sails heralds the start of the yachting season on the lakes. The summer attracts moun-taineers, hikers and watersports enthusiasts. Almost everyone can be seen during the famous Oktoberfest, which starts in the middle of September.

SPRING

SPRING comes early here. At the beginning of April, fruit trees are in blossom, Alpine meadows become carpeted with flowers, mostly crocuses, and the melting Alpine snow creates rushing streams. Numerous festive ceremonies mark the Easter period in Bavaria. Easter traditions centre on the symbolism of the egg. Houses are decorated with

Crocus from a meadow

ornamental twigs with Easter eggs hanging from them, while excited children are up early searching every nook and cranny of their homes for Easter eggs. In May, the blossom of chestnut trees forms a canopy over reawakening beer-gardens.

MARCH

Starkbierfest *(between Ash Wednesday and Good Friday)* Munich. The Festival of Strong Beer commemorates the strong ale that was drunk by Pauline monks as they observed the Lenten fast.
Internationale Jazzwoche *(last two weeks in March)*, international jazz festival taking place in Burghausen.

APRIL

Biennale *(April/May)*, Munich. Germany's largest contemporary music festival.
Augsburger Plärrer *(two weeks after Easter)*, Augs-burg. Biannual event (also held in September). The largest folk festival in Swabia, the counterpart to the Oktoberfest.
Auer Dult (Maidult) *(from the last Saturday in April)*, Munich. Renowned fair held in the Mariahilfplatz in the city's Au district.

MAY

Trachten- und Schützen-festzug *(first Sunday in May)*, Passau. Large procession of folk groups and bands from Bavaria and Austria open this annual fair.
Maibaumaufstellen *(May 1)*. Virtually every Bavarian community honours the custom of Raising the Maypole *(see p28)*.

Typical Fronleichnam (Corpus Christi) procession

Maibockausschank *(May 1–14)*, Munich. The occasion when the strong Bockbier is broached. It begins in the Hofbräuhaus to the sounds of a children's orchestra.
Fronleichnam *(Thursday after Trinity Sunday)*. According to Catholic tradition, this religious festival in honour of Corpus Christi is marked by countless processions. The most picturesque are in Lenggries and Bad Tölz.

The Augsburger Plärrer – the biggest traditional holiday in Swabia

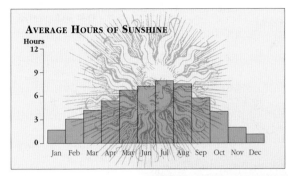

Average Hours of Sunshine
Hours
12
9
6
3
0

Jan Feb Mar Apr May Jun Jul Aug Sep Oct Nov Dec

Sunshine
The greatest number of sunny days are concentrated in the period from June to September. May can also be sunny. December is the least sunny month.

SUMMER

O N SUMMER DAYS the blue skies over Bavaria reach an almost Mediterranean intensity. Cascades of flowers hang from balconies and window boxes. Bathers and watersports enthusiasts are drawn to the crystal-clear rivers and lakes. Almost every resort has its own summer festival, and these celebrations are particularly impressive when they are held by a lakeside. They feature regattas, firework displays and angling contests.

JUNE

König-Ludwig-Feier *(24 August)*, Oberammergau. Festival commemorating the death of Ludwig II, who drowned in the Starnberger See. The occasion is marked with singing, dancing and speeches.
Stadtgeburtstag *(one weekend in June)*, Munich. Festival commemorating the foundation of the city.
Filmfest München *(last week in June)*, Munich. One of Europe's liveliest and most important film festivals.
Tollwood Festival *(second week in June)*, Munich, Olympic Park. Festival of jazz, rock and theatre.

JULY

Kaltenberger Ritterspiele *(first 3 weekends in July)*, Kaltenberg Castle, near

Agnes Bernauer Festspiele in Straubing

Landsberg. Jousting tournaments re-enacting medieval traditions.
Münchener Opernfest-spiele *(1–31 July)*, Munich. Festival of classical opera, ballet, singing and music.
Landshuter Hochzeit *(every three years, the next in 2004)*, Landshut. Spectacle commemorating the marriage of Georg, son of Ludwig the Rich, and Princess Jadwiga *(see p28)*.

Poster for the Auer Dult fair

Schwäbischwerder Kindertag *(1st Wednesday and Sunday in July)*, Donauwörth. Children dressed in historical costume re-enact important events in the history of the town.
Agnes Bernauer Festspiele *(every four years, the next in 2004)*, Straubing. Historical theatre festival telling the story of Duke Albrecht III and Agnes Bernauer, an Augsburg barber's daughter.
Memminger Fischertag *(early July)*, Memmingen. Trout-angling competition.

AUGUST

Auer Dult (Jakobidult) *(July/August)*, Munich. One of three annual fairs held in the Au district of Munich.
Schleißheimer Schloß-konzerte *(July/August)*, Schleißheim. Concerts of classical music.
Gäubodenfest *(around mid-Aug)*, Straubing. Folk festival combined with an agricultural and industrial fair, Bavaria's second largest after the Oktoberfest.
Allgäuer Festwoche *(mid-August)*, Kempten. Exhibition of the Allgäu region's economic and cultural achievements, also including an important folk festival.

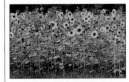

Sunflowers, symbols of summer, a common sight in Bavaria

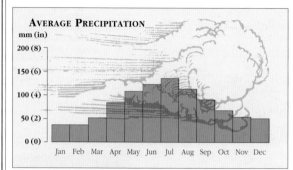

AVERAGE PRECIPITATION

mm (in)

200 (8)
150 (6)
100 (4)
50 (2)
0 (0)

Jan Feb Mar Apr May Jun Jul Aug Sep Oct Nov Dec

Rain and snowfall
Although the autumn drizzle is the most unpleasant, the heaviest rainfall occurs in summer. Intensive snowfall is common in winter, particularly in the Alps and the foothills.

One of the vast beer tents at the Oktoberfest

AUTUMN

BAVARIAN AUTUMNS are often warm and sunny. The forests turn every shade of red and gold, and mushroom-pickers return with baskets filled with many species of edible fungi. The mountain pastures echo to the sounds of herded cows and sheep, and the air is filled with the smell of decaying leaves and smoke.

In autumn the sky becomes dull and overcast, and the shortening days are chilly and damp. The first overnight frosts set in, and mornings often start with a blanket of thick fog, which causes problems for road and air traffic.

SEPTEMBER

Oktoberfest *(16 days leading up to the 1st Sunday in October)*, Munich. The city's world-famous beer festival *(see p29)*.

Viehscheid *(second half of September)*. Traditional celebration of the cattle being brought down from summer pastures in many areas, including Hindelang, Oberstdorf and Königssee.

OCTOBER

Oktoberfest *(see September)*.
Auer Dult (Herbst Dult) *(third Saturday in October)*, Munich. The third of the annual fairs held in the Au district of Munich.
Mode-Woche *(week after the Oktoberfest)*, Munich. The second major fashion event of the year *(see February)*.
Systems *(third week in October)*, Munich. International IT and telecommunications fair held on the grounds of the Neue Messe in Munich.
Medientage München *(around mid-October)*, Munich. Fair dedicated to the mass media.

NOVEMBER

Leonardifahrten und Leonardiritte *(1st Sunday in November)* throughout Bavaria. In many areas, such as Bad Tölz, Schliersee, Murnau and Benediktbeuern, processions on horseback or in painted carts take place in honour of St Leonard, regarded by Bavarians as the patron saint of horses. In Bad Tölz the horses re-enact Christ's journey on the road to Calvary in a procession after receiving a blessing.
St Martin's Day *(11 November)* throughout Bavaria. In almost every town and village processions are held in which children take part, carrying lanterns. Pretzels that they have been given hang from the lanterns. The processions are often led by a horse-rider in a long cloak who represents St Martin.

Bavarian women in a painted cart on St Leonard's Day

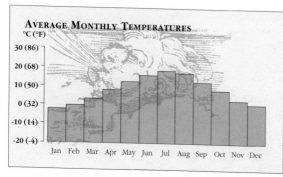

Average Monthly Temperatures
°C (°F)

30 (86)
20 (68)
10 (50)
0 (32)
-10 (14)
-20 (-4)

Jan Feb Mar Apr May Jun Jul Aug Sep Oct Nov Dec

Temperatures
Temperatures are highest in the summer, although temperatures rarely exceed 30°C (86°F). Winters are frosty and snowy, although they can be mild. The coldest temperatures are naturally in the mountains.

WINTER

As autumn draws to a close, people light the Advent candles on the Advent wreaths in their homes every week, while the smell of baking biscuits wafts through the air. At the beginning of December skiers set out on excursions, and if the lakes and canals are sufficiently thickly frozen, they are soon covered with skaters. Winters in southern Bavaria are unpredictable. They may be icy and snowy, or mild and snow-free. December is marked by the carnival spirit. Village carnivals are colourful affairs. At events associated with driving off winter with witchcraft, masks and costumes are a common sight.

The Skifasching (skiing carnival) in Firstalm

PUBLIC HOLIDAYS

Neujahr *New Year*
Epiphany (6 January)
Karfreitag *Good Friday*
Ostern *Easter*
Maifeiertag *May Day*
Christi Himmelfahrt
Ascension
Pfingsten *Whitsun*
Fronleichnam
Corpus Christi
Mariä Himmelfahrt
Assumption (15 August)
Nationalfeiertag
German Reunification Day
(3 October)
Allerheiligen *All Saints*
(1 November)
Weihnachten *Christmas*
(25/26 December)

DECEMBER

Christkindlmarkt *(early December to Christmas Eve),* throughout southern Bavaria. Christmas fair inaugurating the Christmas season with the ritual raising of the Christmas tree in the town or village square.
Sylvester *(31 December).* Sumptuous balls and receptions mark the New Year, which is ushered in with lavish firework displays.

Oberstdorf in winter during the Four Ski-Jump Tournament

JANUARY

Four Ski-Jump Tournament *(1–4 January),* Oberstdorf, Garmisch-Partenkirchen. Famous ski-jumping tournament.
Schäfflertanz *(Epiphany to Shrove Tuesday),* Munich. The Dance of the Coopers street festival held every seven years to commemorate the passing of the plague in the 15th century.

FEBRUARY

Tanz der Marktfrauen *(last day of Carnival),* Munich. Market women of the Viktualienmarkt dress up and perform a dance.
Skifasching *(last Sunday of Carnival),* Firstalm. Bavaria's most renowned skiing carnival, including a competition for the best fancy dress. Also held in Garmisch-Partenkirchen.
Mode Woche, Munich. Famous fashion designers, models and clients meet for this biannual event.

THE HISTORY OF MUNICH AND BAVARIA

O VER THE CENTURIES, *despite its location in the heart of Europe, southern Bavaria gradually built up its distinct character, becoming a geographically and culturally unified entity. Although it never played a leading role, it was one of the strongest duchies in Germany. The Wittelsbach dynasty ruled Bavaria until 1918, when the Free State of Bavaria (Freistaat Bayern) was proclaimed. After World War II Bavaria opposed centralization.*

EARLY SETTLEMENT

The first farming communities settled in southern Bavaria in the 4th millennium BC. Traces of their presence, in the form of the foundations of peasant huts, were found near Kelheim in the 1960s. During the period of the Altheim culture (about 2000 BC), peasant settlements were often surrounded by fortified ditches. During the Bronze Age (1800-1200 BC) the pace of cultural development accelerated, and a wealth of items from burials and many everyday tools of that period have been discovered. During the Hallstatt period, iron began to be used in preference to bronze.

THE CELTS

The Hallstatt period was marked by the appearance in Bavaria of the Celts, whose origins are not clear to this day. The Celts were distinguished by their loose tribal and family ties. The Vindelici tribe of Celts settled in

Lion statue outside the Residenz in Munich

the territory between the rivers Inn and Lech, and their capital was Manching, near Ingolstadt. The Bavarian Celts maintained links with the Mediterranean world, particularly with the Etruscans. They imported Etruscan, and sometimes Greek, luxury goods. Many later Bavarian towns, among them Regensburg (Ratisbon), Kempten, Straubing and Passau, were founded by the Celts.

THE ROMAN EMPIRE

In 15 BC the Roman army, under Drusus and Tiberius, conquered the Celts and reached the Danube. This became the frontier of the Roman Empire and a fortified wall was built to defend it. Southern Bavaria was divided into the provinces of Raetia and Noricum. The city of Vindelicorum, today Augsburg, was founded by the Emperor Augustus, whose name it still bears. It became the administrative centre of this part of the Roman Empire.

TIMELINE

10,000 BC Start of the Neolithic period	3000–2000 BC Appearance of the Altheim culture	1600 BC Bronze Age	700–500 BC Appearance of the Halstatt culture	15 BC Roman soldiers invade the area between the Alps and the Danube.	AD 162–80 The Marcomanni launch attacks that devastate southern Bavaria
150,000 BC	**3000 BC**	**1500 BC**	**600 BC**	**300 BC**	**AD 1**	**AD 300**
150,000–100,000 BC First human settlement in the Danube valley	2000–1800 BC Appearance of the first bronze artifacts	1200 BC Appearance of the earliest Beaker culture	500 BC First Celtic settlements in Bavaria	*Gilt mask from the Roman period*	AD 233–83 Fifty years of conflict between the Romans and Germanic tribes

◁ **Portrait of Ludwig I, king of Bavaria**

THE END OF THE ROMAN EMPIRE

After two centuries of peaceful development, Raetia and Noricum were attacked by two Germanic tribes, the Marcomanni and the Alamanni. The first attacks were repulsed by Emperor Marcus Aurelius, but the province suffered destruction in the mid-3rd century by invasions and civil war. Towards the end of the 3rd century stability returned for about 100 years, but after AD 400 a new wave of Germanic invasions toppled Roman control.

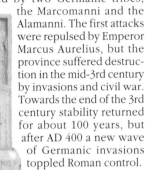

Roman stella from Augsburg

From those war-torn and troubled times there are records of the activities of the early Christians – St Afra, the martyr who was burned in Augsburg, and St Severinus, who revived missionary activity in the region.

THE GREAT MIGRATION AND EARLY CHRISTIANITY

The origins of the Bavarians are still imperfectly known. Most historians believe that a new tribe, whom the Romans knew as the Baiovarii, appeared south of the Danube, in the area of present-day southern Bavaria, in 450–550. They are thought to have originated from a Germanic tribe centred in Boiohaemum, what is today the Czech Republic. The Baiovarii were joined by remnants of other Germanic and Celtic tribes and by Romanized people. At the same time, settlers started appearing to the west of the River Lech. The Alamanni tribes became the neighbours of the Baiovarii to the west, while to the north, the region a few dozen kilometres beyond the Danube was conquered by the Franks. This situation continued virtually unchanged to the present day, with the addition of the territories beyond the River Lech and Bavaria's acquisition of the Franconian lands after 1803.

Most of the inhabitants of the region retained their pagan beliefs for some time, and Christianity took hold only very slowly. Irish, Anglo-Saxon and Frankish missionaries started preaching in the region in the early 7th century. At the turn of the 7th century, numerous bishops were active in Bavarian lands: Emmeram in Ratisbon, Korbinian in Freising, and Rupert in Salzburg. In 739 there were bishoprics in Ratisbon, Freising, Passau and present-day Salzburg. They were set up and run by the Anglo-Saxon missionary bishop, St Boniface. It is noteworthy that the importance of their sees continued for the next millennium. A key role in the establishment of Christianity and the nurturing of cultural development from the late 7th century and throughout the 8th century was played by the many Benedictine monasteries, particularly by those of Weltenburg and Benediktbeuern.

Roman mosaic with hunting scenes from a villa near Westerhofen

TIMELINE

450–550 Emergence of the Bavarian tribes	**476** Fall of the Roman Empire	**555** Garibald I becomes Prince of Bavaria	**c. 620** First monastery founded in Weltenburg	

400	450	500	550	600	650

400–30 Pressure from Germanic tribes overthrows Roman rule in Bavaria	**482** Death of the missionary St Severinus in Bavaria	**c. 630** *Lex Baiuvariorum,* the first book of Bavarian law, is written

Fragment from a Longobardi helmet

RULE OF THE BAVARIAN TRIBES

The Duchy of Bavaria was founded in the mid-6th century. The ruling Agilofing dynasty probably originated from the territories of the Merovingian state to the west, and was its vassals. The first known Duke of Bavaria was Garibald I (555–91). According to the *Lex Baiuvariorum*, the first legal code issued in those lands, the ducal throne was to belong to the Agilofing dynasty for all time.

Being dependent on the powerful Merovingians and weaker than the Frankish dukes to the north, Bavaria's Agilofing rulers were forced to resort to constant manoeuvring to retain their position. One of the ways in which they managed to preserve their rule was by strategic marriages with the Allaman, Longobardi and Frankish dynasties. Their activity within the state was limited to military leadership, while in peacetime they took charge of the judiciary. Despite this, the Agilofing dukes played a major role in Bavaria's development. Not only did they lay the foundations of the future state of Bavaria by ensuring its territorial unity, but they also played an important role in championing Christianity.

The main centre of ducal and ecclesiastic power was Ratisbon, on the River Danube. The duchy itself grew slowly and by peaceful means, and almost unnoticed it expanded into what was later to become Austria. Under the rule of Tassilo III (748–88), the last ruler of the Agilofing dynasty, the duchy extended as far as Carinthia. However, the growing might of the Agilofing dynasty and of its state alarmed the Frankish ruler Charlemagne, who defeated Tassilo in 788 and in so doing put an end to the Bavarian tribes' first state. Bavaria lost its independence and became part of the Frankish state, while Tassilo himself was confined to a monastery.

After the division of the Frankish empire under the terms of the Treaty of Verdun in 843, Bavaria became one of the centres of the East Frankish Empire (which was the embryo of the later Germany). The Emperor Arnulf of Carinthia resided in Ratisbon at the end of the 9th century.

The Cross of Tassilo from the church in Polling

Chalice of Tassilo, c. 777

Initial from an illuminated manuscript, depicting the martyrdom of St Emmeram, Bishop of Ratisbon

---

A fibula decorated with a geometric pattern

907 Hungarian tribes overrun Bavaria

788 Tassilo III is overthrown by Charlemagne

938 Emperor Otto's campaign against Duke Eberhard of Bavaria

750	800	850	900	950	1000

739 Bishoprics established in Freising and Passau

843 Division of the Frankish empire

900 Death of Emperor Arnulf leads to a period of instability

954 Hungarian tribes invade Swabia

738 St Boniface begins evangelizing Bavaria

Friedrich Barbarossa bestowing power on the Ottonians and Wittelsbachs

THE EARLY MIDDLE AGES

At the end of the 8th century, rulers proceeded to unify the Bavarian tribes and founded a new duchy. Throughout the 9th century the Bavarian dukes were in conflict with the Saxons, who took the Bavarian throne in 919. These conflicts ended in their defeat, and in the 10th century the German kings decided to appoint their own vassals to the Bavarian ducal throne, or to rule the duchy directly.

The following centuries brought a degree of stability with the rule of the Welf dynasty. Duke Henry the Lion founded Munich in 1158 and with the support of Bavaria and his possessions in Saxony waged a war against the Emperor Friedrich Barbarossa. He was finally defeated in 1180, and Bavaria lost the lands east of Salzburg. The same year, Frederick Barbarossa conferred the title of Duke of Bavaria on Otto I Wittelsbach. This powerful dynasty was to rule Bavaria right up until 1918, a

Late Gothic sculpture from Ottobeuren Abbey

record length of time for any German dynasty. The Wittelsbachs gradually built up their family possessions in central Bavaria, repelling successive attacks by rival families. In 1214 they annexed part of the Rhineland Palatinate, and by 1253 Bavaria was one of the largest ducal territories in the fragmented German empire.

THE LATE MIDDLE AGES

Under Ludwig IV of Bavaria, the duchy was at the height of its powers. Ludwig added the Margravate of Brandenburg, the Tyrol and part of the southern Netherlands to Bavaria. In 1314 he became king of Germany, and 14 years later he was crowned Holy Roman Emperor. External glory was reflected in internal changes. The Emperor introduced civic and land laws, and built up an administrative system with new central institutions.

From the end of the 14th century, tax affairs were decided by representatives of three ranks: knights, clergy and burghers. From the 15th century this group assumed the form of an assembly called the Landtag or Landschaft. After the death of Ludwig IV, Bavaria was shaken by an endless succession of conflicts and local wars.

TIMELINE

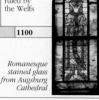

1070 Bavaria is ruled by the Welfs

1180 Otto Wittelsbach is made Duke of Bavaria

c.1200 The final edition of the *Nibelungenlied* appears in Passau

1328 Ludwig IV of Bavaria becomes German emperor

1100	1150	1200	1250	1300

Romanesque stained glass from Augsburg Cathedral

1158 Foundation of Munich by Duke Heinrich de Löwe

1214 The Palatinate is incorporated into Bavaria

1255 Munich becomes the capital of the duchy

1317 Fire destroys a large part of Munich

The sons of Ludwig IV attempted to divide the state into small duchies ruled by each of them. In spite of the poverty and sacrifice brought by the resulting wars, this situation had a positive aspect. The division and rivalry of the various ducal courts encouraged the development of culture.

Landshut underwent a period of splendour and in 1475 it was the venue of the sumptuous wedding of the daughter of Casimir Jagiellon, king of Poland *(see p28)*. However, in the Swabian territories on the River Lech, territorial disintegration continued in the 15th century. A leading role was played by the empire's principal city, Augsburg. The territory under the control of the Bishop of Augsburg also held a prime position.

Renaissance tombstone from the church in Oettingen

imperial parliament in Augsburg, the Protestants presented the articles of their faith, known as the Confessions of Augsburg, to the Emperor. Some Bavarian Protestants were forced to renounce their faith, while the following edict of 1571 finally removed all supporters of the Reformation from Bavaria. In the war of 1546–7 between Karl V and the Protestant dukes, Bavaria took the Emperor's side. The first Bavarian Jesuits fought actively against the Reformation. The great Michaelskirche in Munich was built in the late 16th century as a symbol of Bavarian Catholicism. In return for their allegiance to Rome, the younger sons of the Wittelsbachs were given sees in the west and north of the Empire, thus further strengthening the position of the Wittelsbachs on the German political scene.

THE RENAISSANCE AND COUNTER-REFORMATION

In 1506 the Bavarian states forced the adoption of a regulation that forbade the division of duchies: from then on, the throne passed to the eldest son. The Bavarian duchies were strengthened by the fact that their lands were not affected by the German peasants' wars of 1524-6.

The rulers of Bavaria were firmly opposed to the Protestantism that was spreading through the territories of Swabia and Franconia. In 1530, at the

Handing the Confessions of Augsburg to Emperor Karl V

1385 The first residence in Munich is built by Duke Stephan III

1516 The dukes of Bavaria issue the Reinheitsgebot, the world's first decree, enforced to this day, on brewing beer

1530 Protestants submit the Confessions of Augsburg to Karl V at the imperial parliament

1350	1400	1450	1500	1550

1369 The population of Munich exceeds 10,000

Martin Luther, father of the Reformation

1506 The states of Bavaria issue a decree forbidding the division of the country

1517 Luther's 95 "theses" launch the Reformation

1555 The imperial parliament declares a religious peace

THE AGE OF MAXIMILIAN I

Duke Wilhelm V, who came to the throne in 1579, brought the state to the edge of bankruptcy, abdicating in 1598 in favour of his son Maximilian I (1573–1651). During his 50-year reign, Maximilian reorganized the administration of the state and the military, streamlined the fiscal system and reigned in a kind of early absolutism. In the face of worsening religious and political conflicts in the empire, which ultimately led to the outbreak of the Thirty Years' War, Maximilian I took charge of the Catholic camp. In 1618 he supported the Habsburgs against the rebellious Bohemian state, and Bavarian troops played a decisive role in the defeat of the Bohemians at the Battle of White Mountain in 1620.

Bust of Maximilian I

As a reward for his part in this victory, Maximilian I was given the title of Prince Elector in 1623. The lands of the Upper Palatinate, which were added to Bavaria, were subjected to a brutal regime of re-Catholicization. During the second part of the Thirty Years' War, attacks by Swedish and Franco-Swedish forces caused a great deal of devastation and severely impoverished the country.

Finally, thanks to French support, Maximilian succeeded in retaining all conquered lands and the title of Elector at the peace congress in Münster. Pro-French policy would dominate Bavarian policy from then up until German Unification in 1871.

Maximilian's style and method of rule were emulated by later Bavarian leaders, including Duke Maximilian Montgelas and Franz-Josef Strauß. Bertel Thorvaldsen's equestrian statue of Maximilian in Munich commemorates his achievements.

DREAMS OF POWER

Maximilian II Emanuel, who married the daughter of the Polish king Jan III Sobieski, was known as the "White Knight". One of the most colourful figures in Bavaria's history, he had dreams of great conquests and of winning the crown. He allied himself with the Viennese court, and took part in the Battle of Vienna, where the Turks were defeated, in 1683. He was rewarded with the regency of the southern Netherlands. Entangled in the Wars of the Spanish Succession, he changed sides and in 1702 formed an alliance with Louis XIV.

However, in 1704 the Franco-Bavarian

Maximilian Emanuel receiving a Turkish emissary after his victory at Vienna

TIMELINE

1609 Maximilian I, Duke of Bavaria, founds the League of Catholic Rulers of the Empire

1618 An uprising in Prague sparks the Thirty Years' War

1623 The Duke of Bavaria is declared elector

1648 The Peace of Westphalia ends the Thirty Years' War. Bavaria retains the lands of the Upper Palatinate won in 1620–22

| 1600 | 1620 | 1640 | 1660 | 1680 |

1620 Maximilian I is victorious at the Battle of White Mountain, fought against rebellious Bohemian states

1645–8 Swedish and French troops devastate Bavarian lands

1683 An anti-Turkish coalition led by Jan III Sobieski is victorious at the Battle of Vienna

Patrona Bavariae *from the wall of the Residenz in Munich*

army was de-feated by Habsburg troops and Maximilian II Emanuel fled to France. Bavaria then suffered ten years of harsh Austrian rule during which protests by desperate peasants were suppressed with bloodshed.

Rococo window arch at the Residenz in Munich

Maximilian II Emanuel did not return to the elector's throne until a peace treaty was signed in 1715. Although he was a prominent patron of the arts and a popular leader, his lengthy and turbulent rule had weakened Bavaria's position.

Rococo monstrance from Passau

REFORM, ANNEXATION AND ENLIGHTENMENT

In 1740–45, despite Maximilian II Emanuel's disastrous anti-Habsburg policy, his son Karl Albrecht made a further attempt to become involved in the Austrian succession. As Karl VII, Emperor of Austria, he was, however, unable to repel the troops of Maria Teresa. At the Treaty of Füssen in 1745 his successor, Maximilian III Joseph, was forced to renounce claims to the Austrian throne.

During the long and peaceful reign of Maximilian III Joseph, in which the ideology of enlightened absolutism was put into practice, there were important agricultural reforms, as well as the foundation of the Bavarian Academy of Sciences in 1759. Another development was the famous Nymphenburg porcelain factory.

The king's death in 1777 ended the direct Wittelsbach line. Emperor Joseph II's orders to annexe Bavaria caused Prussian objections and led to the accession of Karl Theodor, an indirect descendant of the ruling family of the Palatinate. Karl Theodor continued his predecessor's policy of enlightenment, while the spirit of scientific enquiry was cultivated in Bavarian abbeys, which contributed to knowledge and culture.

With the outbreak of the Napoleonic Wars (1799–1815), Bavaria tried to remain neutral but was unable to protect its possessions in the Palatinate from French occupation.

Ornamental interior of the church of Weltenburg Monastery, one of many built in the Baroque period

1714 The Peace of Rastatt between Bavaria and the Habsburg Empire		1740 War of Austrian Succession breaks out, with Bavaria on the anti-Habsburg side	1759 Foundation of the Bavarian Academy of Sciences	1789 Start of the French Revolution
1700	1720	1740	1760	1780
1701–02 The Elector Maximilian II Emanuel makes an alliance with France against the Habsburgs		1745 Peace of Füssen between Bavaria and Austria	1777–9 War of Bavarian Succession	

Ornamental Rococo window of a town house in Straubing

The Wittelsbach Dynasty

IN 1180 Bavaria was given in lien to Otto I Wittelsbach, whose family ruled Bavaria until 1918. In 1329 the family was divided into a Bavarian and Palatinate line, which branched out even further. The Wittelsbachs occupied the German imperial throne on two occasions (in 1328 and 1742). In 1806 Napoleon proclaimed Maximilian I Joseph king. The family traditionally patronized the arts, which reached their apogee in the 19th century. The decline of the Wittelsbach dynasty began with Ludwig II, the "dilettante" king , and finally ended with the abdication of Ludwig III.

Wilhelm IV (1508–50) periodically shared his rule with his brother, Albrecht IV.

Otto II (1231–53) reformed the administrative and judicial system.

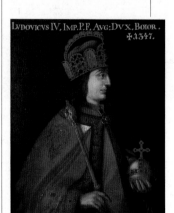

Otto I (1180–83) was the first Wittelsbach on the Bavarian throne.

Ludwig II, the Severe (1253–94) shared power with his brother Henry XIII. He moved the duchy's capital from Landshut to Munich.

Stephan II (1349–75) was one of six sons of Ludwig IV, who shared power among themselves.

Albrecht III, the Pious (1438–60) secretly married Agnes Bernauer, a baker's daughter, who was drowned in the Danube on his father's orders.

1150	1225	1300	1375	1450	1

1150	1225	1300	1375	1450	1

Ludwig I of Kelheim (1183–1231) extended Bavarian territory into the Rhineland Palatinate. He was stabbed on the bridge at Kelheim by an unknown assassin.

Johann II (1375–97), son of Stephan II, built the new Residenz in Munich with his three co-ruling brothers.

Ernest (1397–1438) ruled Bavaria for over 40 years, averting wars and conflicts.

Albrecht IV, the Wise (1467–1508) was the first humanist to occupy the Bavarian throne. He ended the influence of the Italian Renaissance.

LVDOVICVS IV, IMP. P. F. AVG : DVX, BOIOR.
✝ 1347.

Ludwig IV of Bavaria (1294–1347) was crowned king of Germany in 1314. He became Emperor in 1328, and this brought him into conflict with the Pope.

Maximilian II Emanuel (1679–1726), an ambitious but unfortunate ruler, caused Bavaria to fall under Austrian rule.

Maximilian II (1848–64), a highly educated ruler, was a great patron of science and the arts.

Karl Theodor (1777–99), a descendant of the Palatine family, united Bavaria and the Palatinate, which had been separated since 1329.

Ludwig II (1864–86) is remembered as an insane ruler who had fairy-tale residences built for him.

Wilhelm V, the Pious (1579–97) brought Bavaria to bankruptcy and abdicated in favour of his son Maximilian.

Karl Albrecht (1726–45) was crowned king of Bohemia, and later became Karl VII, Emperor of Germany.

Ferdinand Maria (1651–79) had a peace-seeking policy.

Ludwig III (1913–18) was the last and the most unfortunate king of Bavaria.

1600	1675	1750	1825	1900

1600	1675	1750	1825	1900

Maximilian I (1597–1651) was one of the leaders of the Habsburg-Catholic faction during the Thirty Years' War.

Ludwig I (1825–48) was a lover of the arts, antiques and women.

Maximilian I Joseph (1799–1825), crowned in 1806 while still a child, issued the Bavarian Constitution in 1818.

Albrecht V (1550–79) founded a fine library and also created the first art collection in Germany.

Luitpold (1886–1912) ruled the country as prince regent on behalf of the ailing king Otto I.

Maximilian III Joseph (1745–77) was more of an aesthete and composer, and did not have any great political ambitions. He was the last of the old Bavarian line of Wittelsbachs.

The Wittelsbach rulers of Bavaria

GOLDEN AGE OF THE WITTELSBACHS

The modern state of Bavaria was established at the beginning of the 19th century and it has survived more or less intact to this day. In 1803 Napoleon dissolved the German Empire's old territorial structures, and with his approval in 1803–06 Bavaria doubled its territory, incorporating the Swabian lands up to Ulm, and the Franconian lands. In 1806 Maximilian Joseph, again with Napoleon's approval, was crowned king, acquiring the title of Maximilian I Joseph.

Territorial expansion was accompanied by far-reaching internal reforms. In 1803 Maximilian I Joseph and his aide Count Maximilian Montgelas disbanded the monasteries and

Maximilian I Joseph, king of Bavaria

reorganized the country's administration. In late 1813 they deftly switched allegiance from Napoleon to the anti-Napoleonic coalition. Thus, at the Congress of Vienna they were able to retain the bulk of the territory that they had acquired with Napoleon's aid.

From 1815 to 1866 the Bavarian kings manoeuvred between the Prussians and Austrians, managing to conduct an independent foreign policy. This ended when the Prussians defeated the Bavarian-Austrian alliance.

Cartouche with Bavarian crest

In the latter half of the 19th century Bavaria made significant cultural and political advances. Education was developed and the re-established University of Munich flourished. Thanks to Ludwig I, Munich acquired impressive new parks, gardens and buildings. The visual arts and drama flourished, briefly overtaking those of Vienna and Berlin. Maximilian I Joseph's reign saw great progress in science and industry, and the emergence of "Maximilian" architecture. Ludwig I's patronage of the arts was continued by his grandson Ludwig II.

In 1866 Bismarck forced Bavaria to join the Prussian camp, which was supported by groups from the state bureaucracy and Franconian Protestant quarters.

TIMELINE

1803 Montgelas dissolves the Bavarian monasteries	**1813** Bavaria joins the anti-Napoleonic coalition	**1818** Bavaria becomes a constitutional monarchy		**1848** The revolution in Munich leads to the abdication of Ludwig I

1800	1815	1830	1845

1805 Bavaria forms an alliance with Napoleon

1806 Bavaria becomes a kingdom

1815 At the Congress of Vienna, Bavaria retains almost all its territorial gains from the Napoleonic period

The dancer Lola Montez, mistress of Ludwig I

UNDER PRUSSIAN RULE

Their country's participation on the victors' side in the Franco-Prussian war of 1870–71 won many Bavarians over to the idea of a unified Germany. Ludwig II, who ruled Bavaria at the time, increasingly avoided any involvement in politics and escaped more and more into the world of Wagner's music, tales of chivalry and fairy-tale castles. The day-to-day running of the country was left to an anonymous group of government officials in Munich.

When the regency was taken over by Prince Luitpold after Ludwig II's tragic death, little changed. Luitpold, a popular ruler, attempted to offset political dependency on Berlin with a liberal cultural policy which contained a distinct anti-Prussian element. Under Luitpold's rule, Munich enjoyed the highest period of cultural and artistic development that it has ever experienced. Luitpold's son and heir, Ludwig III, who was thoroughly pro-Prussian, quickly lost his popularity.

After Germany's defeat at the end of World War I, on 7 November 1918 the rule of the Wittelsbachs in Munich was overthrown, and the Free State of Bavaria (Freistaat Bayern) was proclaimed. This has been Bavaria's official name ever since. Between February and May 1919 the far-left Bavarian Soviet Republic ruled Munich and part of Bavaria. This weakened Bavaria's moderate forces and radicalized the right, which started to embrace extremist groups, such as Hitler's. In the general ferment of the Weimar

Ludwig II, much admired among Bavarians

Republic, Bavaria became a bastion of stability, with a slightly dictatorial right-wing government. The failure of Hitler's attempted putsch in 1923 helped to stave off Nazism for a while, but the mild sentences imposed on the leaders of the fascist Brownshirts only helped to increase their popularity.

From 1923 to 1933 the country was ruled by the Bavarian People's Party, whose policy was to oppose that of liberal and "red" Berlin. However, attempts to weaken Prussia's position in the Reich were unsuccessful, and political and cultural decline ensued. From 1918 to 1933 Munich's position as a cultural metropolis was taken over by Berlin.

Cartoon from a 1908 issue of the satirical journal *Simplicissimus*

66 Prussian War against Austria and Bavaria

1870–1871
Franco-Prussian War, in which Bavaria takes part

1900 Population of Munich reaches 500,000

Art Nouveau decoration on a house in Munich

9 November 1923 Hitler's attemped putsch in Munich

| 1875 | 1890 | 1905 | 1920 |

1886 Tragic drowning of King Ludwig II in the Starnberger See

Frieze from the Propyläen in Munich

1 August 1914
Outbreak of World War I

7 September 1918
Revolution in Munich overthrows the Wittelsbach dynasty

The Castles of Ludwig II

KING LUDWIG II of Bavaria, fondly known as "Kini" to his subjects, has remained a cult figure to this day. With his mad fantasies and lack of interest in politics, he seemed to come from another world. The king's passions were architecture and music, and his friendship with Richard Wagner influenced his entire life. He dragged the country into financial ruin as he built one magnificent country home after another, all the while dreaming of new ones. Gradually he became withdrawn and, deemed insane, was finally removed from power. At the age of 42 he drowned in the Starnberger See in mysterious circumstances.

This turret is reached by a spiral staircase leading from a picturesque gallery.

Ludwig II's Night Sleigh Ride
This painting by Richard Wenig, and the actual sleigh, can be seen in the Marstall-museum in Nymphenburg. The king adored his nocturnal escapades, which helped him avoid the harsh realities of daylight.

Throne Room of Neuschwanstein Castle
The Throne Room was designed in Byzantine style. It is decorated with gilded mural paintings, mosaics and a huge chandelier. A splendid gold and ivory throne planned for Ludwig II (see p226) was never made.

The Minstrels' Room
is a lavishly painted official reception room.

NEUSCHWANSTEIN CASTLE

The castle was built in 1868–86. Assiste by the painter and designer Christian Jank, Ludwig II fulfilled his vision of ar old German castle, although he only lived here for 172 days.

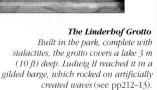

The Linderhof Grotto
Built in the park, complete with stalactites, the grotto covers a lake 3 m (10 ft) deep. Ludwig II reached it in a gilded barge, which rocked on artificially created waves (see pp212–13).

Hall of Mirrors in Herrenchiemsee Palace
This showcase gallery was built in 1879–81 along the side of the palace facing the garden. Almost 100 m (328 ft) long, it outstrips the Hall of Mirrors at Versailles, on which it is based. The ceiling frescoes glorify Louis XIV, and night-time concerts (see p198) were illuminated with 1,848 candles placed in the gilded candelabras and chandeliers.

Moorish Hall in Schachen
With its fountain, rich carpets, ottomans, gilded candelabra and vases, the hall of this palace conjures up The Tales of the Thousand and One Nights *(see p213).*

The upper courtyard leads into the main part of the castle, containing the reception room and apartments.

The gatehouse, flanked by turrets and set with crenellations, is decorated with the royal coat of arms.

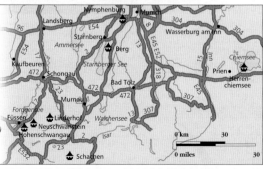

LUDWIG'S CASTLES

Ludwig II was obsessed with creating the perfect residence. In Alpine surroundings he built Neuschwanstein Castle *(see p226).* His fascination with the world of the Bourbons was expressed in the Linderhof *(see pp212–13)* and Herrenchiemsee *(see p198)* palaces.

Adolf Hitler signing the Munich Agreement

IN THE SHADOW OF THE NAZIS

The rulers of Bavaria underestimated the danger of the burgeoning Nazi movement. The participants in Hitler's 1923 putsch were given light sentences, with Hitler spending only eight months behind bars. In 1925 the NSDAP (Nazi Party) was reactivated, and in 1926 the ban on public speeches by Hitler was lifted. By 30 January 1933 Hitler had seized power, and in March he overthrew the Bavarian government and stripped Bavaria of its autonomy. Munich became Capital of the Movement; the Führer wanted it to become the Reich's ideological and cultural centre. The first concentration camp was built in nearby Dachau. During the Winter Olympics in Garmisch-Partenkirchen and the Summer Olympics in Berlin in 1936, the Nazis were at pains to present a positive image to the world. In 1937 Hitler embarked on an overt clamp-

Concentration camp prisoner's shirt

down in cultural policy. An exhibition of Degenerate Art was held in Munich, and later in other cities, its aim being to stigmatize modern "degenerate" art. The Haus der Kunst was built for annual exhibitions of German art. The large-scale redevelopment of Munich began, and the Königsplatz became the venue for Nazi rallies.

In 1938 the Munich Agreement, by which Czechoslovakia was partitioned, was signed and two years later the first Allied bombs fell on Munich. Hitler was associated with Bavaria until the end of his life, frequently visiting its capital and his residence near Berchtesgaden. Relatively few Bavarians spoke out against Hitler, a notable exception being the White Rose student group, and the opposition movement did not play a significant role here. In April 1945 an attempt was made to organize the final resistance here, but Hitler's "Alpine Fortress" ultimately proved to be of no use.

Hikers at the Kehlsteinhaus, the surviving part of Hitler's residence

TIMELINE

9 March 1933 Hitler presses the Bavarian government to resign	**1934** Hitler abolishes independence of German states, including Bavaria **29 September 1938** Munich Agreement	**30 April 1945** American troops enter Munich **1 October 1946** The first elections in Bavaria bring victory to the CSU		**14 June 195** Celebrations Munich's 700 anniversary
1930	**1935**	**1940**	**1945**	**1950**	**1955**	**1960**
30 January 1933 Hitler becomes Chancellor of the Reich		**1 September 1939** German attack on Poland launches World War II *February 1936 – the 4th Winter Olympics are held in Garmisch-Partenkirchen*	**20 September 1949** Appointment of the government of the Federal Republic of Germany	**1957** The population of Munich reache 1 million

Oktoberfest – the world's best-known beer festival

MODERN BAVARIA

The ravages of war were less severe in Bavaria than they were in other parts of Germany. In April and May 1945 Bavaria was occupied by American troops and until 1949 it formed part of the American occupation zone. Despite a great influx of displaced people, most of Bavaria's inhabitants were spared the worst of postwar deprivation because of the agricultural strength of the region. The Federal Republic of Bavaria, set up in 1949, made efforts to take an independent position as the region with the best preserved sense of historical and geographical identity, and constantly opposed any attempts at centralization. One of the external manifestations of this trend towards autonomy was the success that the local

Christian Democrats had in keeping their own organization distinct from the CDU (Christian Democratic Union), and in setting up their own CSU (Christian Social Union). It ruled Bavaria continuously from 1949. The main figure in the CSU, until his death in 1988, was the temperamental Franz-Josef Strauß, an unquestioned leader of the German right.

The CSU, appealing to regional tradition even to the extent of anti-Prussian separatist sentiment, skilfully pursued a policy of industrialization after 1960. Electronics and computer manufacture developed strongly, as did the car manufacturers BMW and Audi. During the 1972 Summer Olympics, the region glittered not only with its celebrated modern architecture, but also with its openness and liberalism. The Olympic ideal of peace was, however, marred by bloodshed in an attack by Palestinian separatists.

Franz-Josef Strauß

In the years leading up to the reunification of Germany, Munich was regarded as "Germany's secret capital". But 1989 and the revival of Berlin's role means that Munich and Bavaria now face fresh challenges.

FC Bayern Munich, one of the world's best soccer teams

1972 The 20th Olympic Games are held in Munich	**1974** The 10th World Soccer Championship finals are held in Munich	**1980** Pope John Paul II visits Altötting during his pilgrimage to Germany	*The BMW logo, one of the symbols of modern Bavaria*

1970	1975	1980	1985	1990	1995	2000

1966 Construction of the Munich U-Bahn and S-Bahn network begins

Poster for the Munich Olympics

1988 Death of Franz-Josef Strauß

3 October 1990 Reunification of Germany weakens Bavaria's political role

1992 The opening of Munich's new airport

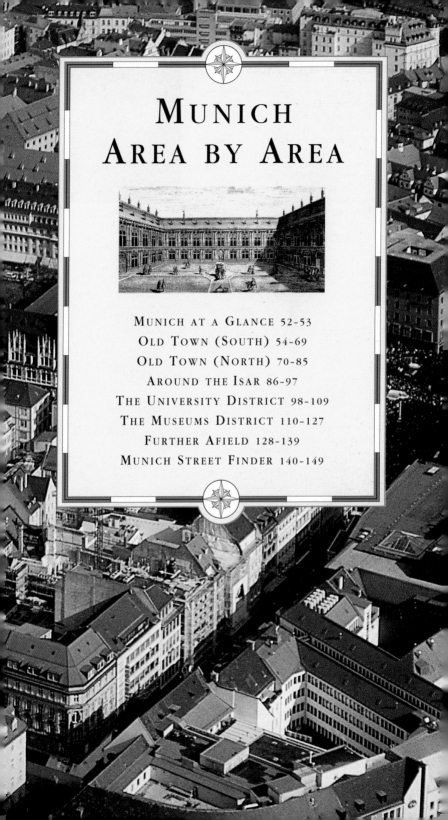

MUNICH
AREA BY AREA

Munich at a Glance

MUNICH IS Germany's third-largest city, and before the fall of the Berlin Wall it was dubbed the "unofficial capital of the country". Another name for it was the "village with a million inhabitants". Its metropolitan bustle, prosperity and high-tech industries exist alongside a rural, traditional atmosphere. The city has many parks, including the landscaped Englischer Garten, with the pretty River Isar that flows through it, and on fine days there are splendid views of the Alps, all of which combine to give the capital of Bavaria its unique atmosphere. It is also a city of culture.

Munich has many historic monuments as well as outstanding museums and art galleries and several theatres.

Alte Pinakothek
Susanna and the Elders *by Albrecht Altdorfer is one of the gallery's masterpieces of German Renaissance art (see pp118–21).*

The Glyptothek
Peace, a Roman copy of a sculpture by Cephisodotus, is one of the many classical sculptures on display in the Glyptothek, built by Ludwig I specifically to house such works of art (see p116).

MUSEUMS DISTRICT
(See pp110–27)

Theatinerkirche
This elegant Baroque church with its twin-towered façade is a prominent feature of the city's skyline (see p79).

OLD TOWN (SOUTH)
(See pp54–69)

Asamkirche
The interior of the Church of St Johann-Nepomuk exemplifies Baroque illusionism. Space, architectural elements, stuccowork, frescoes and the interplay of light and shadow combine to create the illusion of wave-like motion (see pp66-7).

0 metres   750

0 yards   750

Siegestor
Based on the Arch of Constantine in Rome, this is a monument to the Bavarian army. It is crowned by a statue symbolizing Bavaria riding in a chariot drawn by four lions (see p104).

UNIVERSITY DISTRICT
(See pp98–109)

Bayerisches Nationalmuseum
This museum contains interiors taken from elsewhere in Bavaria and preserved in their entirety. An example is the Gothic Weberstube from Augsburg (see pp108–9).

Friedensengel
The Angel of Peace, standing on the right bank of the Isar, can be seen from afar. The column, 18m (59 ft) high, is topped by a gilded bronze angel (see p92).

AROUND THE ISAR
(See pp86–97)

OLD TOWN (NORTH)
(See pp70–85)

Maximilianeum
This building, in what is known as the Maximilian style, now houses the Bavarian parliament (see p91).

The Residenz
The Brunnenhof is one of the seven courtyards in the Residenz. It takes its name from the Mannerist Wittelsbach Fountain (Brunnen) that stands in the centre (see pp74–7).

OLD TOWN (SOUTH)

THREE GATES, the Karlstor, Sendlinger Tor and Isartor, mark the boundary of the southern part of the Aldstadt (Old Town). Marienplatz is the main square in this district, and it is also the central point of the whole of Munich. Marienplatz was once a market square, and it has witnessed all of the most important events in Munich's history.

Both tourists and local people come to admire the many fine

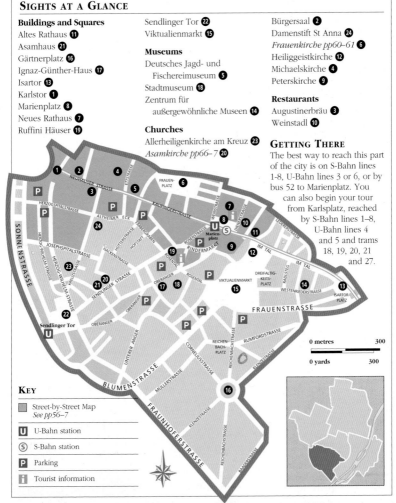

Putto from the plinth of the Mariensäule

historic buildings, including the Frauenkirche, with its distinctive outline, and Peterskirche, the city's oldest church. South of Marienplatz is the Angerviertel. Because it was safe from flooding by the River Isar, this area was chosen by the legendary monks who founded Munich and gave the city its name. Life in the Angerviertel centres around the Viktualienmarkt, which has been held here for almost 200 years.

SIGHTS AT A GLANCE

Buildings and Squares
Altes Rathaus ⑪
Asamhaus ㉑
Gärtnerplatz ⑯
Ignaz-Günther-Haus ⑰
Isartor ⑬
Karlstor ①
Marienplatz ⑧
Neues Rathaus ⑦
Ruffini Häuser ⑲

Sendlinger Tor ㉒
Viktualienmarkt ⑮

Museums
Deutsches Jagd- und Fischereimuseum ⑤
Stadtmuseum ⑱
Zentrum für außergewöhnliche Museen ⑭

Churches
Allerheiligenkirche am Kreuz ㉓
Asamkirche pp66–7 ⑳

Bürgersaal ②
Damenstift St Anna ㉔
Frauenkirche pp60–61 ⑥
Heiliggeistkirche ⑫
Michaelskirche ④
Peterskirche ⑨

Restaurants
Augustinerbräu ③
Weinstadl ⑩

GETTING THERE

The best way to reach this part of the city is on S-Bahn lines 1-8, U-Bahn lines 3 or 6, or by bus 52 to Marienplatz. You can also begin your tour from Karlsplatz, reached by S-Bahn lines 1–8, U-Bahn lines 4 and 5 and trams 18, 19, 20, 21 and 27.

KEY

▦	Street-by-Street Map *See pp56–7*
Ⓤ	U-Bahn station
Ⓢ	S-Bahn station
🅿	Parking
ℹ	Tourist information

◁ **The Fish Fountain on Marienplatz, which has been redesigned with 19th-century elements**

Street-by-Street: Around Marienplatz

E**VER SINCE** Munich was founded, Marienplatz has been the city's architectural and commercial hub. The geographical centre of the city is marked by the Mariensäule (Column of the Virgin), from which all distances in Munich are measured. The square and the streets around it, which have been pedestrianized since the Munich Olympics in 1972, are always full of visitors. In one hour up to 18,000 tourists and shoppers pass through this area, rising to 22,000 on Saturdays.

Virgin on the Mariensäule

Karlstor
This gate was retained when the old city walls were demolished in 1791 **1**

HERZOG-WILHELM-STR.

NEUHAUSER STR.

KAPELLENSTR.

HERZOGSPITALSTR.

Asamkirche ↓

EISENMANNSTR.

Bürgersaal
The austere façade of this church is decorated by a statue of the Madonna and Child by Franz Ableitner set over the portal **2**

Neuhauser Straße
is Munich's largest shopping street. It is filled with typical 19th-century buildings and with cafés and shops that enjoy the highest turnover in the whole of Germany.

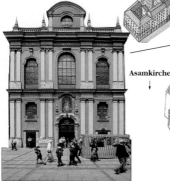

Augustinerbräu
This pub, one of the oldest in Munich, has elaborate interior decoration and a picturesque beer-garden courtyard **3**

STAR SIGHTS

★ **Frauenkirche**

★ **Michaelskirche**

★ **Neues Rathaus**

★ **Michaelskirche**
The nave of the Church of St Michael, roofed by impressive barrel vaulting, is separated from the presbytery by a triumphal arch **4**

KEY

− − − Suggested route

0 metres   100

0 yards   100

Deutsches Jagd- und Fischereimuseum
The German Hunting and Fishing Museum, located in a former Augustinian church, is reached from the presbytery side **5**

LOCATOR MAP
See Street Finder, maps 3, 5 & 6

★ Frauenkirche
The figure of the Madonna and Sorrowful Christ comes from a 13th-century basilica. The Baroque gates were carved by Ignaz Günther **6**

★ Neues Rathaus
The figures in the New Town Hall's chiming clock enact a joust and perform the Dance of the Coopers **7**

Peterskirche
The high altar of the Church of St Peter is decorated with a figure of the saint carved by Erasmus Grasser. Around it are the four Church Fathers, by Egid Quirin Asam **9**

KAUFINGERSTR.

ROSENSTR.

Viktualienmarkt

MARIENPLATZ

RINDERMARKT

STR.

Heiliggeistkirche

Altes Rathaus
The tower of the Old Town hall was recon-structed after World War II on the basis of plans dating from 1493 **11**

Karlstor ●

KARL'S GATE

Karlsplatz 5. **Map** 3 A2 (5 A2) **U** or
S Karlsplatz-Stachus. 🚋 18, 19, 27.

A VESTIGE of the medieval town's fortifications, this gate stands at the western entrance to the Old Town. Originally known as the Neuhauser Tor, the gate received its present name in 1791 in honour of Prince Karl Theodor, who recommended the demolition of the old walls to enable the city to expand.

Initially, the Karlstor had three towers. The tallest of them, the central tower, was destroyed in 1861 when the gunpowder that was stored there exploded. The gate was rebuilt, to a Neo-Gothic design by Domenico Zanetti. The bronze figures in the walls of the arches were taken from the old fountain in Marienplatz in 1865.

The medieval Karlstor, seen from the Old Town

Bürgersaal ●

Neuhauser Str. 14. **Map** 3 A2 (5 B3).
U or **S** Karlsplatz-Stachus. 🚋 18, 19, 20, 21, 27. **Lower church hall** ◯ 8am–8pm daily. **Upper church hall** ◯ 11am–1pm daily.

THE NAME of this church reflects its original purpose as the headquarters of the Marian congregation. It was designed by Giovanni Antonio Viscardi and consecrated in 1778. The rather austere façade fronts a two-storey interior. The lower church contains the tomb of the beatified Rupert Mayer, a staunch fighter against the

The dazzling interior of the Bürgersaal, featuring 19th-century frescoes

Nazis. The upper church, which was the main meeting-place of the Marians, glitters with Rococo stuccowork by Joseph Georg Bader and paintings by Anton von Gumpp, among others. During World War II the interior was damaged by fire, and some of the decoration has been restored. Surviving original features include the bas-relief on the high altar by Andreas Feistenberger, dating from 1710, the famous Guardian Angel of 1763 and the group of figures crowning the pulpit by Ignaz Günther.

Augustinerbräu ●

AUGUSTINE BREWERY

Neuhauser Str. 27. **Map** 3 A2 (5 B3).
📞 23 18 32 57. **U** or **S** Karlsplatz-Stachus. 🚋 18, 19, 20, 21, 27. ◯ 10am–midnight. 🍴

TWO ADJOINING houses with picturesque 19th-century façades form part of the oldest brewery in Munich. The Augustinerbräu was founded by Augustinian

Al fresco seating outside the Augustinerbräu

monks and was mentioned as early as 1328. The historic interior of the brewery hall is a fine and today rare example of the aesthetics and atmosphere of a Munich restaurant pre-dating World War I. An unusual feature is the Muschelsaal (Shell Hall), whose walls are lined with seashells, pebbles, decorative mouldings, busts and antlers. The brewery is divided into a restaurant and beer hall, with a delightful beer garden.

Michaelskirche ●

ST MICHAEL'S CHURCH

Neuhauser Str. 6. **Map** 3 B2 (5 B3).
U or **S** Karlsplatz-Stachus. 🚋 18, 19, 20, 21, 27. ◯ 8am–7pm daily.

THE FOUNDER of this church, built for the Jesuit order which was active in this area from 1559 onwards, was Prince Wilhelm V. Construction began in 1583, but when the tower collapsed in 1590, it was decided to enlarge the transept and to add a choir to designs by Friedrich Sustris.

The Michaelskirche, which aimed to bolster the Counter-Reformation and reinforce the Jesuits' presence, is the largest late Renaissance religious building north of the Alps. It is reminiscent of the church of Il Gesú in Rome.

The three-tier façade, with its double doorway, is an outstanding example of Mannerist architecture. Between the pilasters there are windows and rows of niches containing the figures of Bavarian and imperial rulers engaged in the expansion and defence of Christendom. The ground floor is dominated by a bronze figure of St Michael slaying the Dragon, with a figure of Christ the Saviour on his shield, made by Hubert Gerhard in 1585. The two portals, designed by Friedrich Sustris, lead in to a strikingly spacious interior. The barrel vaulting over the nave spans the second-largest space after St Peter's Basilica in Rome. The elongated choir ends with the massive high altar, where a painting by Christoph Schwarz depicts the fall of the rebellious angels. In the crypt beneath the choir lie members of the Wittelsbach family, including Maximilian I and Ludwig II, and the church's founder. Beside the church is a monastery and a college. The latter was built in 1585–97, also by Sustris. It is known as the Alte Akademie.

Statue from the Michaelskirche

Deutsches Jagd- und Fischerei- museum ❺

GERMAN HUNTING AND FISHING MUSEUM

Neuhauser Str. 2. **Map** 3 B2 (5 B3).
📞 22 05 22. Ⓤ or Ⓢ Marienplatz.
🚋 18, 19, 20, 21, 27. ◯ 9.30am–
5pm Tue–Wed and Fri–Sun;
9:30am–9pm Mon and Thu. ♿

THE LARGEST collection of field sports equipment in the world is displayed in a white Augustinian basilica. The building's ecclesiastical origins are concealed by the shops in the aisle, through which the museum is entered from the street. The church was built in the late 13th century. It was rebuilt several

times, and became the first building in Munich to be decorated in the Baroque style. In 1911 it was converted into a concert hall, and in 1966 the collection of the German Hunting and Fishing Museum, founded in 1934, was moved here from Schloss Nymphenburg. The collection includes hunting weapons, bags and sleighs, and 500 stuffed animals and birds in re-creations of their natural surroundings. There are also trophies and pictures of hunting scenes. The angling section illustrates the development of fishing tackle, and shows numerous specimens of fish.

Frauenkirche ❻

See pp 60–61.

Neues Rathaus ❼

NEW TOWN HALL

Marienplatz 8. **Map** 3 B2 (6 D3).
📞 23 39 29 88. Ⓤ or Ⓢ Marienplatz. 🚋 ☐ **Viewing tower:**
◯ May–Oct: 8:30am–7pm Mon–Fri,
10am–7pm Sat–Sun; Nov–Apr:
9am–4:30pm Mon–Fri. **Clock
chimes:** 11am daily; May–Oct also
noon, 5pm, 9pm.

IN THE SECOND half of the 19th century, the civic authorities decided to build new headquarters for themselves. The chosen site was the south side of Marienplatz and 24 houses were demolished to clear a large plot of land. Construction lasted from 1867 to 1919. This monumental building with its six courtyards is a prime example of German pseudo-historical architecture, in this case mock-Netherlands Gothic. The decoration of the façade abounds in sculptures alluding to Bavaria's legends and history, images of local saints and many allegorical figures. The steeple is topped by a bronze figure of the Münchner Kindl (Munich Child), the symbol of the Bavarian capital. The clock in the tower is the fourth-largest chiming clock in Europe. Every day a concert is played on its 43 bells, with coloured copper figures dancing to its rhythms. The figures dance in two scenes – a knightly tournament of honour of the wedding of Duke Wilhelm V and Renata of Lotharingia, and the Schäfflertanz, or Dance of the Coopers *(see pp32–3)*, which is performed in the streets of Munich to this day to commemorate the passing of an epidemic of the plague in 1515–17. In the evening, in the bays of the tower's seventh storey, appear the figures of a nightwatchman blowing on his horn and the Angel of Peace blessing the Münchner Kindl. The viewing tower commands a fine view of the city.

The Neues Rathaus, a highly ornamented 19th-century public building

Frauenkirche ❻

A medallion from the façade

THE FRAUENKIRCHE, the largest Gothic assembly building in southern Germany, was built in just 20 years from 1468–88, a record time for the period. It stands on the site of an earlier Romanesque parish church. The imposing triple-naved brick building was begun by Jörg von Halsbach, and was continued after his death by Lukas Rottaler. The domes that crown the west towers, rising to a height of almost 100 m (330 ft), were not completed until 1525. Since 1821, the Frauenkirche has been the seat of the archbishopric of Munich-Freysing.

The onion domes crowning the towers are typical of the Renaissance.

View of the Church
With its twin towers, the church's distinctive silhouette is Munich's oldest and best-known symbol. By law, no new building that may obscure the view of the church is allowed.

STAR SIGHTS

★ **Emperor's Tomb**

★ **Stalls**

★ **Statue of St Christopher**

The façade has a rather severe aspect. The towers have blind windows at their angles and are pierced by arched doors and windows that echo the shape of the central portal.

Entrance

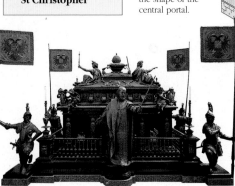

★ **Emperor's Tomb**
A Mannerist canopy of black marble covers the tomb of Emperor Ludwig IV of Bavaria. The sarcophagus is surrounded by the figures of four kneeling knights, personifications of War and Peace, and putti.

Chorhauptkapelle
This painting by Jan Polack (c.1510), in the main chapel of the choir, shows the Virgin protecting members of the patrician Sänfl family.

VISITORS' CHECKLIST

Frauenplatz 1. **Map** 3 B2 (5 C3).
Ⓢ or Ⓤ *Marienplatz.*
52 19. 7am–7pm
Sat–Wed, 7am–8pm Thu, 7am–6pm Fri. 2pm daily.
Tower *Apr–Oct:* 10am–5pm, except Sun and public holidays.

★ Statue of St Christopher
This carved statue, made in a local workshop c.1525, is an example of the dramatic style of the late Gothic period.

★ Stalls
Like the other figures that decorate the stalls, this bust of St James was made by Erasmus Grasser.

Cathedral Interior
Legend tells that the cathedral's builder wagered with the Devil that no window could be seen from within. From the spot where the Devil made his footprint, only a wall of pillars is seen.

"Memminger Altar"
This altar was built in 1994, incorporating reliefs by Ignaz Günther and a Rococo Madonna.

Marienplatz, Munich's bustling and historic central square

Marienplatz ❽

St Mary's Square

Map 3 B2 (6 D3).
Ⓢ or Ⓤ *Marienplatz*. 🚋 *Dec.*

Ever since the city was planned by Heinrich der Löwe, Marienplatz has been Munich's focal point. Until 1807 it was a market-place. It acquired its present name in 1854, when Munich's citizens asked the Virgin Mary to protect them from a cholera epidemic. For centuries the square was the place where major public events, proclamations, tournaments and executions took place. Today it is the venue for the famous Weihnachtsmarkt (Christmas Fair), which is held in the days leading up to Christmas. The square is dominated by the Neues Rathaus (New Town Hall).

Crowds of tourists and local people gather in the square every day to watch the mechanical figures on the clock tower perform their concert. The Mariensäule (Column of the Virgin) in the square was erected in 1638 in gratitude for the end of the Swedish invasion.

The golden statue of the Virgin (1590) is by Hubert Gerhard and the four putti around the plinth (1638) are by Ferdinand Murmann. The putti are shown overcoming hunger, war, heresy and pestilence. Another attraction of the square is the 19th-century Fischbrunnen (Fish Fountain), which was rebuilt after being destroyed in World War II.

Peterskirche ❾

St Peter's Church

Rindermarkt 1. **Map** 3 C, D2 (6 D3).
Ⓢ or Ⓤ *Marienplatz*.
Church 🕐 *7am–8pm Mon–Sat.*
Tower 🕐 *9am–6pm, 10am–6pm Sun and public holidays.*

St Peter's church, standing on the highest point of the Old Town, is Munich's earliest public building. Built in the 11th century, the basilica formed part of the monastery from which the city received it name (*Mönchen* meaning "monks"). In 1278–94 it was replaced by a new church in the Gothic style. In the 14th century the twin towers of the west front were replaced with a single tower. In the 17th century the church was redecorated in Baroque style, and in the 18th century was remodelled in the Rococo

The Peterskirche, with its famous tower, Munich's oldest church

style. The stuccowork is by Johann Baptist Zimmermann and others. The church's famous tower, known as Alter Peter (Old Peter), has eight clocks, seven bells and a viewing gallery that offers a splendid view over the Old Town. The interior of the church has unusually lavish decoration. The high altar is crowned with a statue of St Peter (1492) by Erasmus Grasser, surrounded by the Church Fathers (1732) by Egid Quirin Asam. The choir contains five figures (1517) by Jan Polack with scenes from the life of St Peter.

Side entrance to the Weinstadl, an ornate late Gothic doorway

Weinstadl ❿

Wine Merchants'

Burgstraße 8. **Map** 3 C2 (6 D3).
📞 *22 80 74 20.* Ⓢ or Ⓤ *Marienplatz.* 🕐 *11:30am–11:30pm Mon–Sat.*

A visit to Munich's oldest surviving town house is the perfect excuse to enjoy a glass of wine in a late Gothic cloistered courtyard. In 1510 the town council bought this pair of houses between Burgstraße and Dienerstraße. The house on Burgstraße accommodates the offices of the city writers' guild (Stadtschreiberhaus), while the house on Dienerstraße contains the Weinstadl. The house has an interesting façade with a large window in the centre. The perfectly preserved large main doorway conceals the entrance passage, a typical feature of old Munich houses.

To the right of the façade is a small late Gothic side entrance framed by a donkey-back arch. The façade, which had been under restoration, was unveiled in 1964, revealing most of the restored Renaissance decoration executed by Hans Mielich in 1552. An attractive addition to the courtyard is a late Gothic tower with a spiral staircase.

Altes Rathaus ⓫

OLD TOWN HALL

Marienplatz 15. **Map** 3 C2 (6 D3).
Ⓢ or Ⓤ *Marienplatz.* ⬤ *to visitors.*
Spielzeugmuseum Ⓒ 29 40 01.
◻ *10am–5pm daily.* ▨

THE ORIGINAL old town hall, dating from 1310, was replaced by a new one in 1480 which is known today as the Altes Rathaus (Old Town Hall). It was built by Jörg von Halsbach, who also built the Frauenkirche. The town hall was rebuilt on many occasions, most recently in 1861–4, when it acquired its present Neo-Gothic character. In 1877 and then in 1934 two gateways were cut through in order to accommodate the increasing flow of traffic.

The oldest part of the building is the tower of 1180–1200, part of the original city fortifications. Since 1983 it has housed the Spielzeugmuseum (Toy Museum), which as well as antique doll's houses, tin cars and copper soldiers contains a display tracing the history of the Barbie doll.

The Gothic interior of the Altes Rathaus survives. The ceremonial hall occupying the ground floor has wide wooden barrel vaulting, and a wall with a frieze of 96 coats of arms dating from 1478. There are plans to use this hall to exhibit the Dancing Moors (Moriskentanzer) that Erasmus Grasser carved in 1480. The figures currently on display here are copies of the originals that can be seen in the Stadtmuseum.

The Pentecost, by Ulrich Loth, in the Heiliggeistkirche

Heiliggeistkirche ⓬

CHURCH OF THE HOLY SPIRIT

Im Tal 77. **Map** 3 C2 (6 D3).
Ⓢ or Ⓤ *Marienplatz.*
◻ *7am–noon and 3–6pm daily.*

THE CHURCH of the Holy Spirit is one of Munich's oldest buildings, ranking in importance alongside the Cathedral and the Peterskirche. It stands on the site of a chapel, a hospital and a pilgrims' hostel. In the mid-13th century a hospital church was built here. This was replaced by a church in the 14th century. In 1724 the church was decorated in the Baroque style. The fine vaulting and stuccowork are by the Asam brothers. In 1729 a tower was added. Its Neo-Baroque façade dates from 1895, when the hospital next to the church was demolished.

The interior of the church is a fine example of the combination of Gothic and late Baroque elements. The ceiling frescoes depict scenes from the hospital's history. The high altar was made by Nikolaus Stuber and Antonio Matteo in 1728–30 and rebuilt after World War II.

Clock on the tower of the Altes Rathaus

Original elements of the altar include the painting of the Pentecost (1644) by Ulrich Loth and the flanking angels by Johann Georg Greiff. The bronze figures in the vestibule (1608) by Hans Krumpper originally formed part of the tomb of Ferdinand of Bavaria.

Isartor ⓭

ISAR GATE

Im Tal 43. **Map** 3 C3 (6 E4).
Ⓢ *Isartor.* ▯ **Panoptikum** Ⓒ 22 32 66. ◻ *11am–5:30pm Mon, Tue, Fri, Sat; 10am–5:30 pm Sun.*

ENTRY INTO the city from the southeast is through the Isartor. This gate is the only vestige of the city's original fortifications, and it has been preserved in its original form. The central tower was built in 1337, and in 1429–33 two eight-sided towers, connected by walls, were added. In the 19th century arcades were made in the towers. They were decorated with friezes representing the triumphal procession of Ludwig IV of Bavaria after his victory at the Battle of Mühldorf.

The southern tower houses the **Panoptikum**, a museum dedicated to the actor and comedian Karl Valentin (1882–1948), a master of the absurd who wrote theatre sketches and short films. The collections include many of his scenes, among them *The Vesuvius that Doesn't Smoke Because it is Forbidden in the Museum* and *The Hook on which the Artist Hung his Learned Profession.*

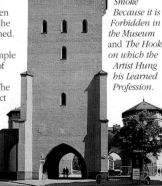
The central fortified tower of Isar Gate

Zentrum für außergewöhnliche Museen ⓮
MUSEUM OF UNUSUAL OBJECTS

Westenriederstr. 41. **Map** 3 C3 (6 E4).
Ⓤ or Ⓢ *Isartor*. 🚋 *17, 18*.
🎫 *29 04 121*. ⏰ *10am–6pm daily*.

THE MUSEUM of Unusual Objects is true to its name. In 1984, the collector Manfred Klauda opened the world's first museum of chamber pots, showing their development over 2,000 years. To this is added a collection of several hundred porcelain chamber pots mainly in the shape of gravy boats designed for the discreet use of ladies in the 18th and 19th centuries during public events.
There is also a room dedicated to Elizabeth of Austria, with personal objects and imperial photographs. A collection of logs from two centuries is shown alongside chastity belts and instruments of torture. Collections of corkscrews, Easter bunnies and pedal cars are also on display, and the Aromas Section contains a staggering collection of perfume bottles. The museum also mounts temporary exhibitions, on such themes as the history of the Christmas Tree, St Nicholas or garden gnomes.

Chamber pot from the Museum of Unusual Objects

Viktualienmarkt ⓯
FOOD MARKET

Between Petersplatz and Frauenstr.
Map 3 C3 (6 D4). Ⓤ or Ⓢ *Marien-platz*. 🚋 *52*.

THIS IS MUNICH'S oldest and most picturesque market. Since the beginning of the 19th century food of all kinds has been sold here – fruit and vegetables, milk, meat, the finest French wines and cheeses, fish and shellfish and exotic delicacies from all corners of the world, albeit at fairly high prices. All sorts of

A colourful stall at the popular, lively and historic Viktualienmarkt

people, from ordinary shoppers to tourists, can be seen here. Local customs include eating white sausage (Weißwürst), sipping hot soup and drinking beer in a beer-garden around a decorated maypole. The last day of the carnival is famed for the masked dance of the market women. The fountain commemorating various cabaret artists, such as Karl Valentin, emphasizes the popular nature of the square.

Gärtnerplatz ⓰

Road map 3 C3 (6 D5). Ⓤ *Frauen-hoferstr.* 🚋 *18, 20.* 🚌 *52, 56.*
Gärtnerplatztheater 🎫 *21 85 19 60, evenings 20 24 11.* **Box office** ⏰ *10am–6pm Mon–Fri, 10am–1pm Sat.* **Jüdisches Museum** Reichenbachstr. 27. 🎫 *20 00 96 93.* ⏰ *2–6pm Tue–Thu, 9am–noon Wed.*

THE HEXAGONAL SQUARE lying at the intersection of Reichenbachstraße, Cornelius-straße and Klenzestraße is named after the prominent 19th-century architect Friedrich von Gärtner. It is the focal point of the district known as the Gärtnerplatz-viertel, which was built in the second half of the 19th century. It was the first large district of purpose-built apartment blocks in Munich to be designed in a unified style.
In 1864–5 a theatre was built on the south side of Gärtnerplatz. It was designed by Franz Michael Reifenstuel and was known as the Gärtnerplatztheater. It was a slightly less up-market response to the courtly Nationaltheater. Its decorative façade stands out among the somewhat monotonous architecture that surrounds it. The **Gärtnerplatztheater** stages minor operas, operettas and musicals. Nearby is the **Jüdisches Museum** (Jewish Museum), which traces the history of the Jews in Bavaria.

Ignaz-Günther-Haus ⓱
IGNAZ GÜNTHER HOUSE

St-Jakobs-Platz 15. **Map** 3 B3 (5 C4).
Ⓤ or Ⓢ *Marienplatz.* Ⓤ *Sendlinger Tor.* 🎫 *23 32 23 70.* ⏰ *2–6pm Mon–Fri, 2–7:30pm Thu, 9am–1pm Sat.*

IGNAZ GÜNTHER (1725–75) was one of Europe's finest Rococo sculptors. He worked throughout southern Germany, but primarily in Munich. His work can be seen in the Peterskirche, Bürgersaal, Frauenkirche, the grounds of Schloss Nymphenburg and Schleißheim Palace as well as the churches and abbeys of Upper and Lower Bavaria. In

The 19th-century Gärtnerplatz, a green space in the city

1754 he became court sculptor to the Wittelsbachs. He moved into the house on St Jakob's Platz in 1761.

The Ignaz-Günther-Haus is a fine example of late Gothic residential architecture. It still has its small courtyard with a central fountain. The reception room on the first floor has an early 16th-century wooden ceiling. The façade on the side of the Oberanger contains a statue of the Virgin carved by Günther and known as the Hausmadonna. This is a copy of the original, which is in the Bayerisches Nationalmuseum in Munich.

The house and studio of the renowned sculptor Ignaz Günther

Stadtmuseum ⓲

TOWN MUSEUM

St-Jakobs-Platz 1. **Map** 3 B3 (5 C4). Ⓢ or Ⓤ *Marienplatz.* Ⓤ *Sendlinger Tor.* ☎ *23 32 23 70.* ☐ *10am–6pm Tue–Sun.* ♿

SIX ADJOINING buildings house the Town Museum. Two of them, the Marstall and the Zeughaus, were built in the 15th century as granaries but later became the city's stables and arsenal. During the rebellions of 1848 the citizens of Munich broke into the Zeughaus tower. However, the weapons that they found there had rusted and were useless.

In the second half of the 19th century, this arsenal building was used as a display space for the embryonic museum of local history. At this time a major campaign was under way to collect antique objects from the city's inns and attics, hospitals, orphanages, churches and pawnshops.

In addition to the 1,500 objects that were amassed in this way, a huge collection of etchings with a Munich theme was purchased. The Museum of History finally opened in 1888. As the collection grew, a total of four additional wings were added to the original buildings. The museum was given its present name in 1954.

The Stadtmuseum as it is today is divided into specialized sections, each of which operates independently, organizing various temporary exhibitions. As well as permanent exhibitions of old weapons, crafts, folk art, townscapes and collections of posters, there are the collections of the Puppet Theatre and Museum of Musical Instruments, the Photographic Museum and the Fashion Museum. Amateur filmmakers can view the rare film archives of the Film Museum, while those interested in interior design will be drawn to the Urban Interiors section. Undoubtedly the most valuable and intriguing items in the museum are the ten famous Moriskentänzer (Dancing Moors), made by Erasmus Grasser in about 1480 and originally designed for the ceremonial hall of the Old Town Hall.

Bas-relief on the façade of the Ruffini Houses

Ruffini Häuser ⓳

RUFFINI HOUSES

Rindermarkt 10. **Map** 3 B2 (5 C4). Ⓤ or Ⓢ *Marienplatz.* 🚌 *52.*

ON A TRIANGULAR PLOT that was once the site of the Ruffini Tower stands a group of residential buildings. Their construction was ordered by the councillors of Munich in 1808 with the idea of reflecting the history of the city's architecture in three obliquely sited houses. The plans were drawn by the renowned architect Gabriel von Seidl.

The three adjoining houses with an internal courtyard were built in 1903–05, and they are distinguished by their colourful, disparate façades. The reliefs on the façade depicting multifarious human subjects and floral motifs are modelled in white stucco set on a gold and sky-blue background.

Rindermarkt, on which the Ruffini Houses are situated, is one of the city's oldest thoroughfares, and was originally the city cattle market. The cattle fountain (Rinderbrunnen), built by Josef Henselmann in 1964, recalls the fact. The nearby water tower, known as the Löwenturm, dates back to medieval times.

Model of a shop with wax figures, an exhibit at the Stadtmuseum

Asamkirche ⑳

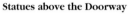

THE ASAMKIRCHE, or Church of St Johann-Nepomuk, was built in 1733–46. It was funded, designed and executed by the Asam brothers, the most famous builders and decorators of the time. Drawing on the full effects of Baroque artistic expression, they created a mysterious theatrical illusion of another world.

Angel on the confessional

The façade, set upon a plinth that imitates natural stone, gives no hint of the splendour within. The nave, with its low-key lighting, is full of striking architectural details, rich stuccowork and masterpieces of fresco painting.

Count Zech's Epitaph
This fine Rococo epitaph, made by Ignaz Günther in 1758, depicts the Grim Reaper taking away someone's life. It stands in the church vestibule.

Statues above the Doorway
The arch over the doorway depicts St John Nepomuk surrounded by cherubs and two angels symbolizing the Secrecy of the Confession and the Profession of Faith.

Church Interior
The exquisite combination of architecture, painting, light and shadow draws attention away from the proportions of the interior. The nave is 28 m (92 ft) long and just 8.80 m (29 ft) wide, proportions that were dictated by the relatively small ground space available.

Bas-relief on the West Doors
The top right-hand carving on the doors of the west façade depicts St John Nepomuk being thrown into prison.

STAR SIGHTS

★ **High Altar**

★ **Painted Ceiling**

Entrance

★ Painted Ceiling

The ceiling is covered with accomplished trompe-l'oeil paintings executed by Cosmas Damian Asam in 1735. They depict scenes from the life and martyrdom of St John Nepomuk.

VISITORS' CHECKLIST

Sendlinger Str. 32. **Map** 3 A3.
U Sendlinger Tor. 🚋 18, 20,
21, 27. 🚌 31, 56. ◯ 8:30am–
6pm daily. ✟ 5pm Mon–Fri;
6pm Sat, 9am, 10:30am Sun.

Detail of the Gallery
The undulating gallery that encircles the interior divides the walls of the nave and the high altar into two distinct parts.

★ High Altar

The high altar contains a glass sarcophagus in which lies a robed wax figure of a prelate representing St John Nepomuk.

Pulpit
The pulpit is reached directly from the adjacent presbytery to the east. It is surrounded by a relief with scenes from the life of St John the Baptist and symbols of the Evangelists.

Façade of the Asamhaus, lavishly decorated with allegorical scenes

Asamhaus ㉑

ASAM HOUSE

Sendlinger Str. 34. **Map** 3 A3 (5 B4). Ⓤ *Sendlinger Tor.* 🚋 *18, 20, 21, 27.* 🚌 *31, 56.* 🔵 *to visitors.*

IT WOULD BE difficult to find a more unusual artist's home. While Cosmas Damian Asam decided to settle in the suburban Maria Einsiedel Palace, which he renovated, his brother Egid Quirin Asam purchased four adjoining properties on Sendlinger Straße in 1729–33. He converted them into his own residence, with a church and presbytery in addition.

This was the first time that an artist had built his own house next to a church of his own design (there was even an interior window looking from the house towards the high altar).

Egid Quirin Asam added stucco decorations to the medieval façades, depicting Christian and Classical motifs – personifications of the fine arts, poetry and music are watched over by St Joseph, patron saint of craftsmen, who is surrounded by symbols of Faith, Hope and Mercy. A relief depicting Perfection and the initials IHS crowning the entire imagery symbolize the Christian concept of heaven.

On the left the artist gives a vision of the world of Antiquity, whose ideals were adopted by Baroque artists. Thus Pallas Athenae leads a childlike figure into the world of art and science under the

THE ASAM BROTHERS

The fresco painter Cosmas Damian Asam (1686–1739) and the sculptor and stuccoist Egid Quirin Asam (1692–1750) were taught by their father, the painter Georg Asam, and studied briefly at the Accademia di San Luca in Rome. Cosmas Damian married twice and had a total of 13 children, while Egid Quirin remained a bachelor. They worked in partnership in Bavaria from 1714 onwards, creating masterpieces of late Baroque art in Weltenburg, Rohr,

Portrait of Egid Quirin Asam in the Asamkirche presbytery

Osterhofen and Munich. They were adept at combining architectural, sculptural and paint effects, creating what was called *theatrum sacrum*. This was based on the inter-action of shapes modelled by means of light and shadow.

aegis of Pegasus, with Apollo watching over them all. These visions are complemented by the world of sensations, which are represented by Cupid, satyrs and fauns.

Sendlinger Tor ㉒

Sendlinger-Tor-Platz. **Map** 3 A3 (5 A4). Ⓤ *Sendlinger Tor.*

THE SOUTHERN end of the bustling thoroughfare known as Sendlinger Straße passes through a large Gothic city gate that is overgrown with vines.

The Sendlinger Tor was first mentioned in 1318 and, with the Karlstor and Isartor, this gate is all that remains of the secondary city fortifications that were built in 1285–1347 during the reigns of Ludwig II the Severe and Ludwig IV of

Bavaria. An important trade route to Italy via Innsbruck once passed along here.

The tall gatehouse that formerly stood in the centre of the Sendlinger Tor was demolished in 1808. The octagonal tower which then functioned as a gatehouse dates from the end of the 14th century. In 1906, because of the increasing volume of traffic, the three arches were converted into a single large arch, with pedestrian arches made through the side towers.

Beyond the gate is Sendlinger Tor Platz, a square named after the tower. It is one of Munich's crossroads, with pedestrian subways leading to the metro station. The Sonnenstraße, which continues from here, was the first 19th-century thorough-fare to be built along the

The medieval Sendlinger Tor, now overgrown with vines

course of the old city walls. Its name, meaning "sun street", reflects its bright, open design compared with the narrow, shady passages of the Old Town. Sendlinger-Tor-Platz has a park on the west side with St Matthew's Church rising over it.

Baroque tombstone set into the façade of the Allerheiligenkirche

Allerheiligenkirche am Kreuz ㉓

ALL HALLOWS' CHURCH

Kreuzstr. 10. **Map** 3 A3 (5 B4).
U Sendlinger Tor, Karlsplatz-Stachus.
8am–8pm daily.

ALL HALLOWS' CHURCH was built in 1478 by Jörg von Halsbach, and was the first cemetery church in the parish of St Peter. In the past, four streets converged here, hence the name "am Kreuz" ("at the crossing").

The church's bare brick walls, Gothic vaults and tall steeple make it a prominent landmark in the densely built-up Kreuzstraße. The interior was refurbished during the Baroque era, so that the only vestiges of its Gothic appear-ance are the web vaulting over the nave, fragments of a fresco of Christ in a mandorla and a crucifix made by Hans Leinberger in 1520.

Fine examples of the transitional style of art that developed between the Mannerist period and led into the Baroque can be seen in the tomb of the banker Gietz

(1627) by Hans Krumpper, and in the depiction of the Virgin appearing before St Augustine on the high altar, which was created by Hans Rotten-hammer in 1614.

Today Aller-heiligenkirche is a Uniate (Greek Catholic) church.

Baroque doorway of the Damenstift St Anna

Damenstift St Anna ㉔

CHURCH OF ST ANNE

Damenstiftstr. 1. **Map** 3 A2 (5 B3).
U Karlsplatz-Stachus, Marienplatz.
8am–8pm daily.

PRINCESS HENRIETTA of Savoy, founder of the Theatine Church, brought the Salesian order of sisters to Munich in 1667. During the 18th century the order acquired its own church, which was designed by the Gunetzrhainer brothers. In time the convent passed into the hands of an order of aristocratic ladies, hence the name "Damenstift". Today the building houses a

high school for girls. The façade is in the late Baroque style, as is the opulent decoration of the interior, which was executed by the Asam brothers. After suffering total destruction during World War II, the painting inside the church was restored in sepia, as black-and-white photographs were the only existing record of the original decorative scheme. The paintings depict the oath of angels, the Glory of St Mary and St Anne, and the concert of angels (above the gallery). The realistic group of the Last Supper to the right of the high altar is unusually lifelike. The life-sized statues sitting at the table and gesticulating were probably copied from Spanish originals. This single-nave church, with side chapels behind mighty arches and a presbytery at one end, is a typically Baroque attempt to combine the centrally planned church with the elongated model.

The intersecting interior spaces of the Baroque Damenstift St Anna

OLD TOWN (NORTH)

The NORTHERN PART of the Old Town (Altstadt) was once defined by the fortified city walls. Today it is enclosed by the Altstadtring (ring road). The principal thoroughfares traversing the Old Town are Theatinerstraße and Residenzstraße. West of Theatinerstraße is the old Kreuzviertel district, with Promenadeplatz its hub.

The Old Town has modern shopping streets, and also many fine 18th-century palaces and churches – two of them being the Theatinerkirche and Dreifaltigkeitskirche. To the east lies

Royal orb

the former Graggenau district. At the Alter Hof (Old Court), the first seat of the Wittelsbach family, there is a maze of medieval streets and buildings, among which is the Hofbräuhaus, Munich's most renowned brewery, and a large group of residences overlooking the Hofgarten (Palace Gardens).

Max-Joseph-Platz, a stately square surrounded by fine Neo-Classical buildings, marks the beginning of the grand Maximilianstraße, which is a practical example of 19th-century ideals of integral town planning.

SIGHTS AT A GLANCE

Churches
Dreifaltigkeitskirche **13**
Salvatorkirche **7**
Theatinerkirche
(St Cajetan) **6**

Museum
Literaturhaus **11**

Garden
Hofgarten **23**

Restaurants
Hofbräuhaus **18**

Theatres
Münchner Kammerspiele
im Schauspielhaus **20**

Historic Buildings
Alter Hof **17**
Eilles-Hof **3**
Erzbischöfliches Palais **8**
Feldherrnhalle **5**

Künstlerhaus **12**
Marstall **21**
Münzhof **16**
Palais Neuhaus-Preysing **10**
Palais Porcia **9**
Palais Törring-Jettenbach **15**
Preysing Palais **4**
Residenz (pp74–7) **1**
Staatskanzlei **22**

Streets and Squares
Max-Joseph-Platz **2**
Maximilianstraße **19**
Promenadeplatz **14**

0 metres   200
0 yards   200

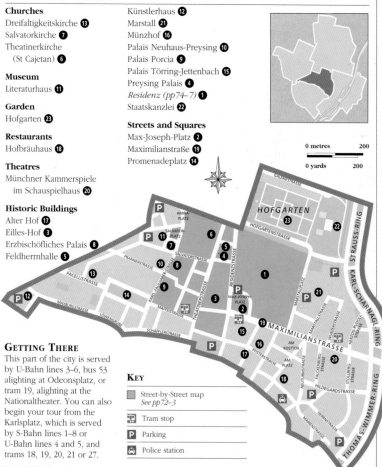

GETTING THERE
This part of the city is served by U-Bahn lines 3–6, bus 53 alighting at Odeonsplatz, or tram 19, alighting at the Nationaltheater. You can also begin your tour from the Karlsplatz, which is served by S-Bahn lines 1–8 or U-Bahn lines 4 and 5, and trams 18, 19, 20, 21 or 27.

KEY

◻ Street-by-Street map
See pp72–3

🚋 Tram stop

🅿 Parking

🚓 Police station

◁ **The Theatinerkirche, built on the model of San Andrea della Valle in Rome**

Street-by-Street: Around the Residenz

Painting from the Palais Törring-Jettenbach

THE RESIDENZ is set in the most elegant part of Munich, an area characterized mainly by the Wittelsbach residences, numerous Baroque palaces and the fine silhouettes of the Theatinerkirche and the opera house. The streets leading to the Altstadtring are lined with cafés and shops selling luxury goods. This area is also the centre of Munich's cultural life, with several theatres as well as concert and banqueting halls within the residences themselves.

Salvatorkirche
Until the end of the 18th century this old chapel stood in the middle of the city cemetery. It is now a Uniate church ❼

★ Theatiner- kirche
The Baroque coat of arms on the façade of the Theatine Church, designed by Ignaz Günther, features the crests of Bavaria and Saxony ❻

Erzbischöfliches Palais
The façade of the Archbishop's Palace was decorated by the great stuccoist Johann Baptist Zimmermann ❽

Eilles-Hof
The arcades of this enchanting late Gothic courtyard, hidden behind the Residenzstraße, are an oasis of peace ❸

Max-Joseph-Platz
This monument to Maximilian I Joseph was erected in the square ten years after the king's death. He had opposed it, believing that the pose did not convey sufficient majesty ❷

MAX JOSEPH PLATZ

Alte Hof

KEY

– – – Suggested route

Feldherrnhalle
*This hall was built
in 1841–44 in honour
of Johann Tilly and
Karl Philipp von
Wrede, the Bavarian
field marshals after
whom it is named.
Their statues stand
inside the loggia* **5**

LOCATOR MAP
See Street Finder maps 3, 5 & 6

Preysing-Palais
*This was the first early Baroque palace in
Munich to be decorated with Regency
elements. It is also the first work of the
court architect Joseph Effner* **4**

★ Residenz
*The wooden carvings that decorate the
interior of the Residenz's Old Theatre feature
allegories of the arts and mythology* **1**

STAR SIGHTS

★ **Residenz**

★ **Theatinerkirche**

---

0 metres	50
0 yards	50

The Nationaltheater, which doubles as the
National Opera, was famed for operas by
Richard Wagner staged here for Ludwig II.

Residenz ❶

Baroque vessel in the Silberkammer

THE RESIDENZ was the home of the Wittelsbach dynasty up until 1918. The buildings date back to 1385, when the Neufeste was built in the part of Munich enclosed by city walls. In the 16th century the Antiquarium and another wing were added, creating the Grottenhof courtyard. The Kaiserhof was added in the 17th century. After rebuilding in the Baroque and Rococo periods, the ensemble was enclosed by Königsbau and Festsaalbau in the 19th century.

Hofkapelle
The Royal Chapel , with intricate ceiling stuccowork, was designed by Hans Krumpper in 1614 .

Staatliches Museum Ägyptischer Kunst
is a collection of Egyptian art formed by Duke Albrecht V for display in the Antiquarium.

Kaiserhof

Patrona Bavariae
The 17th-century façade is decorated with a bronze statue of St Mary, patron saint of Bavaria, by Hans Krumpper.

Grottenhof
The courtyard contains a grotto decorated with volcanic crystals and colourful seashells, and a gilded bronze sculpture of Mercury.

STAR SIGHTS

★ **Antiquarium**

★ **Cuvilliés-Theater**

★ **Schatzkammer**

Nibelungensäle
This mural by Julius Schnorr von Carolsfeld, showing Hagen von Tronje defeating Siegfried, is one of the paintings of the Nibelungenlied.

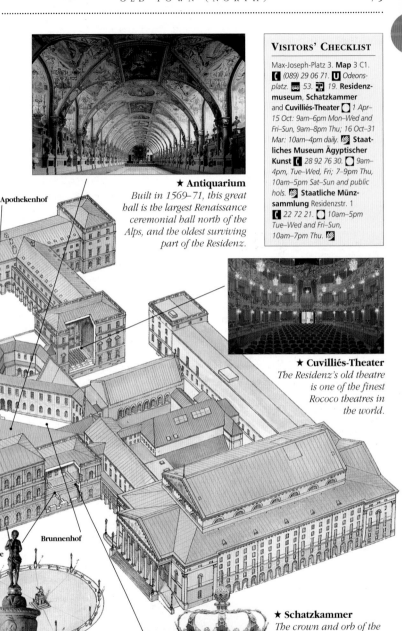

Apothekenhof

★ **Antiquarium**
*Built in 1569–71, this great
hall is the largest Renaissance
ceremonial hall north of the
Alps, and the oldest surviving
part of the Residenz.*

★ **Cuvilliés-Theater**
*The Residenz's old theatre
is one of the finest
Rococo theatres in
the world.*

Brunnenhof

rance

★ **Schatzkammer**
*This 17th-century
ornamental cup is
made of rhinoceros
horn and gold-plated
silver. It can be admired
here alongside
numerous other
works of art.*

★ **Schatzkammer**
*The crown and orb of the
Bavarian kings were made
by Martin Guillaume
Biennais in 1806
when Bavaria was
recognized as a
kingdom and
Maximilian I was
proclaimed king.
However, the
coronation itself did
not take place.*

Exploring the Residenz

Baroque clock by H. Manlich

A THOROUGH EXPLORATION of this unusual palace takes a few days. The first parts to see are the three monumental façades and the many courtyards that are open to the public. The interior of the Residenz is open to the public as the Residenz-museum. It is divided into a section open in the morning and another open in the afternoon. There is separate admission to the Schatzkammer, the Cuvilliés-Theater, the collections of Egyptian art and of coins.

oldest part of the Residenz, which was built in 1569–71 for Prince Albrecht V. The first floor once housed a library and a richly decorated reception hall containing classical sculpture. The final room on this floor is the Schwarzer Saal (Black Hall) of 1590, with trompe-l'oeil paintings on the ceiling. It in turn leads to the Gelbe Treppe (Yellow Stairs), where there is a statue of Venus Italica by Antonio Canova, and rooms in which European and Oriental porcelain and Persian divans are displayed.

Beyond the bedrooms of Maximilian III Joseph and his wife, designed by Cuvilliés in 1763, is the Allerheiligengang (All Saints Passage). It is decorated with 18 paintings by Carl Rottman, which were moved here from the Hofgarten arcades in 1966. The Charlottentrakt that leads away from here is named after Princess Karoline Charlotte Auguste von Bayern, daughter of Maximilian I Joseph, who once lived in the Residenz.

Next is the 17th-century Trierzimmer (Trier Room). The ceiling was painted by Peter Candida and others and the walls are hung with tapestries dating from 1604–15. The St Georgs-Rittersaal (Knights' Hall) leads to the Reiche Zimmer (Rich Room), built in the 1730s to a design by Cuvilliés, with early Rococo decoration. These rooms also include the Grüne Galerie (Green Gallery), Paradeschlaf-zimmer (Parade Bedroom) and Spiegelkabinett (Mirrored Cabinet).

The Grottenhof, which exudes an air of cool Mannerist elegance

THE COURTYARDS

T HE COURTYARD that lies on the side of the Residenzstraße features two Mannerist doorways with figures representing the four cardinal virtues: Justice, Prudence, Fortitude and Temperance.

The south doorway leads into the Kapellenhof (Chapel Yard). It is enclosed by the Residenz's tower, built in 1615. The Grottenhof (Grotto Court) is visible through the gates to the right. This Mannerist courtyard, designed by Friedrich Sustris, encloses the Perseus Fountain.

The north doorway leads to the Kaiserhof, the centre of that part of the Residenz that was built in Maximilian style in the early 17th century. This leads in turn to the monumental Apothekenhof, which is closed on its northern side by Festsaalbau (Ceremonial Hall Wing) of 1835–42.

Parallel to the Antiquarium is the elongated octagonal Brunnenhof, with the famous Wittelsbach Fountain by Hans Krumpper (1611–23). It shows Otto I Wittelsbach surrounded by personifications of the rivers of Bavaria.

MUSEUMS AND ROOMS OPEN IN THE MORNINGS

A CCESS TO the Residenz-museum is from Max-Joseph-Platz and through Königs-bau, built by Leo von Klenze in 1826–35. Visits start from the vestibule and the two garden halls leading to the Ahnen-galerie (Ancestral Gallery) with its lavish stuccowork. and 121 portraits of the Wittelsbachs. After passing François Cuvilliés' porcelain cabinet, visitors reach the Grottenhof and the Antiquarium, the

Tureen from the Silberkammern

The Grüne Galerie, an example of Rococo interiors at their finest

MUSEUMS AND GALLERIES OPEN IN THE AFTERNOON

A NUMBER OF rooms are open to visitors all day. They include the Ahnengalerie (Ancestral Gallery) and Porzellankabinett (Porcelain Cabinet), Reiche Zimmer (Rich Room), Päpstliche Zimmer (Pope's Room) and

The Reiche Kapelle, a masterpiece of encrusted ornamentation

Nibelungensäle. The large collections of European porcelain that are exhibited in the seven Porzellankammern (Porcelain Rooms) are open in the afternoon. Also accessible is the lavishly decorated Hofkapelle, designed by Hans Krumpper in 1601–14. It is adjacent to the Paramentenkammern, a treasury of liturgical objects. The royal staircase leads to the Reliquienkammer, which contains an interesting collection of reliquaries from the different workshops of the Augsburg monasteries.

The Reiche Kapelle is a true masterpiece of religious Mannerist architecture. The private oratory of Maximilian I, it was built in 1607 by Hans Krumpper and sparkles with coloured marble, stuccowork, stone plaques and terracotta reliefs, and scagliola (imitation marble).

The Silberkammern and Hartschiersaal nearby house 3,500 pieces of silver plate from the Wittelsbach Service, made in the 18th and 19th centuries. The Steinzimmer (Stone Rooms) beyond are named after their stone walls.

A visit to the 17th-century part of the Residenz ends in the Vierschimmelsaal (Hall of the Four White Horses) and the Kaisersaal (Imperial Hall), where there is a statue of Tellus Bavarica (1594), which once crowned the circular church in the Hofgarten.

SCHATZKAMMER

IN 1565, ALBRECHT V ordered that the jewels of the Wittelsbachs be sold after his death. This led to the creation of a treasure house. To it Elector Karl Theodor added the contents of the Palatinate treasury from Heidelberg, Düsseldorf and Mannheim. Later, religious works of art confiscated after the secularization of the knightly orders, and the insignia of the newly founded kingdom of Bavaria were added.

Decorative chain made in 1575

Highlights include the royal insignia, the cyborium (covered cup) of Arnulf of Carinthia (c.890), the Rappoltsteiner Cup (1540), a statue of St George (1597) and royal insignia of 1806.

Figure of St George (1597), inlaid with precious stones

CUVILLIÉS-THEATER (ALTES RESIDENZTHEATER)

EUROPE'S FINEST surviving Rococo theatre was designed in 1751–53 by François Cuvilliés in collaboration with Johann Baptist Straub and Johann Baptist Zimmermann.

The predominantly gold and red wood carvings on the balconies, royal loggia and proscenia still survive. The first performance of Mozart's *Idomeneo* took place here in 1781. Destroyed in World War II, the theatre was rebuilt in the Apothekenhof, using the surviving original carvings.

EGYPTIAN COLLECTIONS

OPENED IN 1970, the Egyptian Art Museum is one of the most recently created state museums in Bavaria. The origins of the collection go back to the 16th century, when Albrecht V acquired a number of Egyptian statues. In the 19th century the rulers of Bavaria purchased Egyptian pieces for the Bavarian Academy of Sciences and the Glyphotek. In the 20th century, personal donations substantially enlarged the collection.

Today the museum contains a fine and extensive collection of Egyptian art from the Old, Middle and New Kingdoms, and from the later Ptolemaic and Coptic periods.

Egyptian bronze statuette

COIN COLLECTION

THE RESIDENZ contains the largest coin collection in the world. Its nucleus originated in a collection formed by Albrecht V and Ludwig I. It contains coins and medals dating from all periods and originating from all over the world. Seals, weights and banknotes also form part of the display.

The Neo-Classical National Theatre at Max-Joseph-Platz

Max-Joseph-Platz ②

Map 3 C2 (6 D2). ⑤ *Marienplatz.*
Ⓤ *Odeonsplatz.* 🚋 *19.*
Nationaltheater 🄲 *21 85 19 20.*
⬜ *10am–6pm Mon–Fri, 10am–1pm
Sat (tickets for performances can also
be obtained).*

D URING THE 1820s, Karl
von Fischer and Leo von
Klenze laid out a grand
square outside the Residenz,
flanking it with the
monumental façades of
Neo-Classical buildings:
Königsbau to the north, the
National Theatre to the east,
and the arcaded Törring-
Jettenbach Palace to the
south. The latter now houses
the central post office.

In the square is a statue of
Maximilian I Joseph, the first
king of Bavaria, who drew
up the Bavarian constitution,
the first in Germany, in
1818. The statue was created
by Leo von Klenze and
Christian Daniel Rauch.

The building of the National
Theatre, which doubles as the
National Opera, is modelled
on a Greek temple. The
interior also obeys classical
canons. The large circular
auditorium is decorated
predominantly in purple,
gold, ivory and sky blue. It
is surrounded by five-tiered
galleries, with the royal box
in the centre. The National
Theatre became famous for its
performances of Wagnerian
operas. It was here that
*Tristan und Isolde, Die
Walküre* and *Rheingold* were
first performed. Today it is
the venue for opera festivals.

Eilles-Hof ③

Residenzstr.13 (also accessible from
the side of Theatinerstr. 40–42).
Map 3 C2 (6 D2). Ⓤ or ⑤ *Marienplatz.* Ⓤ *Odeonsplatz.* 🚋 *18.*

B ETWEEN THE Residenz-
straße, Perusastraße and
Theatinerstraße runs a
network of narrow passages
that are filled with small
shops and cafés. The peace in
this area is broken only by
the music of street musicians.

One of the most impressive
courtyards in this part of the
city is the mid-16th century
Eilles-Hof, which once
formed part of a monastery.
The narrow yard is today
surrounded by glazed arched
cloisters with late Gothic
openwork balustrades. It is
one of the last surviving
arcaded courtyards that were
typical of medieval Munich.

Preysing-Palais ④

Residenzstr. 27. **Map** 3 C1 (6 C2).

O N AN IRREGULAR
plot of land
between Theatiner-
straße and Residenz-
straße, which leads to
Odeonsplatz, Count
Maximilian von
Preysing-Hohenaschau
built the first Rococo
palace in Munich. It
was designed by the
court architect Joseph
Effner and built in
1723–8. Novel
designs were used
for the three sides of

the palace (the fourth adjoins
Feldherrnhalle). For the first
time exuberant mouldings
covered the entire façade,
partially obscuring the
architectural divisions of
the building.

The finest example of rich
Baroque design at the palace
is the grand staircase, in the
centre of the north wing. It is
reached today via an internal
passage that was once a hall
and is now lined with elegant
shops. The staircase has
decorative balustrades and is
supported by giant Caryatids,
and the walls are covered
with lavish stuccowork. No
succeeding late Baroque
palace has such a wealth of
interior décor.

**Preysing-Palais, an example of
early Baroque exterior decoration**

Feldherrnhalle ⑤

FIELD MARSHALS' HALL

Odeonsplatz. **Map** 3 C1 (6 C2).
Ⓤ *Odeonsplatz.* 🚌 *53.*

O N THE SITE of the
Schwabinger Tor, a
medieval watchtower, the
architect Friedrich von
Gärtner raised a building that
blends perfectly with the
old and new towns
between which it
stands. The aim had
been to create a
focal point that
would close off
Ludwigstraße and
give the irregular
Odeonsplatz a more
ordered appearance. At
the request of Ludwig I
a loggia in honour of
the heroes of Bavaria
was built, modelled
on the famous
Loggia dei Lanzi
in Florence.

**Statue of Count Tilly
in the loggia of the
Feldherrnhalle**

HITLER AND THE FELDHERRNHALLE

On the evening of 8 November 1923, Adolf Hitler announced the start of the "people's revolution" in the Bürgerbräukeller and ordered the takeover of the central districts of Munich. On 9 November a march of some 2,000 people acting on his orders was stopped by a police cordon outside the Feldherrnhalle in Residenzstraße. Four policemen and 16 of Hitler's supporters were shot. The marchers were dispersed, and Hitler fled to Uffing am Starnberger See, but was arrested and imprisoned. When Hitler finally came to power in 1933, he turned what became known as the Beer-hall Putsch into a central element of the Nazi cult.

The accused in the trial against the participants in the Beer-hall Putsch of 1923

years later, the completion of the façade was entrusted to Cuvilliés and his son, who finished the work in 1768.

The distinctive form of the church brought considerable variety to Munich's cityscape. The huge domes of the towers are 70 m (230 ft) high. The volutes on the towers are inspired by those of Santa Maria della Salute in Venice.

The Cuvilliés' late Baroque façade is brought forward and broken up by pilasters and scrolled cornices. It also has niches with the figures of Ferdinand and Adelaide, Maximilian and Cajetan, the patron saint of the church. The portico contains a cartouche with coats of arms, including those of Bavaria and Saxony.

The white interior, which contrasts with the black confessionals and pulpit, is decorated with stuccowork, allegorical figures and putti. The main altar is flanked by twisted columns.

The crypt contains the tombs of the dukes and kings of Bavaria, among them the founders of the church and their son Maximilian Emanuel and his wife Teresa Kunigunda Sobieska.

The Feldherrnhalle was completed in 1844. It consists of an open hall 20 m (65 ft) high with a triple arcade approached by a stairway in the central span. The statues of lions flanking the stairway were added in 1906. The niches in the arcade contain statues of Count Tilly, a renowned military leader in the Thirty Years' War, and of Count von Wrede, a marshal of the Bavarian Napoleonic era. There is also an allegorical memorial to the Bavarian army of Ferdinand von Miller the Younger, built in 1899.

Theatinerkirche ❻ (St Cajetan)

ST CAJETAN'S CHURCH

Theatinerstr. 22. Ⓢ *Marienplatz.*
Ⓤ *Odeonsplatz.* 🚋 *19.*
🕐 *8am–8pm daily.*

To CELEBRATE the birth of their long-awaited son in 1662, the Elector Ferdinand and his wife Henriette Adelaide of Savoy ordered the construction of a church and monastery for the Theatine order. It was designed by Antonio Barelli of Bologna, who wanted it to be the finest and most highly decorated temple.

Work began in 1663. The church was also designed for use as a court chapel. It was based on Sant' Andrea della

Valle in Rome. Thus a building of pure Roman Baroque form rose in Munich. It is a barrel-vaulted cruciform basilica with an apse, a dome over the crossing and arcades opening onto side chapels. From 1675 work was supervised by Enrico Zucalli, who completed the dome, designed the interior and added twin towers which had not formed part of Barelli's original design. Almost 100

The Baroque Theatinerkirche, one of Munich's finest buildings

The Salvatorkirche, with the Literaturhaus in the foreground

Salvatorkirche ❼

CHURCH OF THE SAVIOUR

Salvatorplatz 17. **Map** 3 B1 (5 C2).
🅄 Odeonsplatz. 🚋 19. 🚌 53.
◯ 10am–8pm daily.

I**N THE LATE** 15th century, the population of Munich increased greatly, and the existing cemeteries at Frauenkirche and Peterskirche were no longer sufficient. A new cemetery was created near the city walls, and cemetery chapels were built – the Kreuzkirche for the parish of St Peter and the Frauenkirche for that of St Mary.

Salvatorkirche was completed in a single year (1493–4). It was built by Lukas Rottaler, who brought the Gothic style to Munich. The combination of brick, stone and terracotta, the intricate fan vaulting and the delicate division of the walls give the church a distinctive

elegance. The whole is complemented by a slender tower ending in a steeple. Vestiges of late Gothic frescoes can be seen over the north door.

In 1829 Ludwig I donated the church to the Orthodox community. The iconostasis (screen) at the end of the nave is in Romanesque style, and the combination of Gothic architecture with Greek Orthodox furniture creates a unique effect. A plaque on the outer wall commemorates those who lie in the cemetery. They include the painter Hans Mielich, the composer Orlando di Lasso, and the architects François Cuvilliés and Johann Baptist Gunetzrhainer.

Erzbischöfliches Palais ❽

ARCHBISHOPS' PALACE

Kardinal-Faulhaber-Str. 12. **Map** 3 B1
(6 D2). Ⓢ 🅄 Marienplatz,
Odeonsplatz. 🚋 19. ◯ to visitors.

T**HIS PALACE**, which consists of four wings enclosing a courtyard, was commissioned by the Elector Karl Albrecht and built by François Cuvilliés in 1733–7. It became the seat of the archbishops of Munich and Freising in 1821. It is the only surviving urban palace built by Cuvilliés.

The building is fronted by finely moulded pilasters. The tympanum contains the crest of Count von Holstein, Karl Albrecht's illegitimate son, the division across the coat of

arms indicating his illegitimate status. A bas-relief over the doorway depicts the Virgin surrounded by cherubs.

The interiors of the palace were completed in about 1735 by Johann Baptist Zimmermann to a design by Cuvilliés. They are among the finest examples of late Baroque decoration in Munich. The courtyard contains a statue of Venus by Johann Baptist Straub.

Monumental sculpture on the façade of the Palais Porcia

Palais Porcia ❾

Kardinal-Faulhaber Str. 12. **Map** 3 B2
(5 C2). Ⓢ Marienplatz. 🅄 Marienplatz,
Odeonsplatz. 🚋 19. ◯ to visitors.

T**HE PALAIS PORCIA** was Munich's first first four-winged Italianate Baroque palace. It was built for the Fugger family in 1693–4 by the architect Enrico Zucalli.

The façade is based on that of Bernini's Palazzo Odescalchi in Rome. The rusticated lower storey, which is pierced by a columned doorway, is surmounted by two upper storeys that are divided by pilasters.

In 1733 the Elector Karl Albrecht dedicated the palace to his sweetheart, Princess Porcia. The interior was re-modelled in the Rococo style to a design by François Cuvilliés, with the involve-ment of Johann Baptist Zimmermann. The balustrade of the balcony was replaced by an ornamental grille.

In 1819 the palace was acquired by the Museum

Medallion with the Virgin above the entrance to the Erzbischöfliches Palais

Literary Society, and in 1820 the rear wing was extended by the addition of a ballroom and a concert hall designed by Leo von Klenze.

Over the following century the building was an important centre of musical life in Munich. In 1934 it housed the Bayerische Hypotheken- und Wechselbank. Bombing raids in 1944 unfortunately destroyed the Rococo interior. However, the general design of the vestibule was restored in 1952, and the Rococo statue of Bellony was moved here from the Archbishops' Palace.

Palais Neuhaus-Preysing ⑩

Prannerstr. 2. **Map** 2 B1 (5 C2).
Ⓢ *Marienplatz.* Ⓤ *Marienplatz, Odeonsplatz.* 🚊 *19.* ● *to visitors.*

THIS PALACE was built in 1740–50, probably by Karl Albrecht von Lespilliez. A small attic was added during the Neo-Classical period.

The building is currently owned by HypoVereinsbank. The interior was completely destroyed during World War II, although the façade somehow survived. The palace was restored and renovated in 1956–8.

A little further along the same street are two fine late Baroque palaces, also designed by Lespilliez: the Palais Seinsheim at No. 7, built in 1764, and the Palais Gise at No. 9, built in 1765.

THE SIEMENSFORUM

The Siemensforum is a showcase that the electronics giant Siemens has built in Munich, and also in Berlin, Zurich, Vienna and Milan. Its purpose is to provide a forum for discussion and information on modern technological advances. As well as organizing congresses, events and exhibitions, the Munich Siemensforum contains a permanent exhibition taken from the Siemens-Museum. The museum was built in 1916 in Berlin to commemorate the 100th anniversary of the birth of Werner von Siemens, the inventor and engineer who founded the company. The museum moved to Munich in 1954.

The history section includes exhibits of the first telegraphic devices, such as the Morse transmitter. The modern section displays modern electronics and microelectronics, which are presented using the latest multimedia technology.

The Siemensforum, an impressive display of modern technology

Literaturhaus ⑪

Salvatorplatz 1. 📞 *29 19 340.*
🕐 *10am–6pm Mon–Fri .*
Exhibition area 🕐 *11am–7pm Mon–Fri, 10am–6pm Sat–Sun.*

MUNICH'S GREAT literary traditions and its influential position in the European publishing market were marked by the opening of the Literaturhaus in 1997.

This monumental building, which blends with the closely aligned façades of town houses and the outline of the Salvatorkirche, dominates Salvatorplatz. Until the

beginning of the 20th century this was the site of the city market. In 1887 a large school building designed by Friedrich Löwel was built here, its open ground floor fulfilling the function of a market hall up until 1906.

In 1993 the building, which had been partially destroyed during World War II, underwent renovation and reopened as the Literaturhaus.

The present building skilfully combines the period style of the lower storeys with a light steel and glass structure for the two upper storeys. These provide a breathtaking view onto the dome of the Theatinerkirche and the city's rooftops.

The Literaturhaus is the home of literary institutions and foundations that organize literary conferences and seminars as well as readings, concerts and receptions.

Part of the ground floor hall is occupied by a display area where temporary exhibitions are held. There is a library on the first floor. One of the institution's great attractions is the literary café. Its decor includes an installation by the American artist Jenny Holzer devoted to the Bavarian poet and novelist Oskar Maria Graf.

Façade of the Palais Neuhaus-Preysing with its rich Rococo stuccowork

The Künstlerhaus, built in northern German Renaissance style

Künstlerhaus

ARTISTS' HOUSE

Lenbachplatz 8. **Map** 3 A1 (5 B2).
(*55 78 65 68.* **(S)** or **(U)** *Karlsplatz-Stachus.* 📭 *18, 19, 20, 21, 27.*
◐ *8:30am–5pm daily.*

T HE KÜNSTLERHAUS, on the
southern side of Lenbach-
platz, was designed by
Gabriel von Seidl and built in
1892–1900. This attractive
building, with wings set
around an inner courtyard, is
in mock northern German
Renaissance style, which is
characterized by stepped
gables and bronze decoration.
 The Munich painter Franz
von Lenbach made a great
contribution to its completion.
Having collected funds, he
set to work on the interior.
The rooms are decorated in
Italian Renaissance and Art
Nouveau styles.
 Despite wartime
destruction, the vestibule and
the Venetian Room – which
today houses a restaurant –
have been preserved. Before
World War I the Künstlerhaus
was a meeting place for
Munich artists, and was
known for its Künstlerfeste
(costume events).

Dreifaltigkeits-
kirche

CHURCH OF THE HOLY TRINITY

Pacellistr. 6. **Map** 3 B1 (5 B2). **(S)** &
(U) *Karlsplatz-Stachus.* 📭 *19.*
◐ *8am–8pm daily.*

I N THE WAR of the Spanish
 Succession (1700–14) the
townswoman Anna Maria
Lindmayr had a vision in
which the city was consumed
by the flames of war. To ward
off such disaster, the burghers
pledged to build a church.
 Work began in 1711, and
the result is an unusually
interesting piece of architecture. The design, inspired by
the Roman architecture of
Francesco Morrominiego, is
by Giovanni Antonio Viscardi,
and construction was
supervised by Enrico Zucalli
and Johann Georg Ettenhofer.
It was completed in 1718.
 The broken façade is set
with a multitude of columns,
pilasters and cornices, and
windows of different shapes
are set in surprising places.
A niche in the upper storey
contains a statue of St Michael
by Joseph Fichtl. The plan
combines elongated and
centralized schemes.

High altar of the Dreifaltigkeitskirche

The interior is profusely
decorated with stuccowork
and with paintings by Cosmas
Damian Asam. The high altar
(1717) has a painting of the
Holy Trinity, to whom the
church is dedicated, by
Andreas Wolff and Johann
Degler. The Rococo
tabernacle of 1760 is by
Johann Baptist Straub.

Promenadeplatz

Map 3 B2 (5 C2). 📭 *19.*

T HIS ELONGATED rectangular
 square, whose origins date
back to the Middle Ages, was
once the site of the salt
market, and storehouses for
salt and the customs house
stood here. At the end of the
18th century, the buildings
were demolished and the
square was planted with
linden trees. Fine palaces and
town houses also rose up all
round the square.
 The square, whose present
name dates from 1805, is
decorated with 19th-century
statues of well-known local
and regional figures.
 On the northern side is the
Bayerischer Hof, a high-class
hotel, where many famous
people have stayed. In
addition to the main building,
in the Maximilian style, the
adjoining Palais Montgelas
also forms part of the hotel. It
was designed for the king's
minister and the creator
of modern Bavaria by
the architect Emanuel
Joseph von Herigoyen
(1811–13). The
decoration is by Jean-
Baptiste Métivier. The
grand interior has been
preserved, including the
Royal Hall, Montgelas
Hall and Library, all in
Empire style. It was
beside the building on
Kardinal-Faulhaber-
straße that Kurt Eisner,
first president of the
Bavarian Republic, was
shot in 1919.
 Situated on the other
side of the square, at
No. 15, is the house
belonging to the archi-
tect Johann Baptist
Gunetzrhainer.

The Neo-Renaissance loggia of the Palais Törring-Jettenbach

Palais Törring-Jettenbach ⓕ

Residenzstr. 2. **Map** 3 C2 (6 D2).
[55 22 62 20. **Ⓢ** or
Ⓤ Marienplatz. **Ⓤ** Odeonsplatz.
⊞ 19. **◯** 8am–7pm Mon–Fri,
8am–2pm Sat.

THE BAROQUE PALACE that originally stood on this site was at odds with ideas of town planning that had inspired the creation of Max-Joseph-Platz, particularly after the Neo-Classical wing of Königsbau and the Opera House were built.

In 1835–8 Ludwig I commissioned Leo von Klenze to rebuild the original palace, extending it and creating a façade based on that of the Ospedale degli Innocenti in Florence. The Baroque doorway was moved inside, as were two of the nine sculptures by Johann Baptist Straub (the remaining

seven are in the Bayerisches National-Museum). The new arcade-style loggia was painted in ochre, contrasting with the red walls behind. This aristocratic palace is now Munich's central post office.

Münzhof ⓖ

STATE MINT

Hofgraben 4. **Map** 3 C2 (6 E3).
Ⓢ or **Ⓤ** Marienplatz. **⊞** 19.
◯ 8am–4:15pm Mon–Thu,
8am–2pm Fri.

TWO DUCAL SEATS in Munich are associated with Albrecht V – the Alter Hof and the mid-14th century Neufeste (now destroyed), which were separated by a stable building. Designed by the architect Bernhard Zwitzel of Augsburg, they were built by Wilhelm Egckl.

The courtyard was surrounded by a three-storey loggia housing the stables and coach-houses. They also contained Albrecht V's library and some of the earliest collections of art in Europe. Despite a marked adherence to the Italian Renaissance, the building shows Albrecht's own interpretation.

When it was rebuilt in the 19th century as the state mint, it was given a Neo-Classical east façade. The north façade, meanwhile, is in the Maximilian style.

Alter Hof ⓗ

OLD RESIDENCE

Burgstr. 8. **Map** 3 C2 (6 D3).
Ⓢ or **Ⓤ** Marienplatz. **⊞** 19.

THE FIRST FORTIFIED residence built for the Wittelsbachs within the walls of Munich was constructed in 1253–5. The purpose was to protect them not only from outside invaders, but also from rebellious citizens. In 1328–47 the Alter Hof was the residence of Emperor Ludwig IV of Bavaria. In the second half of the 14th century construction began on a larger residence, and gradually the seat of power was moved there. From the 14th century the Alter Hof only housed the duchy's administrative offices.

This delightful residence is a rare example of medieval secular architecture. The west wing ends with a gatehouse decorated with the crests of the Wittelsbachs, and it retains its original Gothic character. Another original feature is the distinctive bay window known as the Monkey Tower. According to legend, when Ludwig IV was a baby he was carried off by a monkey from the royal menagerie. The monkey climbed to the top of the tower, and it took a long time for it to be coaxed into returning the child.

Monkey Tower in Alter Hof

Renaissance triple-tier arcades create an orderly sense of space in the Münzhof

The Hofbräuhaus – the best-known address in Munich

Hofbräuhaus ⓲

Platzl 9. **Map** 3 C2 (6 E3).
Ⓢ or Ⓤ *Marienplatz.* ◯ 9am–11:30pm. ⓒ 22 16 76. ▣

MUNICH'S GREATEST tourist attraction, and the epitome of the Bavarian lifestyle, is the Hofbräuhaus. An inn, it formed part of the Royal Brewery that was founded by Wilhelm V in 1589. The opening ceremony of the inn in 1830 was attended by Ludwig I. Extended on numerous occasions, the building was given its present Neo-Renaissance exterior in 1896.

The ground floor contains the Schwemme, a large hall with a ceiling painted in 1971. The hall can hold 1,000 drinkers seated at long tables, strains of folk music audible over the talking and laughter.

On the first floor is the vaulted Festsaal, a ceremonial hall seating 1,300, and many smaller side-rooms known as *Trinkstuben*. In summer the beer-garden, with chestnut trees and a bubbling fountain, is a popular place. Every day 10,000 litres (17,600 pints) of beer are consumed here.

Maximilianstraße ⓳

Map 3 C2 (6 D, E2). Ⓤ *Odeonsplatz.* Ⓢ or Ⓤ *Marienplatz.* ▥ 19.

WHEN HE CAME to power, Maxmilian I Joseph continued the passion for building that had gripped his father Ludwig I. His wish to make his own architectural mark on Munich manifested itself in Maximilianstraße. Built in 1852–5, this was a reaction to the outmoded Neo-Classicism of Ludwig-straße. Maximilianstraße was built to connect the Residenz and the Old Town with the green areas along the banks of the Isar. It is divided into two parts, the showpiece square closed off by the Maximilianeum, and the commercial part within the Old Town. The division is further accentuated by the modern ring road. Today, this luxurious boulevard is one of the world's most exclusive and expensive streets.

Friedrich Bürklein, who designed the thoroughfare, created a novel architectural and decorative scheme that combined English Gothic with Italianesque arcades and depended on new skeleton construction methods. The arcades of the imposing Neo-Gothic buildings contain Munich's luxury shops such as Bulgari, Laroche, Hermès, Armani and the eccentric local men's fashion designer Rudolf Moshammer.

The famous Kempinski Vier Jahreszeiten hotel and the Ethnographic Museum are the only buildings not designed by Bürklein.

The opera house, the theatre, the many art galleries, where private views are a social event, and the clientele of the bustling cafés combine to create a thriving urban atmosphere in the area.

Münchner Kammerspiele im Schauspielhaus ⓴

MUNICH CHAMBER THEATRE

Maximilianstr. 34–35.
Map 4 D2 (6 F3).
ⓒ 23 33 70 00. Ⓤ *Lehel.*
● until 2003 due to restoration.

THE SCHAUSPIELHAUS is one of the few surviving Art Nouveau theatres in Germany. It was built in 1900–01 and adjoins the backs of two buildings in Maximilian style. The architect was Richard Riemerschmid and the modern stage equipment was created by Max Littmann.

The interior is also in Art Nouveau style. The walls of the auditorium are bright red with ornamental outlines. The green ceiling has six stucco beams and imaginative floral strands lit by spotlights in the shape of flower buds. The typical Art Nouveau device of softening lines with floral motifs can be seen everywhere – around the stage and the balconies and on door handles. The decorative stage curtain was made in 1971. Equally imaginative and colourful are the foyers on the two floors and the ticket office.

The theatre, which was originally named the Schauspielhaus (Playhouse), was renowned for the controversial works performed there, such as Frank Wedekind's *The Awakening of Spring*. The theatre's avant-garde traditions continued in the postwar period.

The interior of the Art Nouveau-style Munich Chamber Theatre

The Bavarian State Chancellery, a pompous presence and the subject of dispute

Marstall ⑳

ROYAL STABLES

Marstallplatz 4. **Map** 3 C1 (6 E2). **U** *Odeonsplatz.* 🚃 19. 🚌 21 85 20 28.

LEO VON KLENZE's first major work on the Residenz was the royal stables, on which he worked from 1820 to 1825. The large hall-like building is based on Renaissance and Baroque palace architecture.

The row of semi-circular windows is topped by medallions depicting horses' heads. Busts of Castor and Pollux, the sons of Zeus who (particularly in the case of Castor) were excellent horse-men, crown the columns at the entrance. The reliefs on the gates depicting the epic battle between the Lapiths and the Centaurs were made by Johann Martin von Wagner in 1821.

Medallion from the Marstall

Today the Marstall houses the Marstalltheater, which is known for its experimental performances combining theatre with dance and music.

Staatskanzlei ⑳

BAVARIAN STATE CHANCELLERY

Map 4 D1 (6 F1). **U** *Odeonsplatz.*

AFTER A DISPUTE between the city council and the government that went on for almost 30 years, the Bavarian State Chancellery was finally completed in 1992. A design proposed in the 1980s, by which the ruins of the former army museum at the end of the Hofgarten would be linked to a modern architectural complex, seemed too invasive to most of Munich's residents. It interfered with green areas, and the wings of the new building would mean the demo-lition of the 16th-century garden wall. After protests and litigation brought by the town council, supported by art historians and building conserva-tionists, the government altered the original plans.

Hofgarten ㉓

PALACE GARDEN

East side of the Hofgarten. **Map** 3 C1 (6 E1). **U** *Odeonsplatz.*

THE HOFGARTEN, with its references to Italian models, is one of the largest Mannerist gardens north of the Alps. It was laid out in front of the south wing of the Residenz in 1613–17. The geometrically designed gardens are divided by two straight main paths that intersect at right angles. At the intersection is the polygonal Hofgartentempel, or Temple of Diana, built by Heinrich Schön in 1615. The figure of Diana crowning the cupola was completed by Hubert Gerhard in 1594 (the present one is a copy). In 1623 Hans Krumpper remodelled the figure, transforming it into a symbol of Bavaria and adding putti bearing the ducal insignia.

The garden is bounded to the west and north by a gallery built in the reigns of Albrecht V and Maximilian I. The art gallery built in the north of the garden in 1781 was the precursor of the present Alte Pinakotek and Neue Pinakotek. The rooms now house an art gallery and the **German Theatre Museum**, the oldest of its kind in Europe. Its collections illustrate the history of drama in all parts of the world.

The triumphal arch of the entrance gate is Leo von Klenze's first work in Munich. The carvings are by Ludwig Schwanthaler and the frescoes, by Peter Cornelius, depict the history of the Wittelsbachs and Bavaria. The northern arcades feature land-scapes by Richard Seewald of 1962. South of the gardens rises the imposing Festsaal-bau, with von Klenze's huge doorway of 1835–42.

The Mannerist Temple of Diana in the centre of the Hofgarten

AROUND THE ISAR

THE ISAR, the river that flows through Munich, is quite attractive in the stretch between two bridges, the Luitpoldbrücke (Prinzregentenbrücke) and Corneliusbrücke. The Prater-insel and Museumsinsel, two islands linked to the city by several footbridges, also con-tribute to a striking townscape.

The main attractions that draw visitors to this part of Munich are in the area of the Luitpoldbrücke, Maximiliansbrücke and Ludwigs-brücke. On the steep right bank of the Isar are the Maximilansanlagen, green

A bust on the façade of the Maximilianeum

areas densely planted with trees and favourite places for walks and cycle rides.

The Maximilianstraße leads to the Maximilianeum, the great parliament building, which appears to be drawn like a theatre curtain across this wide thoroughfare. Everything exudes an air of dignity. Here are the monument to Maxi-milian II, the Ethnographical Museum and the Upper Bavarian gov-ernment building. This section of the Maximilianstraße is flanked by Lehel, the fashion quarter, one of Munich's prettiest districts.

SIGHTS AT A GLANCE

Churches
Annakirche ❶
Klosterkirche St Anna ❷
Nikolaikirche ❿

Museums and Galleries
Alpines Museum ❻
*Deutsches Museum
  see pp 94–7* ⓮
Villa Stuck ❽
Völkerkundemuseum ❹

**Historic Buildings
and Monuments**
Friedensengel ❾
Ludwigsbrücke ⓭
Maximilianeum ❼
Monument to Maximilian II ❺
Müllersches Volksbad ⓬
Regierung von
  Oberbayern ❸

Other Sights
Gasteig ⓫

GETTING THERE
The best way to reach this part of the city is on trams 17 and 19 or U-Bahn lines 4 and 5, to Lehel or Max-Weber-Platz. Sights further south are served by tram 18 or S-Bahn lines 1-8, those further north by tram 18 or bus 53.

KEY

▨	Street-by-Street map pp88–9
Ⓤ	U-Bahn station
Ⓢ	S-Bahn station
⬚	Tram stop
Ⓟ	Parking

0 metres 100
0 yards   100

◁ **The entrance to the Müllersches Volksbad, which has several swimming pools and baths**

Street-by-Street: Along Maximilianstraße

Relief from St Anne's Church

MAXIMILIAN II, with the aid of his court architect Friedrich Bürklein, translated his vision of urban planning into reality in the Maximilianstraße. Designed in what became known as the Maximilian style, it opens out from the Old Town into a kind of forum flanked by monumental buildings. It is completed by a circus with a monument of the king contemplating his creation. The scheme is dominated by the Maximilianeum, the Bavarian parliament building, on the opposite side of the river.

Haus der Kunst

ST-ANNA-STR.

BÜRKLEINSTR.

Regierung von Oberbayern
These Neo-Gothic buildings house the government of Upper Bavaria ❸

ST-ANNA-STR.

PFARRSTR.

Residenz

MAXIMILIANSTR.

★ **Klosterkirche St Anna**
The niche in the finial of St Anne's church holds a statue of its patron saint ❷

Monument to Maximilian II
This statue, 13 m (42 ft) high, was carved by Ferdinand von Miller, to a design by Kaspar Zumbusch, in 1875. The king, whose great ambition was to be a professor rather than a monarch, is surrounded by figures symbolizing Peace, Liberty, Justice and Strength ❺

Völkerkunde-museum
The rich collection of the Ethnographical Museum illustrates the culture and everyday life of non-European peoples ❹

STEINSDORFSTR.

The Isar, although flanked by embankments, retains its woodland charm.

| 0 metres | 100 |
| 0 yards | 100 |

KEY

– – – Suggested route

STAR SIGHTS

★ **Klosterkirche St Anna**

★ **Maximilianeum**

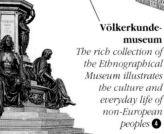

Annakirche

The monumental apse of St Anne's Church, built in Neo-Romanesque style, was painted by Rudolf von Seitz in 1892. It shows the Holy Trinity surrounded by St Mary, St Anne and the Apostles ❶

LOCATOR MAP
See Street Finder maps 4 & 6.

The Maximiliansbrücke was built in 1904–6 to a design by Friedrich von Thiersch that incorporates Neo-Romanesque decoration. The figure of Athena expresses the idea of Munich as Athens on the Isar.

Friedensengel

ERSCHSTR.

STERNSTR.

ISAR

PRATERINSEL

MAXIMILIANSBRÜCKE

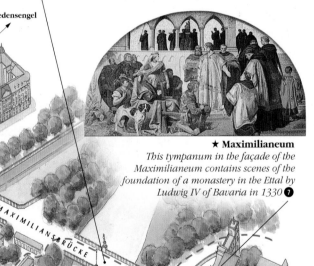

★ Maximilianeum

This tympanum in the façade of the Maximilianeum contains scenes of the foundation of a monastery in the Ettal by Ludwig IV of Bavaria in 1330 ❼

Alpines Museum

This museum is dedicated to the Alps and mountaineering displays, including equipment from 1900 ❻

Neo-Romanesque doorway of Annakirche

Annakirche ❶

PARISH CHURCH OF ST ANNE

St-Anna-Platz 5. **Map** 4 D2. Ⓤ *Lehel.* 🚋 *20.* ⬭ *8am–6pm daily.*

A COMPETITION for the design of a parish church for the Lehel district was held in 1895. The winner was Gabriel von Seidl. Work began in 1887, continuing until 1892. The design of the church is based on that of the Romanesque imperial cathedrals of the Rhineland, in the great German nationalist style that was prevalent after 1871.

The monumental triple-nave basilica has a square plan, the transept and apse ending in a chapel and the west front having a large tower and a Neo-Romanesque doorway. The interior is decorated with late 18th- to early 19th-century wall paintings. An interesting feature is the hybrid iconography in the figure of Christ on the west front, dating from 1910, in which He is depicted on horseback holding a bow and an olive branch.

Klosterkirche St Anna ❷

ABBEY CHURCH OF ST ANNE

St-Anna-Platz 21. **Map** 4 D2 (6 F2). Ⓤ *Lehel.* 🚋 *17, 19.* ⬭ *6am–7pm daily.*

I N 1725 LEHEL, then still a suburb, was settled by an order of Hieronymite monks. A monastery church was built here in 1727–33. Designed by Johann Michael Fischer, it was a real architectural jewel for the city: Munich's first Rococo religious building. The oval interior is lined with scalloped niches that are separated by arches supported on pilasters. The interior decoration was executed by the Asam brothers. The ceiling paintings, which glorify St Anne, were executed by Cosmas Damian Asam and completed in 1730. In 1737 the Asam brothers completed the high altar and most of the side altars, their stuccowork and paintings harmonizing with the fluid forms of the interior. The pulpit and tabernacle, by Johann Baptist Straub, date from around 1756.

Cartouche from the Klosterkirche St Anna

After suffering war damage, the interior was restored on the basis of a record of colour photographs.

Regierung von Oberbayern ❸

UPPER BAVARIA GOVERNMENT BUILDING

Maximilianstr. 39. **Map** 4 D2 (6 F3).

T HIS MONUMENTAL building, the seat of the government of Upper Bavaria, is one of the finest examples of the Maximilian style. The eponymous king, Maximilian II, strove to create a new architectural style, distancing himself from the severe Classicism of his father, Ludwig I. The result was an eclectic mixture of elements drawn from such diverse styles as English Gothic and Moorish architecture.

Solid and imposing, the Regierung von Oberbayern was built in 1856–64 to a design by Friedrich Bürklein. The façade, 170 m (558 ft) long, was conceived as part of the grand new city plan. It is vertically divided into 17 bays of arched windows arranged above an imposing arcade. Its strong horizontal lines and its ornamentation are highly reminiscent of those of English Gothic cathedrals. Indeed, the pseudo-ecclesiastical appearance of the building was designed to underline its civic importance and dignity. This symbolism is further reinforced by the large statue of Justice that crowns the building.

Part of the façade of the Upper Bavaria Government building

Völkerkundemuseum ❹

STATE MUSEUM OF ETHNOGRAPHY

Maximilianstr. 42. **Map** 4 D2 (6 F3). 📞 *21 01 360.* Ⓤ *Lehel.* 🚋 *17, 19.* ⬭ *9:30am–5:10pm Tue–Sun.* ♿

T HE BUILDING THAT was eventually to become the State Museum of Ethnography was built in 1859–65 to a design by Eduard von Riedl. It is in the Maximilian style and the façade is set with eight figures personifying the virtues of the Bavarian people: patriotism, diligence, magnanimity, piety, loyalty, justice, courage and wisdom.

The building was originally intended to house the collections of the Bavarian National Museum. From 1900 to 1923 it served as the first main building of the Deutsches Museum.

Caryatids flanking the entrance to the Völkerkundemuseum

Since 1926 it has been the home of the State Ethnographic Museum, the second largest in Germany after that of Berlin.

The collection itself dates from 1782, when curiosities from the collections of Bavarian rulers were displayed in the galleries of the Residenz. The museum collection now consists of some 300,000 pieces relating to the life and culture of non-European peoples. The Far East (China and Japan), South America (Peru) and East and Central Africa are particularly well represented.

Because of the size of the collection, many exhibits are displayed on a rotating basis.

Monument to Maximilian II ❺

Rondo Maximilianstr. **Map** 4 D2. 🚋 19.

As you walk along Maximilianstraße you pass a circus that has at its centre a statue of Maximilian II, patron of the arts and industry, and inspirer of the new architectural style to which he gave his name. Maximilian II conceived the urban planning of this part of the city. The monument was erected by the citizens of Munich in homage to their ruler and in honour of the monarchy.

The bronze statue, designed by Kaspar Zumbusch and cast in 1875, stands on a red marble plinth surrounded by personifications of the four royal virtues. Four putti hold the coat of arms of the four tribes of Bavaria: the Franconians, Bavarians, Swabians and Palatines.

Alpines Museum ❻
MUSEUM OF THE ALPS AND MOUNTAINEERING

Praterinsel 5. **Map** 4 E3. 🆔 21 12 240. 🕐 1–6pm Tue–Fri, 11am–6pm Sat–Sun. 🖼

The museum stands in scenic parkland in the southern part of Praterinsel, one of the islands in the Isar in central Munich. The building that it occupies, dating from the late 19th century, was presented to the German-Austrian Mountaineering Association in 1938.

The museum's exhibits illustrate both the scientific and the aesthetic aspects of the Alps. The displays, with a geological section on Alpine rocks and minerals, relate to their exploration and study, and include many paintings and drawings of Alpine scenery.

A book from 1897, Alpines Museum

The museum also houses the world's largest library of books on Alpine subjects, and has a mountaineering archive. An information centre serves the needs of mountaineers intending to set out on expeditions into the Alps.

Maximilianeum ❼

Max-Planck-Str. 1. **Map** 4 E2. 🆄 Max-Weber-Platz. 🚋 18, 19. 🚌 53.

The largest building on Maximilianstraße is, not surprisingly, the monumental Maximilianeum. It was built as a commission from Maximilian II by Friedrich Bürklein in 1857–74 and stands on an elevation on the right bank of the Isar.

The building was the headquarters of a royal fund that gave gifted school students the opportunity to study at university without paying fees. Since 1949 it has been the seat of the Bavarian parliament (and until 1999 the Bavarian senate).

It took 17 years to complete the Maximilianeum, progress being hampered by the sloping terrain of the river bank. The focal point of the slightly concave façade is the tall, triple-arched projecting entrance, topped by the figure of an angel. Wings, arcaded in their lower storey, extend on either side. The terracotta façade is decorated with busts and statues, while coloured mosaics on a gold background fill the semicircular blind windows over the upper storey. The interior is decorated with historical and allegorical paintings by Wilhelm and Friedrich von Kaulbach.

The Maximilianeum, seat of the Bavarian parliament

Die Sünde, a portrait of sin by Franz von Stuck, in the Villa Stuck

Villa Stuck **8**

Prinzregentenstr. 60. **Map** 4 F1.
[**] 45 55 51 25. **U Prinzregenten-platz, Max-Weber-Platz. **[**] 18.
**[**] 10am–6pm Tue–Sun.

FRANZ VON STUCK (1863–1928), the talented son of a miller from Lower Bavaria, made a giddy career for himself in Munich. He not only achieved great success as a painter, sculptor and graphic artist, but also became a professor at the Academy of Fine Arts, was given an aristocratic title and earned himself the title "prince of art".

In 1897–8 Stuck built himself a magnificent home, to which a large studio was added in 1913–14. Both the architectural conception and the interior decoration of the house were his own work. In it, he combined Neo-Classical, Art Nouveau and Symbolist elements, thus underlining his tenet that art and life were connected.

The house contains finely decorated reception rooms which, after the artist's death, were used for meetings by Munich's high society. The walls of the drawing rooms and studios are covered with mosaics and paintings in a Pompeian style. As well as ostentatious furniture, there are examples of Stuck's own sculpture. The museum also has an Art Nouveau display and hosts visiting exhibitions.

Friedensengel **9**
ANGEL OF PEACE

Prinzregentenstr. **Map** 4 F1. **[**] 18.
**[**] 53.

HIGH ON THE right bank of the Isar stands the Angel of Peace, a monument raised to mark 25 years of peace after the Franco-Prussian War of 1870–71, in which Germany was victorious.

Commissioned by the city council, the monument was designed by the architect Jacob Möhl in 1891 and built in 1896–9 by Heinrich Düll, Max Meilmeier and Georg Pezold. It stands on the Maximilian Terraces, which are supported by a wall pierced by three niches. The central niche is in the form of a grotto that acts as a backdrop to the fountain. The monument is flanked by a stairway with a decorative balustrade. The plinth, on a tall podium, is in the form of an open hall with caryatids and columns. It contains portraits of the rulers and generals of the Franco-Prussian War.

The monument was modelled on the Erechtheum on the Acropolis in Athens. Inside the hall, gold mosaics depicting the allegories of Peace, War, Victory and Culture cover a pedestal from which rises a Corinthian column 25 m (86 ft) high.

The Angel of Peace

The golden figure of the angel, 6 m (19 ft) high and crowning the column, imitates the Greek statue of Nike Paioniosa on Mount Olympus.

Nikolaikirche **10**
CHURCH OF ST NICHOLAS

Innere Wiener Str. 1 **Map** 4 E3.
U Rosenheimer Platz. **[**] 18.
**[**] daily.

BESIDE THE Gasteig Culture Centre, in the middle of a small, tranquil wood, stands the little church of St Nicholas. Its whitewashed walls and onion dome bring to mind the churches of rural Bavaria.

The building, first mentioned in 1315, was originally part of a leper hospital. It was rebuilt in the Renaissance and Baroque periods. After suffering destruction in World War II, it was restored and a late Baroque altar from Garmisch was added. Adjoining the church is the Altöttinger Kapelle, a chapel with an arcaded ambulatory. It is a copy of the famous church at Altötting. Originally built in Baroque style, it has been given several facelifts since then, the latest being in 1916. The Crucifixion group once formed part of an ancient Calvary. The modern crucifix standing amid the Baroque figures replaces the 18th-century original one that was destroyed during World War II.

The tiny Church of St Nicholas, which has a provincial atmosphere

The modernist, fortress-like Gasteig Cultural Centre

showers and baths, there is also a barrel-vaulted men's swimming pool, a domed ladies' swimming pool and a Roman bath. In the basement is a grooming centre for dogs.

The whole building reflects the new concepts of hygiene that were coming into vogue in the late 19th century, together with an interest in Roman bathing traditions. From an architectural point of view, the building is notable for the Neo-Baroque, Art Nouveau and Moorish elements that it incorporates.

Gasteig ⓫

Rosenheimer Str. 5. **Map** 4 E4.
🎫 48 09 80. **Ⓤ** Rosenheimer Platz.
🚋 18. **◯** 8am–11pm daily. **Library** 10am–7pm Tue–Fri, 10am–8pm Mon.

GASTEIG CULTURAL Centre is one of the largest of its kind in Europe. Built from 1978 to 1985, it covers more than 23,000 sq m (247,300 sq ft) and stands on the site of the Bürgerbräukeller, the beer hall where Hitler survived an attempt on his life when a bomb was planted there in 1939. The beer hall was demolished in the 1970s.

The modern glass, steel and brick building dominates the surrounding area like a fortress. It houses four major institutions: the Volkshochschule (an adult education centre), the municipal library, the Richard Strauss Conservatoire and the Philharmonia. The semicircular concert hall, with seating for 2,500, is lined with wood to enhance the acoustics. Besides the three other halls – the Carl Orff performance hall, the Small Concert Hall and the Black Box chamber theatre, there are many smaller auditoriums, workshops and rooms that are a focal point in the cultural life of Munich.

The complex contains a large forum where major performances take place, and where there are also shops and cafeterias. The south entrance is graced by a fountain in the shape of an enormous wind instrument.

Müllersches Volksbad ⓬
MÜLLER BATHS

Rosenheimer Str.1. **Map** 4 E3.
🎫 23 61 34 29. **Ⓤ** Rosenheimer Platz. **🚋** 18, 20.
◯ 7:30am–11pm daily. 🦽

ANYONE WHO IS keen on swimming or interested in interior design should visit this complex. It was built in 1897–1901 by the engineer Karl Müller to an architectural design by Carl Hocheder. At the time the baths – the first public baths in Munich – were considered to be the finest in Germany.

The men's and women's pools were originally separate. In addition to the many relaxation rooms,

The tower of the Müllersches Volksbad

Ludwigsbrücke ⓭

Zweibrückenstr./Rosenheimer Str.
Map 4 D3 (6 F5). **Ⓤ** Rosenheimer Platz, Isartor. **🚋** 16, 17.

THE HISTORY of Munich began at Ludwigsbrücke in 1158, when Heinrich der Löwe destroyed the toll bridge over the Isar belonging to the Bishop of Freiburg. Prince Heinrich wished the Salzstrasse, the salt route that had existed since Roman times, to cross the Isar near the place where Benedictine monks had established a settlement. He therefore built a new toll bridge, and the settlement became a centre of trade, having trading rights and issuing its own coinage.

The present bridge dates from 1935. It is decorated with figures personifying Industry and River Navigation (these were made in 1892 for the previous bridge) and Art (made in 1979).

Beside the bridge, on Museumsinsel, is the Fountain of Father Rhine, built in 1897–1902 by the sculptor Adolf von Hildebrand. The bronze statue of Father Rhine originally formed part of the fountain that stood outside the theatre in Strasbourg. When it was brought to Munich, it was placed in the centre of a fountain and was surrounded by putti standing on plinths.

Deutsches Museum ⑭

THE DEUTSCHES MUSEUM, the oldest and largest museum of technology and engineering in the world, draws over 1.4 million visitors each year. It was founded in 1903 by Oskar von Miller, an engineer. The building in which it is housed, located on the island in the Isar, was designed by Gabriel von Seidl in 1925. The collections cover most aspects of technology, from its history to its greatest achievements. The museum also houses the world's largest library of technology.

Exterior of the Museum
The building combines Neo-Baroque, Neo-Classical and modern elements.

Decorative Arts
This plate with the portrait of a lady from Ludwig I's "gallery of beauty" is an example of reproduction techniques applied to porcelain. The ceramics section illustrates the development of faience, stoneware and porcelain.

★ Physics
Galileo's workshop features a large collection of the scientific equipment used by the famous astronomer and physicist to establish the basic laws of mechanics.

Second floor

First floor

★ Pharmaceuticals
Among the exhibits in this recently created section is a model of a human cell magnified 350,000 times and graphically illustrating how it functions.

Main entrance

Ground floor

MUSEUM GUIDE
The museum's 17,000 exhibits are displayed over six floors. While those on the lower floors include heavy vehicles and sections on chemistry, physics, scientific instruments and aeronautics, those on the middle floors relate to the decorative arts. The upper floors are devoted to astronomy, computers and microelectronics.

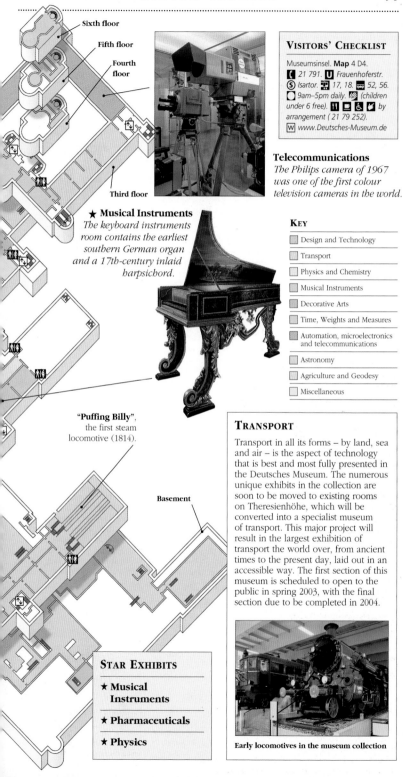

Sixth floor

Fifth floor

Fourth floor

Third floor

VISITORS' CHECKLIST

Museumsinsel. **Map** 4 D4.
21 791. 🚇 *Frauenhoferstr.*
🚊 *Isartor.* 🚌 *17, 18.* 🚌 *52, 56.*
🕘 *9am–5pm daily.* 🎟 *(children under 6 free).* 🚻 🛗 ♿ 🎫 *by arrangement (21 79 252).*
🌐 *www.Deutsches-Museum.de*

Telecommunications
The Philips camera of 1967 was one of the first colour television cameras in the world.

★ Musical Instruments
The keyboard instruments room contains the earliest southern German organ and a 17th-century inlaid harpsichord.

KEY

- ☐ Design and Technology
- ☐ Transport
- ☐ Physics and Chemistry
- ☐ Musical Instruments
- ☐ Decorative Arts
- ☐ Time, Weights and Measures
- ☐ Automation, microelectronics and telecommunications
- ☐ Astronomy
- ☐ Agriculture and Geodesy
- ☐ Miscellaneous

"Puffing Billy",
the first steam
locomotive (1814).

Basement

TRANSPORT

Transport in all its forms – by land, sea and air – is the aspect of technology that is best and most fully presented in the Deutsches Museum. The numerous unique exhibits in the collection are soon to be moved to existing rooms on Theresienhöhe, which will be converted into a specialist museum of transport. This major project will result in the largest exhibition of transport the world over, from ancient times to the present day, laid out in an accessible way. The first section of this museum is scheduled to open to the public in spring 2003, with the final section due to be completed in 2004.

Early locomotives in the museum collection

STAR EXHIBITS

- ★ **Musical Instruments**
- ★ **Pharmaceuticals**
- ★ **Physics**

Exploring the Deutsches Museum

To VIEW ALL THE EXHIBITS on every floor in detail would take a whole month as the entire route through the museum is 16 km (10 miles) long. It is best to concentrate on just a few of the 40 sections. The attractive way in which the exhibits are laid out is very effective, and there are plenty of items that visitors can operate themselves, so this is a museum that children will enjoy too. There are also regular demonstrations of working machinery and film shows.

DESIGN AND TECHNOLOGY

THE MUSEUM CONTAINS displays of such classic aspects of engineering as machine-building, mining, metallurgy, and hydraulic and civil engineering. The display of machines and turbines features many prototypes and the first diesel engine. The demonstrations of high-voltage currents and artificial lightning are particularly impressive, as is the re-creation of a mine.

Figures of miners at work in a re-created coal mine from c.1925

PHYSICS, CHEMISTRY AND PHARMACEUTICALS

THE PHYSICS and chemistry section is outstanding. There are fascinating reconstructions of the laboratories of great scientists and also a collection of the original instruments used in the some of the greatest scientific discoveries, as well as many pieces of prototype apparatus.

The exhibits are complemented by interesting demonstrations of the latest technology in optics, nuclear physics and chemistry. In the pharmaceuticals section the

exhibits graphically illustrate the different biochemical processes that take place in the human body.

MUSICAL INSTRUMENTS

THIS SECTION is displayed in chronological order. The centrepiece of the keyboard instruments section is the earliest harpsichord, which was made in 1561.

The sections on wind, stringed and percussion instruments are equally fascinating. There are also music machines and modern electronic keyboards. In the acoustic hall visitors can try out the synthesizer, creating an almost endless range of weird sounds or analysing their own voice.

DECORATIVE ARTS

THE DECORATIVE ARTS are illustrated by a number of thematic displays. The section opens with glass and ceramics manufacturing techniques from the earliest times to the present.

There is an exhibition of paper manufacturing and printing technology, including an impressive display of industrial textile machinery.

The exhibition of the development of film and photography begins with Daguerre's original equipment from 1839 and ends with the latest digital technology.

The display of technical toys goes all the way from simple building blocks to the most sophisticated modern modelling kits. On the same floor is a realistic re-creation of Altamira cave, in Spain, with its Stone Age paintings.

A quadrant (an instrument for measuring azimuths) made in 1760

TIME, WEIGHTS AND MEASURES

A FINE DISPLAY of clocks and watches illustrates the problems of measuring time. The clocks begin with the simplest forms, such as sundials and sand-clocks, and progress to highly intricate and lavishly decorated mechanical clocks. There are also gigantic clock-tower mechanisms and elaborately ornamented grandfather clocks from various periods, as well as more modern clocks and watches.

The weights and measures section illustrates the unification of measurements, and shows various types of measuring equipment.

An Augsburg clock with the figure of a dancing bear, 1580–90

ASTRONOMY

WITH OVER 180 exhibits, the astronomy section explores such major and still incompletely understood questions as the structure of the universe and the nature of solar energy. It also charts the development of this field of human enquiry with a variety of measuring instruments and models of spaceships, and with models of solar systems and galaxies. It also addresses the problems of radiation and the enigma of black holes. In the observatory visitors can view the stars through giant telescopes.

A highly ornamental brass calculating machine from 1735

AUTOMATION, MICROELECTRONICS AND TELECOMMUNICATIONS

THE PURPOSE of this section is to illustrate the genesis and development of modern technology. It opens with the first calculating machines, developed by Blaise Pascal (1642), Gottfried von Leibniz (1700) and Braun (1735), and the first computer, the earliest built by Konrad Zuse in 1941. There is also an interesting display of the latest information technology.

The development of microelectronics is illustrated with models of the simplest diodes, transistors, resistors, condensers and semi-conductors. The importance of crystals in semiconductors and other aspects of modern electronics is also illustrated.

For non-specialists, the use of high-tech applications in everyday life is of particular interest. Broadcasting and the disseminating of information, by means of radio, television, fibre optics and computers, also have important displays.

THE ZEISS PLANETARIUM

One of the world's best-equipped planetariums occupies the sixth floor of the museum. An artificial sky is created by a Zeiss computer-controlled projector. The dome, 15 m (49 ft) across, is used for the projection of images of the sun, the moon and the planets, along with 8,900 stars and 25 constellations and nebulae. You can watch the movements of heavenly bodies as they change position through the year and view them from different points on the earth. There are also laser shows (Cosmic Dreams, Pink Floyd and Laser Magic II), for which special spectacles are provided. Tickets for the Zeiss Planetarium are sold separately.

AGRICULTURE AND GEODESY

THIS SECTION illustrates the development of farming equipment from the simplest tools to ploughs and modern farm machinery. The geodesic displays show methods of measuring the earth and the development of topography, from early surveying equipment and maps and globes to modern satellite surveying.

TRANSPORT

THE LARGEST SECTION of the museum, and the most popular with visitors, is dedicated to land, water and air transport, as well as space flight. The section opens with an exhibition of cars, bicycles and carriages, including the earliest bicycles. The displays of cars and motorcycles include the first car made by Carl Benz, in 1886. There are also models of cars from the first half of the 20th century, and the very latest examples of automotive engineering.

Another attraction is the well-illustrated history of railways, which is represented by a large collection of engines and carriages, including *Puffing Billy*, the first steam engine (1814), and the first electric engine (1879), old signalling equipment and modern computer-controlled model railways.

The aircraft hall is two storeys high, enabling some of the exhibits to be suspended from the ceiling. The hall illustrates the history of flight, from Otto Lilienthal's glider of 1891, to World War II aircraft and the latest development in aircraft technology. The hall on the second floor is dedicated to space flight. The water transport section has an impressive collection of sailing ships, lifeboats and fishing boats, and a 1906 submarine.

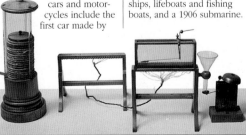

Electrochemical telegraph apparatus dating from 1809

THE UNIVERSITY DISTRICT

THE AREA to the north of the Old Town is a varied district in terms both of its architecture and its atmosphere. Ludwigstraße is lined exclusively with elegant Neo-Classical buildings, most of them government offices and public buildings, including the Bavarian State Library and the university.

West and north of Ludwigstraße the atmosphere changes completely. The buildings here are in a variety of styles spanning the 19th and 20th centuries. The area abounds in trendy shops, bookshops and pubs and it is filled with crowds of young

Art Nouveau ornament

students. Full of history and local colour, this area, known as Schwabing, is fascinating to visit. Leopoldstraße, its bustling main boulevard, comes as a great contrast to Ludwigstraße.

To the east of Schwabing is the Englischer Garten, with the museums of Prinzregentenstraße on its southern side. The park is a welcome oasis to the footsore visitor and to those seeking a moment's peace. Here you can rest among abundant greenery, sunbathe (even nude), cool off in the water or enjoy a cold beer in one of the beer-gardens at the Chinese Tower.

SIGHTS AT A GLANCE

Churches
Ludwigskirche **5**

Museums and Galleries
Archäologische Staatssammlung **11**
Bayerisches Nationalmuseum pp108–109 **13**
Haus der Kunst **14**
Schack-Galerie **12**

Historic Buildings
Akademie der Bildenden Künste **8**
Bayerische Staatsbibliothek **4**
Jugendstilhaus in der Ainmillerstraße **10**
Ludwig-Maximilians-Universität **6**
Pacelli Palais **9**
Siegestor **7**

Streets and Squares
Ludwigstraße **3**
Odeonsplatz **2**
Wittelsbacherplatz **1**

KEY

	Street-by-Street map *See pp100–101*
U	U-Bahn station
	Tram stop
	Bus stop
P	Parking

GETTING THERE

This part of the city is best reached on U-Bahn lines 3 and 6, alighting at Universität or Giselastraße. The museums on Prinzregentenstraße are most conveniently reached by tram 17 or bus 53.

◁ **Leopoldstraße 77, a typical Munich building in the Art Nouveau style**

Street-by-Street: Along Ludwigstraße

Sᴵɢʜᴛsᴇᴇɪɴɢ in this part of the city is fascinating for some but less appealing for others. The district's monumental Neo-Classical architecture was designed to a unified urban plan. There are no shops or pubs here. Instead the streets are lined with palaces whose façades are reminiscent of Italian Romanesque or Renaissance architecture, and the long avenues are punctuated by large squares. It is hard to imagine that the bustling, culturally varied Schwabing district is just next door.

Ludwig-Maximilians-Universität
The university building, looking onto Amalienstraße, has an eclectic façade with an arcaded lower storey **6**

★ Wittelsbacherplatz
Ludwig I's palace, built on Wittelsbacherplatz in 1825, was briefly the residence of its creator, Leo von Klenze **1**

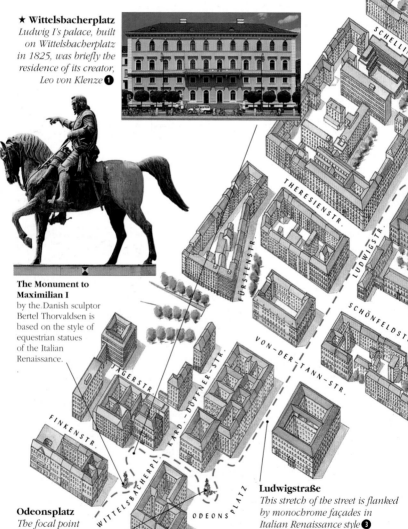

The Monument to Maximilian I
by the Danish sculptor Bertel Thorvaldsen is based on the style of equestrian statues of the Italian Renaissance.

Odeonsplatz
The focal point is the monument to Ludwig I **2**

Ludwigstraße
This stretch of the street is flanked by monochrome façades in Italian Renaissance style **3**

SCHELLINGSTR.

THERESIENSTR.

LUDWIGSTR.

SCHÖNFELDSTR.

FÜRSTENSTR.

VON-DER-TANN-STR.

JÄGERSTR.

KARD.-DÖPFNER-STR.

FINKENSTR.

WITTELSBACHERPL.

ODEONSPLATZ

| 0 metres | 100 |
| 0 yards | 100 |

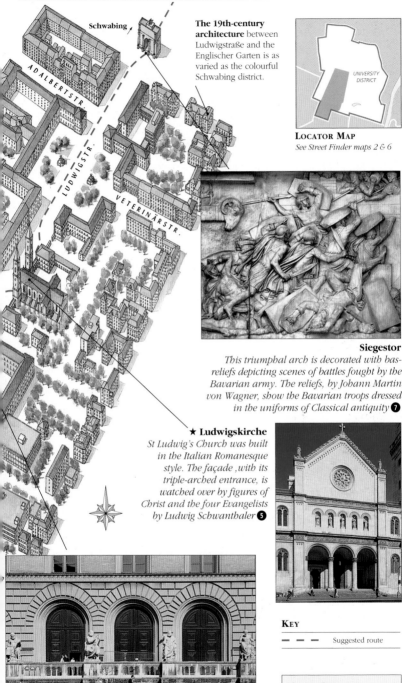

The 19th-century architecture between Ludwigstraße and the Englischer Garten is as varied as the colourful Schwabing district.

LOCATOR MAP
See Street Finder maps 2 & 6

Siegestor
This triumphal arch is decorated with bas-reliefs depicting scenes of battles fought by the Bavarian army. The reliefs, by Johann Martin von Wagner, show the Bavarian troops dressed in the uniforms of Classical antiquity **7**

★ **Ludwigskirche**
St Ludwig's Church was built in the Italian Romanesque style. The façade ,with its triple-arched entrance, is watched over by figures of Christ and the four Evangelists by Ludwig Schwanthaler **5**

Bayerische Staatsbibliothek
A long flight of steps leads to the entrance of the Bavarian State Library. The balustrade is decorated with statues of Thucydides, Homer, Aristotle and Hippocrates by Ludwig Schwanthaler **4**

KEY

– – – Suggested route

STAR SIGHTS

★ **Ludwigskirche**

★ **Wittelsbacherplatz**

The Palladian façade of Arco-Zinneberg Palace on Wittelsbacherplatz

Wittelsbacherplatz ❶

Map 3 C1 (6 D1). Ⓤ *Odeonsplatz.* 🚌 *53.*

THIS SQUARE is situated on Briennerstraße, one of the city's most elegant streets, which leads off from Odeonsplatz. Wittelsbacherplatz was laid out in the 1820s to a design by Leo von Klenze, and is one of Munich's finest squares. It is lined on three sides by Neo-Classical palaces, and the square itself is laid with paving slabs and stones arranged to form various patterns.

Von Klenze lived in the Ludwig-Ferdinand Palais on the south side of the square. From 1878 the palace belonged to Duke Ludwig Ferdinand, after whom it was named. It is now owned by the Siemens corporation.

On the west side of the square is Arco-Zinneberg Palace, also designed by Leo von Klenze, which today houses upmarket shops. To the east is the Odeon and the Palais Méjean, which was rebuilt after being destroyed in World War II.

In the centre of the square stands a monument to the Elector Maximilian I. It was designed by the prominent Danish Neo-Classical sculptor Bertel Thorvaldsen and was unveiled in 1839.

Odeonsplatz ❷

Map 3 C1 (6 D1). Ⓤ *Odeonsplatz.* 🚌 *53.*

IN THE EARLY 19th century, when the Schwabinger Tor was demolished, a decision was made to impose order on the haphazard arrangement of buildings to the north of the Residenz and the Theatinerkirche. In 1817 Maximilian I Joseph approved Leo von Klenze's plan for the Odeonsplatz, unaware that its originator was in fact his son, Ludwig I. The heir to the throne wished to create a magnificent square marking the start of the main thoroughfare to the northern districts and also acting as a triumphal entry point into Munich.

The Odeonsplatz takes its name from the Odeon, a concert hall built by Leo von Klenze in 1826–8 as a counterpart to the Leuchtenbergpalais of 1816–21. Set back from the square, both buildings serve to elongate it.

The equestrian statue of Ludwig I flanked by personifications of Religion, Art, Poetry and Industry in the centre of the square was created by Max Widmann in 1862. It faces the side of the square containing the Market Hall of 1825–6 and the arch

Monument to Ludwig I on Odeonsplatz

leading to the palace court. On the side of the Old Town, the square is bounded by the Feldherrenhalle.

Ludwigstraße ❸

Map 2 D5, 2 E5. Ⓤ *Odeonsplatz, Universität.* 🚌 *53.*

ONE OF THE most splendid city streets in Europe is Ludwigstraße. It was built from 1815 to 1852, the general plan and the first group of buildings being designed and completed by Leo von Klenze. The street begins at Odeonsplatz, whose Italian Renaissance-style palaces harmonize perfectly with the buildings at the beginning of Ludwigstraße. In 1827 the project was taken over by Friedrich von Gärtner, who was responsible for the buildings south of Theresienstraße, which he gave Romanesque and Byzantine elements. The principal buildings on this part of the street are the Bavarian State Library, Ludwigskirche and university buildings.

In the mid-19th century, the Feldherrenhalle and Siegestor were added, at the south and north ends of the street respectively. In building this triumphal route, Ludwig I departed from the city's planning rules to satisfy his aesthetic and political ideals.

The Odeon concert hall before it was destroyed in 1944

The fountain in the centre of Geschwister-Scholl-Platz at Ludwig-Maximilians-Universität

Bayerische Staatsbibliothek ❹

BAVARIAN STATE LIBRARY

Ludwigstr. 16. **Map** 2 E5.
🚇 Odeonsplatz, Universität. 🚌 53.
📞 28 63 80. 🕐 9am–9pm Mon–Fri,
10am–5pm Sat–Sun. ♿ telephone
in advance.

THE BAYERISCHE Staats-
bibliothek, Germany's
second largest municipal
library after that in Berlin,
has its origins in the
collections of books
that were amassed by
Duke Albrecht V and
Wilhelm V in the
16th century. It was
enhanced from 1663,
when the Elector
Friedrich Maria
ordered that one
copy of every new
book published in
Bavaria or
published by a
Bavarian abroad
should be kept in the library.
An enormous addition to the
royal collection of books –
particularly of early editions –
was made when the Jesuit
order was disbanded in 1773
and again when the monas-
teries were dissolved in 1803.

Statue of Hippocrates outside the library

Today the Bayerische
Staatsbibliothek contains
almost 6 million volumes,
including 71,500 manuscripts,
290,000 maps and almost
20,000 current periodicals.

The library was the first
architectural project undertaken by Friedrich von
Gärtner, who started in 1832
and completed it in 1843. The
building echoes the style of
Italian Renaissance palaces.
The great interior staircase is
flanked by figures of Classical
sages carved by Ludwig
Schwanthaler and overlooked
by figures of the library's
founders, Albrecht V and
Ludwig I.

Ludwigskirche ❺

ST LUDWIG'S CHURCH

Ludwigstr. 20. **Map** 2 E5.
🚇 Universität. 🚌 53. 🕐 7am–8pm
daily (except during services).

ITS FAÇADE set with pointed
twin steeples, St Ludwig's
Church is in sharp contrast
to the neighbouring
Staatsbibliothek. It
was built in the Italian
Romanesque style by
Friedrich von Gärtner
in 1829–43. The niches
in the façade contain
figures of Christ and
the four Evangelists.
The wings connect
the church to the
presbytery and
to Friedrich von
Gärtner's house. The
interior is decorated
with Italian Renaissance-
style paintings by Peter
Cornelius and his
pupils. The painting
of the Last Judgment
is the second largest
in the world after
Michelangelo's in the
Sistine Chapel.

The Neo-Romanesque façade of St Ludwig's Church

Ludwig-Maximilians-Universität ❻

LUDWIG MAXIMILIAN UNIVERSITY

Geschwister-Scholl-Platz/ Professor-
Huber-Platz. **Map** 2 E4. 🚇 Universität.
📞 21 800. 🕐 7:30am–9pm
Mon–Fri. ♿

THIS INSTITUTE of higher
education is named in
honour of its first sponsors.
In 1472 Ludwig der Reiche
(the Rich) founded a Jesuit
Studium Generale in
Ingolstadt. In 1773 it became
a university. Maximilian I
Joseph moved it to Landshut
in 1800 and in 1826 Ludwig I
transferred it to Munich. The
university has been located
on Ludwigstraße since 1840.

Today there are some
60,000 students. The noisy
crowds of young people
ensure that the streets in the
vicinity are always full of life.
The university's assembly hall
and seminar rooms are set
round two quadrangles. The
latter are named after Hans
and Sophie Scholl and
Professor Kurt Huber, who
together founded the
White Rose movement
that opposed Hitler.
In 1943 members of
the group distributed
anti-Nazi leaflets at
the university, an
event that is
commemorated by
the "fossilized" sheets
of paper in the
paving of the
main building's
courtyard. The
group was
arrested and
most of its
members were
executed.

The monumental Siegestor, crowned by the personification of Bavaria

Siegestor **7**
VICTORY GATE

Ludwigstr. **Map** 2 E4.
U Universität.

FOLLOWING THE early 19th-century fashion for erecting triumphal arches, Friedrich von Gärtner designed the Siegestor for Ludwig I. The monument was built in 1843–50, and with its three grand arches it echoes the architecture of the Feldherrenhalle *(see pp 78–9)*. The building stands on Ludwigstraße at the intersection with Leopoldstraße, Schwabing's fine main street.

The design of the Siegestor is based on the Arch of Constantine in Rome. It honours the Bavarian army and its role in the country's victory against Napoleon. The arch is covered in bas-reliefs depicting battle scenes, medallions, personifications of the Bavarian provinces, and figures of Victory at the top of the columns. The arch is crowned by the figure of Bavaria riding in a chariot drawn by four lions. The inscription that was added in 1958 states that the arch, which is "dedicated to victory, destroyed during the war", appeals for peace.

Passing through the Siegestor and entering Leopoldstraße, there is a notable change of atmosphere. The architectural uniformity of Ludwigstraße is replaced by stylistic variety in houses of the late 19th and early 20th centuries. The cafés, restaurants, music shops, book-stores, cinemas and discos here make for a vibrant atmosphere that persists into the small hours. This is the heart of the renowned Schwabing district.

Akademie der Bildenden Künste **8**
ACADEMY OF FINE ARTS

Akademiestr. 2. **Map** 2 E4.
C 38 520. **U** Universität. **&**
● closed to the public.

DURING THE 19th century Munich was one of the most important centres of painting, although it was regarded as being rather conservative.

Munich's artistic community developed around the Academy of Fine Arts, which was founded in 1808. Many painters who subsequently became famous studied here, including the Germans Wilhelm Leibl and Franz Marc, the German-Swiss Paul Klee, the Russian-born Wassily Kandinsky, and the Italian Giorgio de Chirico.

The Academy of Fine Arts was originally housed in the Jesuit College of Michaelskirche, moving to its present location in 1886. The architect of the new building was Gottfried Neureuther, who based his design on that of a three-storey Italian palazzo.

The façade is pierced by a series of arched windows and the building is approached by a driveway leading to a grand staircase, with equestrian statues of Castor and Pollux.

Pacelli Palais **9**

Georgenstr. 8–10. **Map** 2 E3.
U Universität, Giselastr. ● closed to the public.

THIS GRAND city palace provides an opportunity to compare two distinct architectural styles that were prevalent in Munich around 1900. The right-hand half of the building is in a late historical style, with columns, tympanums, small towers, carved loggias and sculptures. The flat but colourful Neo-Classical decoration on the left-hand half is typical of the Munich Art Nouveau style. It is now a private residence.

Art Nouveau decoration on the Pacelli Palais

Jugendstilhaus in der Ainmillerstraße **10**
ART NOUVEAU HOUSE

Ainmillerstr. 22. **Map** 2 E2. 🔲 27.
● closed to the public.

THE HOUSE at Ainmillerstraße 22 was the first residential building in Munich to be given an Art Nouveau (Jugendstil) façade. It was designed by Ernst Haiger and Heinrich Helbig in 1899–1900. The highly intricate scheme features decorative floral and mock-antique motifs.

Highly ornamental terracotta frieze on a window at the Akademie der Bildenden Künste

Schwabing

AT THE END of the 19th century Schwabing was well known as a bohemian district inhabited by writers and avant-garde artists. *Simplicissimus*, an anti-authoritarian satirical magazine, and the Elf Scharf-richter cabaret associated with it, were both located here. Many writers' cafés determined the atmosphere of the district. It had its heyday in the years preceding

Logo of Alter Simpl, a local cult café

World War I, when the writers Thomas Mann and Frank Wedekind and the artists Wassily Kandinsky and Paul Klee lived here. Paradoxically, after 1918, it became the favourite haunt of Adolf Hitler, who set up the offices of the *Völkischer Beobachter* newspaper here. After 1945 the district strove to revive its former glory with the help of local artists and students.

The suburbs of Munich *are seen here in a painting by Wassily Kandinsky. The Russian-born painter lived in Schwabing from 1902 to 1914, becoming a German citizen in 1927.*

Art Nouveau window decoration *on the house at Leopoldstraße 77 is a fine example of the trend for geometrical Art Nouveau typical of houses in Schwabing.*

Artists from Schwabing *formed the avant-garde Neue Künstlervereinigung in Munich in the early 1900s. This photograph was taken on the balcony of Kandinsky's house at No. 36 Ainmillerstraße. It shows, from left to right: Maria and Franz Marc; Bernhard Koehler, Kandinsky (seated), Heinrich Campendonk and Thomas von Hartmann. In 1911 the Der Blaue Reiter group was established in Munich, with Kandinsky at the forefront.*

This front door *decoration on the Jugendstilhaus in Ainmillerstraße shows Art Nouveau asymmetry and symbolism. It reflects local artistic bohemian culture, in which the legendary Countess Reventlow, who propounded a free, erotic lifestyle, was a leading figure.*

Englischer Garten

THE ENGLISCHER Garten (English Garden) is so named because it is naturalistically laid out, in the manner of English landscaped grounds. One of Europe's largest city parks, it came into existence thanks to the vision of Sir Benjamin Thompson, an American officer on whom the Elector Karl Theodor bestowed the title Count von

Bas-relief on the Rumford Memorial

Rumford. As Bavaria's Minister of War, he ordered that the swampy terrain around the Isar be developed for military use. It became a municipal park, with many landscaped features designed by Rumford, Reinhold von Werneck and Friedrich Ludwig von Sckell, in 1789. Today the park is a valued green area for the people of Munich.

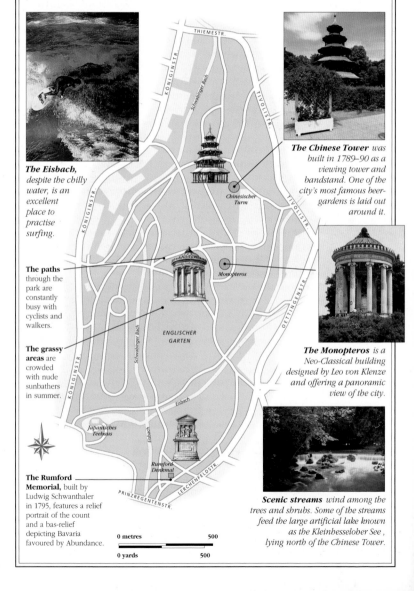

The Eisbach, *despite the chilly water, is an excellent place to practise surfing.*

The paths through the park are constantly busy with cyclists and walkers.

The grassy areas are crowded with nude sunbathers in summer.

The Rumford Memorial, built by Ludwig Schwanthaler in 1795, features a relief portrait of the count and a bas-relief depicting Bavaria favoured by Abundance.

The Chinese Tower *was built in 1789–90 as a viewing tower and bandstand. One of the city's most famous beer-gardens is laid out around it.*

The Monopteros *is a Neo-Classical building designed by Leo von Klenze and offering a panoramic view of the city.*

Scenic streams *wind among the trees and shrubs. Some of the streams feed the large artificial lake known as the Kleinhesseloher See, lying north of the Chinese Tower.*

0 metres   500

0 yards   500

Archäologische Staatssammlung ⑪

ARCHAEOLOGICAL MUSEUM

Lerchenfeldstr. 2. **Map** 4 E1.
 21 12 402. 17. 53.
 9am–4:30pm Tue–Sun.

THE ARCHAEOLOGICAL Museum, at the southern end of the Englischer Garten, is a modern glass and steel construction consisting of six blocks arranged in chequer-board formation. Formerly known as the Museum of Prehistory, it is one of the largest regional museums of archaeology in Germany.

The collections date back to the foundation of the Bavarian Academy of Sciences in 1759. The exhibits, which span a period of time from as early as 100,000 BC to AD 800, are chronologically presented in three separate sections: Pre-historic, Roman and Early Medieval.

A Celtic staff, probably for use in rituals

Implements and jewellery, coins and religious artifacts illustrate the history of human settlement in Bavaria. There is a rich collection of Roman exhibits, including bronze masks from Eining, the Straubing Treasure and many mosaics from Roman baths. A popular attraction is the mummified body of a 16th-century woman that was discovered in marshland.

Schack-Galerie ⑫

Prinzregentenstr. 9. **Map** 4 E1.
 10am–5pm Wed–Mon.
 23 80 52 24. 53. 20.

THIS INTERESTING collection of 19th-century paintings was formed by Friedrich von Schack (1815–94), a wealthy baron from Mecklenburg. As well as an art collector, he was a man of letters, a trans-lator and a traveller. In 1857 Schack bought a palace near the Propyläen, which he used to house his ever-growing art collection. Von Schack's main interest lay in contemporary Munich painters, and he often sponsored young artists who had not yet gained due recog-nition. Under the terms of his will, von Schack's art collect-ion was bequeathed to the Emperor Wilhelm II, who then decided to give the collection a home in Munich, commissioning a building especially for it. Designed by Max Littman and completed in 1910, the building has a Neo-Classical façade and is similar to the Berlin castle of the collection's founder, who is praised in an inscrip-tion on the façade.

In 1939 the Schack-Galerie was merged with the Bavarian State Art Collection. In 17 halls, it presents German painting from the late Romantic period. Among the 270 paintings are works by Moritz von Schwind, including *Turnip-counter* and *King Olch*, Arnold Böcklin's *Villa by the Sea* and *Triton and the Nereids*, and Anselm Feuerbach's *Portrait of a Roman Woman* and *Paolo and Francesca*. Also of interest are the paintings by Karl Spitzweg, Franz von Lenbach and Hans von Marées, and copies of Old Master paintings made by young artists sponsored by von Schack.

Façade of the Schack-Galerie, based on von Schack's Berlin castle

Bayerisches Nationalmuseum ⑬

See pp108–109.

Poster for an exhibition at the Haus der Kunst

Haus der Kunst ⑭

ART HOUSE

Prinzregentenstr. 1. **Map** 4 D1.
 21 12 70. during exhibitions 10am–10pm Tue–Thu, 10am–6pm Sat–Mon.

SINCE THE END of World War II, the Haus der Kunst has housed a fine collection of modern art. Built between 1933 and 1937, the Neo-Classical building is the work of a Nazi architect, Paul Ludwig Troost; Adolf Hitler laid the foundation stone and the building became the model for the nascent National Socialist architecture.

The museum opened its doors in 1937 with a display of propaganda art, which was proclaimed by the Nazis as "truly German". This was followed by a second presentation, "The Exhibition of Degenerate Art", in which several masterpieces of modern art were ridiculed.

Despite its original intended purpose, the building is now a dynamic museum of modern art that is famous far beyond the bounds of Munich for its regular special exhibitions. Its rich collection includes many representative works by major German artists of the 20th century, alongside modern works by such important foreign artists as Picasso, Matisse, Mondrian and Magritte. As well as Expressionist and Abstract paintings, examples of modern sculpture are on display in the museum.

Bayerisches Nationalmuseum ⑬

IN ARCHITECTURAL TERMS, the Bavarian National Museum was intended to embody the idea of a 19th-century artistic shrine. It was built by Gabriel von Seidl in 1894–5, and features a mixture of styles that expresses the richness and variety of the collections within. The decoration of the interior was devised with the exhibits in mind. The nucleus of the collection is that of the Wittelsbachs, which Maximilian II donated to the country in 1855. One of Germany's largest history museums, its collections span Classical antiquity to the 19th century.

A 16th-century suit of armour

Model of Munich
Commissioned by Albrecht V, this wooden model was made by Jacob Sandtner in 1570.

First floor

Bauernstube (Farmhouse Parlour)
These pieces of traditional furniture were made by Anton Perthaler of Lower Bavaria in the late 18th century.

Ground floor

★ Judith with the Head of Holofernes
This alabaster figure was made by Conrad Meit in 1515, with the figure of Judith being depicted as a nude.

Main entrance

★ Christmas Crib
In this 18th-century Neapolitan crib, realistic figures stand among the picturesque rocks and fantastic architecture.

Basement

Harpsichord
This harpsichord in the Musical Instruments Hall was made in Paris in 1754 by Jean Henri Hemsch.

VISITORS' CHECKLIST

Prinzregentenstr. 3. **Map** 4 E1.
U Lehel. **T** 17. **M** 53. **C** 211 24 01. ◯ 10am–5pm Tue–Wed & Fri–Sun, 10am–8pm Thu. **H** ✎ **&** by arrangement

★ St Mary Magdalene
This statue of the saint borne by angels was made by Tilman Riemenschneider in 1490–92 for an altarpiece.

MUSEUM GUIDE
The collections are laid out on three floors connected by grand staircases. The basement contains a collection of Christmas cribs (mainly Neapolitan and South German) and a section devoted to folk art. Painting, sculpture and crafts up to the 18th century are exhibited on the ground floor. The upper floor contains collections of musical instruments, porcelain and Biedermeier art.

STAR EXHIBITS

★ **Christmas Crib**

★ **Judith with the Head of Holofernes**

★ **St Mary Magdalene**

Gothic Hall
Laid out like a church, the hall contains religious art and tombstones of around 1500, including paintings by Johann Polack.

Romanesque Sculpture
Sculpture and architectural details dating from the first half of the 13th century and originating from the Wessobrunn Benedictine monastery fill this sculpture hall.

KEY

☐ Folk art

☐ Cribs

☐ Late 16th-century art

☐ 17th and 18th-century art

☐ Thematic exhibition, including musical instruments and porcelain

☐ Non-exhibition space

THE MUSEUMS DISTRICT

A COMPETITION for an architectural design to embellish the area along the Royal Route between the Residenz and Schloss Nymphenburg was announced in 1807. The winning design was one jointly produced by Friedrich Ludwig von Sckell and Karl von Fischer, although it was later modified by Leo von Klenze.

The axis of this area, known as the Maxvorstadt, is Briennerstraße.

Coat of arms on the façade of the Palaeontology Museum

Maximilian I Joseph and Ludwig I dreamed of turning Munich into a city of the arts, commissioning the Alte Pinakothek and Neue Pinakothek, and grand buildings on Königsplatz. The 19th-century painter Franz von Lenbach had an imposing villa (now an art gallery) built on the square. The omnipresence of art here is underscored by the district's many private galleries, antique shops and bookstores.

SIGHTS AT A GLANCE

Museums and Galleries
Alte Pinakothek pp118–21 **8**
Galerie im Lenbachhaus **6**
Glyptothek **5**
Museum "Reich der Kristalle" **10**
Neue Pinakothek pp122–5 **9**
Paläontologisches Museum **7**
Pinakothek der Moderne **11**
Staatliche
  Antikensammlungen **3**

Historic Buildings
Dürkheim Palais **12**

Justizpalast **15**
Propyläen **4**

Churches
Basilika St Bonifaz **2**

Streets and Squares
Karlsplatz **14**
Karolinenplatz **1**
Lenbachplatz **13**

Gardens
Alter Botanischer Garten **16**

Other Sights
Löwenbräukeller **17**

GETTING THERE

The best way to get to the Museums District is on U-Bahn line 2, alighting at Königsplatz, and then by tram 27, alighting at the Pinakothek or Karolinenplatz stop.

KEY

▨	Street-by-Street map See pp112–13
U	U-Bahn station
S	S-Bahn station
🚊	Tram stop
P	Parking

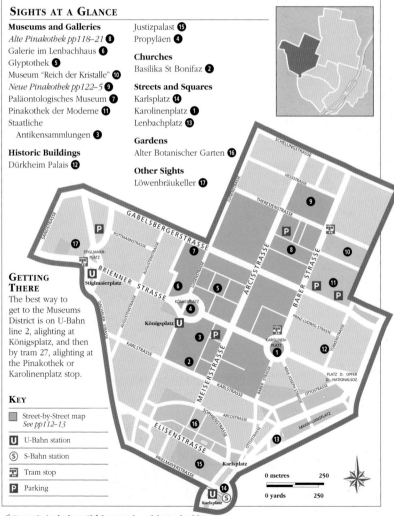

◁ **Fountain in the beautiful front garden of the Lenbachhaus**

Street-by-Street: Around Königsplatz

SEVERAL DAYS are needed for a thorough exploration of this part of the city. The many museums here contain world-class art – from prehistoric to modern. On Königsplatz, Greek and Roman sculpture can be seen in the Glyptothek, and Classical and other antiquities in the Antikensammlungen. The Alte Pinakothek and Neue Pinakothek nearby contain some of the richest collections of European painting in the world. The Lenbachhaus is renowned for works by the Blaue Reiter group. Those interested in natural history will enjoy the Palaeontology Museum.

A Cupid in the garden of the Lenbachhaus

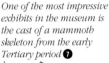

Paläontologisches Museum
One of the most impressive exhibits in the museum is the cast of a mammoth skeleton from the early Tertiary period **7**

Galerie im Lenbachhaus
The restored interior of the Lenbachhaus sets in its context the bourgeois lifestyle of Franz von Lenbach, the famous late-19th century Munich portraitist **6**

Propyläen
The frieze decorating the side towers of the Propyläen, with motifs and scenes from the Greek War of Independence, is by Ludwig Schwanthaler **4**

Staatliche Antikensammlungen
Among the museum's treasures is a collection of antique art and artifacts **3**

Basilika St Bonifaz
This church contains the tomb of Ludwig I **2**

★ **Glyptothek**
The Glyptothek's Ionic colonnade with pediment is flanked by statues of great artistic figures from Classical antiquity: Hephaestus, Prometheus, Daedalus, Phidias, Pericles and Emperor Hadrian **5**

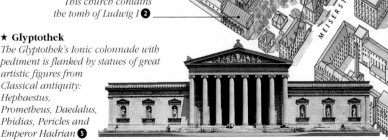

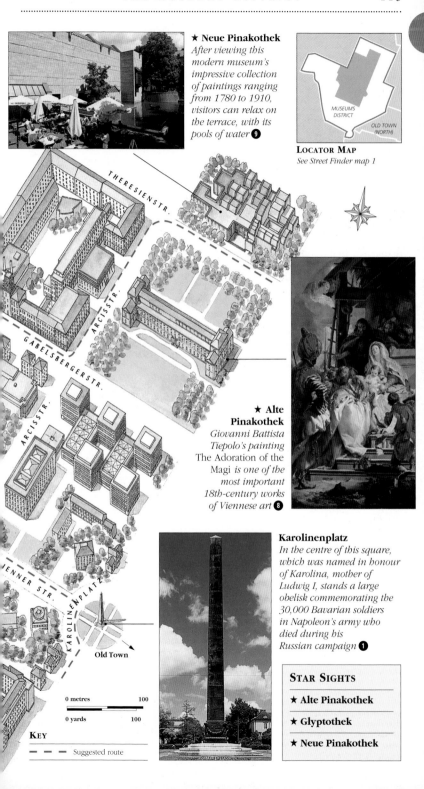

★ **Neue Pinakothek**
After viewing this modern museum's impressive collection of paintings ranging from 1780 to 1910, visitors can relax on the terrace, with its pools of water ❾

LOCATOR MAP
See Street Finder map 1

★ **Alte Pinakothek**
Giovanni Battista Tiepolo's painting The Adoration of the Magi *is one of the most important 18th-century works of Viennese art* ❽

Karolinenplatz
In the centre of this square, which was named in honour of Karolina, mother of Ludwig I, stands a large obelisk commemorating the 30,000 Bavarian soldiers in Napoleon's army who died during his Russian campaign ❶

Old Town

0 metres   100
0 yards   100

KEY

‑ ‑ ‑ Suggested route

STAR SIGHTS

★ Alte Pinakothek

★ Glyptothek

★ Neue Pinakothek

The Amerikahaus on Karolinenplatz

Karolinenplatz ❶

Map 1 C5, 3 A1. 🚊 27.

Maximilian I Joseph, who continued the development of Munich that was begun by his predecessor Karl Theodor, focused his attention on the area around Briennerstraße. The Royal Route connecting the Residenz with Schloss Nymphenburg was opened up, and it became the focal point of the development of this suburb, which was named Maxvorstadt in the king's honour.

In 1809–12 a square was built at the junction of Briennerstraße and Barerstraße. This was Karolinenplatz, the first star junction in Munich. Designed by Karl von Fischer, it was modelled on the Place de l'Étoile in Paris. In the centre of the square stands a bronze obelisk 29 m (95 ft) high, designed by Leo von Klenze and cast from Turkish guns captured at the Battle of Navarino in 1827. The obelisk commemorates the 30,000 Bavarian soldiers who died during Napoleon's Russian campaign of 1812.

On the northwestern side of the Karolinenplatz is the Anthropologische Staatssammlung, the only anthropological collection of its kind in Germany, with a curious assortment of skulls. On the western side is the Amerikahaus, an American cultural centre, built in 1955–7.

Basilika St Bonifaz ❷

BASILICA OF ST BONIFACE

Karlstr. 34. **Map** 3 A1, 5 A1.
🕗 8am–8pm daily. 🚊 27.

The basilica of St Boniface, which was commissioned by Ludwig I, functioned as the parish church of the Maxvorstadt but was later dedicated to the Benedictine monks who moved to Munich. The church, which takes the form of an early Christian basilica, was built in 1835–48 by Georg Friedrich Ziebland.

Behind the portico, which is supported by Ionic columns, are three arched doorways. The central one is flanked by statues of St Peter and St Boniface, and the arch is crowned by a portrait of the architect himself – a rare occurrence – in medieval dress. The location of the church and monastery at the rear of the Kunstausstellungsgebäude (now the Antikensammlung) illustrates contemporary ideas about architecture, in which religion was to be linked with art and science, as represented by the Benedictine order.

The basilica, which was built after the destruction brought by the Franco-

Central section of the façade of the Basilika St Bonifaz

Prussian War, carries no memory of the original double-aisled church, which had colourful paintings and an open-beam roof supported on 66 monolithic columns. Of its furnishings, the white marble tomb of Ludwig I survives, with the tombstone of his wife Theresa behind it.

Staatliche Antiken-sammlungen ❸

THE NATIONAL COLLECTION OF ANTIQUITIES

Königsplatz 1. **Map** 1 B5. 📞 59 83 59. Ⓤ Königsplatz. 🚊 27.
🕗 10am–5pm Tue–Sun, 10am–8pm Wed. 🎫

In 1838 Ludwig I, temporarily at loggerheads with the court architect Leo von Klenze, commissioned Georg Friedrich Ziebland to design the southern side of the Königsplatz. The king wished for an exhibition hall that would adjoin the Benedictine monastery and Basilica of St Boniface at the rear. The building, completed in 1848, was modelled on the design of a late Classical Greek temple, its proportions differing from those of the Glyptothek on the opposite side of the square. Over the large colonnaded portico is a tympanum containing a figure of Bavaria as patroness of art and industry. From 1898 to 1916 the hall housed the gallery of the Munich Secession (Art Nouveau movement), after which it was taken over by the Neue Staatsgalerie. Since 1967 it has housed the National Collection of Antiquities.

This impressive collection includes an important assemblage of Greek and Etruscan vases, plus fine pottery and glass, bronze and terracotta figures and jewellery. The core of the collection was donated by Ludwig I, a passionate collector and an ardent admirer of the ancient world.

Greek kylix (drinking vessel), Staatliche Antikensammlung

Propyläen ❹

Map 1 B5. **Ⓤ** *Königsplatz.*

FROM 1815, Ludwig I and Leo von Klenze planned the layout of the Royal Square, or Königsplatz, west of Karolinenplatz. The latter was laid out as an almost perfect square, with the Glyptothek and what is now the Antikensammlungen facing one another on opposite sides. To the west of the square was a gate built by Leo von Klenze in 1854–62, named the Propyläen.

According to the designs of the king and the architect, the buildings on three sides of the square would each represent one of the orders of architecture. The Propyläen would represent the Doric order, the Glyptothek the Ionic, and the exhibition hall the Corinthian.

The Propyläen was based on the Propylaeum in Athens, which consists of a central entrance way crowned by a grand tympanum and flanked by towers. Munich's Propyläen was intended to function as the western gate into the city, the Neo-Classical equivalent of the medieval Isar Gate. When, however, the city's development rendered it superfluous, Ludwig I and von Klenze emphasized the Hellenistic character of the Propyläen, turning it into a kind of monument to the Greek War

of Liberation against Turkey (1821–9). In so doing they strove to underline the dynastic connections between Bavaria and the newly independent Greek state.

An inscription inside the gate commemorates those who fought in the war against the Turks. The reliefs surrounding the building, by Ludwig Schwanthaler, show scenes from Greek battles. The main focus is the relief, also by Schwanthaler, on the tympanum facing the square, in which personifications of Religion, Science and Art, Trade, Building and Agriculture pay homage to Otto I Wittelsbach, the first ruler of the new Greek state. Just before the official opening of the Propyläen on 23 October 1862, Otto I was toppled from the Greek throne and had to make a humiliating return to Bavaria.

Königsplatz was given a new ideological slant by Adolf Hitler. In 1933–7, two large buildings were raised in the adjoining streets to house the central organs of Nazi power. One was Führerbau, where the British prime minister Neville Chamberlain signed the infamous Munich Agreement in 1938, and the other Verwaltungsbau. Before them two mock Greek temples were built for the tombs of the martyrs of the Beer-hall Putsch of 1923 *(see p79)*. The square became a focal point for Nazi rallies and parades.

After World War II the memorials were demolished, and in 1947 the Nazi party building became the central building of the Institute of Art History.

LEO VON KLENZE (1784–1864)

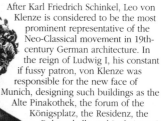

After Karl Friedrich Schinkel, Leo von Klenze is considered to be the most prominent representative of the Neo-Classical movement in 19th-century German architecture. In the reign of Ludwig I, his constant if fussy patron, von Klenze was responsible for the new face of Munich, designing such buildings as the Alte Pinakothek, the forum of the Königsplatz, the Residenz, the Ruhmeshalle and Ludwigstraße. He was responsible for planning Munich as the new Athens, as well as the Walhalla near Ratisbon, the Befreiungshalle in Kelheim and the New Hermitage in St Petersburg.

Bust of the architect crowned with laurel

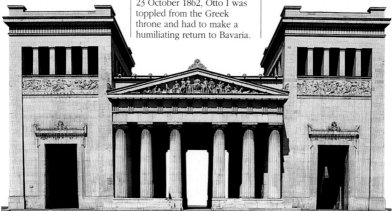

The Propyläen, a grand city gate in the Neo-Classical style, designed by Leo von Klenze

Glyptothek ❺

GLYPTOTECA

Königsplatz 3. **Map** 1 B5. 📞 *28 61 00.* Ⓤ *Königsplatz.* ⭕ *10am–8pm Tue, 10am–5pm Wed, 10am–8pm Thu, 10am–5pm Fri–Sun.* ♿

T HE IDEA of building a museum to house Greek and Roman sculpture originated in 1805, when Ludwig I, the future king, was on his first tour of Italy. His passion for collecting led to the formation of a considerable collection of antique statues, which he purchased in Italy and Greece.

In 1816 Leo von Klenze was assigned the task of designing a museum to house this collection. It was named the Glyptothek, from the Greek word *glypte*, meaning "carved stone". It is regarded as von Klenze's finest Neo-Classical work. The bas-relief in the tympanum over the portico depicts Athena surrounded by artists. The windowless walls of the building are set with niches containing figures that together make up a gallery of great artists, ranging from the mythical Hephaestus and Prometheus to some fine artists of the Renaissance to Antonio Canova and Ludwig Schwanthaler.

The museum's hall contains the world's finest collection of

Bas-relief from the tomb of Mnesarete, of around 380 BC

Statue of Cupid in the garden of Lenbachhaus

antique sculpture. Prize exhibits include Archaic figures from the Temple of Aphaia on Aegina of 500 BC, the famous Barberini Faun of 220 BC and the Rondanini Alexander of 338 BC.

Galerie im Lenbachhaus ❻

LENBACHHAUS ART GALLERY

Luisenstr. 33. **Map** 1 B5. 📞 *23 33 20 00.* Ⓤ *Königsplatz.* ⭕ *10am–6pm Tue–Sun.* ♿

T HE PORTRAITIST Franz von Lenbach (1836–1904), one of the greatest painters of 19th-century Munich, commissioned Gabriel von Seidl to build him a grand residence behind Königsplatz. The residence, completed in 1891, originally consisted of a residential area and a separate studio wing. These were joined together in 1912. The house and its garden are in the style of an Italian suburban villa, with Renaissance and Baroque elements.

In 1924 the property was bought by the municipality for use as an art gallery, for which a north wing was added. The grand interior of the Lenbachhaus, with many of the artist's paintings and sketches, has been preserved. The exhibition area contains galleries in which Munich painting from the Gothic to

the Art Nouveau periods is displayed, the 19th and early 20th centuries being well represented with works by Karl Spitzweg, Wilhelm Leibl and Lovis Corinth. The museum is also renowned for its fine paintings by artists of the Blaue Reiter group, which was active in Munich from 1911 to 1914 *(see p211)*. In 1957 Gabriele Münter, Wassily Kandinsky's partner up to 1914, offered the museum her private collection of pictures from his defining Munich and Murnau period. This offers the opportunity to explore the evolution of Kandinsky's art before his abstract period.

Another donation of works by Alexej Jawlenski, August Macke, Franz Marc and the young Paul Klee has enriched the collection. In 1971 the museum acquired the archives and works of the book illustrator Alfred Kubin. More recent additions are works by modern artists such as Andy Warhol, Joseph Beuys and Anselm Kiefer. In 1994, the Kunstbau, a hall for temporary exhibitions, was built in the adjoining U-Bahn station under Luisenstraße.

Paläontologisches Museum ❼

PALAEONTOLOGY MUSEUM

Richard-Wagner-Str. 10. **Map** 1 B5. 📞 *21 80 66 30.* Ⓤ *Königsplatz.* ⭕ *8am–4pm Mon–Thu, 8am–2pm Fri, 10am–4pm first Sun of the month.* ♿

S INCE 1950, the Bavarian palaeontological collection has occupied an eclectic building dating from 1899–1902. It was built by Leonhard Romeis as a crafts school, as the decorative motifs in the main entranceway reveal. The main hall is an arcade with a glass roof, where the skeletons of large animals are exhibited.

The collection grew from that of the Bavarian Academy of Sciences, founded in 1759, and of Munich University.

The displays are divided into various thematic groups: the development of mammals, animals of the Tertiary period and the Ice Age; the geological history of Munich; fossilized fish and reptiles from Jurassic sites in Bavaria and Württemberg; fossil plants; and the Ries meteorite crater near Nördlingen. Skeletons found in Bavaria include those of a mastodon, woolly rhinoceros, crocodile and giant tortoise. Fossilized palm trees show the existence of a tropical climate here in prehistoric times.

Main entrance to the Palaeontology Museum

Alte Pinakothek ❽

See pp118–21.

Neue Pinakothek ❾

See pp122–5.

Museum "Reich der Kristalle" ❿
MINERALOGY MUSEUM

Theresienstr. 41 *(entrance in Barerstr.)* **Map** 1 C5. **☎** 23 94 43 12. **Ⓤ** *Theresienstr.* **🚋** 27. **🕐** 1–5pm Tue–Fri, 1–6pm Sat–Sun. **♿**

THE EXHIBITS here are part of the great collection of the Mineralogische Staatsammlung, which originated with collections of rocks and minerals formed in the 18th century. The museum owes its exceptionally valuable

collection of minerals to Duke Maximilian Leuchtenberg, whose career included the supervision of mineral extraction in the Urals and Siberia. In 1858 his collection was added to that of the Bavarian Academy of Sciences.

The present museum is in a modern building. Visitors can enjoy a fine collection of colourful and often unusually shaped mineral formations from all over the world, and study the structure and appearance of crystals. Exhibitions devoted to special topics are also held.

A crystal in the Museum "Reich der Kristalle"

Pinakothek der Moderne ⓫

Ainmillerstr. 11. **Map** 1 C5. **Ⓤ** *Theresienstr.* **🚌** 53. **🚋** 27. **🕐** *First part of the building opens to the public in 2002.* **W** *www.pinakothek-der-moderne.de*

WORK ON a vast modern building to house 20th-century and contemporary art began in 1996. The gallery was intended to complement the Alte Pinakothek, whose exhibits go up about 1800, and the Neue Pinakothek, which is devoted to art of the 19th century. The building was designed by the Munich architect Stephan Braunfels,

whose goal was to create a spacious, highly transparent structure. Two entrances lead into diagonal tunnels that in turn lead to a central rotunda.

The collection of the Pinakothek der Moderne features outstanding 20th-century paintings, from Cubism (with works by Pablo Picasso and Georges Braque), the Neue Sachlichkeit and paintings by Giorgio De Chirico and Max Beckmann through to Pop Art, Minimal Art, Photorealism and the Junge Wilde movement of the early 1980s. Besides paintings, the gallery also houses collections of sculpture – including the well-known sculpture by Joseph Beuys entitled *The End of the World* – as well as drawings, installations and photographs.

The collection will be enhanced by private donations (including the gift of the Brandthorst Collection), and will include ultramodern art. Further additions are to be the collections of the Staatliche Graphische Sammlung (with graphic art dating from the 15th century to the present day), the Neue Sammlung (industrial designs from the Bayerisches Nationalmuseum) and the Architekturmuseum der TU, the largest collection of its kind in Germany.

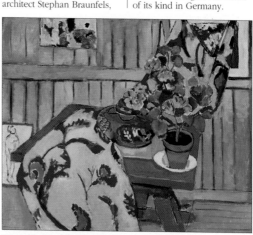

Painting by Henri Matisse in the Pinakothek der Moderne

Alte Pinakothek 🄭

T HE ALTE PINAKOTHEK, one of the world's most famous art galleries, opened in 1836. It is a building in the Italian Renaissance style, designed by Leo von Klenze. The history of its collections goes back to the Renaissance, when Wilhelm IV the Steadfast (ruled 1508–50) decided to adorn his residence with historic paintings. His successors were equally keen art collectors and, by the 18th century, an outstanding collection of 14th- to 18th-century paintings had been amassed.

St Luke Painting the Madonna (c. 1440)
This painting by the Netherlandish artist Rogier van der Weyden is one of his most widely copied works.

★ The Battle of Alexander (1529)
This famous painting by Albrecht Altdorfer depicts the decisive moment in Alexander the Great's victory over the Persians.

★ Pietà (c. 1495)
The rich, contrasting colours, strong effects of light and shadow and homogeneous composition of this painting are typical of the work of Sandro Botticelli.

Adoraton of the Magi
(c. 1502)
This scene by Hans Holbein the Elder forms part of an altarpiece from Kaisheim.

Ground floor

Main entrance

STAR EXHIBITS

★ **The Battle of Alexander**

★ **The Deposition**

★ **Pietà**

GALLERY GUIDE

The collections are laid out on two floors. The ground floor is occupied mainly by German painting up to 1500. On the first floor are works by German painters after 1500, as well as Dutch, Netherlandish, Flemish, French, Italian and Spanish paintings.

Portrait of Karl V (1548)
Titian painted this portrait of the emperor when he was in Augsburg for peace negotiations, known as the Peace of Augsburg.

VISITORS' CHECKLIST

Barerstr. 27. **Map** 1 C5.
23 80 52 16.
Königsplatz. 53. 27.
10am–5pm Tue–Wed,
Fri–Sun; 10am–10pm Thu.
Children under 14 free

Peasants Playing Cards (c.1632)
This is an expressive, semi-satirical scene from Flemish peasant life painted by Adriaen Brouwer.

★ The Deposition (c.1634)
In this dramatic painting, Rembrandt consciously challenged Rubens with his own vision of Christ's sacrifice.

Italian Baroque painting is represented by such masters as Tiepolo and Guido Reni.

KEY

◻ German painting

◻ Netherlandish painting

◻ Flemish painting

◼ Dutch painting

◻ Italian painting

◻ Spanish painting

◼ French painting

◻ Non-exhibition space

First floor

Portrait of the Marquise de Pompadour (1756)
One of the finest French Rococo paintings by François Boucher, this is currently on loan to the Neue Pinakothek (see pp122–5).

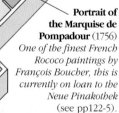

Land of Cockaigne (1562)
The Flemish artist Pieter Bruegel painted this visual satire on the mythical land of plenty, condemning gluttony and indolence.

Exploring the Alte Pinakothek

AFTER WORLD WAR II, the Alte Pinakothek was rebuilt by Hans Döllgast. The entrance hall, ticket office, bookshop and cafeteria are on the ground floor, as are the section on German Gothic painting, the Breughel Room and the temporary exhibitions gallery. The collections on the first floor are grouped according to the great national schools. The larger paintings are exhibited in the main rooms, and smaller ones in the side galleries.

The Abduction of the Daughters of Leukippos (1618) by Rubens

Four Apostles (1526), a pair of panels by Albrecht Dürer

GERMAN PAINTING

THE ALTE PINAKOTHEK is renowned for its important collection of German late Gothic and Renaissance art. The section opens with a collection of paintings by the Cologne School, from the Master of St Veronica (c. 1420), to the fine altar of St Bartholomew (1500–10), which anticipates the Renaissance. Late 15th-century painting is represented by Michael Pacher's *Altar of the Church Fathers*, with a bold handling of perspective.

The collection of paintings by Albrecht Dürer documents the development of his work from a *Self-Portrait* of 1500 to the *Four Apostles* of 1526. Two paintings by Matthias Grünewald show a strong Renaissance influence, as does the *Crucifixion* (1503) by Lucas Cranach the Elder. Albrecht Altdorfer of Regensburg, a painter of the Danube School, is represented by his *Battle of Alexander* with its pioneering use of landscape.

Mannerism is exemplified by the allegories by Hans Baldung Grien and Hans von Aachen's *Allegory of Truth*. Painting of the 17th century includes works by Adam Elsheimer and Johann Liss.

NETHERLANDISH PAINTING

THIS SCHOOL, which split into the Flemish and Dutch schools at the end of the 16th century, is introduced by the fine works of Rogier van der Weyden, particularly his Cologne Altarpiece with the famous *Adoration of the Magi*.

Hans Memling's *Seven Joys of the Virgin* depicts scenes from the life of Christ in an extensive symbolic landscape. A glimpse of the grotesque world of Hieronymus Bosch is given by a fragment of his *Last Judgement*, while a completely different climate bathes Pieter Breughel's *Land of Cockaigne*. An outstanding example of the assimilation of Italian Renaissance style is *Danae* by Jan Grossaert.

FLEMISH PAINTING

THE LARGEST collection of works by the great 17th-century painter Peter Paul Rubens can be seen here. They range from the intimate *Rubens and Isabella Brandt in the Honeysuckle Bower* (1609), painted to celebrate the artist's marriage, to *The Abduction of the Daughters of Leukippos* and *The Battle of the Amazons* in the High Baroque style. Here also are the large-scale *Last Judgement, Fall of the Rebel Angels* and *Women of the Apocalypse,* as well as sketches for the scenes from the life of Marie de Medici.

This section also includes paintings by Rubens' pupils Anthony van Dyck and Jacob Jordaens, and the peasant scenes of Adriaen Brouwer, the most notable of which is *Peasants Playing Cards.*

The Adoration of the Magi (c.1455) by Rogier van den Weyden

DUTCH PAINTING

THE GALLERY'S rich collection of 17th-century Dutch art represents the Golden Age of Dutch painting. It includes an outstanding series of Passion scenes by Rembrandt that were executed in the 1630s and are important examples of the Baroque style.

Outstanding among the wealth of portraits is a self-portrait by Carel Fabritius and the *Portrait of Willem van Heythuysen* by Frans Hals.

Landscape painting is represented by the work of Jacob van Ruisdael and by the townscapes and river scenes of Han van Goyen. Among the genre painters, Jan Steen, Gabriel Metsu and Gerard Terborch are particularly noteworthy names.

Portrait of Willem van Heythuysen (1625–30) by Frans Hals

ITALIAN PAINTING

SUCH IS THE comprehensive nature of the gallery's collection that it is possible to make a thorough study of Italian painting here. Most of the early works came to the gallery thanks to Ludwig I's infatuation with the art of this particular period.

Paintings of the 14th century include Giotto's *Last Supper*. Florentine art, which flowered a century later, is represented by the religious paintings of Fra Filippo Lippi and Dominico Ghirlandaio. Other highlights include

The Annunciation (c. 1473) by Antonello da Messina

Leonardo da Vinci's *Madonna and Child* (c. 1473), Perugino's *Vision of St Bernard* and works by Raphael, outstanding among which is the *Madonna dei Tempi* (1507).

The Venetian School is represented by Titian's *Crown of Thorns* and Tintoretto's series of battle scenes glorifying the Gonzaga family. Great works of the 18th century include the religious canvases of Tiepolo and the fascinating Venetian townscapes of both Canaletto and Francesco Guardi.

SPANISH PAINTING

ALTHOUGH IT is smaller than other sections in the gallery, the collection of Spanish painting is no less interesting and includes works by the major masters of the Spanish School. The dramatic *Disrobing of Christ* by El Greco is one of three versions of this famous work. There are also paintings by Diego Velázquez, as well as the Mannerist scenes from the *Legend of St Catherine* by Francisco de Zurbarán, one of his finest works.

Also of interest are Murillo's paintings, in particular his genre scenes depicting street urchins in Seville. Other notable works include studio paintings by the lesser-known Claudio José Antonílez of about 1670.

FRENCH PAINTING

DESPITE THEIR political connections with France, the Wittelsbachs did not collect French art on a large scale. The museum has three small paintings by Nicolas Poussin that, as early works, are not representative of his mature style. The work of Claude Lorrain is better documented, exhibits including his melancholic *Banishment of Hagar*.

By contrast, 18th-century French painting is well represented, most of the works having been acquired with the help of various banks. Noteworthy among them are paintings by Jean-Baptiste Pater and Nicolas Lancret, followers of Antoine Watteau, and Jean-Marc Nattier's excellent *Portrait of the Marquis of Baglion*. The work of François Boucher is generously represented, from the exquisite *Portrait of the Marquise de Pompadour* to his intimate study of the young Louise O'Murphy, mistress of Louis XV.

The eroticism of the Rococo age is illustrated by sketches by Jean-Honoré Fragonard, while Jean-Baptiste Greuze's moralistic *Grievance of Time* heralds the sentimentality of Neo-Classicism.

Disrobing of Christ (c. 1585) by El Greco

Neue Pinakothek ⑨

THE NEUE PINAKOTHEK, which contains 19th-century paintings displayed in a building designed by August von Voit, opened in 1853. From 1909 to 1911, under the curatorship of the art historian Hugo von Tschudi, the collection of academic paintings was extended in an avant-garde direction. The building itself was destroyed during World War II, and between 1976 and 1981 a new gallery, designed by Alexander von Brancas, was constructed. Today the museum's exhibits consist primarily of German and French paintings dating from 1780 to 1910.

★ **Italia and Germania**
(1828) *This painting by Friedrich Overbeck looks back to the Renaissance.*

Heroic Landscape with Fishermen (1818)
In this Romantic painting by Théodore Géricault, the Neo-Classical landscape is bathed in a romantic light.

Ground floor

Neptune's Horses (1892)
This work by Walter Crane, alluding to Classical antiquity, fuses Pre-Raphaelite expression and Art Nouveau ornament.

Basement

STAR EXHIBITS

★ **Breakfast in the Studio**

★ **Italia and Germania**

★ **Seni at the Dead Body of Wallenstein**

Main entrance

Restaurant and cafeteria

Disabled access

GALLERY GUIDE
The collections are arranged in 22 halls and 11 rooms. The recommended route for visitors, tracing a figure of eight, takes the collections in chronological order. The halls, of varying size, height and level, are arranged around two inner courtyards.

Portrait of the Marquesa de Caballero (1807)
In his role as court painter, Francisco de Goya executed many portraits of Spanish royalty and aristocracy such as this one.

★ Seni at the Dead Body of Wallenstein (1855)
This illustration by Karl Theodore von Piloty of a scene from Schiller's famous play enjoyed enormous popularity during the 19th century.

Play of the Waves (1883)
Arnold Böcklin interpreted this mythological scene in a subtly erotic Neo-Baroque manner.

Still Life with Aparagus (c.1885)
The artist Karl Schuch remains underrated to this day. His painting of asparagus spears was influenced by the work of Édouard Manet.

★ Breakfast in the Studio (1869)
This outstanding painting by Édouard Manet, with strongly constrasting dark and light tones, dates from the end of his pre-Expressionist period.

KEY

☐	Neo-Classicism and Romanticism
☐	Nazarenes and Biedermeier
☐	Realism and late Romanticism
☐	History painting
☐	Böcklin, Marées and late Realism
☐	Impressionism
☐	Symbolism and Art Nouveau
☐	Temporary exhibitions
☐	Non-exhibition space

Exploring the Neue Pinakothek

THE NEUE PINAKOTHEK is admirably designed for visitors. The recommended route for viewing the collections starts and ends in a large hall, and can easily be extended or shortened. Glass roofs allow the rooms to be illuminated by natural light. The varied rhythm of the itinerary and the size and height of the rooms, which are situated at different levels, keep the experience interesting and full of stimulating variety.

The Sudeten Mountains in Mist (1820) by Caspar David Friedrich

NEO-CLASSICISM AND EARLY ROMANTICISM

THE SCULPTURES of Paris by Antonio Canova and of Adonis by Bertel Thorvaldsen show these artists' different approaches to Neo-Classicism. Ascetic Neo-Classicism was also shaped by Jacques-Louis David with his *Portrait of the Marquise Sorcy de Thélusson* (1790). Neo-Classical landscape painting is represented by German painters including Jacob Philipp Hackert.

Also on display are a series of melancholy landscapes by the German Romantic painter Caspar David Friedrich. The Dresden school of landscape painters is represented by Carl Gustav Carus and Johan Christian Dahl, among others. *Heroic Landscape with Fishermen* by Théodore Géricault imbues the Neo-Classical landscape with a Romantic atmosphere. The paintings of Eugène Delacroix, such as *Valentine Dying* (1830) and *The Death of Ophelia* (1838) treat the Faustian and Shakespearean themes so beloved of the Romantic painters.

THE NAZARENES AND BIEDERMEIER

THE GALLERY's body of Nazarene paintings formed the basis of its collection when it first opened in 1853. *Italia and Germania*, the allegory by Friedrich Overbeck in which the two figures sit in a sisterly embrace, expresses the artistic relationship between the two nations. Joseph Anton Koch's paintings *Heroic Landscape with Rainbow* (1815) and *View of the Environs of Olevano* (1830) combine Romantic impulses with the religious mood characteristic of the Nazarenes.

Although they are artistically quite different, the genre paintings of the Austrian artist Ferdinand Waldmüller and the fairy-tale cycles of Moritz von Schwind (such as *Symphony*) both express a specific urban view of happiness in line with the Biedermeier style's *Gemütlichkeit* (domestic harmony).

REALISM AND LATE ROMANTICISM

IN THE EARLY 20th century the Neue Pinakothek started to acquire French paintings of the Realist school, whose

The Poor Poet (1839) by Carl Spitzweg

Don Quijote (1868) by Honoré Daumier

origins date from about 1850. The gallery's acquisitions from that time include studies by Camille Corot, notably some of his Italian vignettes. There is also a collection of works by Gustave Courbet, among which images of rocks in landscapes predominate. The contrast between different paintings by the caricaturist Honoré Daumier is superb: while *Dramatist on Stage* (1860) shows the world of Parisian theatre, his incomparable *Don Quijote* (1868) conveys the symbolic character of the knight from La Mancha. With his satirical *The Poor Poet* (1839), Carl Spitzweg created almost a cult character in Germany.

HISTORY PAINTING

HISTORICAL SUBJECTS were a favourite theme in the 19th century. This section opens with Wilhelm von Kaulbach's vast canvas *The Destruction of Jerusalem* (1846), in which the sacking of the city by the Emperor Titus is given an allegorical setting. Kaulbach also painted canvases showing the virtues of Ludwig I, who was a prominent patron of the arts. Historical painting is represented to a significant degree by Karl von Piloty, with his famous *Seni at the Dead Body of*

Wallenstein (1855) and the much later *Thusnelda in the Triumphal Procession of Germanicus* (1873), a Neo-Baroque vision of what was seen as the coming triumph of the Germanic nations.

BÖCKLIN, MARÉES AND LATE REALISM

AFTER THE unification of the German Empire in 1871, German art fragmented into various movements. Hans von Marées of the Rhineland sought new ways of treating Classical themes. The Neue Pinakothek houses its principal works, including the triptych *Hesperides II* (1884) and *Three Riders* (1887).

Anselm Feuerbach's superb handling of colour expresses a tragic interpretation of Classical themes, as in his *Medea* (1870), while Arnold Böcklin's world of Classical mythology is in harmony with Neo-Baroque trends (as in his *Play of the Waves*). Here also is a substantial collection of works by the Munich Realist Wilhelm Leibl, including *Portrait of Mrs Gedon* (1869), as well as paintings by Carl Schuch and Wilhelm Trübner.

Hesperides II (1884) by Hans von Marées

Boys on the Beach (1898), Max Liebermann

IMPRESSIONISM AND POST-IMPRESSIONISM

WITH REGARD to Impressionist painting, what the Neue Pinakothek lacks in quantity it makes up for in the importance of its collection. Mention should be made of masterpieces by Édouard Manet, such as *Barque at Argenteuil* (1874), Claude Monet's *Bridge at Argenteuil* (1874) and in particular of Paul Cézanne's

Railway Track (1870). In the latter, a milestone in his artistic development, the artist shows for the first time his tendency to endow natural forms with geometric shapes. Edgar Degas' delightful *Women Ironing* (1869) is accompanied by a number of his portraits and statuettes of dancers. The gallery also has paintings by Auguste Renoir, Camille Pissarro and Alfred Sisley.

German Impressionists are also well represented. On display are early works by Adolph von Menzel and paintings by Lovis Corinth, Max Slevogt and Max Liebermann, including his carefree *Boys on the Beach*. The room containing paintings by Paul Signac inaugurates the gallery's Post-Impressionist section. Paul Gauguin is represented by works from his Breton period as well as by *Birthday* (1888), a classic painting from his Tahitian period. Most notably, the Neue Pinakothek has a representative collection of works by Vincent van Gogh. Prominent among them are *Sunflowers* (1888) and two landscapes: *View of Arles* (1889) and *Plain at Auvers* (1890). All three paintings express the artist's delight in the beauty of the sun, the sky, flowers and crops.

SYMBOLISM AND ART NOUVEAU

THE INTERACTION between the two artistic movements Symbolism and Art Nouveau is superbly illustrated by *Neptune's Horses* by Walter Crane. James Ensor's expressive *Masks* and paintings by Edvard Munch and Maurice Denis can also be seen here.

Of equal interest are works by artists such as Pierre Bonnard and Édouard Vuillard who continued the Impressionist tradition. The erotic and eschatological themes typical of Symbolism can be seen in Egon Schiele's *Agony* (1902), for example. The *Portrait of Margarethe Stonborough-Wittgenstein* (1905) by Gustav Klimt comes at the end of the Neue Pinakothek's exhibits.

Sunflowers (1888) by Vincent van Gogh

Dürckheim Palais ⓬

Türkenstr. 4. **Map** 3 B1. 🚋 27.
⬤ closed to the public.

BUILT IN 1843–4 for the chief
steward of the court,
Count Georg Friedrich von
Dürckheim-Montmartin, the
palace was designed by
Friedrich Jakob Kreuther.
Up until 1909 the building
housed the Prussian
Embassy. Today it is used
by Bayerische Landesbank.
The modern building of the
bank next door to the palace
creates a strong sense of
aesthetic dissonance.

The façade of the palace,
with its distinctive brick and
terracotta reliefs, makes
reference to early Italian
Renaissance architecture. The
main entrance, which was
originally centrally placed on
the building, was moved to
the right in 1912. The palace
is a classic example of the
transitional style of
architecture that links the
work of Friedrich von Gärtner
and the Maximilian style.

**Triad of windows on the ground
floor of Dürckheim Palais**

Lenbachplatz ⓭

Map 3 A1. Ⓢ and Ⓤ Karlsplatz/
Stachus. 🚋 18, 19, 20, 21, 27.

THIS IRREGULARLY shaped
square lies between
Maximiliansplatz, the Alter
Botanischer Garten and
Karlsplatz. The buildings that
line it were not conceived as
a single urban plan, and are
typical of the late 19th
century. Standing in imposing
groups and laid out in
irregular fashion around the
square, they create a set of
contrasting perspectives.

On the west side stand the
law courts (Justizpalast) and
on the south side rises the
bizarre outline of the

People relaxing beside the fountains of Karlsplatz

Künstlerhaus. On the north
side is the **Stock Exchange**
(Börse). Built in 1868–98, it is
an example of pompous Neo-
Baroque, its splendour reflecting the power of the financial
institution within. The neighbouring **Bernheimerhaus**, at
No. 6, was built in 1889. In
architectural terms, it was
regarded as the ultimate residential building in Munich, a
novelty at the time being the
exposed iron structure of the
ground floor and the huge
picture windows.

On the east side of the
square, bordering Maxi-
miliansplatz, is Munich's finest
fountain, the **Wittelsbacherbrunnen**, built by Adolf von
Hildebrand in 1893–5 to
commemorate the completion
of the city's new water-supply
system. The fountain
symbolizes both charity and
the destructive power of
water. While water cascades
from a large double bowl
mounted on a throne, the
fountain is dominated by two
allegorical figures – a stone-
throwing youth on a steed,
and a woman seated on a
bull and holding a goblet.

Karlsplatz ⓮

Map 3 A1 (5 A2).
Ⓢ and Ⓤ Karlsplatz/Stachus.
🚋 18, 19, 20, 21, 27.

AFTER THE city's fortifications
were blown up in 1791
on the orders of Karl
Theodor, a vast square was
laid out on the western side
of the Old Town. It was
named Karls-platz in honour
of the ruler, as was the gate
called the **Karlstor**, which
was pre-served. The square
also had a popular name –
Stachus – which is still used
today. It refers to the most
popular inn in Munich, which
since 1759 has stood on the
southwest side of the square.

In 1899–1902 the architect
Gabriel von Seidl added two
semicircular wings, known as
the Rondelbauten, to the
Karlstor. These three-storey
Neo-Baroque buildings, with
two tower-shaped projections,
have numerous shops in their
ground-floor arcades. Another
architectural feature of the
square is the mock-historic
law courts (Justizpalast)
on its northwest side.
Until the 1960s,
Karlsplatz was one
of the busiest
traffic inter-
sections in
Europe.
When the
ring road

Allegorical statue on the Wittelsbacherbrunnen on Lenbachplatz

around the Old Town was completed, the west part of the square was closed to traffic and a large fountain installed. The fountain is now a favourite meeting place for the inhabitants of Munich and a resting place for tourists. In the 1970s the area beneath the square was converted into a major metropolitan hub and shopping centre.

Detail of the ornamental attic of the Justizpalast

Justizpalast **⑮**

LAW COURTS

Elisenstr. 1a. (Karlsplatz) Prielmayerstr. 7. **Map** 3 A1 (5 A2). **⑤** 55 97 01. **Ⓢ** and **Ⓤ** Karlsplatz/ Stachus. ⛋ 18, 19, 20, 21, 27.

On the northwest side of Karlsplatz stands one of the best-known late 19th-century landmarks in Munich. The law courts, built in 1887–97 by Friedrich von Thiersch, are an example of pure Neo-Baroque architecture, with discreet Neo-Mannerist elements.

The building's great novelty at the time was its vast steel and glass dome, which acted as a skylight. The interior – particularly the main hall and the main stairway, which are directly beneath the dome – has an extraordinary wealth of detail in its design.

North of the Justizpalast are the Neues Justizgebäude (New Law Courts). Built in 1906–08, also by Thiersch, they are in the Neo-Gothic style and have a clocktower and gables.

Alter Botanischer Garten **⑯**

OLD BOTANICAL GARDEN

Map 3 A1 (5 A1). Between Elisen-and Sophienstr. **Ⓢ** and **Ⓤ** Karlsplatz/ Stachus. ⛋ 18, 19, 20, 21, 27.

Visitors to Munich who find themselves in need of respite from the bustle of the city centre will find a sanctuary in the Old Botanical Gardens north of the Justiz-palast. Laid out on a semi-circular plan in 1804–14, they were designed by Ludwig von Sckell, who was also respon-sible for the Englischer Garten.

The entrance to the gardens is through an early Neo-Classical gate built by Emanuel Joseph von Herigoyen in 1811 and bearing a Latin inscrip-tion by Goethe. In 1854 the greenhouse was demolished to make space for the Glas-palast. Modelled on London's Crystal Palace, it was built to house the First Industrial Exhibition. The Glaspalast burned down in 1931, destroying at the same time an exhibition of German Romantic painting.

In 1914 new botanical gardens were laid out in Nymphenburg, and the Old Botanical Gardens were converted into a muni-cipal park. A restaurant (today the Park Café) was built in 1935–7, as well as an exhibition hall designed by Oswald Bieber. The sculptor Josef Wackerle created the Neptune Fountain, which has a figure based on Michelangelo's David. The café garden, shaded by exotic trees, is an ideal place to relax and enjoy a cold beer.

The Neptune Fountain in the Old Botanical Garden

Löwenbräukeller **⑰**

Stiglmaierplatz 2 /Nymphenburger-straße. **Map** 1 A5. **⑤** 52 60 21. **Ⓤ** Stiglmaierplatz. ⊙ 9am–1am daily

Visitors entering the city from the west along Nymphenburgerstraße will see from afar the marble statue of the lion that crowns the Löwenbräukeller on Stigl-maierplatz. This famous Munich brewery has its own inn, which is large enough to hold 4,000 drinkers.

The picturesque brewery and inn were built in 1883 by Albert Schmidt and were refurbished by Friedrich von Thiersch at the turn of the 19th and 20th centuries. The sides of the octagonal tower are decorated alternately with the brewery's emblem – a white griffin – and the city's coat of arms. The tower rises above an arcaded entrance hall with a roof terrace. In summer drinkers are drawn to the beer garden shaded by large chestnut trees.

The building of the world-famous Löwenbräukeller

FURTHER AFIELD

MANY OF Munich's attractions lie outside the city centre and, thanks to a highly efficient transport system, they are easily reached. To the north, for instance, is the famous Olympiapark and the BMW factory's modern complex of buildings. To the west lies the Nymphenburg district, with its palace, park and botanical gardens. Southeast of the

Sculpture in the Nymphenburg gardens

Old Town is Theresienwiese, where the famous Oktoberfest is held, and unfailing attractions to the south are the Hellabrunn Zoo, in Thalkirchen, and the Bavaria Film Museum, in Geiselgasteig. To the east are some masterpieces of religious architecture – the great Mariä Himmelfahrtskirche in Ramersdorf, and Michaels-kirche in Berg am Laim.

SIGHTS AT A GLANCE

Palaces and Historic Buildings
Asam-Schlössl **12**
Blutenburg **15**
Grünwald **11**
Nymphenburg pp130–33 **1**

Museum
BMW-Museum **4**

Districts
Berg am Laim **7**
Ramersdorf **8**

Parks and Open Spaces
Botanischer Garten **2**
Olympiapark **3**
Theresienwiese **13**
Tierpark Hellabrunn **9**

Others
Au **6**
Bavaria-Filmstadt **10**
Hypo-Hochhaus **5**
Neue Messe München **14**

KEY

▦	Central Munich
▢	Outskirts of Munich
▬	Motorway
▭	Major road
═	Minor road
—	Railway line
🚉	Railway station

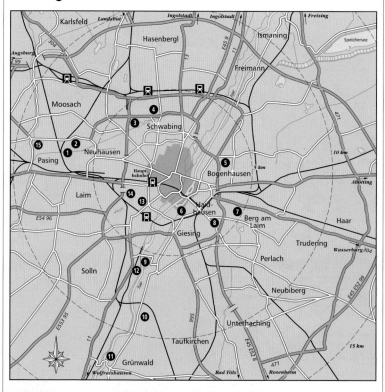

◁ **The Olympiapark, with the Olympiaturm, and the buildings of the BMW factory in the background**

Nymphenburg ➊

Aᴄᴛᴇʀ ᴛʜᴇ ʙɪʀᴛʜ of Maximilian Emanuel, the heir to the throne, his father, Duke Ferdinand Maria, presented his wife with a suburban palace. The queen named it Nymphenburg (Nymphs' Castle) and supervised the building work that ensued. Maximilian continued his mother's work, creating with the architect Joseph Effner one of the finest palaces and gardens in Europe. Later, buildings were added around the courtyard fronting the palace. In the 19th century the formal French gardens were converted into an English landscaped park incorporating the existing canals.

Porcelain parrot at the factory

★ Amalienburg
Built by François Cuvilliés, the Amalienburg was a small hunting lodge. Its circular hall was covered with fine shellwork, and the windows and mirrors created the illusion of great space.

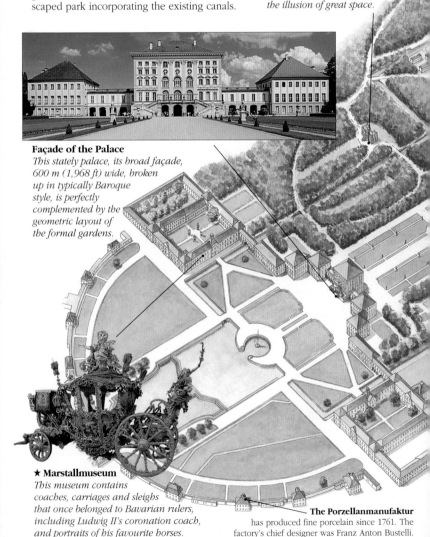

Façade of the Palace
This stately palace, its broad façade, 600 m (1,968 ft) wide, broken up in typically Baroque style, is perfectly complemented by the geometric layout of the formal gardens.

★ Marstallmuseum
This museum contains coaches, carriages and sleighs that once belonged to Bavarian rulers, including Ludwig II's coronation coach, and portraits of his favourite horses.

The Porzellanmanufaktur
has produced fine porcelain since 1761. The factory's chief designer was Franz Anton Bustelli.

Garden
The formal French garden at the rear of the palace, with an 18th-century canal, forms the main axis of the entire palace and its gardens.

VISITORS' CHECKLIST

Nymphenburg 17 90 80.
www.schloesser.bayern.de
Rotkreuzplatz. 12, 17. 41.
1 Apr–15 Oct: 9am–6pm Mon–Wed & Fri–Sun, 9am–8pm Thu; 16 Oct–31 Mar: 10am–4pm daily.
Museum Mensch und Natur
9am–5pm Tue–Sun (closed throughout 2002).

Badenburg
The bathing hall and the first heated tiled pool are surrounded by a viewing gallery.

★ Pagodenburg
This pavilion was used for receiving visitors and for relaxation. The ground floor is covered with 2,000 Dutch Delft tiles depicting figures and landscapes.

The orangery was, at the time it was built, the first in Germany to be heated by hot water.

The Museum Mensch und Natur is dedicated to the structure of the earth and the workings of the human body.

STAR FEATURES

★ Amalienburg

★ Marstallmuseum

★ Pagodenburg

Magdalenenklause
This folly, built as a chapel in a grotto with hermits' cells, reflects the Baroque idea of withdrawal from courtly life into a world of peace and contemplation.

Schloss Nymphenburg

A staircase lantern

THE OLDEST part of the palace is the central section, built in 1675 in the form of an Italianate villa. In 1702 Maximilian Emanuel commissioned the construction of side pavilions, which were connected to the villa by galleries. Soon after 1715, when Joseph Effner took charge of building work on the palace, the Steinerner Saal (Audience Hall) with stunningly lavish interior decoration was built, along with the other rooms in the wings, and the stables and orangery.

Italianate Villa
The façade of the oldest, 17th-century wing of the palace, facing the garden, is fronted by a double stairway supported on three arches.

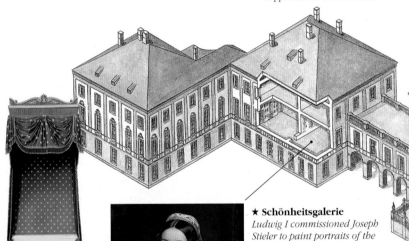

★ Schönheitsgalerie
Ludwig I commissioned Joseph Stieler to paint portraits of the city's beautiful women. As well as portraits of noblewomen, the Gallery of Beauties was hung with pictures of dancers, townswomen and "The Beauty of Munich", a tailor's daughter.

★ Royal Bed
The royal bedchamber in the south wing of the palace is decorated with fine paintings. and filled with mahogany furniture, including the Royal Bed, where Ludwig II was born.

Portrait of Karl Albrecht as Emperor Karl VII
This majestic portrait was produced in the studio of the court painter George Desmarées in 1742. The pendant is the portrait of the Empress Maria Amalia, which hangs in the same room.

STAR FEATURES
★ Royal Bed
★ Schönheitsgalerie
★ Steinerner Saal

Paintings

The walls and ceilings of the palace halls are covered with colourful paintings framed with stuccowork. The finest is the ceiling of the Steinerner Saal, in which mythological scenes are shown in idyllic garden settings.

Balustrades

decorated with vases line the stairways leading to the palace gardens.

Lackkabinett

This corner cabinet with Chinese motifs is exquisitely decorated with black lacquer on wood panelling. The Chinese theme is reinforced by the Rococo painting of the ceiling.

Entrance

★ Steinerner Saal

Upon entering the palace, visitors walk into a spacious hall with windows on either side decorated in a resplendent Rococo style.

Vorzimmer

This anteroom in the north part of the palace is richly decorated in French Regency style. Paintings, stuccowork and wood carvings cover the walls, while the ceiling is decorated with Classical subjects.

Botanischer Garten ❷

BOTANICAL GARDEN

Menzingerstr. 12. 📞 *17 86 13 10.*
🚋 *12.* 🕐 *9am–7pm; in winter until 4:30pm.* **Greenhouses** 🕐 *9–11:45am, 1–6:30pm; Nov–Jan: until 4:30pm.*

NORTH OF the gardens of Schloss Nymphenburg, new botanical gardens were laid out in 1909–14. Covering

The Botanical Garden with its stunning variety of plants

2 sq km (.75 sq mile) and containing over 15,000 species of plants growing in artistic arrangements, this is one of the finest botanical gardens in Europe.

Entry to the garden is through the Botanical Institute, which is fronted by the colourful Schmuckhof (Decorative Yard). Passing through it visitors see a section on ecology and genetics, followed by a rose garden and a plantation of rhododendrons and protected species, and of medicinal plants and crops. There is also an arboretum with rare trees. Beyond this is a section illustrating the vegetation of meadows, plains, swamps and sandy and arctic environments. There is also a rockery.

The impressive greenhouses shelter tropical plants, cacti and fruit trees, unusual orchids and giant water lilies.

Vehicles displayed at the BMW-Museum

BMW-Museum ❹

Petuelring 130. 📞 *38 22 33 07.*
Ⓤ *Olympiazentrum.* 🚌 *36, 41, 43, 81, 84, 136, 184.* 🕐 *9am–5pm daily (last admission 4pm).* 📷 ♿ **Cinema**

IN THE EARLY 1970s, the BMW car manufacturing group built a series of ostentatious architectural structures that went some way to rival the architectural development of the neighbouring Olympia-park. The designer in charge of the concept, Karl Schanzer of Vienna, used the idiom of architectural symbolism.

Olympiapark ❸

MUNICH'S Olympic Park was built for the 20th Olympic Games, which the city hosted in 1972. The modern complex of sports facilities overlies an area formerly used as drill grounds and later as an airfield. The artificial lake is fed by the Nymphenburg Canal and the hills were made from the rubble removed from the city after World War II. The whole complex is dominated by the Olympic Tower.

GEORG-BRAUCHLE-RING

HANS-BRAUN-BRÜCKE

ERNST-CURTIUS-WEG

Werner-von-Linde-Halle

Tennis-anlage

Olympia-stadion ①

SPIRIDON-LOUIS-RING

Olympiahalle ②
The sweeping roofs, designed by the engineer Otto Frei, take the form of a canopy of steel netting and acrylic slabs supported on masts up to 80m (260 feet) high.

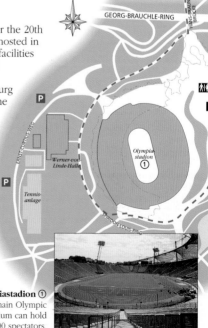

Olympiastadion ①
The main Olympic stadium can hold 60,000 spectators.

Schanzer envisaged the 19-storey office building that dominates the complex as resembling the four cylinders of a car engine. The building, clad in silver aluminium, has a ground plan in the form of a clover leaf.

At the foot of the building, and counterbalancing its imposing structure, is what could be described as a shrine – the BMW-Museum. Built in concrete and taking the form of a bowl 41 m (135 ft) across, this window-less, silver-painted structure contains exhibits illustrating the history of the factory's production. A spiral ramp connects five platforms where the first cars, including the famous Dixi, are displayed, along with motorbikes, racing cars of the 1950s and 1960s, the modern BMW range and futuristic prototypes. Film and slide shows complete the exhibition. This is one of newest museums in Germany, and the presentation is changed every few years.

Hypo-Hochhaus ❺

Arabellastr. 12. **U** Richard-Strauss-Str. **C** 92 440.

UNLIKE MANY other major cities throughout the world, central Munich is not overshadowed by forests of skyscrapers housing the head-quarters of banks, tall buildings and hotels. Munich's modern urban agglomerations have been built outside the

Hypo-Hochhaus's silver-clad futuristic headquarters

Mittlerer Ring (ring road). One example of this is Arabella Park, a group of multifunctional exclusive residential developments, hotels and office buildings. The buildings of the Bayerische Hypotheken und Wechselbank were built here in 1975–81 to designs by Walter and Bea Betz.

The architects achieved a unique effect. The 114-m (375-ft) skyscraper consists of three blocks of different sizes that are joined by gigantic rings supported by four cylindrical towers. The glazing and the silver panels covering the exterior of the buildings create an effect of levity and cool elegance.

It is worth walking round the building to experience the unusual metamorphosis of forms that is produced from different viewpoints. Despite its architectural significance, Hypovereinsbank's head-quarters is a typical example of the megalomania of major financial institutions today.

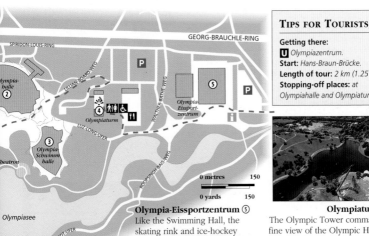

GEORG-BRAUCHLE-RING

SPIRIDON-LOUIS-RING

LILIAN BOARD WEG

WALTHER BRITHE WEG

TOOT POTUSH BAS WEG

Olympia-halle ②

Olympiaturm

LUZ-LONG-UFER

Olympia Schwimm halle ③

Theatron

Olympia-Eissport-zentrum

⑤

④

Olympiasee

WILLI-GEBHARDT-UFER

TIPS FOR TOURISTS

Getting there:
U Olympiazentrum.
Start: Hans-Braun-Brücke.
Length of tour: 2 km (1.25 m).
Stopping-off places: at Olympiahalle and Olympiaturm.

0 metres 150
0 yards 150

Olympia-Eissportzentrum ⑤
Like the Swimming Hall, the skating rink and ice-hockey stadium is open to the public.

Olympiaturm ④
The Olympic Tower commands a fine view of the Olympic Hill, the lake and the stadium, where the Bayern München and TSV 1860 München soccer teams play.

Schwimmhalle ③
The Swimming Hall is one of the finest in Europe. The complex comprises five pools, saunas, a jacuzzi and a diving platform, as well as a grassed relaxation area.

KEY

— Suggested route

☼ Viewpoint

P Parking

A performance at the puppet theatre in Au

Au **❻**

Map 4 D5. 🚊 *25, 27*. 🚌 *52, 56.*
🚡 *Auer Dult: Mariahilfplatz.*
Maidult: starts around 1 May;
Jakobidult: starts Sat after 25 Jul;
Herbstdult: starts third Sat. in Sep.
Otto Bille's Marionettenbühne 📞
15 02 168. ◐ *During performances.*

UP UNTIL the 15th century, the district of Au was part of the floodplain of the River Isar, and it was only after the river was controlled that people started to settle here. Au was incorporated into Munich in 1854. Until the early 20th century, the poorer population of the city lived in Au, and picturesque cottages typical of old Munich can still be seen there today.

Three times a year, for nine days, Au is transformed into a centre of games and entertainment. During Auer Dult, stalls, shooting galleries and merry-go-rounds are set up on Mariahilfplatz. This local event goes back to the 14th century and is associated with the fairs after St Jacob's Day.

The town square is dominated by a Neo-Gothic church. Built in 1831–9, it was the first instance of the Gothic revival in southern Germany.

The old puppet theatre, known as Otto Bille's Marionettenbühne, is a great attraction for children.

Berg am Laim **❼**

🚊 *19.* 🚌 *93, 137.* **Michaelskirche**
Clemens-August Str. 9a.
◐ *8am–6pm daily.*

THE NAME Berg am Laim reflects its position: along Harlbacher Bach is an elong-ated hill *(Berg)*, from which clay *(Lehm)* was extracted.

By the beginning of the 18th century, the area had been taken over by Clemens Joseph, Bishop of Cologne, who founded the Brother-hood of St Michael here. His successor, Clemens August, ordered the construc-tion of Michaelskirche. For this he commissioned the most prominent figures of his time: the architect Johann Michael Fischer, the painter and stuccoist Johann Baptist Zimmermann and the sculptor Johann Baptist Straub. Work lasted from 1737 to 1751 and the result was one of the finest Rococo churches in Germany.

While the twin-towered façade is the quintessence of late Baroque style, the interior has Rococo furnishings and paintings. The painting of St Michael overcoming Satan on the high altar (1694) is by Johann Andreas Wolff, and the figures of putti and angels are ascribed to Ignaz Günther. The pulpit, crowned with a statue of St Michael bearing the Bavarian flag, is by Benedikt Haßler. The dome and ceiling are painted with scenes from the life of St Michael.

The pulpit in Michaelskirche in Berg am Laim

In 1941–3 over 300 Jews from Munich were rounded up by the church and the monastery before being deported to a concentration camp. A modest memorial is dedicated to them.

Ramersdorf **❽**

Ⓤ *Karl-Preis-Platz and Innsbrucker Ring.* **Mariae Himmelfahrt**
Aribonenstr. 9. ◐ *8am–6pm.*

RAMERSDORF is one of Munich's industrial centres. In the midst of small factories, garages and a close network of streets is an oasis of peace: the village church of Mariae Himmelfahrt. This is one of the oldest pilgrimage churches in Bavaria.

Since the 14th century processions of people have made their way here to worship a relic of the Holy Cross that is kept in a precious monstrance. Since 1465 another object of worship has been the figure of the Madonna Enthroned carved by Erasmus Grasser.

While the exterior of the church has retained its Gothic character, the interior is Bar-oque. The Gothic cloisters are deco-rated with stucco-work and have 17th-century altars. The cemetery is worth a visit, as is the Alter Wirt, an inn dating from 1663 that was frequented by pilgrims and travellers on the road bet-ween Salzburg and Augsburg.

The Baroque interior of the pilgrimage church in Ramersdorf

Tierpark Hellabrunn ❾

MUNICH'S ZOO was established in 1911. It has over 4,800 animals representing 480 species and covers an area of 3.6 sq km (890 acres). The species are arranged by continent and by their geographical occurrence. The design of the enclosures, which skilfully re-create natural environments, makes Hellabrunn one of the most beautiful zoos in the world. The zoo specializes in breeding animals that are under threat of extinction.

VISITORS' CHECKLIST

Tierparkstr. 30. **✆** *62 50 820.*
U *Thalkirchen.* **🚌** *52.*
○ *Apr–Sep: 8am–6pm daily;*
Oct–Mar: 9am–5pm. 🎫 👍 🍴

★ Elephants
The elephants live in a hall covered by a dome of reinforced concrete, the first of its type in the world.

Isar Entrance

Flamingo Entrance

Alpine Ibex
These protected animals are rarely seen in the wild. In the zoo, they live in a rocky paddock planted with alpine vegetation.

The Kiang
is a wild ass from Tibet that lives in herds.

The mhorr gazelle no longer exists in the wild.

The Gardens
The animals are not the only attraction here. The layout of the zoo includes peaceful areas for walking and relaxation.

KEY

Alpine ibex ③
Aquarium ⑤
Children's Zoo ⑭
Chimpanzees ④
Elephants ⑥
Gazelles ⑧
Kiang ⑫
Lions ⑦
Mesopotamian deer ⑪
Pelicans ①
Penguins ⑬
Przewalski's horse ②
Rhinoceros ⑩
Siberian tigers ⑨

★ Rhinoceros
The sheer size and primitive shape of these animals never fail to fascinate. They live in the zoo in a re-created natural environment.

| 0 metres | | 150 |
| 0 yards | | 150 |

STAR SIGHTS

★ Elephants

★ Rhinoceros

The realistic reconstruction of the U-boat from the film _Das Boot_

Bavaria-Filmstadt ⑩

Geiselgasteig. Bavariafilmplatz 7.
Ⓤ Silberhornstr, Wettersteinplatz
(some distance away). 🚋 25.
Ⓢ Rosenheimer Platz (some distance
away). 📞 64 99 23 04.
🅾 Mar–Apr: 9am–4pm daily;
May–Oct: 9am–5pm daily; Nov–Feb
10am–3pm daily. 🎬. **Stuntshow:**
Apr–Oct: 11:30am, 1pm, 2:30pm.
Cinema: Apr–Oct: 10am–5:30pm
daily.

Commonly known as
Hollywood on the Isar,
Bavaria-Filmstadt is one of
Europe's major film studios.
Set up in 1919, they were
originally located in the
Stachus district. Among the
prominent people who have
worked here have been
directors such as Alfred
Hitchcock, Orson Welles,
Billy Wilder, Ingmar
Bergmann and Rainer Maria
Fassbinder, and film stars
including Gina Lollobrigida,
Romy Schneider, Elizabeth
Taylor, Sophia Loren, Richard
Burton and Burt Lancaster.
Every year scores of films for
the big screen and television
are made at the Filmstadt
("cinema city"), which
opened to the public in 1981.

The 90-minute tour of the
studios takes visitors on a
miniature railway and on foot,
through some fascinating film
sets. The set for _Enemy Mine_
plunges into the world of
science fiction, while fantasy
and fable reign on the set of
The Neverending Story.
Entering the 57-m (187-ft)
reconstruction of the U-boat
used in the Oscar-winning
film _Das Boot_ is an

unforgettable experience.
Another lasting impression is
made by the backdrops used
in the production of _Asterix
and Obelix_, set in the age of
the Romans and Gauls.

Other major attractions are
the heart-stopping exploits of
stuntmen and the show of
film tricks on seats that move
with the action. By arrangement, groups of young
people can make their own
films here, directing, cutting
and watching the final results.

**Grünwald Burg's Gothic gatehouse,
set with coats of arms**

Grünwald ⑪

Grünwald Burg. Grünwald Zeillerstr. 3.
🚋 25. 🚌 224. 📞 64 13 218.
🅾 10am–4:30pm Wed–Sun.
⬤ 31 Oct–15 Mar.

Grünwald, on the southern
outskirts of Munich, is
one of the city's most exclusive villa suburbs. It is also a
good starting point for walking and cycling tours.

The district's greatest
attraction is Grünwald Burg,
a well-preserved medieval
castle whose origins go back
to the 12th century, although
Roman fortifications predate
it. In 1270 the building came
into the possession of the
Wittelsbachs. In the 15th
century a gatehouse was
constructed: its stepped
gable is set with 11 coats
of arms, those of Bavaria at
the apex and those of Poland
and Jerusalem among the
others further down. From
1602 to 1857 the castle
accommodated a prison
and a gunpowder store.

The archaeological collections housed here illustrate
the history of the castle and
of Roman art in Bavaria.
There are lapidariums and
frescoes, a kiln and a reconstruction of a Roman kitchen.

Asam-Schlössl ⑫

Thalkirchen. Maria-Einsiedel-Str. 45.
Ⓤ Thalkirchen. 🚌 57 (summer
only).

In 1724 Cosmas Damian
Asam acquired a 17th-
century property in the Isar
valley. He intended to use it
as an out-of-town residence
and studio. Asam, a twice-
married father of 13, was
beginning to find his previous
residence in Theatinerstraße
rather overcrowded.

With the help of his brother
Egid Quirin Asam, Cosmas
Damian rebuilt the house that
he had bought, converting the
second floor into a spacious
studio lit by a huge semi-
circular window. The house
was named Maria Einsiedel in
honour of the Swiss pilgrimage church that the brothers
had decorated. The artist
covered the façade of his new
home with paintings. He
decorated the third floor with
a statue of Moses bearing the
Ten Commandments, and a
painting of the antique sculpture known as The Borghese
Fencer, crowned by an angel
among clouds.

Over time, the building has
been converted for a variety
of purposes. It currently
houses a restaurant.

Theresienwiese ⓭

Theresienwiese Ruhmeshalle-Theresienhöhe Bavaria. 🕾 89 29 06 71. ◻ Apr–Oct: 10am–noon, 2–5:30pm Tue–Sun.

T HE EVENTS that took place in Munich on 17 October 1810 had far-reaching consequences. This was the day on which the marriage of Theresa von Sachsen-Hildburghausen and Ludwig I, the future king, took place. To mark the occasion, horse races, a cattle fair and a folk festival were held in meadows outside the city. The folk celebrations were repeated in following years, and this custom grew to become the Oktoberfest (see p29), the largest folk festival in the world. The festival grounds were named Theresienwiese in honour of the bride.

The beer festival is not, however, the only attraction of Theresienwiese. On an elevated ridge with a grand stairway stands the Neo-Classical Ruhmeshalle (Hall of Fame), built by Leo von Klenze in 1843–53. It is an open hall fronted by 48 Ionian columns and containing the busts of 77 prominent Bavarians. In front of the hall stands a gigantic figure of Bavaria as a Germanic goddess carrying a sword and an oak wreath and accompanied by a lion. This unusual work by Leo von Klenze and Ludwig Schwanthaler, which stands 18m (59 ft) high, was the first monumental cast iron figure to be made. It predates New York's Statue of Liberty by some 30 years. Visitors can view the city from a platform in the figure's head.

The main entrance to the Neue Messe, with the flags of many nations

Neue Messe München ⓮

Am Messesee 2. 🅄 Messestadt-West, Messestadt-ost.

I N 1992 the international airport at Riem was closed and the site, where building work took place from 1995 to 1998, was transformed into a huge exhibition area.

This was the Neue Messe München, which came to stand as an example of modern functional yet elegant architecture. It was designed by Bystrup, Bregenhoj & Partners, architects from Copenhagen, the winners of the international competition that was announced in 1991.

A sequence of 12 halls is arranged along the Atrium, an arterial axis 600 m (1,968 ft) long. The main entrance is flanked by the multifunctional ICM (International Congress Centre Munich) building. The entire covered area of 200,000 sq m (50 acres) stands in front of a large lake. Major international events that are held in the

Neue Messe include an information and telecommunications fair, a fashion show, a crafts show and a mineralogy congress.

Blutenburg ⓯

Blutenburg. Ⓢ Obermenzing (some distance away). 🚌 75. **Internationale Jugend-bibliothek:** 🕾 89 12 110. ◻ 10am–4pm Mon–Fri.

O N A man-made island in the River Würm stands Blutenburg, a small hunting lodge surrounded by greenery and water. From 1425 the lodge belonged to the Wittelsbachs and its residents included Duke Albrecht III, his son Sigismund, the later Princess Henriette Adelaide, Theresa Kunigunde Sibieska and Maximilian I Joseph.

The lodge now houses the **International Jugend-bibliothek**. Containing over 500,000 volumes in 110 languages, the library is the largest collection of children's and young people's literature in the world and is under the patronage of UNESCO.

The only original part of the lodge that still stands is St Sigmund's Chapel (1488), built by the architects of Munich's Frauenkirche. The frescoes on its exterior walls are among the few surviving examples of late Gothic mural painting. The interior of the chapel, covered with intricate rib vaulting, contains some treasures of religious art, including altarpieces of 1491 by Jan Polack and late Gothic sculptures and stained glass.

The doorway of Blutenburg's Gothic chapel

The great statue of Bavaria fronting the Ruhmeshalle in Theresienwiese

MUNICH STREET FINDER

Map references given for historic
buildings and other sights
throughout the chapter on
Munich refer to the maps included
in the following pages.

The key map below shows
the area of Munich covered by
the *Street Finder*. Buildings and
monuments in pink are star
sights that are covered in detail
in the chapter; those in brown
are sights and places that are

**Bavaria on the
Ruhmeshalle**

worth seeing. Streets shown in
yellow are closed to traffic.

The *Street Finder* maps
include U-Bahn and S-Bahn
stations as well as main car parks,
hospitals, post offices, police
stations, tourist information
centres and taxi ranks in
Munich. The word *Straße (Str.)*
indicates a street, *Platz* a
square, *Brücke* a bridge and
Bahnhof a railway station.

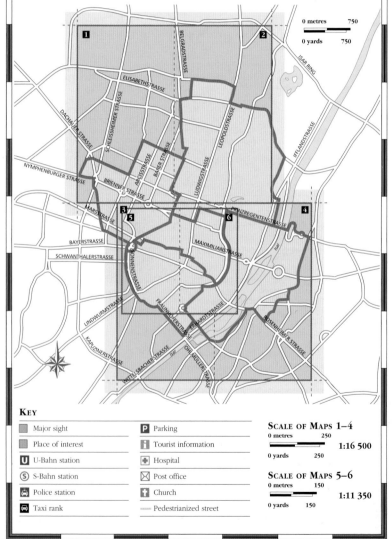

KEY

▮ Major sight	**P** Parking
▮ Place of interest	**ℹ** Tourist information
U U-Bahn station	**✚** Hospital
S S-Bahn station	**⊠** Post office
🚓 Police station	**✝** Church
🚕 Taxi rank	—— Pedestrianized street

SCALE OF MAPS 1–4

0 metres   250

0 yards   250

1:16 500

SCALE OF MAPS 5–6

0 metres   150

0 yards   150

1:11 350

Street Finder

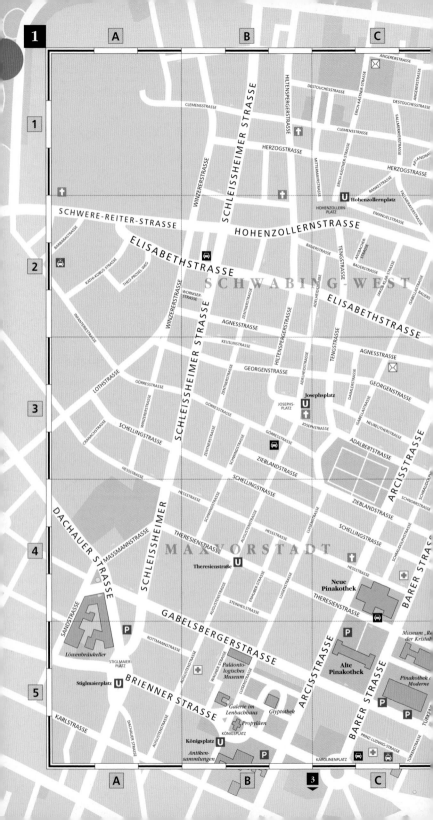

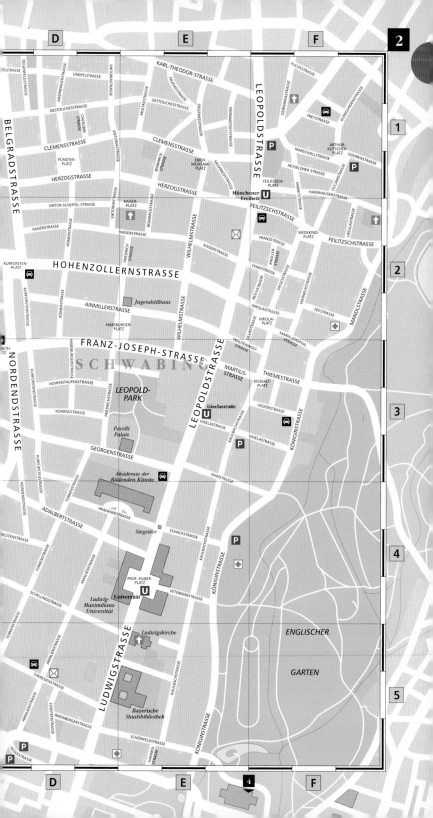

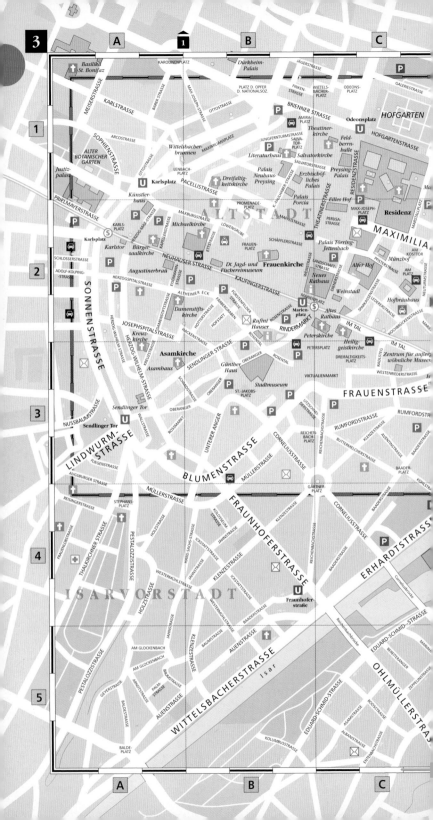

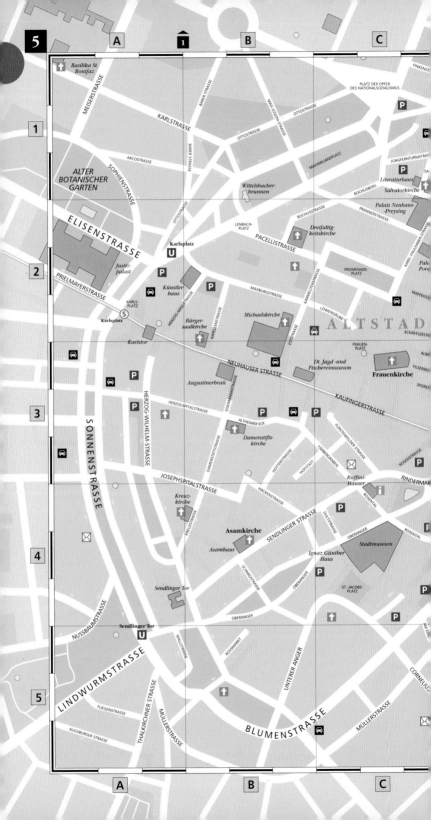

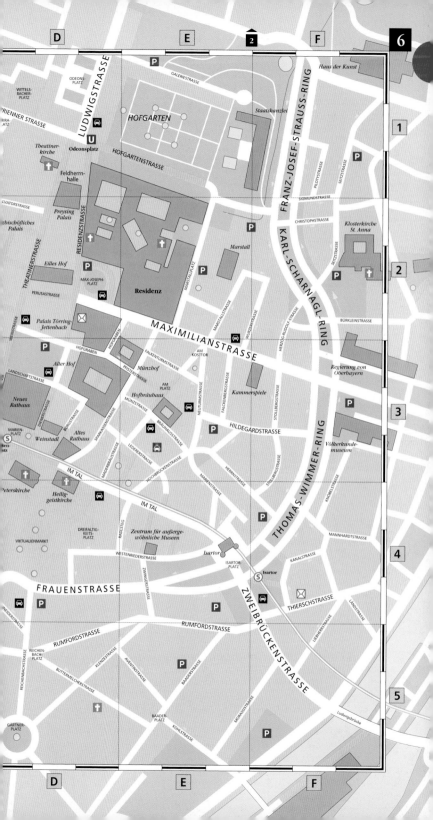

THE BAVARIAN ALPS AREA BY AREA

The Bavarian Alps at a Glance

THE BAVARIAN ALPS have much to offer tourists. Well endowed with ski lifts and shelters, the Alps offer ideal conditions for skiers, while the many lakes draw watersports enthusiasts and ice-skaters. The mountainous regions of the Bavarian Forest are a delight, both for their primeval natural surroundings and for the affordable prices to be found here. Many of the region's towns and villages contain buildings of great splendour and architectural importance.

Augsburg
Because of its many canals which are crossed by bridges, this town is known as the Venice of the North (see pages 244–9).

Neuschwanstein
This castle is the embodiment of Ludwig II's idea of a romantic seat of power. It has a fantastical setting, and its design, particularly that of the towers, was the model for the Disneyland's fairy-tale castle (see pp226–7).

SOUTHERN SWABIA
Pages 234–251

THE ALLGÄU
Pages 218–33

UPPER BAVARIA (SOUTH)
Pages 202–17

Ottobeuren
The Rococo stalls of this renowned Benedictine church are part of the overall decorative scheme (see p224).

Oberammergau
Like many others here, this house, built in 1775, is covered with Lüftlmalerei. Oberammergau is the centre of this type of trompe-l'oeil decoration (see p212).

0 km   30

0 miles   30

Altmühl
*Picturesquely
set on a hill,
Prunn Castle
overlooks the
River Altmühl
with its wooden
bridge – the
oldest and
longest in
Europe*
(see p179).

Hallertau
*This region is renowned for its hop
plantations, which supply the country's
brewing industry, so satisfying the
Bavarians' demand for beer, their
favourite drink* (see p155).

**UPPER
ARIA (NORTH)**

LOWER BAVARIA

**UPPER BAVARIA
(EAST)**

Herrenchiemsee
*Bavaria's largest palace, with
the most extensive grounds,
features sculpture created
for Ludwig II* (see p198).

Linderhof
*The gardens
surrounding
Ludwig II's
favourite palace
were modelled on
those of Versailles.
The fountains
and cascades
add a magical
dimension*
(see p196).

Schwarzeck
*Schwarzeck is one of the many
hiking and skiing stations around
Berchtesgaden, reached by a steep
and winding road* (see p196).

UPPER BAVARIA (NORTH)

onsisting of flat countryside traversed by the river valleys of the Danube and its tributaries the Isar, Ilm, Paar and Altmühl, this region of Upper Bavaria (Oberbayern) is not as varied as the south. However, it has plenty of historic monuments, as at Eichstätt and Freising, and architectural gems such as the palace at Schleißheim.

During the Jurassic period, 150 million years ago, a lagoon existed at the northern edges of this region. This became what is today the valley of the meandering River Altmühl, the location of the largest nature reserve in Germany. Many Jurassic fossils have been unearthed here, particularly in the area around Eichstätt.

More recent history concerns Dachau, a charming little town just 20 km (12 miles) northwest of Munich. Its name has become synonymous with one of the earliest concentration camps to be set up in Germany, in 1933. The camp is still surrounded by barbed wire and guard towers still stand. The site functions as a museum of the Nazis' cruel system of forced labour and extermination in which millions of victims of the Third Reich lost their lives. It is preserved as a memento and a warning to present and future generations.

The northern part of Upper Bavaria is mainly farmland. Extensive asparagus plantations stretch out around Schrobenhausen, while in a region of the Amper and Danube valleys, an area known as Hallertau, endless forest-like plantations indicate the large-scale production of the hops that are used in the brewing of beer, Bavarians' favourite drink. Hallertau forms part of the Hopfenstraße, or German Hop Trail. Along the way lies Ingolstadt, whose main claim to fame nowadays is the Audi car plant.

Here, too, are many fine historic buildings. The imposing outlines of castles tower over towns such as Beilngries, Eichstätt, Ingolstadt and Neuburg, on the northern fringes of this region. There is also a wealth of ecclesiastical buildings, the most prominent among which are the churches and abbeys at Scheyern, Indersdorf and Fürstenfeldbruck.

The imposing Baroque façade and formal gardens of the Neues Schloss in Schleißheim

◁ < The town of Eichstätt, situated in the picturesque valley of the River Altmühl

Exploring Upper Bavaria (North)

A NY EXPLORATION of the northern part of Upper Bavaria should take in the Baroque Neues Schloss at Schleißheim, the grandest building in the area, set in extensive parkland. Equally interesting is the town of Freising, with its fine cathedral and the Diözesanmuseum, which contains one of the most resplendent collections of religious art in Germany. Nature-lovers looking for beautiful countryside should head for Ries and its environs, and the northern part of this area, where hop plantations stretch to the horizon.

GETTING AROUND

Several roads traverse northern Upper Bavaria. Motorways A9 and A93 lead to the north of Germany via Nuremberg and Regensburg. Motorway A8 leads west to Stuttgart, and motorway A92 connects the region with southern Bavaria. The S-Bahn local rail network and Deutsche Bahn national rail network provide links between towns. Franz-Josef-Strauß Airport, near Freising, provides air links with other cities in Germany and the rest of Europe.

SEE ALSO

• *Where to Stay* p261.

• *Where to Eat* pp272–3.

The grand Baroque staircase of the Neues Schloss in Schleißheim

Nürnberg

Würzburg

KIPFENBER

EICHSTÄTT ①

Altmühl

13

INGOLSTAD

Donauwörth

④

Donau

NEUBURG
AN DER DONAU

D O N A U M O O S

Paar

SCHROBEN-
HAUSEN ●

300

Augsburg

Augsburg

E528

KLOSTER ⑫
INDERSDORF

Augsburg

FÜRSTENFELDBRUCK ⑬

471

2

GERMERING ●

Memmingen

E54 96

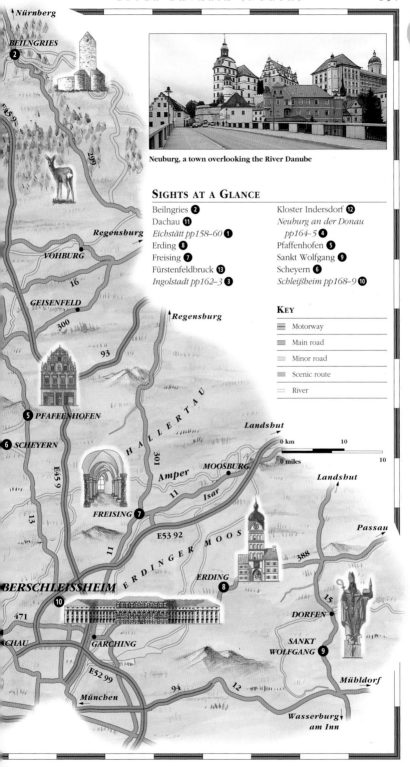

Neuburg, a town overlooking the River Danube

SIGHTS AT A GLANCE

KEY

▰	Motorway
▰	Main road
▰	Minor road
▰	Scenic route
═	River

Eichstätt ➊

Painting on a town house

Eichstätt, a see and centre of religious life since 741, is probably one of the prettiest towns in Bavaria. It stands in an exceptionally scenic location in the valley of the River Altmühl. The town's appearance was largely determined by 30 years of work by Gabriel de Gabrieli, a prominent architect of the first half of the 18th century who was also active in Vienna. The town's unique atmosphere is further enhanced by the Catholic university and its students.

Tenement houses lining Marktplatz

🔲 Marktplatz

Marktplatz, north of the cathedral, is the focal point of the burghers' district. It is surrounded by the houses of prominent merchants, and these magnificent abodes alternate with modest craftsmen's houses. On the west side of the square stands the town hall, whose tower dates from 1444. The façade and upper part of the tower were built in 1823–4.

Eichstätt's other squares – Residenzplatz, Domplatz and Leonrodplatz – were also key elements in the urban planning of the town.

The magnificent tomb of St Willibald in the cathedral

Residenzplatz is one of the finest squares in the whole of Germany. It lies south of the cathedral and has a trapezoid shape. The two-storey buildings that line the square were originally part of the chapterhouses that were designed by Gabriel de Gabrieli.

Domplatz, with the cathedral on its northeastern side, is laid out on the site of the former cemetery.

On Leonrodplatz stands the church and former Jesuit abbey, as well as the former cathedral deaconry.

🔲 Dom St Salvator und St Willibald

Domplatz.

Eichstätt's cathedral has a late Gothic nave and presbytery, the latter flanked by twin Romanesque towers. The Baroque façade was built by Gabriel de Gabrieli in 1715.

The Gothic cloisters on the south side of the cathedral adjoin the presbytery. The west wing of the cloisters contains a double-naved moratorium containing the Gothic tombs of priests, chaplains and benefactors of the cathedral. Distinctive

among the many works of art to be seen in the cathedral is the statue of St Willibald, who became the first bishop of Eichstätt in the 8th century. The statue, carved in the late Gothic style, was made in 1514. In 1745 Matthias Seybold built a two-sided altar with a canopy to cover the statue of the saint and the tomb containing his relics. This altar is located on the elevated part at the west end of the cathedral.

🔲 Fürstbischöfliche Residenz

Residenzplatz 1. 🔲 9am–3pm Mon–Fri, 10am–11:30am & 2–3:30 pm Sat–Sun.

The former bishop's residence, which adjoins the cathedral on its southern side, was built in 1700–27 to a rectangular plan with a central courtyard. The interior is decorated with stuccowork and Rococo frescoes, and features a fine Rococo staircase and Hall of Mirrors, all dating from the 18th century.

The main staircase of the former bishop's summer residence

🔲 Schutzengelkirche

Ostenstr.

This former Jesuit church was built in 1617–20 under the direction of Johann Alberthal. Having suffered destruction in 1634, in the course of the Thirty Years' War, it was rebuilt in 1660. The interior was lavishly decorated by Franz Gabriel and Johann Rosner, among others, in the first half of the 18th century. To the south of the church

Romanesque rotunda in the Kapuzinerkirche

are the buildings of the former Jesuit College, dating from the 17th and 18th centuries, with two courtyards and cloisters. The college is now used as a seminary.

⛪ Kloster Notre Dame du Sacré Coeur

Notre Dame 1. **Informationszentrum Naturpark Altmühltal** 📞 *(08421) 98 760.*

This convent was built for a foundation established in 1711 for the education of young girls. Work on the convent began in 1712, and on the church in 1719, both

to designs by the architect Gabriel de Gabrieli.

The church has a centralized plan. The façade is divided by huge pilasters and decorated with a sculpture of the Immaculate Conception above the portal. Today, the church and the convent are the headquarters of the information centre for Altmühl Valley National Park.

⛪ Kapuzinerkirche Hl. Kreuz und zum Heiligen Grabkirche

Kapuzinergasse 2.

This modest church of the Capuchin monks was built in 1623–5 and enlarged in 1905. To the south of the nave stands an oval stone-built Romanesque rotunda crowned by an open gallery and a dome supported on tall, slender columns. It was built in 1160 in imitation of the Church of the Holy Sepulchre in Jerusalem.

VISITORS' CHECKLIST

Road map C2. 🏠 *13,000.* 🚉
🚌 *Bahnhofplatz 17.*
📞 *(08421) 30 29.* ℹ️ *Domplatz 8, (08421) 98 800.*
🌐 *www. eichstaett.de.*
@ *tourismus@eichstaett.btl.de*
🎉 *Fliegerfest (May/Jun), Burgfest auf der Willibaldsburg (Jul/Aug), Brauereifest (Aug), Volksfest (Aug/Sep).*

⚓ Fürstbischöfliche Sommer Residenz

Ostenstr. 24.

The former bishop's summer residence, also designed by Gabriel de Gabrieli, dates from 1735–7. The ground and upper floors and narrow side galleries now house the offices of the Catholic university. The residence is set in geometrically laid out parkland that merges into a landscaped park descending in terraces to the River Altmühl.

The Baroque façade of the former bishop's summer residence

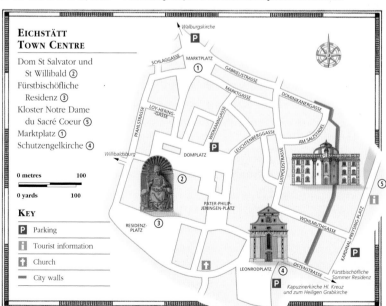

EICHSTÄTT TOWN CENTRE

Dom St Salvator und St Willibald ②
Fürstbischöfliche Residenz ③
Kloster Notre Dame du Sacré Coeur ⑤
Marktplatz ①
Schutzengelkirche ④

0 metres   100
0 yards   100

KEY

🅿️ Parking

ℹ️ Tourist information

✝️ Church

— City walls

🏛 Walburgskirche

Westenstr.

This church was built on the spot where the relics of St Walburg were buried in 875. The present monastery dates from 1629–31. In the chapel behind the high altar is St Walburg's tomb, the church's most holy feature and the object of pilgrimages. The chapel, which contains numerous votive images placed there in gratitude to the saint, is decorated with intricate wrought-iron grilles. The altarpiece consists of Gothic carvings depicting St Walburg, his parents and his brother, St Willibald.

♣ Willibaldsburg

Burgstr. 19. **Jura-Museum**
📞 *(08421) 29 56, (08421) 47 30.*
🕐 *Apr–Sep: 9am–6pm, Thu–Sun;
Oct–Mar: 10am–4pm Thu–Sun.* **Ur-
und Frühgeschichtliches Museum**
📞 *(08421) 89 450.*
🕐 *Apr–Sep: 9am–6pm Thu–Sun;
Oct–Mar: 10am–4pm Thu–Sun.*

This castle, on a hill south-west of the town, overlooks the Altmühl river valley. It can be reached by car through a tunnel 63m (206 ft) long. The castle has an elongated design and is surrounded by 17th-century fortifications. From 1335 to 1725 it was the seat of bishops but was partly demolished in the 19th century. The present approaches to the castle were built in the first half of the 17th century. The castle walls contain the ruins of a residence built for Bishop Martin von Schaumberg (1560–90).

The western section of the hill is occupied by a three-winged building with central cloisters, and a main building with small towers. Both were built by Elias Holl, who was brought to Eichstätt by Bishop Konrad von Gemmingen in 1609. Together with Augsburg town hall, they are regarded as Germany's most important late Renaissance buildings.

The north wing houses the **Jura-Museum**, with a rich collection of fossils from the Jurassic period. The south wing contains the **Ur- und Früh-geschichtliches Museum** (Museum of Prehistory), with fascinating displays.

Beilngries ❷

Road map D2. 🏘 *9,000.* 🚌 🚉
ℹ *Hauptstr. 14, (08461) 84 35.*
🌐 *www.beilngries.de*

THE BEST WAY to reach Beilngries is by road or boat from Kelheim along the scenic Altmühl valley. The town still has its defensive walls, which are set with nine towers and reinforced by a fosse (moat). Among the historic buildings on Haupt-

Romanesque tower, a vestige of the medieval castle outside Beilngries

straße is the late 16th-century house at No. 25, known as the **Kaiserbeckhaus**, which has a cantilevered upper storey supported on corbels.

The imposing Neo-Baroque **Walburgskirche** was built in 1912–13 to a design by Wilhelm Spannagl. The span of its vaulting and the ingenuity of its circular windows are impressive.

On a steep hill outside the town once stood a medieval castle, vestiges of which are two tall Romanesque **towers** flanking the gatehouse. In 1760–4 the castle was converted into the **Bishop's hunting lodge**. Its main decorative motifs are deer, which led to its being called Schloss Hirschberg ("Deer Mountain"). The Imperial Hall and the Knights' Hall are decorated with paintings by Michael Franz and have Rococo stuccowork. The palace chapel, built with material from the walls of the Romanesque castle chapel, was designed by Alexander von Branc in the 1980s.

Ingolstadt ❸

See pp162–3.

Neuburg an der Donau ❹

See pp164–5.

FOSSILS FROM THE JURASSIC ERA

About 150 million years ago, the region of the Altmühl river valley in northern Upper Bavaria and southern Franconia lay beneath a shallow lagoon that was separated from the open Jurassic sea by a reef of corals and sponges.

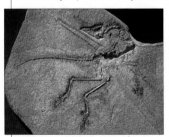

A fossil of *Archaeopteryx lithographica* in the Jura-Museum in Eichstätt

Today collectors search quarries for fossils of ammonites, small crustaceans, insects and marine plants. For a modest sum impressive specimens can also be purchased from the quarry workers. A rich collection of fossils is on view in the Jura-Museum in Willibaldsburg castle in Eichstätt.

Pfaffenhofen ❺

Road map D3. 🏛 *21,600.* 🚌 🚆
(08441) 49 150 ❗ *Hauptplatz 47,*
(08441) 49 150.
🌐 *www.pfaffenhofen.de*

T HE TOWN, situated on
the River Ilm, lies at the
western extremity of the hop-
growing region. It was once
surrounded by fortifications
set with 17 towers and
pierced by four gates. Around
the pleasant square, which
has been extended to form a
wide street, stands the Gothic
Johann Baptist-Kirche and
a Neo-Gothic **town hall**. A
tall, square tower with a
steeple stands beside the
church presbytery. The
Mesnerhaus, a residential
house dating from 1786,
contains a **museum**
with a sizeable
collection of art dating
from the 16th to the
19th centuries.

🏛 **Museum im
Mesnerhaus**
Scheyrerstr. 5.
📞 *(08441) 27 444.*
🕐 *11am–3pm Sat.*

**Soaring Gothic tower of Johann
Baptistkirche, Pfaffenhofen**

Scheyern ❻

Road map D3. 🏛 *4,200.* 🚌 🚆
in Pfaffenhofen. ❗ *Ludwigstr. 2,*
(08441) 80 640.

S CHEYERN LIES southwest of
Pfaffenhofen. In 1119,
when the seat of the Scheyern
family was converted into a
monastery, it was occupied
by monks of the Benedictine
order. After the first wave of

Façade of the Benedictine monastery in Scheyern

the dissolution of the
monasteries, the Benedictines
left but returned in 1837 at
the request of Ludwig I.

The triple-nave basilica
of **Mariä Himmelfahrts-
kirche** was remodelled in
the Baroque style in 1768–9,
with decorative mouldings
by the Wessobrunn stuccoists.
The Chapel of the Holy Cross
contains a Baroque altar with
a late Renaissance crucifix of
1600. The centrepiece of the
tabernacle is a Byzantine
relic of the True Cross,
which is kept in a magnificent
monstrance made by
Johann Georg in 1738.

Freising ❼

Road map D3. 🏛 *45,000.* 🚌 🚆
Ⓢ ❗ *Marienplatz 7, (08161) 54
122.* 🌐 *www.Freising.de*

T HE SEAT OF a bishopric from
720, the town was for
centuries the residence of the
bishops of Freising and
Munich. The hill on which the
cathedral stands is known as
Mons Doctus (Learned
Mount). The cathedral
dates from the mid-
13th century, with
the cloisters added
in the 15th century.
It was remodelled
in 1723–4 with
the involvement of
the Asam brothers
(see p68).

An outstanding
feature of the interior
is a Pietà of 1492 by
Erasmus Grasser and
Gothic stalls dating
from 1485–8. The
Romanesque crypt
contains a column
known as the

**Oriel window of
Freising town hall**

Bestiensäule, which is
decorated with carvings
symbolizing the fight against
evil. Beside the crypt is the
Maximilankapelle, with
stuccowork and paintings
by Hans Georg Asam.

The late Gothic **cloisters**
feature paintings by Johann
Baptist Zimmermann of 1717
and tombstones dating from
the 15th to the 18th centuries.
The cloisters are linked to the
Gothic **Benediktuskirche** of
1345, and a stunning Baroque
cathedral library designed by
François Cuvilliés.

The Gothic **Johannis-
kirche**, in front of the
cathedral, is linked to the
bishop's residence, which
has fine Renaissance cloisters.
On the cathedral hill is the
Diözesanmuseum, the
largest museum of religious
art in Germany.

In the town at the bottom
of the hill are the church or
St Peter und Paul, designed
in the early 18th century by
Giovanni Antonio Viscardi,
with paintings by Johann
Baptist Zimmermann, and the
late Gothic
Georgskirche, with a
Baroque tower, as
well as the Neo-
Renaissance **town
hall** of 1904–05.

On Weihenstephan
hill stands the world's
oldest **brewery**,
founded in 1040. The
Benedictine monas-
tery now houses
certain departments
of Munich's Technical
University.

🏛 **Diözesanmuseum**
Domberg 21. 📞 *(08161)*
48 790. 🕐 *10am–5pm*
Thu–Sun.

Ingolstadt ❸

Fountain statue

L UDWIG THE RICH founded Bavaria's first university here in 1472. Initially a centre of humanism, it later became a focal point of the Counter-Reformation. In the 16th century Ingolstadt was the largest fortified town in southern Germany, and was defended by Swedish soldiers during the Thirty Years' War. It suffered severe bomb damage during World War II but was restored soon after. Today Ingolstadt is known principally for the Audi cars manufactured here and for its oil refinery. However, it has some noteworthy buildings.

Alte Anatomie, now the Deutsches Medizinhistorisches Museum

The Baroque interior of the Bürgersaal St Maria de Victoria

🔒 Bürgersaal St Maria de Victoria

Konviktstr. ⬜ 9am–noon & 1pm–5pm Tue–Sun. 🖼

This hall was built in 1732-6 as the meeting place of the Marian students' association. The stuccowork is by Egid Quirin Asam, and the painting by his brother Cosmas Damian Asam, who exploited to superb effect the various points of perspective as he covered the ceiling with extensive frescoes. The sacristy contains a famous monstrance of 1708 by the Augsburg goldsmith Johannes Zeckl, depicting the defeat of the Turks at the Battle of Lepanto in 1571.

🏛 Kreuztor and City Walls

The city walls, together with their semicircular towers, were built from 1362 to 1440. Of the four original city gates, only the western one, known as the Kreuztor, survives. It is considered to be one of the finest of its kind in Germany.

The Taschenturm, a tall tower with stepped gables, also survives. Of the forti-fication towers, built from 1539 to 1579 and demolished in 1800, only the ruins of casemates and bastions still stand today.

In the band of greenery around the town stand forti-fications that were begun in 1823 by Ludwig I, built to designs by Leo von Klenze under the direction of the military engineers Michael von Streiter and Karl Peter Becker. The best-preserved element is the Reduit Tilly, a redoubt that served as a bridgehead to the opposite bank of the Danube.

🔒 Liebfrauenmünster

Kreuzstr. 1.

This great 15th-century church with diagonally set twin towers is one of the largest Gothic brick buildings in Bavaria.

The high altar, completed in 1572, commemorates the centenary of the foundation of Ingolstadt's university. The altar, 9 m (30 ft) high, incorporates 91 paintings by Hans Mielich. Other features of the interior are the Renaissance stalls and pulpit, the Gothic and Renaissance stained glass, and the monument to Johannes Eck, Martin Luther's greatest opponent, who died in 1543.

🏛 Alte Anatomie

Anatomiestr. 18/20. **Deutsches Medizinhistorisches Museum.** 📞 (0841) 30 51 860. ⬜ 10am–noon & 2pm–5pm Tue–Sun. 🖼

This fine Baroque building, completed in 1723, originally housed the university's Department of Medicine and is now home to a museum of medical history. The pleasant courtyard has a garden where medicinal herbs are grown.

The Gothic Kreuztor, Ingolstadt's western gate

♠ Neues Schloss

Paradeplatz 4. **Bayerisches Armeemuseum** 📞 *(0841) 93 770.*
◯ *8:45am–4:30pm Tue–Sun.* 📷

The Neues Schloss (New Castle) was built in the first half of the 15th century. Set with corner towers, the two-storey castle has the appearance of an impregnable stronghold. A Renaissance gateway leads into the inner courtyard. Today the castle houses the **Bavarian Army Museum**, with displays of items captured in the wars against the Turks.

♠ Herzogskasten

Hallstr. 4.

This ancient castle, standing on the southwestern corner of the city walls, was built in 1255. The oldest secular

VISITORS' CHECKLIST

Road map D2. 🏠 *117,000.* 🚌
📮 *(0841) 93 41 825.*
🚉 *Rathausplatz 2, (0841) 30 51 098.* 🅦 *www.ingolstadt.de*
@ *touristinformation@ingolstadt.de*
🎭 *Ingolstädter Bürgerfest (first weekend in Jul).*

The Neo-Renaissance Altes Rathaus, with its elaborate gable

building in Ingolstadt, it was a ducal residence until it was superseded by the Neues Schloss, which was built in the 15th century. The castle then was converted into a

granary. Rising two storeys high, it has a very tall roof with a Gothic stepped gable. It now houses a library.

🏛 Altes Rathaus

Rathausplatz 2.

The elegant town hall was lavishly remodelled in the Neo-Renaissance style by Gabriel von Seidl in 1882–3. Its sculptural decoration was designed by Lorenz Gedon. The building incorporates a former residence.

⛪ Moritzkirche

Hieronymus Str. 3.

Begun in the mid-14th century and completed in 1489, the church is a Gothic basilica with a 14th–15th-century watchtower known as the Pfeifturm.

The hospital nearby, completed in 1434, served as the main university building from 1472 to 1800.

The Neues Schloss, an elegant and imposing residence

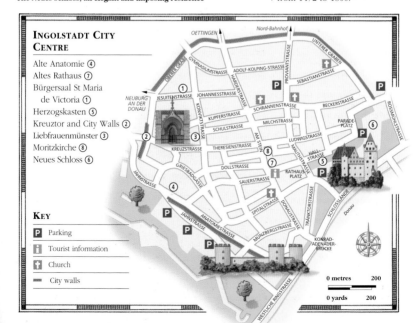

INGOLSTADT CITY CENTRE

KEY

🅿 Parking

🛈 Tourist information

⛪ Church

▬ City walls

0 metres 200

0 yards 200

Neuburg an der Donau ❹

Sɪᴛᴜᴀᴛᴇᴅ on the River Danube (Donau), Neuburg is considered to be one of Bavaria's most beautiful towns. The atmosphere from the time when it flourished as a ducal residence lives on in the streets and squares of the Obere Stadt (Upper Town). These are rivalled by the Obere Vorstadt, an early centre of the Counter-Reformation, which has an Ursuline convent as well as patricians' town houses and the palaces of the court elite. Along the Danube lies the Englischer Garten, a park traversed by the road to the 16th-century castle of the Wittelsbachs in nearby Grünau.

Oberes Tor, gateway to the Upper Town

⊞ Oberes Tor and Town Walls

In the 14th century Obere Stadt was enclosed by walls, towers and galleries. Considerable vestiges of the upper town remain, notably Oberes Tor, the main gate. It was rebuilt in 1541, when it was flanked by circular towers and topped with a Renaissance gable.

⛪ Peterskirche

Amalienstr. 40.
The church stands on the site of the oldest church in Neuburg, first mentioned in 1214. It was designed by Johann Serro of Graubünden and built in 1641–6. The triple-nave open interior is decorated with Baroque painting and stuccowork.

⊞ Amalienstraße

Of the many fine gabled houses that line this street, two are especially worthy of note. One is the Eylhaus, the old post office, built in 1720 and located next to Weveldhaus, and the other the Court Pharmacy, first mentioned in 1713. Both have ornamental gables. Equally elegant are the 17th- and 18th-century houses that can be seen in Herrenstraße.

🏛 Stadtmuseum Weveldhaus

Amalienstr. A19.
📞 (08431) 49 334.
The two-storey late Gothic Weveldhaus was built in the 16th century, and was redecorated in 1715 by Gabriel de Gabrieli, who added a fine Baroque portal. The building now houses a museum that contains many artifacts relating to the history of the town and the surrounding area.

⊞ Karlsplatz

There are few town squares in Bavaria more charming than Karlsplatz. Surrounded by trees, it has a Mariensäule (Column of the Virgin) and a fountain in the centre. The square is dominated by the façade of Hofkirche, which occupies its entire eastern side. The square boasts exquisite proportions and fine, elegant buildings.

Baroque doorway of the Weveldhaus on Amalienstraße

On the northern side of the square stands the Renaissance town hall of 1603–09. Its double exterior stairway leads to the grand entrance on the first floor. Beside it stands the Taxishaus (named after the von Thurn und Taxis family). It was completed in 1747 and its façade is decorated with elaborate polychrome stuccowork. Further on is the Zieglerhaus, with fine wrought-iron grilles and an elegant gate.

On the west side of the square is the pleasantly proportioned and decorated Lorihaus and the library building, its Rococo façade facing onto Amalienstraße. Built in 1731–2, it was furnished in 1802 with furniture from the Kaisheim monastery library.

Mariensäule on Karlsplatz

⛪ Pfarrkirche Mariä Himmelfahrt

Karlsplatz 10.
The former Hofkirche (Court Church) was founded by the Protestant rulers of Neuburg in reaction to the building of the Jesuit Michaelskirche in Munich. Work began in 1608 but was interrupted by the death of Philip Ludwig. In 1617 his Catholic successor brought the Jesuits to Neuburg and donated the church to them. It was completed in 1627.

The late Renaissance building, with a flat façade and a central octagonal domed tower, was decorated with fine stuccowork in 1616–18. The paintings by Peter Paul Rubens that once graced the altar are now in the Alte Pinakothek in Munich. Interesting features of the presbytery are the ducal loggia and the stairway to the crypt, the dukes' final resting place. A passage connects the church to the neighbouring castle.

Interior of Pfarrkirche Mariä Himmelfahrt

⛪ Schloss

Residenzstr. 2. 🅲 (08431) 88 97.
🕐 10am–5pm Tue–Sun. 🎫

The history of Neuburg Castle goes back to Roman times, when the fort of Venaxamodorum stood here. It has been in the possession of the Wittelsbach family since the 13th century. The present-day castle was built in 1530–45 and was redecorated in the Renaissance style in 1667–70. It has a pentagonal outline and is set with two circular towers that look onto the Danube. The attractive Renaissance courtyard is surrounded by a double-tiered gallery. The west side

of the courtyard has sgraffito decorations and two stone figures of dukes, probably dating from the second half of the 17th century. The west wing has a Renaissance chapel with galleries and ceiling frescoes painted by Hans Bockberger in 1543. These were plastered over in 1616, when Protestant fervour celebrated its triumph over Catholicism, but they were uncovered again in 1934–51.

An underground passage beneath Neuer Bau, the north wing, leads from the Danube to Obere Stadt. The Baroque grottoes are open to visitors. The Blue Grotto is lined with decorative shell patterns.

🏰 Former Jesuit College

Am Unteren Tor.

This 17th-century college building has a modest but imaginatively designed façade. On the first floor is the former assembly hall, which is renowned for its excellent acoustics.

Stone figures in the arcaded courtyard of the Schloss

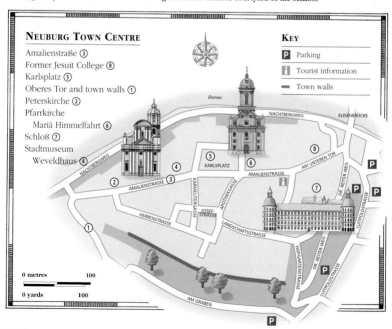

NEUBURG TOWN CENTRE

Amalienstraße ③
Former Jesuit College ⑧
Karlsplatz ⑤
Oberes Tor and town walls ①
Peterskirche ②
Pfarrkirche
  Mariä Himmelfahrt ⑥
Schloß ⑦
Stadtmuseum
  Weveldhaus ④

KEY

🅿 Parking

🅸 Tourist information

▬ Town walls

0 metres   100
0 yards   100

The Landshutertor in Erding, crowned by a Baroque dome

Erding ⓐ

Road map D3. 👥 *31,000.* 🚌 🚉 Ⓢ 🛈 *Landshuterstr., (08122) 40 80.* 🌐 *www.erding.de*

THIS TOWN is bounded by the rivers Fehlbach and Sempt, which join in the south of the conurbation. The historic buildings are grouped along two intersecting axes: Landshuterstraße, which culminates in the elongated Schrannenplatz, and the streets of Lange Zeile.

At the west end of Schrannenplatz is the Gothic **Johanneskirche**, built in the late 14th to early 15th centuries. It has an unusual layout, with the presbytery facing the square. Outside the presbytery stands a tall, 10-storey **belfry**, its façade decorated with friezes and blind windows. Inside the church the most interesting feature is the larger-than-life figure of Christ on the Cross, carved by Hans Leinberger in about 1525.

On the opposite side of Landshuterstraße stands the Gothic town gate known as the **Landshutertor**, or Schöner Turm. Flanked by towers, its façade is divided by rows of arched blind windows and it is covered by a shingle-clad Baroque dome, making it one of the most outstanding town gates in southern Bavaria. At Landshuterstraße 1 is the former

Statue of St Wolfgang

residence of the counts of Preysing, dating from 1648, which is now the town hall. Opposite stands the Gothic **Hospital Church of the Holy Spirit**, while at No. 3 Schrannenplatz is the 14th-century **Frauenkirche**.

Sankt Wolfgang ⓥ

Road map E4. 👥 *4,000.* 🚌 🚉 *Dorfen. Hauptstr. 9, (08085) 18 80.* 🌐 *www.st.wolfgang-ob.de*

THE TOWN is named in honour of St Wolfgang, the Bishop of Ratisbon (Regensburg), who was canonized in 1052. According to legend the saint, while on his way to Mondsee monastery, discovered a spring with miracle-working waters here. In the early 15th century a **chapel** was built over the spring. **Wolfgangskirche** was built to the south of the chapel in 1430–77. This two-nave, web-vaulted church is an outstanding example of late Gothic Bavarian brick architecture. The foundations contain the Stone of St Wolfgang, a piece of red marble bearing what is said to be the saint's footprint. Substantial fragments of the original Gothic altar of about 1485 also remain. There is also a carving of St Wolfgang with St George and St Sigismund by Heinrich Helmschrot of Landshut (or his studio), and paintings of scenes from the life of St Mary.

In the elongated northern nave, and a few steps higher up, is the original **chapel** with the miracle-working spring, which attracts pilgrims. In the early 18th century it was decorated with fine stuccowork with acanthus motifs. The small figure of St Wolfgang that stands on the Rococo altar was made in 1470 and is said to have miraculous powers. Before the altar is a deep covered well. Visitors can lie down beside it and drink its curative water using a ladle.

The town hall is another interesting building. It was originally a presbytery, built by Johann Baptist Gunetzrhainer.

Oberschleißheim ⓧ

Road map D3. 👥 *12,000.* Ⓢ 🛈 *Freisinger Str. 15, (089) 315 61 30.*

THIS TOWN is best known for its three impressive **palaces** *(see pp168-9)*, set in the gardens of the Hofgarten. But also of interest is the **Flugwerft Schleißheim**, a museum located on one of the oldest aerodromes in Germany. Part of the Deutsches Museum, the museum is located in restored buildings dating from 1912–19, in a new exhibition hall and on the apron. Some 50 aircraft and helicopters are on display. There is also an exhibition illustrating the development of flight and of space flight.

🏛 **Flugwerft Schleißheim**
Effnerstr. 18. 📞 *(089) 31 57 14 0.* 🕐 *9am–5pm daily.* 🏷

Otto Lilienthal's aeroplane, built in 1894, Flugwerft Schleißheim

The gardens of the Renaissance castle in Dachau

Dachau ❶

Road map D4. 🏛 38,000. Ⓢ ▯
ℹ Konrad-Adenauer - Str. 1, (08131)
84 566. 🗓 www.dachau.de
🎭 Dachauer Volksfest (Aug).

SET ON A steep hill, this picturesque little town on the River Amper has a panoramic view of nearby Munich, although its name has become synonymous with the martyrdom of hundreds of thousands of people.

In 1933 the first Nazi **concentration camp** was set up here and it was in use up until 1945, during which time 30,000 prisoners perished here. The site of the camp was opened to the public as a place of remembrance in 1965.

One of the buildings contains the **KZ Gedenkstätte Dachau**, a museum which documents the history of the concentration camps and the crimes against humanity that were committed here before and during World War II.

On the hill at the edge of the town, a **palace** was built on the site of a 15th-century castle as a summer residence for the Wittelsbachs. Of the original four wings constructed in 1558–77, only the southwest wing remains. The ceremonial hall on the first floor, which survives, was decorated in 1564–5 by Hans Wissreuter.

The focal point of the town is a triangular plaza on which the town hall and the church

stand. Hans Krumpper's late Renaissance **Jakobskirche** was built in 1624–5. It incorporates an earlier presbytery with a fine tower dating from about 1425 and extended in 1676–8 with the addition of a dome.

🏛 KZ-Gedenkstätte Dachau (Museum)
Alte Roemerstr. 75. ▮ (08131) 66 99 70. ◯ 9am–5pm Tue–Sun.

Kloster Indersdorf ❷

Road map C3.
🚌 Ⓢ ▯ Markt Indersdorf.
ℹ Markt Indersdorf, Marktplatz 1, (08136) 93 40.
🗓 www.markt-indersdorf.de

THIS FORMER Augustinian abbey built in the early 11th century stands on the north bank of the River Glonn. Vestiges of a 12th-century triple-nave Romanesque basilica with a twin-towered façade and Gothic remodelling are discernible in the later **Klosterkirche Mariae Himmelfahrt**. The latter was lavishly furnished during the 18th century. Franz Xavier Feichtmayr the Elder added the interior Rococo stuccowork in 1754–6, and the paintings of scenes from the life of St Augustine were executed by Matthäus Günther, assisted by Johann Georg Tiefenbrunner.

The extensive **abbey buildings** of 1694–1704, designed by Antonio Riva, are set around two courtyards south and east of the church.

Gate and guard tower of Dachau concentration camp.

Gothic Madonna in Fürstenfeld-bruck's Baroque church

Fürstenfeldbruck ❸

Road map C4. 🏛 33, 000. Ⓢ ▯
ℹ Hauptstr. 31, (08141) 28 107.
🗓 www.fuerstenfeldbruck.de
🎭 Volk- und Heimatfest (Jun–Jul); Brucker Altstadfest (Jul); Leonhardifahrt (Oct–Nov); Christkindlmarkt (Dec); Luzienhäuschen-schwimmen (13 Dec).

THE FINEST AND most important building in the town is the former **Cistercian abbey**, situated on the way to Augsburg and built in 1263–90. Its establishment was funded by Ludwig II, the Severe, after the execution of his wife Maria of Brabant, who was unjustly accused of infidelity. In 1691–1754, remodelled by Giovanni Antonio Viscardi, it became one of the largest Baroque abbeys in Bavaria.

The monumental façade of **Mariae Himmelfahrtskirche** conceals an interior of fine stuccowork by Pietro Francesco Appioani, vaulting lavishly painted by Cosmas Damian Asam and a high altar of 1760–62 designed by his brother Egid Quirin Asam.

The monastery, its interior decorated with stuccowork and painting in 1924, now houses a police college and museum. Many historic town houses line the main street. The old town hall, refurbished in 1866–8, features paintings dating from 1900.

On St Luke's Day, in memory of the flood of 1725, children float model houses illuminated with candles across the Amper, which flows through the town.

Schleißheim Palace

Mask on the Neues Schloss

ORIGINALLY INTENDED to rival the splendour of Versailles, the palace at Schleißheim was the architectural setting for the imperial ambitions of Maximilian Emanuel. The architect was Enrico Zucalli, and work started in 1701. It was then interrupted, but restarted in 1717 under the direction of Joseph Effner, who deviated from the original plans. The 330-m (1,082-ft) long Neues Schloss has an overpoweringly lavish interior, which was decorated by Cosmas Damian Asam and Johann Baptist Zimmermann. Today, as well as admiring the elaborate interior decoration, visitors can see the palace's outstanding gallery of Baroque painting.

Doors
The doors leading into the vestibule were carved by Ignaz Günther in 1736 and are counted among his masterpieces.

Altes Schloss
In the late 16th century Wilhelm V built himself a modest country seat. Under the direction of his son, Maximilian I, Heinrich Schön the Elder remodelled it in 1616–23, with mouldings and paintings by Peter Candid. It was rebuilt after World War II.

A gateway with clock tower built in about 1600 leads into the courtyard in front of the Altes Schloss.

★ Neues Schloss
The vestibule, decorated with fine stuccowork and frescoes, leads into a Rococo dining-room on one side and to a grand staircase on the other.

| 0 metres | 150 |
| 0 yards | 150 |

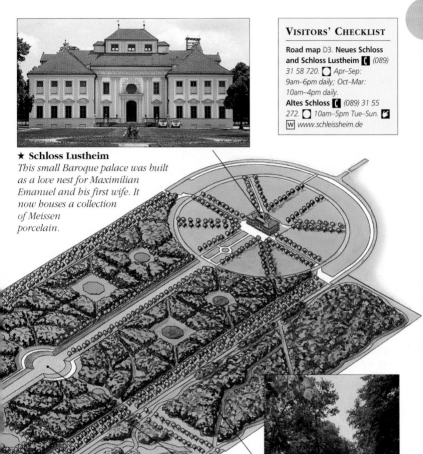

VISITORS' CHECKLIST

Road map D3. **Neues Schloss
and Schloss Lustheim** ☎ (089)
31 58 720. ◐ Apr–Sep:
9am–6pm daily; Oct–Mar:
10am–4pm daily.
Altes Schloss ☎ (089) 31 55
272. ◐ 10am–5pm Tue–Sun. ☒
Ⓦ www.schleissheim.de

★ Schloss Lustheim

*This small Baroque palace was built
as a love nest for Maximilian
Emanuel and his first wife. It
now houses a collection
of Meissen
porcelain.*

Canals
*Lustheim's
canals form the axis
of the park layout. In
front of Neues Schloss the
water flows into a basin with a
cascade and fountains.*

★ Park
*This is the only Baroque park
in Germany that has survived
in its original form. It is
characterized by canals and
pathways that mark out
geometrical patterns of greenery.*

MAXIMILIAN EMANUEL

In 1701 the Elector Maximilian
Emanuel ordered the extension
of Schleißheim and the rebuilding of Nymphenburg. Defeat
in the war against Austria
caused work to be temporarily
suspended, so that he did not
see its completion. Despite this
his patronage brought Bavaria
into the mainstream of the
high Baroque, giving the
Wittelsbach family a name for
splendour and prestige.

STAR SIGHTS

★ **Neues Schloss**

★ **Park**

★ **Schloss Lustheim**

LOWER BAVARIA

L OWER BAVARIA (NIEDERBAYERN), *bordering Austria and the Czech Republic in the east, is both a distinct cultural entity and a separate administrative area. With a pristine natural environment, it is an oasis of peace, while its fine Baroque buildings leave an indelible impression on the visitor. With none of the bustle of big cities, towns like Landshut and Passau have retained an old-world flavour.*

Lower Bavaria encompasses most of the Bayerischer Wald (Bavarian Forest), which includes a nature reserve and a national park. Increasing numbers of holiday-makers are appreciating the unspoiled natural environment here. As recently as the 1960s, out-of-the-way villages delighted visitors with their tumbledown thatched cottages. Today such sights are confined to the open-air museums of the Museumsdorf Bayerischer Wald and the Freilichtmuseum Finsterau.

The local people, known for their hospitality and friendliness, work in the region's forestry, tourist and glassware industries. Calm and restrained, they have a strong sense of their own worth. When Franz Xaver Krenkl, a Lower Bavarian, beat the royal carriage on its journey to Munich in his own cart, his comment was simply "Wer ko der ko" ("He who can, can").

From the Benedictine monastery at Weltenburg to the town of Kelheim the River Danube flows between high limestone cliffs overgrown with dense mixed foliage. On both sides of the river unique rock formations create fantastic shapes, and they have been named accordingly. Sailing along this stretch of the Danube is an unforgettable experience, as is the view down onto the river from the gallery around the Neo-Classical Liberation Hall in Kelheim. A canal completed in 1986 joins the Danube at Kelheim, providing a waterway link with the Rhine and the Main, using a stretch of the River Altmühl. This valley is as magical as that of the Danube.

Initiatives to industrialize Lower Bavaria have resulted in the construction of two modern factories in Dingolfing, where the famous BMW cars are produced.

Passau's beautiful Old Town, on the banks of the River Danube

◁ **Baroque interior of the Benedictine Abbey library in Metten**

Exploring Lower Bavaria

LANDSHUT is the capital of Lower Bavaria. Every four years tourists flock here to witness the Landshut Wedding, a great historical spectacle that is held at the foot of Trausnitz castle *(see p31)*. Passau, set on a bend in the Danube, is equally picturesque. From here the "Asam Trail" begins, taking in the churches that the Asam brothers decorated in Aldersbach, Osterhofen, Straubing, Rohr and Weltenburg *(see p68)*. The piety of the local people can be seen in the many pilgrimage churches, the best known being at Bogenberg, known as the Mount Athos of Lower Bavaria, and Geiersberg, near Deggendorf.

Bavarian coat of arms on the town gate in Vilshofen

Map showing locations including:
Regensburg, Cha, RIEDENBURG, ALTMÜHL ESTUARY VALLEY, Regensburg, KELHEIM, BOGENBERG, WELTENBURG, STRAUBING, ABENSBERG, GEISELHÖRING, Donau, NEUSTADT, ROHR, Ingolstadt, ROTTENBURG, LANDA, Geisenfeld, DINGOLFING, MAINBURG, München, Freising, LANDSHUT, München, VILSBIBURG, Wasserburg am Inn, Altötting, Erding

0 km   15
0 miles   15

Barrage on the River Altmühl at Haidhof

GETTING AROUND

Lower Bavaria borders Austria and the Czech Republic. Three motorways pass through the region. The A92 links Landshut and Deggendorf, following the course of the River Isar, and the A3 links Regensburg and Passau, along the course of the River Danube. Regensburg can also be reached by A93. The railway network is sparse but there is a good bus service.

SIGHTS AT A GLANCE

Aldersbach **15**
Bogenberg **6**
Fürstenzell **12**
Landshut pp174–7 **1**
Metten **7**
Museumsdorf
  Bayerischer Wald **10**

Ortenburg **13**
Osterhofen **17**
Passau pp184–7 **11**
Rohr **2**
Sammarei **14**
Sankt Hermann **8**
Straubing pp180–81 **5**

Vilshofen **16**
Weltenburg **3**

Tours
Nationalpark
  Bayerischer Wald **9**
Altmühl Estuary Valley **4**

KEY

▬ Motorway
▬ Main road
▭ Minor road
▬ Scenic route
═ River

Cham

*Plzeň
(Pilsen)*

VIECHTACH
BODENMAIS
ZWIESEL
REGEN
85
11

SANKT HERMANN **8**
BISCHOFSMAIS

NATIONALPARK
BAYERISCHER
WALD

FINSTERAU

Prague

METTEN **7**
Donau
DEGGENDORF
E56 3
533
GRAFENAU **9**
533
NATIONALPARK
BAYERISCHER WALD

PLATTLING
Isar
MUSEUMSDORF
BAYERISCHER WALD **10**
TITTLING
85
12
FREYUNG

WALDKIRCHEN

OSTERHOFEN **17**
VILSHOFEN **16**
Donau
8
ALDERSBACH **15**
SAMMAREI **14**
ORTENBURG **13** **12**
FÜRSTENZELL
11
PASSAU
Linz →
HAUZENBERG
OBERNZELL
388
Linz
Linz

BAD GRIESBACH
E56 3
12
PFARRKIRCHEN
388
EGGENFELDEN
POCKING
Inn
20
Altötting
12
Altötting
SIMBACH
Ried
Linz
Salzburg
Salzburg

SEE ALSO

• *Where to Stay* p261.

• *Where to Eat* p273.

The stone-built Roman viaduct
at Dingolfing

Street-by-Street: Landshut ●

Griffin on a house in the Schirmgasse

L ANDSHUT, THE CAPITAL of Lower Bavaria, grew up around Trausnitz castle and flourished in the 14th and 15th centuries. In 1475 it was the scene of a grand and lavish wedding when Duke Georg of the House of Wittelsbach married the Polish Princess Jadwiga, daughter of Casimir Jagiellon. Wedding guests included the Emperor Frederick III and his son Maximilian. The event is commemorated today by a great spectacle, the Landshut Wedding *(see p31)*.

★ Stadtresidenz
This palace, built for Duke Ludwig X in 1536–43, was the first Renaissance palace in Germany.

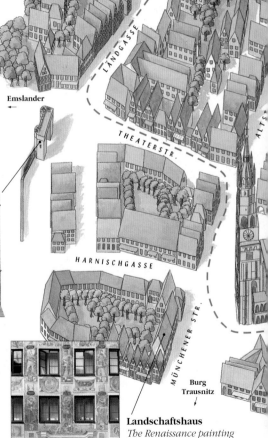

Emslander

Ländtor
The Gothic gateway leading into the city from the side on the River Isar is a vestige of the old city fortifications.

Landschaftshaus
The Renaissance painting executed in 1599 on the walls of the house at Altstadt 28 is a good example of this kind of exterior decoration in Landshut.

Burg Trausnitz

STAR SIGHTS
★ **Martinskirche**
★ **Stadtresidenz**
★ **Town Hall**

★ **Town Hall**
The Gothic town hall has a fine Renaissance oriel window. The interior paintings and stained-glass windows on the theme of the Landshut Wedding date from 1860.

VISITORS' CHECKLIST

Road map E3. 👥 60,000.
🚌 🚆 *Bahnhofplatz.*
ℹ️ *Altstadt 315, (0871)
92 2050.* 🌐 *www.landshut.de*
📅 *Landshuter Hochzeit
(Landshut Wedding) (Jul, every 4
years; next in 2004), Landshuter
Hofmusiktage (Jul, every 2 years),
Landshuter Flohmarkt (May),
Altstadtfest (Jul), Bartlmädult (Aug),
Haferlmarkt (Sep).*

Grasbergerhaus
It was in this late Gothic house with stepped gables and street-level arcade that the betrothed Polish Princess Jadwiga stayed in 1475.

★ **Martinskirche**
The spacious interior of this triple-nave church, which took more than a hundred years to build (1389–1500), impresses with its height, its forest of columns and its fine vaulting.

KEY

‒ ‒ ‒ Suggested route

0 metres   50

0 yards   50

Exploring Landshut

Landshut, like Munich, lies between a fork in the River Isar. It stretches out between Trausnitz castle, which is set on a vantage point, and the Cistercian abbey of Seligenthal. The central conurbation is concentrated around two wide parallel streets that function as squares lying on a north-south axis. They are known as Altstadt and Neustadt.

Landshut is perhaps the most quintessentially German of all Lower Bavarian towns. With its historic buildings spared damage during World War II, the town has retained the atmosphere of its earlier days of glory.

🔒 Jesuitenkirche

Spiegelgasse.
The Church of St Ignaz, located on the southern road leading out of Neustadt, was formerly part of a Jesuit monastery. Designed by the Jesuit architect Johannes Holl, it was built from 1613 to 1641. The interior features a fine Baroque high altar dating from 1663.

Side entrance to the Gothic Jodokkirche

🔒 Jodokkirche

Jodokgasse.
This Gothic triple-nave brick basilica, built in 1338–1450, was dedicated to St Jodok, the son of a Breton duke who lived in the 7th century and who became a pilgrim and hermit. In the mid–19th century the church was restored to its original Gothic appearance and was furnished in Baroque style.

Stone reliefs on the Gothic altar in Martinskirche

🔒 Martinskirche

Altstadt 219. 📞 (0871) 92 21 780.
🕐 Apr–Sep: 7:30am–6:30pm daily;
Oct–Mar: 7:30 am–5pm daily.
Three architects collaborated on the building of this Gothic church. One of them was Hans von Burghausen, whose tombstone, dated 1432, is built into its southern wall. At 131 m (430 ft) high, the brick church tower is the tallest in the world; the steeple was added in 1500. The tower commands a splendid view of the town and of the castle and its gardens. The interior of the church abounds in priceless Gothic furnishings.

🔒 Dominikanerkirche

Regierungsplatz.
The Church of St Blasien, part of the former Dominican monastery, was built in 1271–1386 in the form of a triple-nave Gothic basilica. The interior was remodelled in the Rococo style by Johann Baptist Zimmermann and decorated with lavish stucco-work. The Neo-Classical façade was added in 1805.

🔒 Spitalkirche

Heilige–Geist–Gasse.
The late Gothic Church of the Holy Spirit and the building of the former hospital located opposite stand on the south side of the road leading out of Altstadt. The triple-nave church was built by Hans von Burghausen in 1407–61.

The interior features fan vaulting and there is an ambulatory around the presbytery. On the northern side of the presbytery stands a large tower. The entrance to the church, in the west front, is a tall, ornamental portal fronted by a porch whose corners are set with low towers.

🏛 Stadtresidenz

Altstadt 79. 📞 (0871) 92 41 10.
🕐 Apr–Sep: 9am–5pm Tue–Sun;
Oct–Mar: 10am–4pm Tue–Sun. 🎫
This residence, in the Italian Renaissance style, consists of two adjacent buildings.

The Deutscher Bau, built in 1536–7, has a Neo-Classical façade dating from about 1780 on the side looking onto Altstadt. A museum of local history (currently closed but due to reopen in 2004) was laid out here in 1935.

The Italienischer Bau, built in 1537–43, has a fine arcaded courtyard. The building's façade, looking onto Länd-gasse, is decorated with a large cartouche bearing the coat of arms of Ludwig X of Bavaria, for whom it was built. Inside visitors can see the fine reception halls, which occupy two floors, and admire the beautiful Renaissance frescoes depicting mythological scenes.

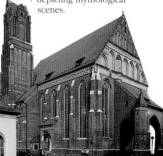

Spitalkirche, on the road leading from Altstadt

Burg Trausnitz

THIS CASTLE, whose history began in the year 1204, was the seat of the von Bayern-Landshut branch of the Wittelsbach family. It was extended in the 14th and 15th centuries, and was converted into a residence in 1568–79. In 1961 a fire destroyed the northwest wing, but painstaking restoration work has allowed it to re-open to visitors. The late Romanesque chapel and the original staircase were spared.

★ Narrentreppe
The Fools' Staircase is decorated with lifesize figures from the Commedia dell'Arte painted in 1578 by Padovano. They commemorate the shows performed by an itinerant Italian theatre troupe for Wilhelm V.

St-Georgs-Rittersaal
The walls of this hall are hung with tapestries illustrating the exploits of Duke Otto Wittelsbach woven to designs by Peter Candid in Paris in 1618.

Arcaded courtyard

STAR SIGHT

★ Narrentreppe

Alte Dürnitz
This spacious two-nave hall is situated on the ground floor and features arches supported on palmate pillars.

The Castle
A steep flight of steps leads up to the castle and its gardens. The castle commands a fine view of the whole town and the valley of the River Isar.

Rohr ❷

Road map D2. 🚌 🚆 *Abensberg.*
🛈 *Marienplatz 1, (08783) 96 080.*
Abbey 📞 *(08783) 96 000.*
🕐 *6am–7pm daily.* 🎫 📷

THIS AUGUSTINIAN abbey dates from the 12th century. In the first quarter of the 13th century, when the church and **abbey** were transferred to the Benedictines, the buildings were remodelled in the Baroque style.

Mariä Himmelfahrt is renowned for its stuccowork and the high altar of 1723 by Egid Quirin Asam. The altar was built in the form of a theatrical stage with wings. The sculptural group on the altar depicts the Assumption of the Virgin. A scene of great drama and expression, it embodies the idea of a *Theatrum Sacrum* and is one of Asam's masterpieces in this genre.

The high altar of the church of Mariä Himmelfahrt in Rohr

Weltenburg ❸

Road map D2. 🚌 🚆 *Kelheim.* ⛴
Monastery 📞 *(09441) 20 40.* 🎫
📷 🖥 *www.klosterschenke-weltenburg.de*

THIS BENEDICTINE **monastery** complex, dating from the early 7th century, stands in a picturesque setting on a terrace beside the Danube.

The Asam brothers added to the complex the splendid Baroque **Georgs- und Martinskirche**, which was completed in 1716. Cosmas Damian was responsible for the architectural designs and

A boat trip through the Danube Gorge from Weltenburg to Kelheim

the paintings, and Egid Quirin Asam built the fine high altar and the statue of St George slaying the Dragon.

There is a beer-garden in the cloisters where visitors can sample the products of the monastic brewery. Boat trips through the Danube Gorge to Kelheim also depart from a quay nearby.

Straubing ❺

See pp180–81.

Bogenberg ❻

Road map F2. 🏔 *10,200.* 🚌
🚆 *Bogen.* 🛈 *Bogen, Stadtplatz 56, (09422) 50 50.* 🖥 *www.bogen.de*

RISING ABOVE the small town of Bogen, the Bogenberg, or "Mount Athos" of Lower Bavaria, was once a Celtic sacred place. Since the Middle Ages it has been a place of pilgrimage. Standing on the top is the Gothic **Hl. Kreuz und Mariä Heimsuchung**,

Angel and candles in the pilgrimage church of Bogenberg

which commands an excellent view over the Danube valley.

Pilgrims come here to honour the miraculous statue of the pregnant Virgin Mary, dating from around 1400, which is clothed in a 17th-century dress and embroidered cloak. Dozens of votive candles flicker in the presbytery. According to an ancient custom, at Pentecost the strongest man from the nearby village of Holzkirchen brings to the church a great candle – *Die lange Stang* – up to 100 kg (220 lb) in weight and 13 m (40 ft) long.

Metten ❼

Road map F2. 🏔 *4,200.* 🚌 🚆 🛈
Krankenhausstr. 22, (0991) 99 80 50.
🖥 *www.markt-metten.de*

THE LOCAL **Benedictine abbey** was founded in about 766. In 1830, after it had been appropriated as a result of the dissolution of the monasteries, it was returned to its industrious owners.

Michaelskirche, which has been rebuilt several times since its foundation in the Romanesque period, was remodelled in 1712–29. The twin-towered façade outlines two circular chapels. The interior has paintings and a high altar by Cosmas Damian Asam.

The most exquisite part of the abbey is the library, built in 1722–9 and decorated with stuccowork by Franz Josef Holzinger. It is one of the finest library buildings in the world. A remarkable pair of Atlases support the low vaulted ceiling.

Altmühl Estuary Valley ❹

THE RIVER Altmühl winds scenically from central Franconia, meandering through the northern part of Upper Bavaria and through Lower Bavaria before flowing into the Danube. The Altmühltal Naturpark, in the river valley, is one of the largest and finest nature parks in Germany. This tour takes visitors along the estuary, ending with the famous canal that connects the River Danube with the Main and the Rhine.

TIPS FOR HIKERS & DRIVERS

Length: *About 20 km (12 miles).*
Stopping-off places: *There are cafés or bars at each of the places along the route. The larger towns have restaurants and some also offer accommodation.*

Schloß Prunn ⑤
This castle, looking as if it had grown from the rocks, houses a museum. The longest wooden bridge in Europe, over the Altmühl, is visible from the terrace.

Rosenburg ⑦
This castle is a centre for the breeding of birds of prey and contains a museum of falconry equipment. Displays with birds of prey, including eagles, are held here every day.

Riedenburg ⑥
The local Crystals Museum is famous for having the world's largest cluster of rock crystal. It weighs 7.8 tonnes and comes from Arkansas in the United States.

EICHSTÄTT

Kelheimwinzer

Saal

REGENSBURG

INGOLSTADT

Essing ④
Here a narrow street leads to a small market square, one of Bavaria's delightful little spots. A medieval gate leads through to the wooden bridge over the former course of the River Altmühl.

Randeck ③
A road running to the foot of the mountain leads to the ruins of an 11th-century castle, which was rebuilt several times, with the town of Essing at its feet.

Tropfsteinhöhle ②
These caves, off the road to Essing, were inhabited during the Stone Age. The temperature inside stays at a constant 9° C (48° C), regardless of external conditions.

Kelheim ①
The Independence Hall, built by Friedrich von Gärtner and Leo von Klenze in 1842–63, commemorates the defeat of Napoleon.

KEY

▨ Suggested route

═ Other road

0 km   10

0 miles   10

Straubing ❺

STANDING on the south bank of the Danube in the fertile Gäuboden valley, Straubing pulsates with life. The medieval appearance of the Old Town has survived basically unchanged, bearing a faithful resemblance to the wooden model made in 1568 by Jakob Sandtner and now on view in the Bayerisches National-museum in Munich. A copy can be seen in the Gäubodenmuseum. Every year in August the town holds the Gäubodenfest, a folk festival second in size only to Munich's Oktoberfest.

Gold mask in the Gäubodenmuseum

🚩 Ludwigsplatz and Theresienplatz

The pedestrianized market square resembles a long, wide avenue cutting through the heart of the Old Town. It is pleasant to wander through the large garden between closely packed stalls and crates full of colourful flowers, fruit and vegetables, and admire the historic buildings. The **Stadtturm**, or tower, offers a sweeping panorama of the town, the Gäuboden and the Bavarian Forest. A Neo-Classical gate built in 1810 divides the market square into two, with **Ludwigsplatz** on the eastern side and **Theresienplatz** on the western.

Ludwigsplatz has two fountains dedicated to the town's patron saints, St Jacob (1644) and St Tiburtius (1685). On Theresienplatz stands a column built in 1709, featuring gilt figures of the Holy Trinity.

Opposite the town gates on the south side of the square is the two-storey **town hall**, its two wings enclosing a courtyard. The town hall was

The Stadtturm (city tower) in the centre of the town square

created in 1380, when two adjacent Gothic houses were conjoined behind a single façade. The stepped gable, however, dates from the 18th century.

🔒 Karmelitenkirche

Albrechtsgasse 20.
This spacious triple-nave Gothic church with a tower was partly remodelled in about 1700 by Wolfgang Dientzenhofer. The lavish

Baroque interior of Ursulinenkirche

17th and 18th-century furnishings successfully harmonize with the later Baroque decoration.

In the church is the tomb of Agnes Bernauer, the beautiful daughter of a barber from Augsburg who was secretly married to Duke Albrecht III and who was tragically drowned in the Danube in 1435 on his father's orders. Every four years in August amateur actors re-create this historical tragedy in the Agnes-Bernauer-Festspiele.

🔒 Ursulinenkirche

Burggasse 9.
This church, which forms part of an Ursuline convent, was built and decorated by the Asam brothers in 1736–41. In their inspired collaboration, Egid Quirin Asam created the architectural design and Cosmas Damian Asam painted the frescoes and the altarpieces *(see p68)*.

♣ Herzogschloss

Schlossplatz 2B. **Museum im Herzogschloss.** 🕻 *(09421) 21 114.* ◯ *10am–4pm Tue–Sun.* ◉ *mid-Jan–mid-March.*
The castle, on the Danube, has an irregular plan and an inner courtyard. Its earliest parts date from the 14th century. The Bernauerturm on the southwestern corner is the turret from which Agnes Bernauer is said to have been thrown into the Danube. The museum is a branch of the Bayerisches Nationalmuseum.

🏛 Gäuboden-museum

Fraunhoferstr. 3.
🕻 *(09421) 81 811.* ◯ *10am–4pm Tue–Sun.*
This local history museum was founded in 1845. Its most renowned exhibit is the Römerschatz, or Roman Treasure, which was discovered in 1950 and which caused a sensation among academics. It is the largest collection of Roman parade armour to have been found anywhere in the

View of the Herzogschloss from the Danube

VISITORS' CHECKLIST

Road map E2. 🏛 *43,000.*
🚉 *Bahnhofplatz.* 🚌
ℹ️ *Theresienplatz 20,*
(09421) 94 43 07.
📠 *(09421) 94 41 03*
🆆 *www.straubing.de*
@ *tourismus@straubing-baynet..de*
🎭 *Gäubodenfest (Aug),*
Agnes-Bernauer-Festspiele
(every four years, next in 2003).

former Roman Empire. The collection includes highly ornamental helmets with visors, shin-guards and metal masks for horses.

🔒 Jakobs-
und Tiburtiuskirche
Pfarrplatz 1a.
This is one of Bavaria's largest and most magnificent Gothic churches, begun in 1400 and not completed for almost a century. The forest of columns in the extraordinarily tall interior support 18th-century barrel vaulting.

The church has preserved its Gothic statues and paintings, including an image of the Mother of God ascribed to Hans Holbein, Baroque paintings and sculptures by the Asam Brothers, and

tombstones. The 15th-century stained-glass windows are the church's finest elements, giving the church interior a unique atmosphere.

Gothic stained-glass window in Jakobs- und Tiburtiuskirche

🔒 Peterskirche
Pointstr. 27.
Peterskirche, a Romanesque basilica dating from around 1200 whose steeples were enlarged in the 19th century, is one of the finest churches of its kind in Lower Bavaria. Among the interior features are a Romanesque Crucifix and a Gothic Pietà dating from about 1340.

The church cemetery is an interesting place to explore, as it is one of the oldest in Germany. It contains three Gothic chapels. One of them, the Bernauerkapelle, was built by Duke Ernst as penance for his son's death in 1435. His symbolic tombstone can be seen within. The walls of the Totenkapelle, built in 1486, bear a cycle depicting the Dance of Death that was painted in 1763.

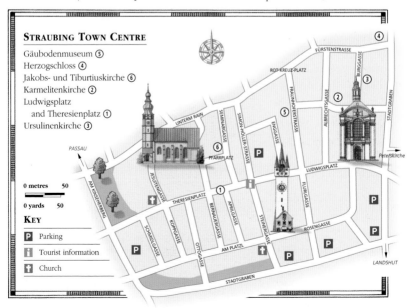

STRAUBING TOWN CENTRE

Gäubodenmuseum ⑤
Herzogschloss ④
Jakobs- und Tiburtiuskirche ⑥
Karmelitenkirche ②
Ludwigsplatz
  and Theresienplatz ①
Ursulinenkirche ③

0 metres   50
0 yards   50

KEY

🅿 Parking

ℹ️ Tourist information

⛪ Church

**The chapel and church at
Sankt Hermann**

Sankt Hermann ⑧

Road map F2. 🚌 🚉 *Regen.* ℹ️
*Bischofsmais, Hauptstr. 34 (09920) 94
04 44.* 🌐 *www.bischofsmais.de*

JUST OUTSIDE Bischofsmais,
on the site of the oldest
hermitage in the Bavarian
Forest, stands a group of
three ecclesiastical buildings.
   In about 1320 St Herman, a
Bernardine monk from the
Niederalteich monastery, lived
here. His cult began in the
17th century, when pilgrimages were made to places that
were associated with him.
   The **Brunnenkapelle**, a
small domed Renaissance
rotunda with a niche for the
miracle-working spring, was
built in 1611. **Hermanns-
kirche**, a Baroque pilgrimage
church, was built in 1653–4.
   The **Einsiedeleikapelle**
was added in 1690. It is a
wooden chapel built in
memory of the saint's
hermitage. Its western part,
the Hermannszelle (Herman's
Cell), is full of wooden legs
and crutches left here by
pilgrims, in thanks for the
miracle cures they received.

Museumsdorf
Bayerischer Wald ⑩

Road map G2. 🚌 🚉 *Tittling.*
📞 *(08504) 84 82.* ⏰ *week before
Easter–Oct: 9am–5pm daily.*
🌐 *www.museumsdorf.com*

NEAR TITTLING, on the east
side of the road from
Grafenau to Passau, this
open-air museum is one of
the largest in Europe. Here
over 140 buildings dating
from the 18th and 19th
centuries have been erected
on a 200,000-sq m (50-acre)
site. As well as traditional

cottages with all their
furnishings, visitors
can see mills, forges,
sawmills and also the
oldest public school
building in Germany.
   Near the museum, in
an **inn** dating from
1829, traditional Bava-
rian specialities are on
offer. Visitors to the
inn include prominent
German figures,
including the former
chancellor Helmut
Kohl and the writer
Friedrich Dürrenmatt.
   The museum is in
the Dreiburgenland, so
named after the three
castles, **Saldenburg**,
Englburg and **Fürst-
enstein**, that are
grouped quite closely
together. They are well
preserved but are not open
to the public.

Passau ⑪

See pp184–7.

Fürstenzell ⑫

Road map G3. 🏛 *7,500.* 🚌 🚉
Passau ℹ️ *Marienplatz 7, (0852) 80
20.* 🌐 *www.fuerstenzell.de*

FOUNDED IN 1274, the
Cistercian abbey here
reached the height of its
artistic development in the
18th century.
   **Mariä Himmelfahrts-
kirche**, built in 1740, was
designed by Johann Michael

**The 19th-century inn at the
Museumsdorf Bayerischer Wald**

Mariä Himmelfahrtskirche, Fürstenzell

Fischer, with stuccowork by
Johann Baptist Modler and
Johann Georg Funk and
elaborate ceiling paintings
by Johann Jakob Zeiller. The
interior features Baroque and
Rococo altars, the high altar
by Johann Baptist Straub,
and a fine Rococo pulpit.
The Gothic tombs of the
Cistercian abbots and the
abbey's founders, which
were transferred here from
the medieval church, are
also of interest.
   The **monastery**, situated
south of the church, was
remodelled in 1674–87, and
extended after 1770. The
Festsaal (State Room), with
frescoes of 1773 in the late
Viennese Neo-Classical style,
is outstanding.
   The monastery library
was decorated in about 1773.
Together with the monastery
library in the town of Metten
nearby, it is the finest
example of artistic patronage
by the Cistercian order in
Germany. The interior is
lined with a gallery supported
on alternating Tuscan
columns and herms (head of
Hermes on a stone pillar).
The bookcases are decorated
with Rococo putti, fencing
figures and Atlases carved by
Joseph Deutschmann.

🏛 **Abbey**
📞 *(08502) 91 100.* ⏰ *3pm
Mon–Sat (library only).* 📷 *compulsory.*

Nationalpark Bayerischer Wald ❾

THIS EXCURSION leads through the Nationalpark Bayerischer Wald, established in 1970 and the first national park in Germany. It is an extensive hilly area of forests, woodland, swamps and meadows, picturesque lakes and interesting rock formations that combine to create unique landscapes inhabited by many species of birds and animals. The Hans-Eisenmann-Haus is the main information centre in the area.

Finsterau ③
The Freilichtmuseum Finsterau is not far from Finsterau, a village with overflowing window boxes, where there is a working smithy and a bakery selling fresh bread.

Hans-Eisenmann-Haus ④
A scenic forest road leads to the house. From here visitors can go to the Pflanzenfreigelände, a reserve with over 500 plant species, or take a trip to the Tierfreigelände, a reserve for wild animals.

St Oswald ⑤
The Waldgeschichtliches Museum illustrates the life and culture of the "forest people". The abbey and church of St Oswald were rebuilt in the Baroque style in 1876. The Brünnlkapelle stands beside a miracle-working spring.

Freyung ①
Schloß Wolfstein contains a museum of field sports. The Schramelhaus (at Abteistraße 6), with the Heimatmuseum, is also worth a visit.

Mauth ②
The village glassworks, the Glasbläserhof Mauth, are fascinating. Glass-blowers can be seen at work and visitors may try their hand at this difficult art.

TIPS FOR DRIVERS

Length of route: 50 km (31 miles).
Stopping-off points: There are bars and restaurants in Freyung, Finsterau, in the open-air museum and at Hans-Eisenmann-Haus.

0 km	15
0 miles	15

KEY

▬ Suggested route

═ Other road

Map labels: NATIONALPARK BAYERISCHER WALD, ZWIESEL, REGEN, Kleine Ohe, Grafenau, PASSAU, Reschbach, 533, 85, 12, PASSAU

Passau ⓫

PASSAU IS ONE of the oldest and most beautiful towns in Bavaria. Nestling in the hills at the confluence of three rivers, it is divided into three districts interconnected by 15 bridges. The Old Town lies on a peninsula between the Danube and the Inn, while Innstadt lies beside the Inn and Ilzstadt beside the Ilz. Passau's fine buildings give it its charm and magic, while the southern wind, felt both in the climate and the art, lends an Italian atmosphere.

Copy of a painting by Lucas Cranach

Towers of the Dom St Stephan – Passau's great Baroque cathedral

🏛 Domplatz

In 1155 the cathedral chapter acquired a plot of land between the cathedral and the western section of the city walls with the aim of building on it chapterhouses arranged around a large square. What were the originally modest chapterhouses were later remodelled in a more ostentatious Baroque style.

Distinctive among them is the Lamberg Chapterhouse, at No. 6 Domplatz, on the west side of the square. Rebuilt in 1724, the chapterhouse is also known as **Lamberg Palace** for its magnificent façade, which is decorated with fine mouldings. The old chapterhouses at Nos. 4 and 5, known as the Barbarahof and Kanonikatshof Starzhausen, today accommodate the presbytery and the seminary.

The square itself features a monument to Maximilian I Joseph. The standing figure of the Bavarian king was created by Karl Eichler in 1824.

🏛 Dom St Stephan

Domplatz 1.

The original cathedral, set on the highest point in the town, was destroyed in the Great Fire of 1662. It was rebuilt in 1668–77 by Carlo Carlone, who created the largest Baroque church north of the Alps, incorporating the surviving Gothic presbytery and transept into the new scheme.

The elegant towers can be seen from afar. The interior contains a stunning wealth of stuccowork and other ornamentation added in 1677–85 by Giovanni Battista Carlone, and paintings by Carpoforo Tencalla.

The burial chapels on the north side of the cathedral include the Gothic Herrenkapelle, which was built in about 1300 for the members of the cathedral chapter and which contains an enormous Romanesque Crucifix dating from about 1190.

Passau Cathedral is famous for its magnificent organ, one of the largest in the world. Occupying the Baroque organ loft, it was built in 1924–8 and refurbished in 1979–81. Organ recitals take place every day at noon from May to October.

⚜ Neue Residenz

Residenzplatz 8. **Treasury and Diocesan Museum.** ☎ (0851) 393241. ⏱ 2 May–31 Oct: 10am–4pm Mon–Fri. 📷

The new bishop's residence, which occupies the south side of Residenzplatz, was built in 1713–30 to plans by Domenico d'Angeli and Antonio Beduzzi. It was refurbished in 1764–71 by Melchior Hefele of Vienna, with stuccowork by members of the local Modler family, the addition of a Neo-Classical façade and interior decoration in the late Baroque style.

The design and decoration of the vestibule and staircase are particularly successful. The reception rooms contain large collections of artifacts from the Diocesan Museum and Cathedral Treasury, some of which can also be seen in the cathedral.

The full splendour of the Dom St Stephan's Baroque interior

The pediment over the façade of the Neue Residenz

♠ Alte Residenz

Theresienstr. 18.
The Old Residence, whose buildings are crowded into a small area between the cathedral and a hillside, is an important landmark visible from the River Inn. The residence probably stands on the site of a bishopric mentioned in 1188. The medieval buildings have been remodelled over the ages, and their present uniform appearance dates from 1680.

The reception rooms were decorated in the 18th century, but soon afterwards the bishopric was moved to the New Residence. The buildings now house the Landgericht, or provincial court.

⚑ Residenzplatz

This square acquired its grand stately character in the Baroque period. Later, stuccowork façades were added to the houses that line it. Particularly noteworthy are the houses at No. 1, built in 1725–30, and No. 13, built in

about 1700. The Neo-Baroque fountain on the square was built by Jakob Bradl in 1903.

🔒 Michaelskirche

Michaeligasse 25.
In terms of architectural importance, the former Jesuit church is second only to Passau's cathedral. It was built and decorated in 1665–77 by members of the Carlone family. Its fine twin-towered façade makes it a

The Schaiblingsturm, part of Passau's medieval defences

VISITORS' CHECKLIST

Road map G3. 🚶 *50,000.*
🚆 🚌 ℹ *Bahnhofstr. 36,
(0851) 95 59 80. Rathausplatz 3,
(0851) 95 59 80.*
ⓦ *www.passau.de*
🎭 *Maidult (May, every two years); Europäische Musikwochen (Jun/Jul); Herbstdult (Sep).*

distinctive feature of the city's skyline. The lavish interior includes a high altar of 1712 by Christoph Tausch of Breslau, side altars of about 1677 and a pulpit and organ loft built in 1717–20.

The former Jesuit college, which was built in 1613–25, is now used as a high school. The courtyard that is enclosed on three sides by the wings of the building has been recently closed off on its northern side by a glazed passage. At the end of the east wing is a tall octagonal tower that once housed an observatory.

⚑ Schaiblingsturm

The 14th-century Schaiblingsturm, on the bank of the River Inn, is a vestige of the old city fortifications. In centuries gone by the tower protected the port on the important salt route.

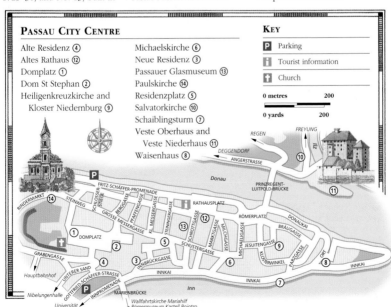

PASSAU CITY CENTRE

KEY

🅿 Parking
ℹ Tourist information
✝ Church

0 metres   200
0 yards   200

The Veste Oberhaus and below it the Veste Niederhaus, overlooking the Danube

🏛 Waisenhaus
Innkai.

This former orphanage, a two-storey building with an inner quadrangle, was built in 1750–62 to a design by Michael Schneitmann. The north wing contains a chapel whose façade and interior feature fine stuccowork executed by Giovanni Martin Luraghi in 1753.

🏛 Heiligenkreuzkirche and Kloster Niedernburg
Jesuitengasse.

This former Benedictine abbey was founded in the 7th century on the site of the Roman castle of Batavis. The present abbey church, which replaces an earlier one built in the early 11th century, is an early Romanesque basilica with two towers and a transept. The presbytery was rebuilt in the Gothic style in the 15th century and the interior was redecorated in the Baroque style after fire damage in 1662 and 1680.

The south transept contains a Romanesque tombstone marking the tomb of the abbess, St Gisela, who was the sister of Emperor Henry II and widow of St Stephen, king of Hungary. In 1420 a sarcophagus with openwork sides was built over the tomb.

🏛 Salvatorkirche
Ferdinand-Wagner-Str.

This pilgrimage church, which stands on the site of a former synagogue, is associated with a pogrom in 1477 against the Jews, sparked off by their alleged sacrilege against the Host. On the west side the church is joined to the rock where the Oberhaus stands. Before a tunnel was made between the upper and lower forts in 1762, the church was accessible only by boat. It is now used as a concert hall.

♣ Veste Oberhaus and Veste Niederhaus
Oberhaus 125. **Oberhausmuseum Passau** ((0851) 49 33 512.
⬤ 9am–5pm Mon–Fri, 10am–6pm Sat–Sun and public holidays.
⬤ 5 Nov–31 Mar except 25–30 Dec & 2–6 Jan.

Work on the imposing Oberhaus (Upper Castle) began in 1219, initiated by the bishop Ulrich II. It is set on a rocky outcrop known as St Georgberg, on the bank of the Danube opposite the Old Town. The main castle consists of Gothic buildings and a chapel. The Niederhaus (Lower Castle) is connected to the Oberhaus by a gallery descending from the polygonal tower. Work on the Niederhaus, on a spit of land between the rivers Inn and Ilz, began in 1250. Both castles, which have been extended and fortified over time, symbolize the power of the church over the town.

The Oberhaus now houses a historical museum. On the route to the Observatoriumsturm (observatory tower) is the Passauer Tölpel (Fool of Passau), a huge head with a mocking expression. This is the remains of a statue of St Stephen of about 1370 that fell from the cathedral during the Great Fire of 1662.

The Niederhaus, whose present apperance dates from about 1444, was the home of the painter Ferdinand von Wagner from 1890 to 1907. He filled the interior with antique furniture and his own paintings. A private residence, it is closed to visitors.

🏛 Altes Rathaus
Rathausplatz. ((0851) 39 60 ⬤ Easter–Oct: 10am–4pm daily.

The Town Hall stands on the site of the former Fish Market alongside the Danube. By the annexation of houses standing between Schrottgasse and Marktgasse, the town hall was constantly enlarged up until the 19th century. The original tower, which was demolished in 1811, was replaced in 1890–91 by a fine Neo-Gothic tower designed by Heinrich

The Altes Rathaus, with Neo-Gothic tower

von Schmidt. It is encircled by a gallery and has a steep sloped roof. Floodmarks on the façade show the high levels reached by the Danube at various times. Entering the building from the side facing Schrottgasse, visitors pass through a late Gothic carved portal of 1510.

The town hall's interior and three courtyards date from the 16th and 17th centuries. The halls, open to the public, contain historical paintings by Ferdinand von Wagner.

🏛 Passauer Glasmuseum

Am Rathausplatz. 📞 (0851) 35 071. ◻ May–Oct: 10am–4pm daily; Nov–Apr: 1–4pm daily. 🖼

Housed in the former Wilder Mann hotel, Passau's museum of glass contains over 30,000 pieces of decorative and household glassware from the 18th to the 20th centuries.

The large collection of Czech glassware and the glass made in the workshops of the Bavarian Forest are particularly remarkable. There is also an interesting section on Art Nouveau glass.

Captivated by the museum's exhibits, the writer Friedrich Dürrenmatt called it "the most beautiful glass museum in the whole world".

Art Nouveau vase in the Glasmuseum

🕊 Paulskirche

Rindermarkt.

The parish church of St Paul was built in 1677 on the site of a medieval church that was destroyed by the Great Fire of 1622. The stuccowork in the interior was executed as recently as 1909. The façade has a tall, picturesque tower which, rising over the Rindermarkt, is a prominent landmark in Passau.

🎭 Nibelungenhalle

Heuwieserstr.

This hall, built in 1935, is the venue for exhibitions and concerts. It is also where the city's ruling dignitaries hold Politischer Aschermittwoch (Political Ash Wednesday), an annual gathering of Bavaria's major political parties.

🎭 Universität

Innpromenade, Innstr., Augustinergasse.

In 1972 the buildings of the former **Augustinian monastery**, founded in about 1070 and turned into barracks in 1803, were converted into a newly founded university. Further buildings were added to the side of the monastery facing the river. These are joined by the **Geisteswissenschaften I** building, constructed in 1976–81 to a design by Werner Fauser. This reinforced concrete structure is rendered in red plaster and combines regional architectural elements with modern spatial concepts.

The **Nikolaikirche**, today a seminary, still has its original Romanesque crypt, although the entire building was re-modelled in the Gothic style in 1348 and again in the Baroque style in 1716–17. The church furniture was moved to the parish church in Vilshofen in 1803.

🕊 Wallfahrtskirche Mariahilf

Mariahilfstiege.

This pilgrimage church, set on the hill known as Mariahilfsberg, dominates the River Inn and Passau's Innstadt district. It commands a fine view of the city and the Dreiflüsseeck – the confluence of the three rivers.

The Capuchin church and monastery, completed in about 1630, are reached by a covered flight of 321 steps. The object of pilgrimage is a copy of a painting of the

Picturesque houses on the banks of the Danube

Madonna and Child by Lucas Cranach the Elder which has been venerated since 1622. The original painting was acquired from a gallery in Dresden by Leopold, Bishop of Passau in 1611. In 1650 the painting was moved to the Jacobskirche in Innsbruck, where it remains to this day.

The strikingly austere interior of Wallfahrtskirche Mariahilf features a silver eternal lamp made by Lucas Lang and presented by the Emperor Leopold I in 1676 on the occasion of his marriage in Passau.

🏛 Römermuseum Kastell Boiotro

Lederergasse 43. 📞 (0851) 34 769. ◻ Mar–Nov: 10am–noon & 2–4pm Tue–Sun; Jun–Aug: 10am–noon & 1–4pm Tue–Sun . ● 1 Dec–28 Feb. 🖼

This Roman fort was built in about AD 250. From then until 400 it was used by Roman soldiers, and in about 460 St Severinus built his cell in the ruins. Excavated in 1974, the ruins, together with the finds unearthed here, are open to visitors.

The imposing buildings of the Wallfahrtskirche Mariahilf

Ortenburg

Road map F3. 🏘 *7,000.* 🚌
🚉 *Vilshofen or Passau.*
ℹ️ *Marktplatz 11, (08542) 16 421.*
🌐 *www.ortenburg.de*

THIS RENAISSANCE **palace**,
which is set on a ridge,
was built in about 1567 on
the site of a medieval castle
belonging to the Bavarian
von Krailburg-Ortenburg
family. Joachim, one of the
family members, brought
the Reformation to the town
in 1563, and ever since then
Ortenburg has been a
Protestant enclave within
Catholic, Counter-Reformation
Lower Bavaria.

The palace is today in
private ownership, but it
contains a museum that is
open to the public. Visitors
can also see such features as
a fine late Renaissance
panelled ceiling dating from
around 1600 in the castle
chapel, the remnants of
trompe-l'oeil frescoes on the
wall of the Knights' Hall and
a torture chamber. The well
outside the palace, which
descends to a depth of 55 m
(180 ft), supplied the
townspeople with water up
until 1927.

The presbytery of the late
Gothic **church**, which has
been a Protestant church
since 1563, contains the
splendid tombs of the owners
of Ortenburg in the 16th and
17th centuries.

**🏛 Schlossmuseum
Ortenburg**
📞 *(08542) 21 74.* 🕐 *Apr–Oct:
10am–5pm daily.*

Courtyard of the Renaissance palace in Ortenburg

The chapel in Sammarei's church,
bedecked with votive images

Sammarei

Road map F3. 🏘 *200.*
🚌 🚉 *Vilshofen or Passau.*
ℹ️ *Ortenburg, Marktplatz 11,
(08542) 16 421, (08542) 16 460.*

SAMMAREI HAS one of the
most remarkable pilgrim-
age churches in the whole of
southern Germany.

An old wooden **chapel**
miraculously survived the fire
that destroyed the neigh-
bouring house of Cistercian
monks from Aldersbach. The
chapel was subsequently
enclosed within the late
Renaissance church of **Mariä
Himmelfahrt**, occupying
part of the presbytery. The
construction of this stone-
built church was supervised
by Isaak Bader the Elder, a
court architect from Munich,
and work began in 1629.
While the church was
completed in 1631, the
interior decoration was not
finished until 1650. The
ambulatory that was created
between the walls of the
chapel and the presbytery
of the church are completely
covered with Baroque votive
images, as are the walls of
the chapel itself.

The chapel is separated
from the nave by a fine high
altar of 1645, which acts as a
kind of iconostasis.

The chapel's late Rococo
altar contains the miraculous
image that is venerated by
pilgrims to the church. It is a
copy of the original *Madonna
and Child* ascribed to Hans
Holbein the Elder in the
church of Jakobs- und
Tiburtiuskirche in Straubing.

**Baroque façade of the Mariä
Himmelfahrt church, Aldersbach**

Aldersbach

Road map F3. 🏘 *4,100.* 🚌 🚉
Vilshofen. ℹ️ *Klosterplatz 1, (08543)
96 100.* 🌐 *www.aldersbach.de*

WORK ON the **Cistercian
monastery** in the town
began at the end of the 17th
century. It was remodelled
by Domenic Madzin in the
first half of the 18th century,
when it became the church of
Mariä Himmelfahrt.

The interior, which is lit by
large windows, is decorated
with exquisite paintings and
stuccowork executed by
Egid and Cosmas Damian
Asam in 1718–20, the first
time that the brothers had
collaborated on a project
(see p68). Among the most
outstanding features are the
choir borne by angels in wide
flowing garments, and the
trompe-l'oeil paintings on the
ceiling over the nave.

The high altar, dating from
1723, is Matthias Götz'
masterpiece. The pulpit, of
1748, and the stalls, of 1762,
are by Joseph Deutschmann.

Vilshofen ⓰

Road map F3. 16,500.
Stadtplatz 29, (08541)
20 816. www.vilshofen.de

FOUNDED IN 1206 at the
confluence of the Vils and
the Danube, Vilshofen centres
around Stadtplatz. This long
street is lined with colourful
houses that were built after
the great fire that destroyed
the town in 1794.

The parish church of
St Johannes der Täufer,
built in the late 14th century,
with two naves, was rebuilt in
1803–04. Its fine Baroque
decoration was executed in
the 18th century, and was
originally intended for the
Nikolakirche in Passau. The
decoration was later transferred to this church.

Another notable feature of
the town is the late Gothic
Barbarakirche, built in the
second half of the 15th
century, and the **Mariähilfs-
kirche**, a former pilgrimage
church built in 1611 by
Antonio Riva. The Mariähilfs-
kirche is decorated with
stuccowork and frescoes
executed by northern Italian
artists, among whom was
Giovanni Petro Camuzzi.

The **gate tower** was built in
1643–7. It was designed by
Bartholomäus Viscardi in the
Mannerist style and has
greyish-white tones and an
onion dome. It has come to
symbolize the town.

The high altar at the Asambasilika in Osterhofen

The most prominent building
in Vilshofen is the
Benedictine abbey of
Schweiklberg, designed by
Michael Kurz and built in
1909–11. The church has two
Art Nouveau steeples.

**The gate tower at the end of the
Straßenmarkt in Vilshofen**

Osterhofen ⓱

Road map F2. 11,600.
Altenmarkt. Stadtplatz 13,
(09932) 40 30.
www.osterhofen.de

THIS SMALL Bavarian town,
whose history goes back
almost six centuries, boasts a
jewel of Baroque architecture,
the **Asambasilika**.

The church was built in
1726 on the site of a medieval
Premonstratensian church. Its
appearance is the result of a
collaboration between the
architect Michael Fischer and
the Asam brothers. While its
exterior is somewhat austere,
with the façade merging with
a wing of the monastery, the
decorative scheme of the
interior is phenomenal.

The unusual shape of the
single-nave interior is created
by its oval side chapels and
serpentine walls. The
architecture, painting and
stuccowork, fused into
a single entity, are highly
distinctive, both as an
ensemble and as individual
elements. While the extensive
ceiling frescoes by Cosmas
Damian Asam create an
illusion of extensive space,
Egid Quirin Asam's stuccowork blurs the boundaries
between reality and illusion.
Absorbing the exquisite
artistry and admiring the
artists' skill can take some
time (*see p68*).

The Asambasilika made
a profound impression on
Pope John Paul II, who
visited Osterhofen during
his pilgrimage to Germany
in 1980.

THE BAVARIAN FOREST

The area between the Danube, Regen and Chamb and
the Czech border is covered by the largest woodland in
Europe. Once Bavaria's most destitute region, it now draws
tourists with its stunning scenery and low prices. The
region is renowned for its locally made glass and crystal,
its hiking trails and skiing areas. The heart of the Bavarian
Forest is the densely wooded National Park Reserve.

A historic Alpine house in the open-air museum at Finsterau

UPPER BAVARIA (EAST)

LYING BETWEEN *the rivers Inn and Salzach, this region is very popular with tourists, who flock here for the breathtaking natural scenery. The steep, snow-covered Alpine slopes, the lush green vegetation of the valleys and the large lakes, such as the Chiemsee and Königssee, all have a magical atmosphere.*

Alexander Humboldt, the famous geographer and explorer, named Berchtesgaden one of the most beautiful places in the world, alongside Naples, Constantinople and Salzburg.

The region is equally appreciated today. The Berchtesgaden National Park, which includes the Königssee and Watzmann, Germany's second-highest peak of 2,713 m (8,900 ft), covers an area of about 210 sq km (80 sq miles) and was established in the southeast of the region in 1978.

The region has more to offer than breathtaking scenery. The Romans discovered health springs here, and the spa of Bad Reichenhall attracts visitors from all over the country. The groundwater contains up to 25 per cent salt, which is extracted in saltworks throughout the region. One of the oldest working saltworks, in use since 1517, is in Berchtesgaden. Here visitors can see excellently preserved tunnels and can cross a 100-m (328-ft) underground lake on a raft.

Many previous rulers of Bavaria felt a special attraction for this area, and Hitler's "Eagle's Nest" residence was located on Mt Kehlstein. A silver urn in a chapel in Altötting contains the hearts of 21 Bavarian kings. The town also attracts many pilgrims, who come to the church with the figure of the Black Madonna, which is famed for its reputed miracle-working powers.

The region is dotted with fine historic buildings. The little churches of Maria Gern and St Bartholomä have a delightful charm. Burghausen boasts the world's longest castle, and one of the islands in Chiemsee was chosen by Ludwig II for yet another of his magnificent residences.

The Kapellplatz in Altötting in winter

◁ Statues outside Herrenchiemsee Palace, Ludwig II's residence on Herreninsel in Chiemsee

Exploring Upper Bavaria (East)

T HE TOWN of Rosenheim on the River Inn could be regarded as the capital of this region. Although not well endowed with historic features, it is well worth a visit in late summer, when the local beer festival takes place. While it vies with Munich's Oktoberfest, it has a much more authentic, local atmosphere. There are historic towns on the rivers Inn, Wasserburg and Rott, the latter containing the grave of the Christian Democrat leader Franz-Josef Strauß. The towns in the Salzach and Traun valleys are also worth exploring. The towns of Tittmoning and Laufen, with their captivating southern atmosphere, are very underrated.

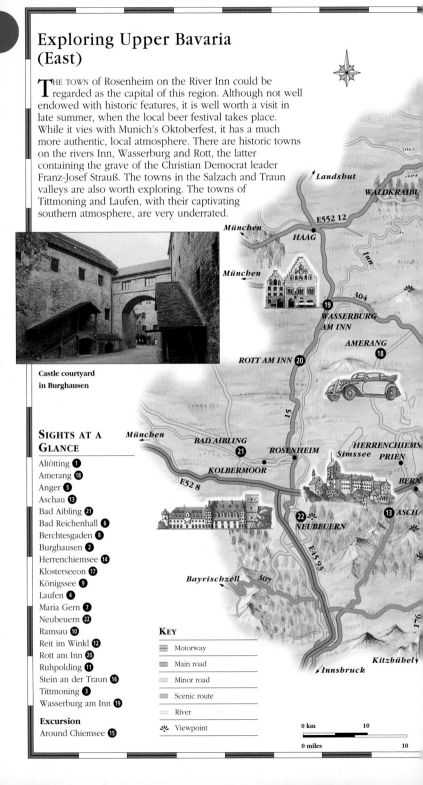

Castle courtyard in Burghausen

SIGHTS AT A GLANCE

Altötting **1**
Amerang **18**
Anger **5**
Aschau **13**
Bad Aibling **21**
Bad Reichenhall **6**
Berchtesgaden **8**
Burghausen **2**
Herrenchiemsee **14**
Klosterseeon **17**
Königssee **9**
Laufen **4**
Maria Gern **7**
Neubeuern **22**
Ramsau **10**
Reit im Winkl **12**
Rott am Inn **20**
Ruhpolding **11**
Stein an der Traun **16**
Tittmoning **3**
Wasserburg am Inn **19**

Excursion
Around Chiemsee **15**

KEY

▬▬▬	Motorway
▬▬▬	Main road
▭▭▭	Minor road
▬▬▬	Scenic route
▭▭▭	River
☀	Viewpoint

0 km   10

0 miles   10

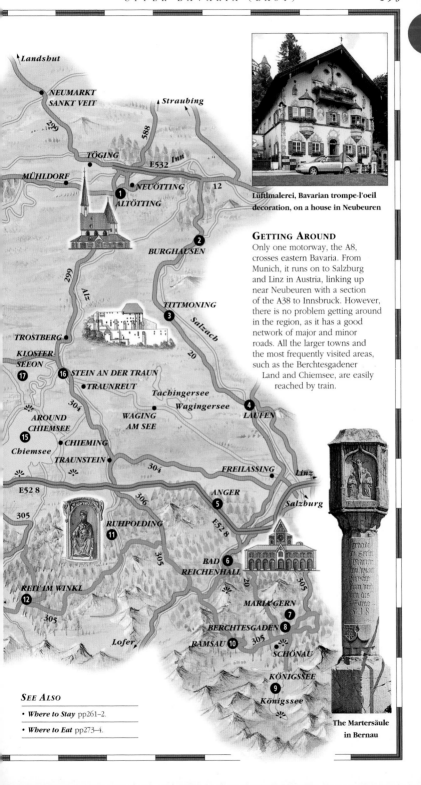

Lüftlmalerei, Bavarian trompe-l'oeil decoration, on a house in Neubeuren

GETTING AROUND

Only one motorway, the A8, crosses eastern Bavaria. From Munich, it runs on to Salzburg and Linz in Austria, linking up near Neubeuren with a section of the A38 to Innsbruck. However, there is no problem getting around in the region, as it has a good network of major and minor roads. All the larger towns and the most frequently visited areas, such as the Berchtesgadener Land and Chiemsee, are easily reached by train.

The Martersäule in Bernau

Burghausen Castle, the longest castle in Europe

Altötting ❶

Road map F4. 👥 11,000. 🚂
ℹ️ Kapellplatz 2a, (08671) 85 858.
🌐 www.altoetting.de

THIS TOWN, established in the 8th century, is one of the earliest Christian sites in Europe. It is also the earliest place of pilgrimage in Bavaria, and is called the Heart of Bavaria by some. Every year about half a million pilgrims come here to pay their respects to the Black Madonna. This early 13th-century statue is kept in the **Heilige Kapelle** (Holy Chapel) which stands in the centre of a large square. The chapel, with a Carolingian apse and a Gothic nave, is surrounded by an ambulatory whose walls are covered with votive images. Pilgrims holding crosses inch up to it on their knees. Pope John Paul II paid a visit to the shrine during his pilgrimage to Germany in 1980.

The treasury of the late Gothic **Stiftskirche** contains valuable votive offerings from the Holy Chapel. The most highly prized of these is the Goldenes Rössl (Golden Steed) of 1404, a masterpiece of French goldwork. The crypt contains the mortal remains of Johann Tilly, the renowned military leader in the Thirty Years' War.

Another feature of interest is the **panorama** re-creating the view from the hill of Golgotha in Jerusalem. It is located in a building dating from 1902–03, and was made by Gebhard Fugel and Joseph Krieger.

🏛 Panorama
Gebhard–Fugel–Weg 10.
📞 (08671) 69 34.
🕐 Mar–Oct: 9am–5pm daily; Nov–Feb: 11am–2pm Sat–Sun. 🎟

ENVIRONS: 2 km (1.5 miles) north, on the River Inn, is **Neuötting**. Notable buildings here include the Gothic Nikolauskirche, designed by Hans von Burghausen, and the late Gothic Annakirche completed in 1515.

Arcade on the the market square in Neuötting

Burghausen ❷

Road map F4. 👥 17,000.
🚂 ℹ️ Stadtplatz 112, (08677) 96 76 931/932. 🌐 www.burghausen.de
🎷 Jazz Festival (Apr); Historisches Burgfest (Jul).

SITUATED ON the River Salzach, which forms the border with Austria, Burghausen is famous for having the longest **castle** in Europe. With its six courtyards, the castle stretches some 1,030 m (3,380 ft) along a ridge between the river and Wöhrsee. The castle was built in 1025 and rebuilt in 1490. The main castle (Hauptburg) contains several **museums**, including a local history museum and a photographic museum. In the rooms that are open to the public, German paintings and furniture are on display.

Angel in Burghausen's Schutzengelskirche

The Old Town, between the castle and the river, has an old-world atmosphere. The market square is surrounded by what are Burghausen's finest buildings: the Gothic **Jakobskirche**, with a Baroque tower, the **town hall**, the mid-16th-century **old Bavarian government building**, with a Renaissance courtyard, the **Schutzengelskirche** of 1731–46, and many historic houses. On the south side of the square is the Jesuit **Josefskirche** of about 1630 and the **Marienbrunnen**, a mid-17th-century fountain.

Tittmoning ③

Road map F4. 🏠 *5,000.*
🚌 🚇 *Laufen, Burghausen.*
ℹ️ *Stadtplatz 1, (08683) 70 07.*
🌐 *www.tittmoning.de*

THE ENTRANCE to this little town on the River Salzach is through a gate in the town walls. The market square is lined with colourful houses with bay windows and wood carvings. Among them is the tall **town hall**, its tower and façade dating from 1711–12. The hill above the town, the summit crowned by a 13th-century **castle**, gives a fine view of the surrounding countryside and the Alps. The **Maria Ponlach** pilgrimage chapel of 1617 is reached by a road round the castle that follows a ravine overlooking the River Ponlach.

Iron bridge at Laufen, crossing over the border with Austria

Laufen ④

Road map F4. 🏠 *6,000.*
🚇 ℹ️ *Im Schlossrondel, (08682) 18 10.*

SET ON A bend in the River Salzach, this town has a southern, almost Italian feel. It was originally a Roman settlement, and flourished during the Middle Ages. Entry into the town is through two medieval **gates**. The streets are lined with arcaded houses with oriels and concave roofs typical of the region.

The 14th-century **parish church** is the oldest single-nave Gothic church in southern Germany. With its

Column of St Mary in Anger's main square

huge roof and late 12th-century Romanesque tower, it dominates the town.

North of the church is the **Dechantshof**, the old archbishop's castle, which contains plaques from the church. Its staircase is decorated with the portraits of bishops. The four-winged **castle**, with an inner courtyard, was built in 1606–08 by Vincenzo Scamozzi.

Anger ⑤

Road map F5. 🏠 *4,300.* 🚌 🚇
ℹ️ *Dorfplatz 4, (08656) 98 89 22.*
🌐 *www.anger.de*

LUDWIG I deemed Anger the prettiest village in Bavaria. Much of its charm has been eroded by the arrival of a motorway and commercial development. However, it still has a delightfully situated late Gothic **church**. The large square, which is lined with interesting houses, has a column with the statue of St Mary in the centre.

ENVIRONS: 2 km (1.5 miles) to the north is **Höglwörth**, a tiny former Augustine abbey built in the 12th century on an island in a lake covered with water lilies.

Bad Reichenhall ⑥

Road map F5. 🏠 *16,500.* 🚇
ℹ️ *Wittelsbacherstr. 15, (08651) 60 63 03.* 🌐 *www.bad-reichenhall.de*

THE TOWN has been known for its salt since Celtic and Roman times, and in the mid-19th century it became an important spa. Noteworthy

buildings include the **Zenokirche**, a former Augustinian monastery dating from the first half of the 12th century. Although it was remodelled after the Gothic period, it retains its original Romanesque portal, which features two lions supporting the columns.

The former **jail** in the large spa park is now used as an inhalations room. In the **Alte Saline**, the old saltworks, which date from 1836–51, Ludwig I ordered a technological **museum** to be built. The exhibits include old salt-making equipment. The saltworks' marble enclosures date from 1524–36 and, together with an underground passage, were designed by the sculptor Erasmus Grasser.

🏛️ Alte Saline mit Salz-museum

An der Salinenstr. 📞 *(08651) 70 02 146.* ⏰ *May–Oct: 10am–11:30am and 2–4pm daily; Nov–Apr: 2–4pm Tue, Thu and the first Sunday in the month.*

The former jail in Bad Reichenhall's spa park

The church in Maria Gern seen against snowy Alpine peaks

Maria Gern ❼

Road map F5. ☷ ▤ *Berchtesgaden.* ❗ *Berchtesgaden, Königseer Str. 2, (08652) 96 70.*

THE PILGRIMAGE church here, the **Marienkirche**, is in a serene and picturesque setting among woodland pastures. Built in 1708–10, its pink pilasters on the exterior make a pleasing contrast with the white walls and the steep polygonal roofs harmonize with the Baroque onion dome of the tower.

The interior is decorated with stuccowork by Joseph Schmidt. The walls of the presbytery are hung with votive images spanning the 12th to the 20th centuries, and the altar has a carving of the Madonna by Wolfgang Huber before which the faithful pray for forgiveness.

The **Ölbergkapelle** below the church dates from 1710.

Berchtesgaden ❽

Road map F5. ☷ 25,000. ▤ ▤ ❗ *Königseer Str. 2, (08652) 96 70, 66 358.* ☒ *www.berchtesgadener-land.com*

THE AREA known as Berchtesgadener Land enjoys an excellent climate. The town is set in beautiful Alpine scenery on the River Ache at the foot of the Watzmann, which at 2,713 m (8,900 ft) is Germany's second highest peak.

The town is an ideal base for hikes throughout the region but with its old-world charm it also has plenty to offer. Here are houses with walls decorated with Lüftlmalerei (*see p208*). One of them, the **Gästehaus zum Hirschen**, an inn dating from about 1600, has paintings depicting monkeys parodying human vices. Another interesting building is the Gothic **Franciscan church**, while a major attraction is the nearby saltworks – the **Salzbergwerk und Salzmuseum**. A little way from the town is the **Kehlsteinhaus**, also known as Hitler's Eagle's Nest (*see p197*). An interesting excursion follows the scenic **Roßfeldringstraße**, which winds along hairpin bends to a height of 1600 m (5,249 ft).

The **Königliches Schloss**, formerly an Augustinian monastery and now owned by the Wittelsbach family, contains a museum with an interesting collection of furniture, paintings and

Gothic woodcarving. The adjoining **church** was remodelled in the Gothic style, although it retains its original Romanesque portal. The façade with its rose window and two towers were added in 1864–8. The Romanesque cloisters, unusual in southern Germany, date from the 12th century.

� **Salzbergwerk und Salzmuseum**
Bergwerkstr. 83. ❘ *(08652) 60 020.* ◯ *May–15 Oct: 9am–5pm daily; 16 Oct–Apr: 12:30pm–3.30pm Mon–Sat.*

� **Königliches Schloss**
Schlossplatz 2. ❘ *(08652) 20 85.* ◯ *Whitsun–15 Oct: 10am–1pm & 2–5pm Sun–Fri; 16 Oct–Whitsun: by guided tour only.* ☑ *11am & 2pm.*

A jetty on Königssee

Königssee ❾

Road map F5. ❗ *Berchtesgaden, Franziskanerplatz 7, (08652) 64 343.* ☒ *www.nationalpark-berchtesgaden.de*

WITH ITS crystal-clear water and fjord-like setting between mountain ridges, Königssee is Bavaria's loveliest lake. The area also forms part of a national park.

The electric-powered boats that are used on the 8-km (5-mile) lake take visitors to the pilgrimage church of **St Bartholomä**, built in about 1700 and set on a peninsula below the eastern escarpment of the Watzmann. Nearby is a well-frequented inn. The boat trip offers views of awesome rock formations, enchanting little spots, waterfalls and echoing cliffs that throw back the sound of the boat's horn. The trip goes all the way to the northern end of Königssee, from where **Obersee** can be reached on foot.

The town of Berchtesgaden, nestling in an Alpine valley

The main street in Reit im Winkl, a popular tourist resort

Ramsau ⑩

Road map F5. 🏔 *1,900.* 🚌 🚉
Berchtesgaden. 🛈 *Im Tal 2, (08657)
98 89 20.*

THIS RESORT town, nestling amid wooded mountain slopes, has one of the most photographed churches in the world.

It is the **Fabian- und Sebastiankirche**, dating from 1512. Its picturesque cemetery, laid out in 1658, contains tombstones spanning the 17th to the 20th centuries. The church is scenically situated above a stream, and stands out wonderfully against the magnificent backdrop of the Reiteralpe.

Ruhpolding ⑪

Road map E5. 🏔 *6,400.* 🚌 🚉 🛈
Hauptstr. 60, (08663) 88 060.
W *www.ruhpolding.de*

THIS TOWN, very popular with tourists, is over-looked by **Georgskirche**, built in 1738–57 with highly deco-rated altars and a pulpit dating from the same period. The right-hand altar features a small Romanesque figure of the Virgin Enthroned, with large almond-shaped eyes, dating from about 1200. Above the church is the old **cemetery**, which has a Baroque chapel and tomb-stones dating from the 18th and 19th centuries.

The old Renaissance **hunting lodge** houses the **Heimatmuseum**, which has a collection of furniture, glass and jewellery spanning the 17th to the 19th centuries. Also on display in the museum is a collection of fossils and interesting minerals that were found in the surrounding mountains. Among the displays at the **Museum für Bäuerliche und Sakrale Kunst** (Museum of Folk and Religious Art) is a fine collection of church ornaments, as well as royal jewellery and crowns.

🏛 **Heimatmuseum**
Schlossstr. 2. 📞 *(08663) 41
230.* 🕐 *2–5pm Tue–Fri .*
🏛 **Museum für Bäuerliche und Sakrale Kunst**
Roman Friesingerstr. 1.
🕐 *9:30am–noon & 2–4pm Thu–Sat,
2–4pm Sun.*

The Madonna of Ruhpolding

Reit im Winkl ⑫

Road map E5. 🏔 *3,000.* 🚌 🚉
Marquartstein. 🛈 *Rathausplatz 1,
(08640) 80 020, (08640) 80 029.*
W *www.reit-im-winkl.de*

THIS SMALL TOWN, at an altitude of almost 700 m (2296 ft), may not have any buildings of historic interest, but it is still a very popular tourist resort. Picturesquely set in the middle of the forest, with its colourful storybook houses and narrow streets, it is easy to see why it so appealing. Many people come here, especially in winter, as the area has the best snow cover in the Bavarian Alps. The town is also filled with visitors in summer, especially hikers using it as a base for day trips into the surrounding area or even into the whole Berchtesgadener Land. The road to Ruhpolding, about 24 km (15 miles) distant, is exceptionally scenic. Forming part of the Alpine Route, it winds among lakes which, when seen from above, resemble a necklace of green beads strung on either side of the road that traverses spectacularly beautiful mountain scenery.

KEHLSTEINHAUS – "THE EAGLE'S NEST"

Set on the summit of Kehlstein, this stone building resembling a mountain shelter is known as the Adlerhorst (Eagle's Nest). It was given to Hitler by Martin Bormann on behalf of the Nazi Party in 1939 and became the Führer's favourite residence. The building was attached to the summer residence built in 1933 and is situated on the slopes of Obersalzberg. The approach to Kehlsteinhaus is a masterpiece of engineering. First, a road with stunning views passes through five tunnels, after which there is an elevator whose shaft is cut into the rock. The last stage of the trip is a ride up in a high-speed elevator, which is taken by the thousands of tourists who come here.

Hitler's famous "Eagle's Nest"

Road leading towards the Alps near Aschau

Aschau ⑬

Road map E5. 🚶 4,500. 🚌 🚉
ℹ Kampenwandstr. 38. **📞** (08052)
90 49 37. **W** www.aschau.de

IN THE CENTRE of this small town, set against fine mountain backdrops, stands a twin-towered **church**. Originally built in the Gothic style, it was rebuilt in the Baroque period and in the early 18th century was decorated with stuccowork and paintings of scenes of the life of St Mary. Beside the church is the small **Kreuz-kapelle**, built in the mid-18th century, while opposite, at Kirchplatz 1, is an old **inn**, built in 1680 and today named the Post Hotel.

ENVIRONS: From Aschau a road leads south towards **Schloss Hohenaschau**, which, set on a height, is visible from a distance. This mighty 12th-century fortress was decorated in the Baroque style in the 17th century, although its medieval walls and keep survive. The reception hall on the second floor was decorated in 1682–4 with Baroque mouldings and 12 larger-than-life-size statues of the ancestors of the castle's owners.

♠ Schloss Hohenaschau
📞 (08052) 90 49 37.
🕐 May–Sep:
9:30am–12:30pm Tue–Fri;
Apr & Oct:
9:30am–12:30pm Thu;
Apr–Oct: 1:30pm–5pm Sun
(museum only). 🌐 ✔

Herrenchiemsee ⑭

Road map E4. 🚉 to Stock. 🚢

HERRENINSEL is the largest island in Chiemsee. It has been settled since prehistoric times. Thanks to Ludwig II, it is today among the region's major tourist attractions. The king aimed to build a gigantic palace set in a vast park filled with statues, fountains and a canal along its axis. It was to be the Versailles of Bavaria.

The **Schloss Herren-chiemsee**, based on Louis XIV's great Palace of Versailles, was built to satisfy Ludwig II's absolutist leanings. Built in 1878–86, it was to outdo all previous royal palaces, but it was never finished.

Ludwig II spent a mere nine days in it, and at the time of his death only 20 of the 70 rooms that were planned for the three wings were ready. They show an astonishing lavishness and splendour. Particularly spectacular are the Große Spiegelgalerie (Hall

Fountain at Schloss Herrenchiemsee

of Mirrors), and the Chambre de Parade. The palace also houses a **museum** dedicated to Ludwig II.

There are also the remains of a church and an August-inian monastery on the island. These are known collectively as **Altes Schloss**.

🏛 Schloss Herrenchiemsee and König-Ludwig II-Museum
📞 (08051) 68870. **🕐** 9am–6pm
daily. 🌐

The medieval castle of Höhlenburg, Stein an der Traun

Stein an der Traun ⑯

Road map E4. 🚌 🚉 **ℹ** Rathaus-platz 3, Traunreut, (08669) 85 70.
W www.traunreut.de

ONE OF Upper Bavaria's most distinctive buildings is **Höhlenburg**, a castle set 30 m (100 ft) above the River Traun. It forms part of a system of three castles. Torch in hand, visitors pass through a series of caves and tunnels. This is said to be the home of the fearful Heinz von Stein, a legendary giant knight who abducted girls. Casemates lead between the medieval upper castle, the lower castle and the new castle, which dates from the 15th century and was rebuilt in the Neo-Gothic style in 1885–9.

♠ Höhlenburg
📞 (08621) 25 01. **🕐** Easter–May:
1:30pm Tue–Sun; Jun–Sep: 1:30pm
& 3pm Tue–Sun; Oct: 1:30pm Tue,
Thu, Sun. 🌐 ✔

Around Chiemsee ⑮

CHIEMSEE, ALSO known as the Bavarian Sea, covers an area of 80 sq km (30 sq miles) and reaches a depth of 73 m (240 ft). Bavaria's largest lake, it is a favourite place for holiday-makers, and its shores are dotted with towns and holiday villages. The Alpine scenery, the watersports facilities and some fascinating buildings are the main attractions here.

Seebruck ⑥
This little town, whose history goes back to Roman times, is today a watersports centre with a large marina.

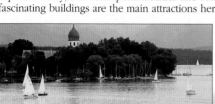

Fraueninsel ⑤
The Benedictine monastery on this island has a Romanesque church with a distinctive onion dome.

Herreninsel ④
This is a favourite destination for visitors, who come to Ludwig II's grand unfinished palace.

0 km   2
0 miles   2

Lambach • Ising
Söll •
Gollenshausen •
Breitbrunn
Kailbach
Rimsting
Prien
Harras •
Chiemsee
Hirschau
E52
Bernau

Gstadt ③
From this town there is a pleasant view of Fraueninsel, which can be reached by boat from here. An interesting sight is Peters- und Paulskirche, decorated in the Baroque style in about 1720.

Urschalling ①
The 12th-century Jakobskirche has some fine mural paintings dating from the 13th and 14th centuries.

Chieming ⑦
Attractions here are the beach, with a 7-km (4-mile) long promenade and houses with Lüftlmalerei *(see p208)* and lavish floral displays.

Stock ②
The Bockerl, a steam railway over 100 years old, provides a link between Stock and Prien. There are also boats to the lake's other islands and towns.

TIPS FOR TOURISTS

Length of route: *about 65 km (40 miles).*
Stopping-off places: *There are many cafés and restaurants in all the small towns round Chiemsee.*

KEY

▬ Suggested route
═ Other route
-- Ferry route

Klosterseeon, the Benedictine monastery, set on a promontory on Klostersee

Klosterseeon ⓱

Road map E4. 🚌 🚃 *Obing.*
🛈 *Obing Kultur- und Bildungs-
zentrum (08624) 89 70.*

ON THE EDGE of Klostersee
stands **Klosterseeon**, a
monastery that was taken
over by Benedictine monks.
The original Romanesque
church was built in stages in
the 11th and 12th centuries.
Remodelled by Konrad
Pürkhel, it acquired its Gothic
appearance in 1433–8. The
ceiling was decorated by
Salzburg painters in 1539.

St Barbara's Chapel
contains the magnificent tomb
of Aribo I dating from about
1400 and ascribed to the Salzburg sculptor Hans Heider.

South of the church is a
monastery with a cloistered
courtyard of 1428–33, which
has Gothic tombstones and
plaques built into the walls.

Amerang ⓲

Road map E4. 👥 *2,500.*
🚌 🚃 🛈 *Wasserburger Str. 11,
(08075) 91 970.* Ⓦ *www.amerang.de*

THE RENAISSANCE **palace** in
this small town was built
by several Italian architects,
prominent among whom
were members of the Scaligeri
family of Verona. Its large
cloistered courtyard is a
venue for open-air concerts.
There is also a museum.

At the other end of the
town is a **Skansen** (open-air
museum) with farmhouses, a
bakery, a mill and a forge.
The **EFA-Automobil-
Museum** (Museum of
German Automobile History)
has 220 cars dating from 1886
to the present.

🏛 **Palace**
⭕ *Whitsun–15 Sep.* 🎫 *11am,
12pm, 2pm, 3pm, 4pm.*
🏛 **Skansen**
Hopfgarten 2. ⭕ *15 Mar–
31 Oct: 9am–6pm Tue–Sun.*
🏛 **EFA-Automobil-Museum**
Wasserburgerstr. 38.
📞 *(08075) 81 41.* ⭕ *Mar–Oct:
10am–6pm Tue–Sun.*

**Amerang's Renaissance palace,
designed by the Scaligeri family**

Wasserburg
am Inn ⓳

Road map E4. 👥 *11,000.*
🚌 🚃 🛈 *Marienplatz 2, (08071)
10 522.* Ⓦ *www.wasserburg.de*

WASSERBURG is set on a
promontory on a
bend in the Inn, and is
one of the best-
preserved historic
towns on the river.
The best view of it
is from the bridge
across the Inn.

The bridge leads to
a picturesque Gothic
gate which in turn
leads into Bruck-
gasse. At No. 25 in
this lane is the
Mauthaus, the
ducal customs
office, dating from
about 1400, with

stepped gables and three
Renaissance oriel windows,
which were added in 1539.

The street leads to Marienplatz, which is lined with
houses. Among them is the
Kernhaus, which once
belonged to the patrician
Kern family. The façade
features decorative mouldings
by Johann Baptist Zimmer-
mann. Opposite stands the
Gothic **town hall**, which
occupies two buildings with
stepped gables. The
Frauenkirche was built in
1368 and is attached to the
watchtower.

The large **Jakobskirche**
was begun in the early 15th
century by Jans von
Burghausen. The **castle**, with
its covered staircase, can be
reached from the church.
Remaining parts of the castle
include the residential wing,
which was converted into a
granary during the
Renaissance, and a 15th-
century chapel. The streets
of the town are lined with
old houses with typical
gateways, courtyards, oriel
windows and
arcades.

The Gothic façade of Wasserburg's town hall

Rott am Inn ⑳

Road map E4. 🏘 *3,500.* 🚌 🚉
ℹ *Kaiserhof 3.* 📞 *(08039) 90 680.*
🌐 *www.rottaminn.de*

THE FORMER Benedictine church of **Sts Marinus und Anianus** was rebuilt in 1759–63 to plans by Johann Michael Fischer, preserving the 12th-century Romanesque tower. The church has one of the finest Rococo interiors, decorated by the greatest artists of the time: the stuccoist Jakob Rauch, the fresco-painter Matthäus Günther and the sculptor Ignaz Günther. Unfortunately the church is currently closed for restoration work.

Franz-Josef Strauß, the former leader of Bavaria's ruling conservative party, is buried in the cemetery of the church, which is regularly visited by members of his CSU party.

The town square in Rott am Inn

Bad Aibling ㉑

Road map D4. 🏘 *13,500.*
🚌 🚉 ℹ *Wilhelm-Leibl-Platz 1, (08061) 90 800.*
🌐 *www.bad-aibling.de*

BAD AIBLING is known for its mud baths, which were in use as far back as Roman times. However, it was only in the mid-19th century that it acquired its present status as a spa town.

There is much of archi-tectural interest here. On a hill stands the church of **Mariä Himmelfahrt**, built in the late Gothic style but later remodelled in the Rococo style by Abraham Millauer to plans by Johann Michael Fischer. **Sebastianskirche** was built on the site of a

16th-century votive chapel after the plague epidemic of 1634, which decimated the local population.

After a series of fires that destroyed most of the town only a few houses survived. One is the 17th-century house at Kirchzeile 13 (today the **Hotel Ratskeller**), which has painted exterior walls and three oriel windows. The **Heimatmuseum** is also worth a visit.

🏛 Heimatmuseum
Wilhelm-Lieblplatz.
📞 *(08061) 87 24.*
🕐 *2:30–5pm Fri.*

ENVIRONS: Some 6 km (4 miles) northwest of Bad Aibling is **Berbling**, with an authentic Bavarian village atmo-sphere. The charming Rococo church, the old houses, the barns, the maypole and the fields that stretch right up to the houses are quintessentially Bavarian. The painter Wilhelm Leibl once stayed here, while he was living in Bad Aibling from 1882 to 1889.

The Renaissance **Maxlrain Palace** lies on the other side of Bad Aibling, 4 km (2.5 miles) to the southwest. It was built in 1582–5 and has a steeply pitched roof and four onion-domed towers. At the neigh-bouring 18th-century inn, beer from the palace brewery is served.

Neubeuern ㉒

Road map E5. 🏘 *4,000.*
🚌 🚉 *Raubling or Rohrdorf.*
ℹ *Marktplatz 4.* 📞 *(08035) 21 65.*
🌐 *www.neubeuern.de*
@ *info@neubeuern.de*

THIS SMALL town situated in the valley of the River Inn is held to be one of the prettiest in Bavaria, if not in the whole of Germany. It owes its present appearance to Gabriel von Seidlow, who rebuilt the town and the medieval castle after two devastating fires in 1883 and 1893. Today it is often used by film-makers. With its **town gates**, **houses** and **church**, all of which are covered with trompe-l'oeil paintings, it possesses everything that a director needs to re-create an old-style Bavarian town.

Oriel window in Neubeuern

Above the houses, decked with greenery and colourful window boxes, towers the **castle** with its tall keep, built in the local historical style in 1904–08. On fine days there is a good view of the Alps from the castle terraces.

ENVIRONS: Some 4 km (2.5 miles) to the southwest is **Samerberg**. From its peak there is a panoramic view of the town of Rosenheim, Simsee and the surrounding area. It is worth taking a roundabout route via the delightful village of **Rohrdorf** to reach the summit.

The Renaissance Maxlrain Palace near Bad Aibling

UPPER BAVARIA (SOUTH)

UPPER BAVARIA'S *southern region looks as if it belongs in the pages of a tourist brochure. It is a region of mountains, lakes and splendid buildings, with plenty to offer holiday-makers, including many opportunities for sporting activities. It borders the River Inn to the east and the Lech to the west. To the south it adjoins the Alps.*

The Werdenfelser Land, the southernmost region of the Bavarian Alps, stretches from Murnau to Garmisch-Partenkirchen. Its name comes from that of the now ruined Werden castle, which once defended the surrounding area. The backdrop of this fine sub-Alpine landscape is made up of the imposing Karwendel, Wetterstein and Ammergauer mountain ranges.

The small towns and villages of the region are the essence of Bavaria. The houses are covered with *Lüftlmalerei (see p208)*, and have wooden balconies that overflow with geraniums and other flowers.

From the pastures you can hear the sound of yodelling, also known as *Almschroa*, which can only be heard in the Bavarian Alps. The traditional costume of the local Bavarians is widely worn *(see p29)*, and not just for show but as everyday wear.

Between the rivers Ammer and Lech, from Wessobrunn to near Steingaden, is the Pfaffenwinkel, or Clerics' Corner, which was given its name in jest in the 18th century because of the proliferation of abbeys, churches and chapels here. The finest among them is the church in Wieskirche, known as the Lord God's Ballroom.

The largest town in the region is Landsberg, whose historic buildings and inviting small streets, alleys and squares make it a very interesting place to explore. The most famous and most visited town in the region is Garmisch-Partenkirchen, where the 1936 Winter Olympics took place.

Traditional festivals and holidays are celebrated enthusiastically in the towns and villages. The best are the painted carts parade and the St Leonard's Day horseback pilgrimage to Mount Calvary in Bad Tölz.

Satellite receivers outside a historic church in Reisting

◁ **Moorings for yachts on Ammersee, one of the region's beautiful lakes**

Exploring Upper Bavaria (South)

THIS REGION is Munich's natural recreation ground. The journey south to Garmisch-Partenkirchen, the area's largest winter sports and hiking centre, takes less than an hour and a fast suburban train connects the Bavarian capital with the Stamberger See and Ammersee. These lakes, together with the Wesslinger See, Wörthsee and Pilsensee, make up the Fünfseenland (Land of Five Lakes) and are also known as Munich's Baths. Rafting expeditions down the Isar start at Wolfratshausen.

SEE ALSO

• *Where to Stay* pp262–3.
• *Where to Eat* pp274–5.

SIGHTS AT A GLANCE

KEY

▬	Motorway
▬	Main road
▦	Minor road
▬	Scenic route
═	River
✷	Viewpoint

Augsburg

Münch

Memmingen

Kempten

LANDSBERG AM LECH **1**

Lech

17

ALTENSTADT
472

SCHONGAU **7**

STEINGADEN **8**

WIESKIRCHE **9**

Ammerse

ANDECHS **3**

2

DIESSEN • **RAISTIN**

WESSOBRUNN **4**

WEILHEIM I. OB.

HOHENPEISSENBERG **6**

Ammer

ROTTENBUCH

23

Staffelsee

MURNAU **10**

OBERAMMERGAU **11**

LINDERHOF **13**

ETTAL **12**

GARMISCH-PARTENKIRCHEN **14**

23

EIBSEE **15** Eibsee

Imst

The highly ornate interior of the church in Steingaden

Sculpture in the gardens of Ludwig II's palace at Linderhof

GETTING AROUND
The southern region of Upper Bavaria is easily reached. The A8, A95 and A96 motorways from Munich lead to the region. The larger towns all have rail links, and those nearer Munich can be reached on the S-Bahn railway. The smaller towns, particularly those in the foothills of the Alps, are all served by convenient bus routes.

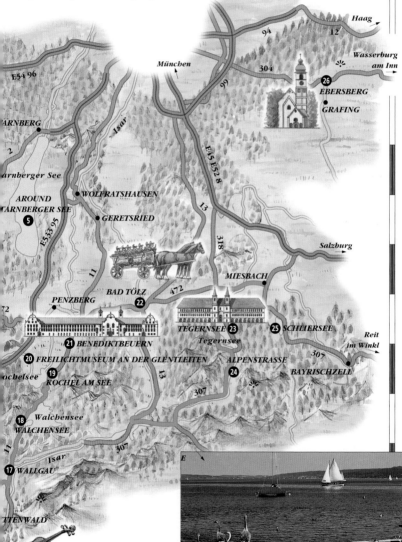

The sandy promenade at Dießen, on Ammersee

Landsberg am Lech ❶

Coat of arms on the Bayertor

L ANDSBERG, which rises in terraces up the steep banks of the River Lech, is well worth more than a brief visit. Enclosed by walls set with towers and pierced by gateways, it largely retains its medieval character. The steep narrow streets, the hidden alleys, the market square and the steep-roofed houses create a special atmosphere. Landsberg was also the place where Adolf Hitler was jailed after his abortive putsch, during which time he wrote *Mein Kampf*.

Gothic bas-relief on the church of Mariä Himmelfahrt

The lavishly decorated stuccowork façade of the Rathaus

Exploring Landsberg

Landsberg's many streets, alleyways and squares abound in fine architecture and historic houses. There are delightful little corners, such as the Hexenviertel, Sellberg and Blattergasse. The Hintere Salzgasse is a particularly striking alley with rows of mid-18th-century single-storey cottages with large, steeply pitched roofs.

⊞ Rathaus

Hauptplatz 1. 📞 (08191) 12 82 68. ☐ May–Oct: 8am–6pm Mon–Fri, 10am–noon & 2–5pm Sat–Sun & public holidays; Nov–Apr: 8am–noon & 2–5:30pm Mon–Thu, 8am–12:30pm Fri.

The Rathaus, or town hall, stands on the west side of the square. The façade and rooms on the second floor have fine mouldings executed by Dominikus Zimmermann in 1718–20. Outside the Rathaus is the Marienbrunnen, a fountain with a statue of the Madonna, dating from 1783.

⊞ Lechwehr

This weir was built in the 14th century at the point where two streams, one of them the Mühlbach, flow into the River Lech. Over the centuries, the weir has been repeatedly washed away by floods and rebuilt. The cascades are scenically set against the backdrop of the Old Town.

⛪ Klosterkirche der Dominikanerinnen Hl. Dreifaltigkeit

Peter Dörfler Str. 🏛

The church, with its uniform Rococo decoration, was built in 1764–6. It stands in the same street as the Dominican convent, whose façade was painted with murals in about 1765. This entire group of buildings was the last work that Dominikus Zimmermann executed before his death.

The Bayertor, one of the finest town gates in Bavaria

⊞ Bayertor and Town Walls

One of the best-known gateways in Bavaria is Landsberg's colourful Bayertor. Built in 1425, it has a 36-m (118-ft) high crenellated tower whose interior contains a stone sculpture of the Crucifixion and armorial cartouches.

The other surviving gates are the Mannerist Sandauertor, dating from 1625–30, the Bäckertor of about 1430, and the Färbertor, built in the later 15th century. The Sandauertor is crowned by the tall, circular Luginsland tower, which functioned as a watchtower during the Middle Ages.

Except for those on the west side, the medieval town walls have been preserved almost in their entirety. The earliest parts, built in the 13th century, can be seen on Vordere Mühlgasse and Hintere Salzgasse. The Schmalzturm, or Schöner Turm, dates from the 14th century. The most recent section of the walls was built in the early 15th century.

⛪ Hl. Kreuzkirche and Neues Stadtmuseum

Von-Helfenstein-Gasse 426. **Neues Stadtmuseum.** 📞 (08131) 94 23 26. ☐ 2pm–5pm Tue–Sun. ● Feb–Mar. 🏛

The Hl. Kreuzkirche was built in 1752–4 to a plan by Ignaz Merani, replacing the previous building of 1580. It was the first Jesuit church in southern Germany. Set high up on a slope overlooking the town, it has a flat façade flanked by belfries with Baroque roofs. The ceiling is decorated with two trompe-l'oeil paintings by Thomas Scheffler, a pupil of the Asam brothers. The paintings create the striking illusion of the Holy Cross falling from above. Monastery buildings stand beside the church. Prominent among them are the former Jesuit college's fine Renaissance cloisters, dating from 1576–1609.

Opposite the church, a little further down the hill, is the former Jesuit college, built in 1688–92 in a refined but pleasingly simple style. Since 1989 the building has housed the local history museum.

The Neues Stadtmuseum and, in the background, Hl. Kreuzkirche

🔒 Mariä Himmelfahrt
Georg-Hellmar-Platz.
The church, built in 1458–88 and retaining its Romanesque tower, was given its present Baroque appearance in about 1700. The windows of the presbytery have late Gothic stained glass, although this is unfortunately obscured by the high altar.

Also in the presbytery, in the Altar of the Rosary made by Dominikus Zimmermann in 1721, is a Gothic figure of the Madonna and Child, an outstanding work executed by Hans Multscher of Ulm in about 1440.

🔒 Johanniskirche
Vorderer Anger.
Built by Dominikus Zimmermann in 1750–52, this church has an oval plan, four semi-circular external corner niches and a separate circular presbytery. Zimmermann, working with Johannes Luidl, was also responsible for the decoration of the interior, which features a magnificent high altar.

🔲 Mutterturm
Von–Kühlmann–Str. 2. **Herkomer Museum.** ((08191) 94 23 26.
◯ 2–5pm Tue–Sun. ⬤ Feb–Mar.
The Mother Tower, built in 1884–7 on the side of the river opposite the town, was the summer residence and studio of Hubert von Herkomer, the painter and dramatist, who died in 1914. Dedicated to his mother (hence the name), the house was built in the style of a Norman castle keep and stands 30 m (98 ft) high.

The museum in the tower contains objects from the artist's studio as well as a selection of his drawings, etchings and paintings.

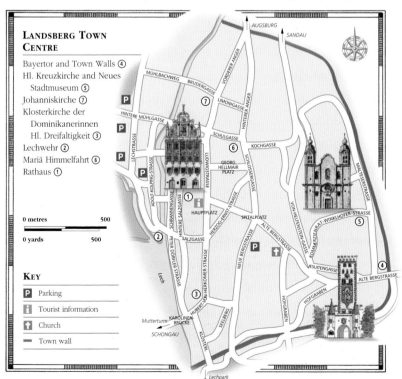

LANDSBERG TOWN CENTRE

Bayertor and Town Walls ④
Hl. Kreuzkirche and Neues Stadtmuseum ⑤
Johanniskirche ⑦
Klosterkirche der Dominikanerinnen Hl. Dreifaltigkeit ③
Lechwehr ②
Mariä Himmelfahrt ⑥
Rathaus ①

0 metres 500
0 yards 500

KEY

🅿️ Parking
ℹ️ Tourist information
✝️ Church
▬ Town wall

Yacht jetty at Dießen on Ammersee

Dießen ❷

Road map C4. 🏘 *8,000.* 🚌 🚉
🛈 *Mühlstr. 4a, (08807) 10 48.*
ⓦ *www.diessen.de*

THIS SMALL fishing town is located on Ammersee, Bavaria's third-largest lake. The area is very popular with people from nearby Munich. Although large numbers of tourists come here, their presence is not especially noticeable. It is pleasant to walk along the lakeside promenade, and especially to visit one of the homely restaurants and to sample Ammersee's speciality, the salmon-like *Renken*.

A few old houses survive here, including the oldest wooden **peasant cottage** in Upper Bavaria, dating from 1491. The most exquisite historic building is the early Rococo **Marienmünster**, a church built for the Augustinian monastery in 1732–5 to a design by Johann Michael Fischer. The fine ceiling paintings, executed by Johann Georg Bergmüller in 1736, depict the saints and blessed members of the von Andechs family. The side altars feature depictions of St Sebastian by the Venetian painter Giovanni Battista Tiepolo and of St Stefan by Battista Pittoni.

Andechs ❸

Road map C4. 🏘 *1,400.* 🚌
🚉 *Herrsching.* 🛈 *Andechser Str. 16, (08152) 93 250.*
ⓦ *www.gemeinde.andechs.de*

ANDECHS IS home to the oldest **church** in Germany. The main part of the building dates from 1420. The church was remodelled in the Baroque style in 1669–1751. The stuccowork and painting are the work of Johann Baptist Zimmermann.

The church attracts some 200,000 pilgrims every year. Because of its situation almost 180 m (590 ft) above the level of Ammersee, together with the Rococo decoration of its late Gothic church, the Benedictine monastery draws large numbers of visitors.

Another reason for the monastery's popularity with visitors is the strong beer that is brewed here. It is served at the monastery's inn and on the terrace, from which there is a breathtaking view over the lake.

The Rococo interior of the church in Wessobrunn

Wessobrunn ❹

Road map C4. 🏘 *1,700.* 🚌 🚉
Weilheim. 🛈 *Zöpfstr. 1, (08809) 313.*

THE EXTERIOR of the former Benedictine abbey here conceals a fine courtyard, lavish stuccowork in the **monastery** and Rococo decoration in the **church**, which was built in 1757–9. Of the original Romanesque buildings, all that remain are the defence tower and the Crucifix in the church. The stuccowork and trompe-l'oeil painting in the cloisters and on the monastery staircase were executed by the workshop of Johann Schmuzer in 1680–96 .

It was here in 814 that the *Wessobrunner Gebet*, the oldest surviving document in the German language, which describes the Creation, was written. It is today preserved in the Stadtmuseum in Munich *(see p 65)*.

LÜFTLMALEREI

Lüftlmalerei is the style of painting that is widely seen on houses in Upper Bavaria and the Allgäu, particularly in the Alpine and sub-Alpine areas. Dating from the 17th century, it was derived from Italian trompe l'oeil painting. A famous exponent of Lüftlmalerei was Franz Seraph Zwinck (1748–92), who lived in Oberammergau in a house called Zum Lüftl. It was probably after his house that this style of painting was named.

Lüftlmalerei in Berchtesgaden

Around Starnberger See ⑤

IT WAS in Starnberger See that Ludwig II, much loved by the Bavarians, drowned in 1886 in a part of the lake near the town of Berg. Like many of Munich's elite, he owned a summer palace on the lake. This scenic region has long enjoyed great popularity. The wealthy citizens of Munich build fine residences here, while those of more modest means come for weekend breaks.

Starnberg ①
Linked to Munich by a railway since 1854, Starnberg boasts luxury villas and has a large marina.

Possenhofen ⑨
Royal visitors to this palace have included Elisabeth, future consort of Franz Joseph of Austria, and Sofia, Ludwig II's betrothed.

Feldafing ⑧
From 1855 to 1863 Ludwig II stayed in a romantic palace on nearby Roseninsel with his cousin Elisabeth (known as Sisi), the future empress of Austria.

Berg ②
The spot where Ludwig II met his death is marked by a Neo-Romanesque chapel built on the lakeshore in 1896–1900.

Assenhausen ③
In an extensive park stands Bismarck's Tower, built in 1896–9 in honour of the German Chancellor.

Tutzing ⑦
A monumental horseshoe-shaped palace surrounded by a landscaped park is currently the home of an evangelical academy.

Bernried ⑥
The Gothic Martinskirche was remodelled in the Baroque style in 1658 by the architect and stuccoist Kasper Feichtmayr.

Ammerland ④
The palace here, built in 1683–5, was presented by Ludwig I to the German poet and painter Franz Pocci in 1841.

0 km | 2
0 miles | 2

TIPS FOR TOURISTS

Length: about 55 km (35 miles).
Stopping-off places: There are many restaurants and cafés in every town on the route. Overnight accommodation is available, although it may be harder to obtain in summer.

Seeshaupt ⑤
This bustling resort, with a marina and elegant lakeside promenade, is very popular with watersports enthusiasts.

KEY

▬ Suggested route

═ Other road

Hohen-peißenberg ❻

Road map C5. 🏛 *4,000.*
🚌 🚉 *Peißenberg or Peiting.*
ℹ️ *Blumenstr. 2, (08805) 92 100.*

THE MOUNTAIN known as Hoher Peißenberg rises east of the town of Peißenberg. The summit, at a height of 988 m (3,241 ft) above sea level, is reached by a scenic winding road. The summit offers an extensive panorama of Upper Bavaria, stretching from Ammersee and Starnberger See to the Alps.

On the summit stands the **Gnadenkapelle,** built in the late Gothic period and remodelled in the Baroque style, the church of **Mariä Himmelfahrt,** built in 1616–19, and a former **chapter-house** of 1619. The chapel contains a miracle-working image of the Madonna Enthroned dating from 1460–80 and brought here from Schongau in 1514.

Michaelskirche font, Altenstadt

Schongau ❼

Road map C5. 🏛 *12,000.* 🚌 🚉
ℹ️ *Münzstr. 5, (08861) 72 16, 71 444.* 🌐 *www.schongau.de*

SCHONGAU is picturesquely located on the river Lech and surrounded by idyllic fields and pastures. The town, whose main street is the wide Münzenstraße, is enclosed by almost completely preserved **town walls** with wooden walkways and towers. They were built in the 14th century and later reinforced in the 17th century.

One of the town's finest buildings is the church of **Mariä Himmelfahrt,** which was built by Dominikus Zimmermann in 1751–3 on the site of a Gothic church. Also of interest is the former **castle** of the Wittelsbachs, dating from the 15th century and refurbished in 1771–2, and the late Gothic **Ballenhaus,** whose ground floor with open-beamed ceiling houses the town hall. The **Stadtmuseum Schongau,** a local history museum, is to be found in **Erasmuskirche,** a former hospital church, established in the 15th century and rebuilt in the 17th century.

🏛 **Stadtmuseum Schongau**
Christophstr. 55. 📞 *(08861) 20 602.*
🕐 *10am–noon & 2–5pm Tue–Sun.*

ENVIRONS: Some 3 km (2 miles) north is **Altenstadt,** which boasts **Michaels-kirche,** the finest surviving monumental Romanesque basilica in Upper Bavaria. Dating from about 1200, it is set on a hill and is surrounded by a wall. The interior is decorated with interestingGothic frescoes. It also contains a crucifix 3 m (10 ft) tall, known as the Great God of Altenstadt, and a carved Romanesque font.

Romanesque cloisters of the abbey in Steingaden

Steingaden ❽

Road map C5. 🏛 *2,900.* 🚌
🚉 *Peiting.* ℹ️ *Krankenhausstr. 1, (08862) 200.* 🌐 *www.steingaden.de*

THIS TOWN has a well-preserved Romanesque **Church of St John the Baptist,** built in the second half of the 12th century and partially rebuilt in the 15th century. It is a columned basilica with a triple apse and twin towers above the west front. The interior was decorated with Rococo mouldings and paintings in 1771–4.

In 1147 the Premonstraten-sians built an **abbey** here, of which the western cloisters, dating from the early 13th century, survive. The architect Dominikus Zimmermann was buried in the Romanesque chapel of St John in 1766.

Wieskirche ❾

Road map C5. 🏛 *2,800.*
🚌 🚉 *Füssen or Peiting.*
ℹ️ *Krankenhausstr 1, Steingaden.*
📞 *(08862) 200.* 🎭 *Festlicher Sommer in der Wies (May–Sep).*

THE ATTRACTIVE pilgrimage church of **Zum Gegeißel-ten Heiland,** nestling in the sub-Alpine scenery, is not only the most resplendent example of South German Rococo, but probably the finest Rococo church in the

Green pastures and a country track near Schongau

world. UNESCO listed it as a World Heritage Site in 1983.

In 1738, the figure of Christ in a small chapel in the fields southwest of the present church is said to have wept genuine tears, and soon afterwards pilgrims began to flock to the site of the miracle. In 1743–4 the Premonstratensian abbot of Steingaden commissioned Dominikus Zimmermann to design a church here.

Built in 1754 and decorated in 1765, the church represents the work of Dominikus and Johann Baptist Zimmermann at its peak. The nave is built to an oval plan and the ceiling is supported by eight pairs of columns. There is an elongated presbytery. The entire building displays an extraordinary fusion of painting, woodcarving and stuccowork and an almost mesmerising interplay of colour and light. The many windows, in fantastic and varied shapes, enliven the exterior and illuminate the interior. Not surprisingly, the church has been called the Lord God's Ballroom.

Murnau ❿

Road map C5. 🏠 *11,300.* 🚌 🚉
ℹ️ *Kohlgruber Str. 1, (08841) 61 410.* 🌐 *www.murnau.de*

MURNAU is situated on an elevation between two lakes, Staffelsee and Riegsee, north of the marsh known as the Murnauer Moos, on what was once the Roman road to Augsburg. During World War II an officers' prisoner-

Rococo interior of the church in Wies, a World Heritage Site

of-war camp existed here. Today Murnau is famous for its breweries.

The **Nikolauskirche** is an interesting building. It was designed by Enrico Zucalli and was completed in 1734, after 17 years' work. The small Baroque **Maria-hilfkirche** stands on Marktstraße, the main street, which commands a view of the Alps to the south.

There are numerous inns and guesthouses, a Neo-Gothic **town hall**, houses with oriel windows and decorative signboards, and narrow, winding alleys which give the town a unique charm. The **monument to Ludwig II**, on Kohlgruber Straße, was erected in 1894 and is the earliest monument to be dedicated to the king.

The finest building in Murnau is the Art Nouveau **Münter-Haus**, where the artist Wassily Kandinsky lived from 1909 to 1914 with his student and lifetime companion Gabriele Münter.

Today it houses a museum dedicated to the famous painter couple, along with works by other members of the Blaue Reiter group.

🏛 **Münter-Haus**
Kottmüllerallee 6.
📞 *(08841) 62 88 80.*
🕐 *2–5pm Tue–Sun.*

DER BLAUE REITER

Cover of the first issue of *Der Blaue Reiter*

Wassily Kandinsky and Franz Marc produced the first issue of *Der Blaue Reiter* in 1911. The journal is now considered one of the most significant manifestos of 20th-century art. The contributors were artists whose aim was to renew art, while retaining their stylistic individuality. They included Paul Klee, Alexej Jawlensky, August Macke and Gabriele Münter. The Blaue Reiter group marked the beginning of lyrical abstract painting.

A colourful flower stall on Unermarkt in Murnau

The Baroque basilica of the Benedictine abbey at Ettal, set in an Alpine valley

Oberammergau ⓫

Road map C5. 🏃 5,000. 🚌 🚊
ℹ️ Eugen-Papst-Str. 9a, (08822) 310.
ⓦ www.oberammergau.de
🎭 Passionspiele (Easter, every
ten years, the next in 2010).

O BERAMMERGAU is one of
the best-known towns in
Upper Bavaria. Its renown
rests on its **painted houses**,
and it is the centre of the
colourful style of trompe-l'oeil
house-painting known as
Lüftlmalerei, which is typical
of the region (see p208).

The town also has an
international reputation for its
Passion play, which has been
performed here at Easter ever
since 1633, when an epidemic
of the plague finally passed.
Originally an open-air event,
the play has been performed
in a purpose-built theatre
since 1930.

The spectacle, which last
for six hours, is performed by
1,400 amateur actors, all of
whom must be local people
or their family members. The
play attracts an audience from
all over the world.

Ettal ⓬

Road map C5. 🏃 1,000. 🚌
🚊 Oberammergau. ℹ️ Ammergauer
Str. 8, (08822) 35 34.
ⓦ www.ettal.de

S ET IN A scenic Alpine valley,
this Benedictine **abbey**
was founded by Ludwig IV in
1330. In 1710, when the
church was remodelled in the
Baroque style to plans by
Enrico Zucalli, a Gothic
rotunda was added. The two-
storey façade that Zucalli
intended was not
completed until the
early 20th century.

The impressive
interior decoration
is in a pure Rococo
style, crowned by the
large dome that is
visible from afar.
The paintings were
executed in
1748–50 by   **Vase in the**
Johann Jakob Zeiller, **Linderhof park**
and the stuccowork,
one of the great achievements
of its time, is by Johann
Georg Üblher and Franz
Xaver Schmuzer. The high

altar has a 14th-century
marble statue of the Madonna
made in the workshop of
Giovanni Pisano. The church,
which attracts many pilgrims,
is surrounded by various
monastic buildings.

Linderhof ⓭

Road map C5. 🏃 5,000. 🚌
🚊 Oberammergau. **Palace**
📞 (08822) 92 030. ⏰ Apr–Sep:
9am–5:30pm daily; Oct–Mar:
10am–4pm daily. 🎫 📷
Park permanently open.
ⓦ www.linderhof.de

O F ALL Ludwig II's
many fairy-tale
residences, the **palace**
at Linderhof best
shows his great fond-
ness for France and
his regard for the
Bourbons and Louis
XIV. The smallest
of Ludwig II's castles
and the one he
visited most often, it was built
by Georg von Dollmann in
1874–8 and is surrounded by
an extensive **park**. The
extravagant luxury of the
interior decoration is based
on French Baroque style.
Although it was intended as a
private residence, the palace
still has an ornate royal
audience chamber. The
other rooms in the palace,
including the Tapestry Room
and Hall of Mirrors, are no
less extravagantly decorated.

The palace is surrounded
by French-style formal
gardens and by Italianate

The Hotel Alte Post in Oberammergau

terraced gardens with cascades, which in turn are surrounded by landscaped grounds. There is an artificial **grotto** dating from 1876–7 with a lake, a stage and a throne with colourful lighting that brings to mind the Venus Grotto in Wagner's opera *Tannhäuser*. Ludwig II would take rides on the lake in a conch-shaped boat.

Another attraction of the park surrounding the palace is the **Moorish kiosk**, made by Karl von Dibitsch in 1850 and purchased by the king in 1876. Inside it is a lavish Peacock Throne. Just as resplendent is the **Moroccan House** of 1878–9, which was installed here in 1989.

Visitors admiring Ludwig II's palace at Linderhof

Garmisch-Partenkirchen ⑭

Road map C5. 🏔 28,000. 🚌 🚊
ℹ️ *Richard-Strauss-Platz 1, (08821) 18 07 00.* 🌐 *www.garmisch-partenkirchen.de*

Two villages, Garmisch and Partenkirchen, separated by the rivers Loisach and Partnach, were conjoined one year before the 1936 Winter Olympics. Thus came into being one of the best-known winter sports centres in Germany, with a convenient motorway link to Munich. The Alpine Ski World Championships were held here in 1978.

Garmisch, the older of the two villages, is mentioned as early as the 9th century. Partenkirchen, which until the 1930s retained its rural character, is 300 years younger. Both parts of the town have many houses with characteristically painted façades, some old and others quite modern.

The finest churches here include **St Anton**, in Partenkirchen, a pilgrimage church dating from the first half of the 18th century, with trompe-l'oeil painting by Johann Holzer. There are also two **churches** in Garmisch dedicated to St Martin. One is medieval, with Gothic frescoes in the interior, and the other is Baroque, with stuccowork executed by Josef Schmuzer in 1730–34 and paintings by Matthäus Günther of 1733.

The **Olympic stadium** in the south part of Parten-kirchen was built in 1935–6. As well as having ski-jumps, it is decorated with larger-than-life sculptures that are typical of Fascist art.

ENVIRONS: A road south of Partenkirchen leads to the scenic **Partnach river gorge** (Partnach-klamm).

Further along, an uphill walk of several hours leads to Ludwig II's hunting lodge in Schachen, just below the summit of Dreitorspitze. Built in 1870 in imitation of a Swiss chalet, the lodge has an ornate Oriental-style interior. The king celebrated his birthdays in the lodge, and also came here on hunting trips.

A house with Lüftlmalerei decoration in Garmisch-Partenkirchen

Eibsee ⑮

Road map C5. 🚌 🚊 *Garmisch-Partenkirchen.*

The greenish-blue waters of this lake, surrounded by wooded mountain slopes, lie 974 m (3,195 ft) above sea level. The scenic paths along its shores lead to secluded jetties for yachts and boats.

A regatta, with processions of yachts and great firework displays, takes place here every summer. Above the lake towers **Zugspitze**, which at 2,962 m (9,717 ft) is the highest peak in the German Alps. The summit can be reached by cablecar or an old funicular train, which passes through many tunnels.

Eibsee, the lake at the foot of Zugspitze

Mittenwald, a town on a former trade route at the foot of the Alps

Mittenwald ⑯

Road map C5. 🏛 *8,400.* 🚌
🚉 🛈 *Dammkarstr. 3, (08823) 33
981.* 🆆 *www.mittenwald.de*

Situated at the foot of the
Karwendel mountain
range, this small town stands
on what was once the main
trade route between Verona
and Augsburg. Up until the
Thirty Years' War, its wealth
was founded on trade but
from the 17th century its
mainstay was craftsmanship,
particularly violin-making.

The beginnings of the local
violin-making trade can be
traced back to 1684, the year
that Matthäus Klotz, a pupil of
the famous Nicolo Amati, was
born. A violin school was
founded in 1853, and in 1930
the **Geigenbau- und
Heimatmuseum** (Museum
of Violin-Making) was
established in the house
where Klotz was born.

Kirche St Peter und Paul
was built in 1738–40 by Josef
Schmuzer. The late Gothic
presbytery survives, and the
tower was completed in 1746.
The Lüftlmalerei on the
façade is an outstanding
example of this type of
decoration *(see p208)*. It is by
Matthias Günther, who also
executed the paintings inside
the church. The monument to
Matthäus Klotz that stands
outside the church was
designed by Ferdinand Miller
in 1890.

Mittenwald is now widely
known as a tourist resort, and
is especially popular with
winter sports enthusiasts.

🏛 Geigenbau- und Heimat-
museum
Ballenhausgasse 11. 📞 *(08823)
25 11.* ⏰ *10am–1pm & 3–6pm
Tue–Fri, 10am–1pm Sat–Sun.*
⬤ *1 Nov–22 Dec.*

Wallgau ⑰

Road map C5. 🏛 *1,400.* 🚌
🚉 *Mittenwald.* 🛈 *Mitten-
walderstr. 8, (08825) 92 50 50.*
🆆 *www.wallgau.de*

This delightful village has
small wooden **cottages**
built in the 17th and 18th
centuries with Lüftlmalerei
(see p208) by Franz Kainer
dating from the 1770s. Most
of the cottages have been
modernized and now function
as hotels, spanning a range of
categories.

The town is popular with
the smart Munich set, who
come to play golf on the fine
local courses, which are set
in breathtaking scenery. The
Gasthaus zur Post is renowned as the place where
Heinrich Heine stayed in 1828
on his journey to Italy.

**One of the many fine golf courses
around the town of Wallgau**

Walchensee ⑱

Road map C5. 🏛 *1,000.* 🚌 🚉
Kochel am See. 🛈 *Ringstr.1, (08858)
411.* 🆆 *www.walchensee.de*

This lake, which lies in an
attractive green valley, is
swept by strong winds, and
is therefore very popular
with windsurfers.

The small **church** near the
lake was built in 1633 and
refurbished in 1712–14.

Environs: In the nearby town
of **Zwergern** stands the
picturesque Margarethen-
kirche, which was built in the
14th century and remodelled
in the Baroque style in 1670.

FRANZ MARC
1880–1916

***Heavenly Horses**, one of
Marc's best-known paintings*

The Munich-born painter
Franz Marc began his
artistic career under the
influence of the Impres-
sionists and of Wassily
Kandinsky, with whom he
set up the group Der
Blaue Reiter *(see p211)*.
Marc adopted Paul
Delaunay's pure palette of
Symbolist colours and the
crystalline forms of the
Italian Futurists. His
paintings of humans and
animals show them in
harmony with their
surroundings. Marc enjoyed
painting from nature
outdoors and was often
visited in his home by
followers of the movement.
He was killed in 1916 at
the Battle of Verdun at
the age of 36.

Beside it stands a monastery known as the Klösterl. Built in 1686–9, it has striking white walls and a tall, steeply pitched roof.

Near **Urfeld**, hidden in the woods, stands a small bust of the great 19th-century German writer Johann Wolfgang von Goethe, who stayed in the town when he set off on his famous Italian travels in 1786.

Walchensee hydroelectric power station above Kochelsee

Kochel am See ⓳

Road map C5. 🏘 *4,200.* 🚌 🚉 **ℹ**
Kalmbachstr. 11, (08851) 338.
ⓦ *www.kochel.de*

KOCHEL IS a popular resort on Kochelsee. The local church, **Michaelskirche**, was built in 1688–90, probably by Kaspar Feichtmayr. The frescoes and stuccowork were added in about 1730.

Two famous figures are associated with Kochel. One is the blacksmith who became the hero of the Bavarian uprising against Austria in 1705 – a statue of him was erected in 1900. The other is the painter Franz Marc *(see p214)*. The house in which he lived is now a

Wooden figure of a fisherman in the lakeside resort of Kochel am See

The extensive cloisters of the monastery at Benediktbeuern

museum of his paintings and the works of other artists of the group Der Blaue Reiter *(see p211)*.

🏛 Franz-Marc-Museum
Herzogstandweg 43. **⬛** *(08851) 7114* ⬜ *1 Mar–15 Jan: 2–6pm Tue–Sun.* 🈺

ENVIRONS: Above Kochelsee is **Walchensee hydro-electric power station**. It was built in 1918–24 to a design by Oskar von Miller, who aimed to electrify the Bavarian rail network and to supply electricity to the whole country. Walchensee power station is still one of the largest in Germany today.

Freilichtmuseum an der Glentleiten ⓴

Road map C5. 🚌 🚉 *Kochel am See, Murnau.* **ℹ** *(08851) 18 50.* ⬜ *Apr–Jun & Sep–Oct: 9am–6pm Tue–Sun; Jul–Aug: 9am–6pm daily.* 🈺

THE LARGEST skansen (open-air museum) in Upper Bavaria opened near Groß-weil in 1976. It re-creates the atmosphere of a traditional Bavarian village, with cottages and workshops. The interiors show the way villagers once lived. The surrounding fields and meadows are cultivated in the traditional way. Cows, horses, sheep and goats graze nearby.

Benediktbeuern ㉑

Road map C5. 🏘 *2,800.* 🚌
🚉 **ℹ** *Prälatenstr. 3, (08857) 248.*
ⓦ *www.benediktbeuern.de*

THE HOLIDAY resort of Benediktbeuern, at the foot of the Bekediktenwand mountains, is known for its former Benedictine **monastery**. Founded in 739 as part of the see established by St Boniface, it was one of the first missionary monasteries that he founded in Bavaria.

Work on the present late Baroque **church**, which stands on the site of a Romanesque church, began in 1682 under the direction of Kaspar Feichtmayr of Wessobrunn. The interior features some fine stucco-work strongly influenced by Italian art. The vaulting over the nave and the side chapels was painted by Hans Georg Asam, father of the renowned Asam brothers, in 1683–7. The monumental altar, built to resemble a triumphal arch, is made out of three different kinds of marble.

By the presbytery, which is fronted by towers, stands the two-storey **Anastasiakapelle**. It was built in 1750–53 by Johann Michael Fischer and has an oval floor plan. The decoration, by Johann Michael Feichtmayr and Johann Jakob Zeiller, is a masterpiece of Bavarian Rococo style.

Also worth visiting are the **monastery buildings**, now owned by Silesians. Dating from 1669–1732, they are arranged around two court-yards. The Alter Festsaal (Old Banqueting Hall), the Kurfürstensaal (Assembly Hall) and the former library, now a refectory, are particularly worth seeing.

Bad Tölz ㉒

Road map D5. 🏠 *17,000.*
🚉 ℹ *Ludwigstr. 11, (08 041)*
78 670. Ⓦ *www.bad-toelz.de*
🎭 *Leonhardifahrt (6 Nov).*

UNTIL QUITE recent times, the inhabitants of Bad Tölz, on the River Isar, made their living through a combination of trade, logging and making and selling their famous painted furniture. When iodine-rich springs were discovered here in 1946, the village became a health spa. To exploit the local mineral water, a water park at

Leonhardiritte **(painted cart), Bad Tölz**

Alpamare, one of the largest in Germany, was built, and transport links, saunas and solariums were installed.

The character of the old town has been well preserved around **Marienstraße**, which leads down to the Isar. Many of the houses, dating from the 17th to the 19th centuries, have characteristic trompe-l'oeil wall paintings and stuccowork, and distinctive overhanging eaves.

The **church** on Kalvarien-berg, one of the prettiest in Bavaria, was begun in 1711 and completed at the end of the 19th century. Particularly impressive is the **Holy Staircase** inside the church. At the festival of St Leonard, patron saint of horses and cattle, a horseback procession ascends Kalvarienberg after the blessing. Processions with horses and painted carts, or Leonhardiritte, take place in the town, too.

Tegernsee ㉓

Road map D5. 🏠 *4,200.* 🚌
🚉 *Tegernsee.* ℹ *Hauptstr. 2,*
(08022) 18 01 40.
Ⓦ *www.tegernsee.de*

FOR the inhabitants of Munich, Tegernsee, within easy reach of the capital, is an upper-class recreation ground. During the Third Reich it was secretly mocked as "Lago di Bonzo".

In the 8th century the Benedictine **monastery** that was founded near Tegernsee became an important centre of culture, and in the 11th century the Romanesque stained-glass windows made here were renowed. Examples can be seen in Augsburg cathedral. In 1823–4 Leo von Klenze converted the monastery into a summer residence for Maximilian I Joseph. Von Klenze also designed a new façade for the monastery church, built by Enrico Zucalli in the Baroque style.

Alpenstraße ㉔

IN 1927, plans were made for a panoramic road that was to pass through the most beautiful parts of the German Alps. The route alternates between the High Alps and the foothills lying between Bodensee and Königssee. It traverses the most scenic areas, allowing travellers to admire Lower Bavaria's stunning scenery. Particularly impressive are the winding sections of the route, such as those around Hindelang and Bayrischzell, which offer breathtaking views.

KEY

▦ Suggested route

⋯ Other road

▦ Scenic route

Jochstraße ②
The scenic road that winds round Hindelang, at altitudes varying as much as 300m (985 ft) along a 7-km (4-mile) long route, offers views of Ostrachtal.

Immenstadt ①
This picturesque little town, which has some fine historic buildings, is situated near the lake, Alpsee.

Zugspitze ③
At 2,962 m (9,721 ft), this peak is the highest in Germany. It is topped by a distinctive cross.

AUGSBURG
MEMMINGEN *Marktoberdorf* *Schongau*
Kempten
Lindau
Bodensee
Sonthofen
Füssen
Forggensee
FELDKIRCH
BAAD
IMST

0 km 20

0 miles 20

The town of Schliersee seen from the lake

Schliersee ㉕

Road map D5. 🏘 7,000.
🚉 **ℹ** *Am Bahnhof, (08026) 60 650.*
🌐 *www.schliersee.de*

Situated east of Tegernsee and known as its "younger brother", Schliersee offers visitors much peace and quiet. The houses on the northern lakeshore all have balconies laden with overflowing window boxes.

The local **church of St Sixtus** has frescoes and stuccowork executed by Johann Baptist Zimmermann in 1714, as well as a distinctive figure of God the Father with

Christ ascribed to Erasmus Grasser, and a Madonna ascribed to Jan Polack. The interesting **Heimat-museum** (local history museum) is housed in an 18th-century hut.

🏛 Heimatmuseum
Lautererstr. **📞** *(08026) 46 71.*
🕐 *15 May–Jun: 4–6pm Tue–Fri, 10am–noon Sat; Jul–Sep: 4–6pm Tue–Fri, 10am–noon Sat–Sun.*

Ebersberg ㉖

Road map D4. 🏘 9,000. 🚉
ℹ *Marienplatz 1, (08092) 82 55 29.*

This little town lies at the southern end of Germany's largest expanse of forest. Of the Augustinian monastery that was founded here in 934 all that remains is the **Sebastianskirche**, built in 1217–31 and remodelled in 1472–1504 in the Gothic style by Erhard Randeck. Notable

among the tombs, which span the 14th to the 16th centuries, is that of the couple who founded the church. In the late Gothic style, it features a model of the church made by Wolfgang Leb in 1501. On Marienplatz, along with Baroque and Neo-Classical houses, is the **monastery inn** (c.1529), today the town hall.

Doorway of Sebastianskirche in Ebersberg, with gilded figures

---

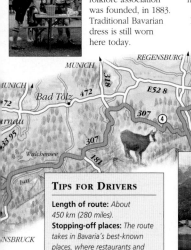

Bayrischzell ④
In this famous health resort beneath the Wendelstein mountains, the first Alpine folklore association was founded, in 1883. Traditional Bavarian dress is still worn here today.

Berchtesgaden ⑥
This architecturally rich town, at the foot of Watzmann, is the hub of the tourist area known as Berchtesgadener Land.

MUNICH   *REGENSBURG*   *Chiemsee*   *Traunstein*   *CHAM*

MUNICH   *Bad Tölz* 318 E52 8   E52 8   *LINZ* *Salzburg*

472   307   ④   305   20

307   181   ⑤   ⑥

Walchensee   *Königssee*   *SPITTAL*

Isar   *INSBRUCK*

Tips for Drivers

Length of route: *About 450 km (280 miles).*
Stopping-off places: *The route takes in Bavaria's best-known places, where restaurants and accommodation are plentiful.*

Hintersee ⑤
The forest covering the foothills around this lake east of Ramsau – one of the many lakes in Berchtesgadener Land – is known as the Zauberwald (Magic Forest).

THE ALLGÄU

THE ALLGÄU *is the part of Swabian Bavaria lying between the Landsberg-Memmingen motorway and the Allgäu Alps. In the east it borders the Lech valley, and in the west Baden-Württemberg, into which it protrudes as far as Bodensee (Lake Constance). The Allgäu is one of the least industrialized regions of Bavaria. Its main sources of wealth are cattle farming, dairy processing and tourism.*

This verdant, hilly region, set against the backdrop of the sheer, craggy peaks of the Alps, attracts holiday-makers from Europe all year round. The gentle climate, the unspoiled scenery, the villages and towns with their historic buildings, and the excellent terrain for various sports makes this a suitable area for the developing tourist trade. The lush meadows and pastures are grazed by the characteristic brown Allgäu cows. The region's dairy produce is famous throughout the country and Germany's largest dairy processing plant is located in Kimratshofen, near Kempten.

Traditions and customs are still very much alive in the region. Local folk costumes, which vary from one district or village to another, are donned not exclusively for special occasions but are worn as everyday clothing.

After World War II, the influx of migrants (many from Sudetenland) considerably altered the structure of the population. The former inhabitants of Gablonz (Jablonec), in the Czech Republic, settled near Kaufbeuren in Neugablonz, bringing with them their traditional trade of jewellery-making.

In the Allgäu Alps, world-class sports are practised. In Oberstdorf, which is famous for its huge ski-jump, there is also a figure-skating school for young men and women from all over the country. The Alpine rockfaces are suitable for both amateur and professional mountaineers, while the cliff-tops are ideal starting-places for colourful paragliders and hang gliders. Neuschwanstein, perhaps the most extravagant of Ludwig II's castles, attracts visitors from all over the world.

Rolling green countryside around Immenstadt

◁ **Neuschwanstein, one of the best known of Ludwig II's castles**

Exploring the Allgäu

THE CAPITAL of the Allgäu is Kempten, a town with Roman origins. Memmingen also has many historic monuments, but these are not the region's main attraction. Tourists are drawn to the castles of Hohenschwangau and Neuschwanstein at the foot of the Alps, which are reached by the Romantische Straße (Romantic Road). Equally splendid are the Renaissance castles of the Fuggers in Babenhausen and Kirchheim, and Ottobeuren Abbey. The south of the Allgäu has breathtaking Alpine scenery, including the Breitach gorge and Sturmannshöhle, a cave with stalactites, near Oberstdorf. This town is renowned for the Four Ski Jumps Tournament.

SEE ALSO

- *Where to Stay* p263.
- *Where to Eat* p275.

BABENHAUSEN

Ulm

E43 7

MEMMINGEN ❶

❶❽ **MARIA STEINBACH**

Leutkirch

The church in Wasserburg on Bodensee (Lake Constance)

Wangen

ISNY

Friedrichshafen

LINDENBERG

WASSERBURG ❶❻

LINDAU ❶❺

Bodensee

Feldkirch

Bregenz

Dornbirn

308 ❶❹ **IMMENSTADT**

SONTHOFE

OBERSTDOR

Baad

SIGHTS AT A GLANCE

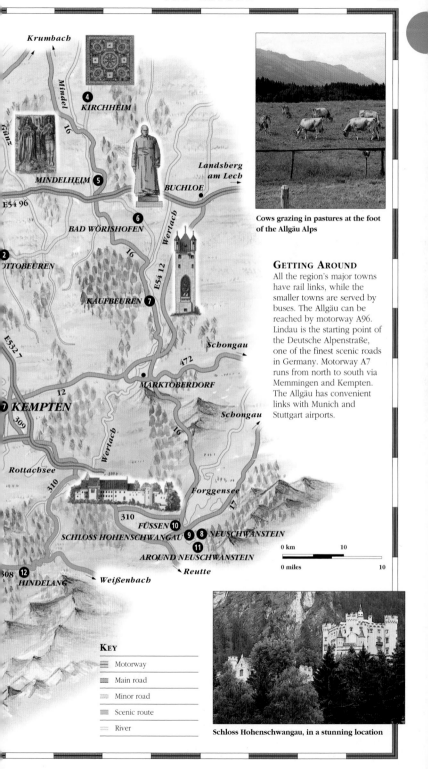

Krumbach

Mindel

Günz

4 KIRCHHEIM

16

MINDELHEIM 5

Landsberg
am Lech

E54 96

BUCHLOE

6 BAD WÖRISHOFEN

2

OTTOBEUREN

16

Wertach

E54 12

E532 7

KAUFBEUREN 7

Schongau

472

MARKTOBERDORF

12

7 **KEMPTEN**

Schongau

309

16

Wertach

17

Rottachsee

310

Forggensee

310

FÜSSEN 10

SCHLOSS HOHENSCHWANGAU 9 8 NEUSCHWANSTEIN

11

AROUND NEUSCHWANSTEIN

↙ Reutte

308 12

HINDELANG ← Weißenbach

Cows grazing in pastures at the foot
of the Allgäu Alps

GETTING AROUND

All the region's major towns
have rail links, while the
smaller towns are served by
buses. The Allgäu can be
reached by motorway A96.
Lindau is the starting point of
the Deutsche Alpenstraße,
one of the finest scenic roads
in Germany. Motorway A7
runs from north to south via
Memmingen and Kempten.
The Allgäu has convenient
links with Munich and
Stuttgart airports.

0 km   10

0 miles   10

KEY

▬ Motorway

▬ Main road

▭ Minor road

▬ Scenic route

▬ River

Schloss Hohenschwangau, in a stunning location

Memmingen ●

MEMMINGEN, a town known as the gateway to the Allgäu, was founded in the 12th century. It stands on the site of an Alemani settlement, on the course of an old Roman road. In 1438 Memmingen became a Free Imperial City, in 1522 it accepted the Reformation, and in 1803 it became part of Bavaria.

Memmingen has retained all the characteristics of a large trading centre. Various residential and artisans' districts have developed both within and outside the town walls. The wide streets often functioned as cargo-handling areas. The mainly timber-framed houses that line them have preserved their Gothic character.

The rich Gothic carvings on the stalls in Martinskirche

The façade of the town hall, with decorative Rococo stuccowork

♨ Hermansbau
Zangmeisterstr. 8. **Stadtmuseum und Heimatmuseum Freudenthal**.
((08331) 85 01 34.
May–Oct: 10am–noon and 2–4pm Tue–Fri, Sun and public holidays.
This late Baroque patrician palace with an arcaded courtyard was built in 1766 for Benedikt Freiherr von Herman. The façade is lavishly decorated with stuccowork, and the central section has a gable with an armorial cartouche.

♙ Martinskirche
Zangmeisterstr. 13. ((08331) 85 69 10. 12 Apr–May: 11am–2pm; June–Sep: 10am–5pm; Oct: 2–4pm.
The Protestant Martinskirche was built in the 15th century, replacing a Romanesque basilica. This late Gothic church has a quadrilateral tower with a later steeple.

The interior has notable wall paintings dating from the 15th and 16th centuries. The most interesting feature of the interior, however, is the presbytery stalls, made by craftsmen from Memmingen in 1501–07. The decorative carvings, with lifelike portraits of the founders, are among the most outstanding examples of late Gothic Swabian art.

♨ Rathaus
Marktplatz 1.
Originally built in 1488, the Gothic town hall was remodelled and enlarged in the 16th century. Its current appearance dates from 1589, the Rococo stuccowork added later to the façade in 1765. This elegant Renaissance building has a projecting central axis with oriel windows on the lower storeys culminating in a polygonal tower, and the wings are flanked by side towers.

♨ Steuerhaus
Marktplatz 16.
The former customs house was built in 1495 to an elongated rectangular plan. It opens on to Marktplatz with an arcade of 20 arches. The second floor and the shaped gables were added in 1708. The painting on the façade dates from 1906–09. The building currently houses various municipal offices.

♨ Westertor and Town Walls
The walls of the old town were completed before 1181. The outer walls were added in the 13th–15th centuries. In the 19th century they were partially demolished, but significant fragments with bastions and walkways have been preserved.

The most noteworthy gate is Westertor, which was rebuilt in 1648 to replace Elias Holl's town gates, and Kemptentor, built in 1383 and topped by a tall brick tower.

♙ Antonierhaus
Martin-Luther-Platz 1.
Strigel- und Antonitenmuseum.
((08331) 85 02 46.
10am–noon and 2pm–4pm Tue–Sat, 10am–12:30 and 1:30–5pm Sun and public holidays.
This former Antonine monastery and hospital, the oldest established by the order, was built in 1383. It stands on the site of an earlier castle.

The four-winged building has internal cloisters with external staircases. Painstakingly rebuilt, since 1996 they have housed a library as well as a café and cultural institutions.

Decorative armorial cartouche on the façade of the Steuerhaus

♠ Fuggerbau

Schweizerbergstr. 6.

The house of the Fugger family *(see p248)* was built in 1581–91 for Jakob Fugger. It is a monumental four-winged building with two square stairwells rising from the corners of the courtyards.

🔒 Frauenkirche

Frauenkirchplatz 4. **(** *(08331) 22 53.*

This three-nave basilica was originally a Romanesque building. It was enlarged at the end of the 14th century, and was remodelled in 1456. From 1565 to 1806 the church was shared by Catholics and Protestants.

The late Gothic paintings on the walls and ceiling were uncovered in 1893. Their state of preservation and wide thematic range make them among the most significant in southern Germany.

🏛 Siebendächerhaus

Gerberplatz 7.

The "House with Seven Roofs", built in 1601, was specially designed for drying

hides. Destroyed in April 1945 and painstakingly rebuilt, it is one of the town's most distinctive buildings.

🎭 Theater

Theaterplatz 2. **(** *(08331) 94 59 16.*

The building on what is now Theaterplatz was originally a monastery's barn. Built in 1680, it became an arsenal and then a theatre in 1803, when the Neo-Classical façade was added.

The distinctive Siebendächerhaus, the "House with Seven Roofs"

> ### VISITORS' CHECKLIST
>
> **Road map** B4. 🕌 *43,000.*
> 🚌 🚊 *Bahnhofplatz.*
> 🛈 *Marktplatz 3, (08331) 85 01 72, 85 01 73.*
> 🔳 *www.memmingen.de*
> 🎭 *Wallensteinspiel (Jul, every 4 years), Fischertag (Jul), Jahrmarkt (Oct), Weihnachtsmarkt (Dec).*

🔒 Kreuzherrenkirche

Hallhof 5. ⬤ *until the end of 2002.*

This two-nave church with a tall onion-domed clock tower was built in 1480–84 in the Gothic style. In 1709 the interior was decorated with lavish Baroque stuccowork by Matthias Stiller and paintings in the style of Johann Baptist Zimmermann.

When the church was deconsecrated in 1803, the interior was horizontally divided so as to make two storeys. After World War II it was restored and since 1947 it has served as Memmingen's exhibition gallery and concert hall.

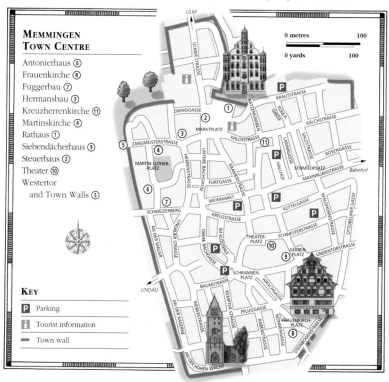

MEMMINGEN TOWN CENTRE

Antonierhaus ⑥
Frauenkirche ⑧
Fuggerbau ⑦
Hermansbau ③
Kreuzherrenkirche ⑪
Martinskirche ④
Rathaus ①
Siebendächerhaus ⑨
Steuerhaus ②
Theater ⑩
Westertor and Town Walls ⑤

0 metres 100
0 yards 100

KEY

🅿 Parking
🛈 Tourist information
▬ Town wall

The lavishly decorated interior of the abbey church at Ottobeuren

Ottobeuren ❷

Road map B4. 🏛 8,000. 🚌
🅿 ℹ Marktplatz 14, (08332)
92 19 50. W www.ottobeuren.de

THE BENEDICTINE abbey in
Ottobeuren, whose begin-
nings go back to the 8th
century, is one of the finest
Baroque monasteries in
Germany. The abbey
**Church of St Theodore
and St Alexander**, rebuilt
and refurbished on numerous
occasions, received its present
appearance in 1748–66, when
it was remodelled by Johann
Michael Fischer.

Nestling in wooded slopes
overlooking the River Günz,
this fine monumental building
is a breathtaking sight. The
lavish interior, in a uniform
Rococo style, features four
domes, the largest of which is
25 m (82 ft) high. The decoration and furnishings are by
various artists, including
Johann Michael Feichtmayr
and Joseph Christian and
Johann Jakob Zeiller.

The **abbey**, to the west of the
church, is known as "the
Escorial of Swabia". Built to
plans by Christoph Vogt
in 1711–31, it is an imposing
quadrilateral edifice with
four cloisters.

Ottobeuren Abbey has been
in the hands of Benedictine
monks since its foundation.
Today the Library, the Abbot's
Chapel, the Theatre Hall and
the Knights' Hall are open
to visitors.

The **Klostermuseum**
contains exhibits that include
sculpture dating from the
12th to the 18th
centuries, the works
of artists who worked
in Ottobeuren (on the
church murals, for
example), clocks and
other artifacts.

The abbey's
Kaisersaal is occupied
by the **Staatsgalerie**,
an interesting art
gallery devoted to the
works, mostly on
religious themes, of
Swabian Gothic

painters. The gallery forms
part of the Bayerische
Staatsgemäldesammlungen.

🏛 **Klostermuseum Abtei
Ottobeuren and Staatsgalerie
Ottobeuren, Kaisersaal**
Benediktiner. ℂ (08332) 79 80.
◯ Apr–Oct: 10am–noon & 2–5pm
daily; Nov–Mar: 2–4pm Mon–Fri,
10am–noon Sat–Sun.

Babenhausen ❸

Road map B4. 🏛 5,600. 🚌
🅿 ℹ Schrannenstr. 7, (08333)
92 36 23. W www.babenhausen-
schwaben.de

THE MOST prominent land-
marks in this town are the
castle and the parish church.

The **castle**, which is
mentioned as early as 1237,
became the property of the
von Rechberg family after
1378. It was probably they
who were responsible for the
steep-roofed two-storey
edifice built here in the 15th
century and incorporated into
the castle. In 1538 the castle
passed into the hands of the
Fuggers (see p249), who
refurbished it in 1541, adding
the west and south wings. In
1955 the **Fuggermuseum**
was founded, with the family
retaining ownership of the
park surrounding the castle.

The **church**, which is
connected to the castle, was
rebuilt in the Baroque style in
1715–30. The interior contains
Baroque altars and a pulpit,
as well as the tombs of the
Rechbergs and Fuggers.

🏛 **Fuggermuseum**
ℂ (08333) 92 09 26. ◯ Apr–Nov:
10am–noon & 2–5pm Tue–Sat,
10am–noon & 1–6pm Sun. 🖼

The castle and church in Babenhausen

Kirchheim ❹

Road map B4. 🏠 1,500.
🚌 🚉 Mindelheim. 🛈 Marktplatz 6,
(08266) 86 080. 🌐 www. kirchheim-
schwaben.de

THE MAIN attraction of this small town is the Renaissance **castle**, owned by the Fugger family since the mid-16th century. The famous Cedar Hall is decorated with wood-carvings on its ceiling and door, and on its window surrounds and chimneypieces.

The altar of **Peter- und Paulskirche** features a painting of the Holy Family ascribed to Domenichino and of the Assumption ascribed to Rubens. Also worth seeing is the tomb of Hans Fugger, who died in 1598. Made of white lime-stone, it was the work of Alexander Colin.

Part of the inlaid ceiling of the Cedar Hall at Kirchheim Castle

Mindelheim ❺

Road map B4. 🏠 13,500. 🚌
🚉 🛈 Beim Rathaus, (08261) 73 73
00. 🌐 www.mindelheim.de
🎪 Frundsbergfest (every 3 years,
the next in 2003).

DURING THE 15th and 16th centuries **Mindelburg Castle**, built by Heinrich der Löwe in 1160, belonged to the Frundsberg family, as did the whole town. The castle was rebuilt in the late 15th to early 16th centuries and again in the late 19th century.

The town's two main streets, Maximilianstraße and Kornstraße, are lined with fine town houses. The former

Jesuit **Maria Verkündigungs-kirche**, built in 1625–6 and refurbished in 1721, has fine stuccowork and altars.

Stephanskirche, built in the early 18th century and rebuilt in the early 20th century, contains the tomb of Duke Ulrich von Teck and his two brides. It is an important work of Swabian Gothic stone carving. In the former chapel of St Sylvester is the **Schwäbisches Turmuhren museum**, displaying belfry clocks.

🏛 **Schwäbisches Turm-uhrenmuseum**
Hungerbachgasse 9.
📞 (08261) 69 64.
🕐 2–4pm Wed.

Knight statue, Kirchheim Castle

Bad Wörishofen ❻

Road map B4. 🏠 14,400.
🚌 🚉 🛈 Bürgermeister-Ledermann-Str. 1, (08247) 96 90 55.
🌐 www.bad-woerishofen.de

THIS SPA RESORT owes its existence to Duke Sebastian Kneipp. Among the 19th-century guest houses here are the **Sebastianeum** at Kneippstraße 8 and the **Kneippianum** at Alfred-Baumgartenstraße 6. The **Justinakirche** and **Klosterkirche** both have decoration by Dominik and Johann Baptist Zimmermann.

🏛 **Sebastian-Kneipp-Museum**
Schulstr. 📞 (08247) 96 90 35.
🕐 15 Jan–15 Nov: 3–6pm Tue–Sun.

Kaufbeuren ❼

Road map D4. 🏠 44,000.
🚌 🚉 🛈 Kaiser-Max-Str. 1, (08341)
40 405. 🌐 www.kaufbeuren.de
🎪 Tänzelfest (Jul).

WITH STEEP, winding narrow streets lined with colourful houses, the hilltop town of Kaufbeuren retains much of its medieval character.

The old town still has its fortifications, complete with walls and defensive towers, one of which is the Fünfkopf-turm, which was built in about 1420. After World War II, Neugablonz, a settlement for refugees from Sudetenland, now part of the Czech Republic, was built here.

The Gothic Fünfknopfturm, part of Kaufbeuren's fortifications

---

SEBASTIAN KNEIPP (1821–1897)

Sebastian Kneipp, a parish priest from St Justin's Church in Bad Wörishofen, introduced a method of therapy involving five factors – water, movement, herbal treatment, diet and inner harmony – but above all cold baths, showers and exercise. In 1903 a monument to Duke Kneipp was erected in the street bearing his name. Portraits of the clergyman (painted in 1936) can be seen on the ceiling of Justinakirche, and the town's former Dominican monastery contains a museum dedicated to him. The local rose-gardens also grew a new variety of rose, the Kneipp Rose.

The Kneipp Monument in Bad Wörishofen

Schloss Neuschwanstein seen against its woodland backdrop

Neuschwanstein ⑧

Road map B5.
i *Neuschwansteinstr. 20, Hohenschwangau, (08362) 81 035.*
w *www.schloesser-bayern.de*

SCHLOSS NEUSCHWANSTEIN, one of Ludwig II's most renowned castles, was built at enormous expense from 1868 to 1892. It received its present name after the king's death in 1886.

The monumental castle, based on Wartburg Castle in Thuringia, was built to plans by the theatre designer Christian Jank, who expressed the king's vision inspired by Wagner's operas *Lohengrin* and *Tannhäuser*. The interior decoration was executed by Julius Hoffmann in 1880.

The castle has a breath-taking situation on an outcrop of rock towering over a gorge in the River Pöllat. There is a particularly memorable view from Marienbrücke, which giddily spans the rushing waters in the ravine below.

⚓ Schloss Neuschwanstein
⏰ *Apr–Sep: 9am–6pm daily, 9am–8pm Thu; Oct–Mar: 10am–4pm daily.*
⏺ *1 Jan, 24, 25, 31 Dec.* 📷 🎫

Schloss Hohenschwangau ⑨

Road map B5. **i** *Alpseestr. 24, (08362) 81 127.*
w *www.hohenschwangau.de*

THIS 14TH-CENTURY castle, which was destroyed during the Napoleonic Wars, was acquired by Maximilian II, the last king of Bavaria, in 1832. The restoration and rebuilding work executed up

to 1854 was primarily the work of Domenico Quaglio.

A bulky building, set with towers and painted yellow, it is situated over a lake against a picturesque backdrop of Alpine scenery.

⚓ Schloss Hohenschwangau
⏰ *Apr–Sep: 9am–6pm daily; Oct–Mar: 10am–4pm daily.* 📷

Statue of the Madonna and Child in St Mang-Kirche at Füssen

Füssen ⑩

Road map B5. 🏙 *16,450.*
i *Kaiser-Maximilian-Platz 1, (08362) 93 850.* **w** *www.fuessen.de*

THE TOWN'S location in the foothills of the Alps, surrounded by lakes and overlooking the River Lech, together with its proximity to Schloss Neuschwanstein and Schloss Hohenschwangau, ensure that it is always full of tourists.

In Roman times Füssen stood on the road connecting northern Italy with Augsburg. In 1313 it passed into the hands of the bishops of

Augsburg, who made it their summer residence. The town's rapid growth was interrupted by the Thirty Years' War and a fire in 1713. After the secularization of the state and its incorporation into Bavaria in 1803, Füssen again enjoyed a period of prosperity, thanks to the interest that the Bavarian kings took in the region.

Füssen has many fine old buildings. The medieval **castle** has an arcaded façade decorated with trompe-l'oeil paintings executed in 1499. Its halls now house the **Filialgalerie der Bayerischen Staatsgemäldesammlungen** (art gallery).

The **Benedictine monastery**, founded in the 9th century, now houses the **Museum der Stadt Füssen**, a local history museum, where a collection of locally made lutes and violins is displayed. Beside it is **St Mang-Kirche**, built in 1720-21. The façade of **Heilig-Geist-Spitalkirche**, painted by Joseph Anton Walch in 1749, is also of note.

🏛 Museum der Stadt Füssen
Lechhalde 3. **C** *(08362) 90 31 45.*
⏰ *Apr–Oct: 11am–4pm Tue–Sun; Nov–Mar: 2–4pm Tue–Sun.* 📷
🏛 Filialgalerie der Bayerischen Staatsgemäldesammlungen
Magnusplatz 10. **C** *(08362) 90 31 45.* ⏰ *Apr–Oct: 11am–4pm Tue–Sun; Nov–Mar: 2–4pm Tue–Sun.* 📷

The painted façade of Heilig-Geist-Spitalkirche in Füssen

Around Neuschwanstein ⑪

THIS TOUR, probably the most scenic in the whole of Bavaria, takes about a day, as it inevitably involves queueing for tickets at both the castles. They are reached from car parks at the foot of Schloss Hohen-schwangau. An effortless way of reaching the giddy heights of Schloss Neuschwanstein is by horse-drawn chaise. Another memorable experience is a boat trip on Alpsee.

Kolomanskirche ①
This small, distinctive Baroque church of 1673–82 stands in isolation at the foot of Schwangauer Berge.

Tegelbergbahn ②
Recently discovered remains of Roman buildings can be seen from the lower station of this cable car, which runs to the summit of Tegelberg.

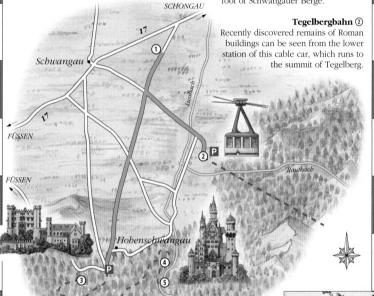

Schloss Hohenschwangau ③
Part of the richly furnished interior of this castle is open to visitors.

Marienbrücke ⑤
The cast-iron bridge that spans the Pöllat gorge is constantly occupied by people fascinated by staring 90 m (300 ft) down into the giddy depths.

KEY

- ▦ Suggested route
- — Suggested walk
- ⋯ Other road
- — Railway line
- P Parking

Neuschwanstein ④
The white silhouette of Ludwig II's castle, set with numerous turrets, has an almost surreal appearance when it is seen against the woodland backdrop, which changes colour through the seasons.

TIPS FOR VISITORS

Length of route: *about 15 km (9 miles).*
Stopping-off places: *Meals and refreshments are available near Schloss Hohenschwangau and Schloss Neuschwanstein.*

The Oberstdorf ski jumps, where the Four Ski Jumps Tournament is held

Hindelang ⓬

Road map B5. 🅜 4,900. 🚌 🚉
Sonthofen. 🅗 Am Bauernmarkt 1, (08324) 89 20.
🆆 www.hindelang.net

Tᴴɪꜱ ʜᴇᴀʟᴛʜ resort is set in beautiful woodland scenery in the Ostrach river valley. The town is best explored by walking down Markt-straße, starting from the Neo-Gothic **church**. The 17th-century **bishop's palace** opposite now houses the town hall. The beautifully restored houses are covered in flowers in summer.

Lüftlmalerei on a hotel in Hindelang

Eɴᴠɪʀᴏɴꜱ: About 1 km (0.6 mile) south of Hindelang is the spa resort of **Bad Oberdorf**. **Hinterstein**, 6 km (4 miles) further on, is popular with mountaineers. The road to **Oberjoch**, 6.5 km (4.5 miles) northeast, known as the Jochstraße, is the most tortuous section of the **Deutsche Alpenstraße**.

Oberstdorf ⓭

Road map B6. 🅜 12,000. 🚌 🚉
🅗 Marktplatz 7, (08322) 19 433.
🆆 www.oberstdorf.de

Tʜᴇ ʙᴇꜱᴛ-ᴋɴᴏᴡɴ health resort and holiday centre in the Allgäu, Oberstdorf, situated in the Iller river valley, is also renowned for its **ski jumps** on the slope of Schattenberg.

One event in the Four Ski Jumps Tournament is held here every year. The best-known ski jump in Oberstdorf is in the Stillach valley. It was the first large-scale ski jump *(Skiflugschanze)* in the world, and competitors can achieve distances of more than 170 m (550 ft). It was built in 1949–50 by the ski jumper and architect Heini Klopfer. The town itself, with its narrow streets and old houses, is extremely attractive. The **Heimat-museum**, with exhibits relating to local history, including the world's largest shoe, is worth a visit.

🏛 **Heimatmuseum**
Oststr. 13. 🅒 (08322) 54 70.
⏺ 15 May–Oct and 27 Dec–15 Apr: 10am–noon & 2–5:30pm Tue–Sat.

Eɴᴠɪʀᴏɴꜱ: The **Breitach river gorge**, 6 km (4 miles) west of Oberstdorf, is a major attraction. A vertiginous track winds for 2 km (1.25 mile) above the water that rushes between sheer cliffs rising to heights of 100 m (325 ft). For the walk, a waterproof overgarment and sturdy hiking boots will be needed.

At the **Sturmannshöhle** cave outside **Fischen**, some 200 steps lead to a large cavern with impressive stalactites and stalagmites. The cave's galleries are connected by rushing under-ground streams that can be heard from the cave mouth.

Immenstadt ⓮

Road map B5. 🅜 14,000. 🚌
🅟 🅗 Marienplatz 3, (08323) 91 41 76. 🆆 www.immenstadt.de
🎿 Klausentreiben (5–6 Dec).

Iᴛ ɪꜱ ʙᴇꜱᴛ to approach Immenstadt from the north, as this route provides a fine view of Alpsee. The town has much to offer to watersports enthusiasts and mountaineers. It also contains many historic buildings. **Nikolauskirche** has been rebuilt several times since the Middle Ages. In 1602–20 a **palace** was built on the market square. One of its apartments has a stucco-work ceiling of about 1720 with hunting scenes and views of castles. The **town hall** was built in 1649 and the local history museum is in a **mill** dating from about 1451.

Eɴᴠɪʀᴏɴꜱ: 2 km (1.25 mile) north is **Bühl**, where Stephanskirche contains a chapel that was built as a replica of the Holy Sepulchre in Jerusalem. The nearby Maria Loretto Chapel with the Cottage of Our Lady of Loretto is made up of the Baroque choir of St Annakapelle.

Lindau ⓯

See pp230–31.

Sarcophagus in Nikolauskirche in Immenstadt

Wasserburg

Road map A5. ⚐ *2,900.*
🚌 🚉 ℹ *Lindenplatz 1, (08382) 88
74 74.* W *www.wasserburg-
bodensee.de*

W ITH A stunningly
beautiful location on the
tip of a promontory on
Bodensee (Lake Constance),
Wasserburg is a charming
village of flower-filled streets
with views of the lake and its
backdrop of hills. Its location
makes it a popular place for
sailing and other watersports.

The village's history dates
from the 8th century, then in
the 10th century a **castle** was
built here to resist Hungarian
invaders. The castle was
modernized in the 13th
century and rebuilt after a fire
in 1358. It is a three-winged
building with an irregular
plan. The east wing is a
vestige of the medieval
structure, while the south
wing dates from the 16th
century and the west wing
from the 18th century. It is
now a hotel.

Georgskirche is equally
historic. It was founded in the
8th century but was later
converted and together with
the cemetery wall was
incorporated into the town's
fortifications. Remnants of
these defences reach down to
the shores of the lake. The
present building is a late
Gothic fortified hall dating
from the second half of the
15th century.

The square tower, built in
1396–1403, was given its
onion dome in 1656. The
church is connected to a
two-storey presbytery.

The **Malhaus** (1597), once
a residence of the Fuggers
(see p248), now houses a
museum illustrating the
culture of the region and
also the fishing industry,
formerly Wasserburg's
main source of livelihood.

🏛 **Museum im Malhaus**
Halbinselstr. 77. 🅲 *(08382) 88 71
97.* ⏺ *May–Oct: 10am–noon
Mon–Tue, Thu–Fri, Sun; 3pm–5pm
Wed, Sat.*

**Georgskirche beside Bodensee
(Lake Constance) in Wasserburg**

Kempten

See pp232–3.

Maria Steinbach

Road map A4. 🚌 🚉 *Leutkirch.*
ℹ *Legau, Marktlegau, (08330) 94
010.*

M ARIA STEINBACH is famed
for its pilgrimage church,
Schmerzhafte Muttergottes,
which is a masterpiece of
Rococo architecture. Situated
on a hill in the idyllic rolling

The Rococo church in Maria Steinbach

landscape of the Iller river
valley, the church was built in
1746–54 on the site of earlier
Romanesque and Gothic
shrines.

The building was inspired
by the works of Dominik
Zimmermann. The undulating
façades, with trompe-l'oeil
painting, conceal a dazzling
interior. The outstanding
mouldings and painting by
Franz Georg Hermann, the
stuccowork of the altars,
pulpit, stalls, confessionals
and organ loft combine to
produce a unified whole.

The figure of the Grieving
Madonna, which since 1730
has been renowned for its
miracle-working powers, was
an object of pilgrimage in
southern Germany during the
18th century.

The group of **presbytery
buildings** set around a
courtyard west of the church
dates from the mid-18th
century. The **Wallfahrtsmuseum** contains a large
collection of votive gifts made
to the Madonna by pilgrims.

🏛 **Wallfahrtsmuseum**
Kirchhof 5 🅲 *(08394) 92 40.*
⏺ *by appointment.*

Bodensee (Lake Constance) and the Alps seen from Wasserburg

Lindau 🅯

Fresco in Peterskirche

Lindau is the only town on Bodensee (Lake Constance), also known as the Swabian Sea, that is officially in Bavaria. The old part of the town, which stands on an island in the lake, is connected to the mainland by a railway and road bridge. Founded as a fishing settlement in Roman times, Lindau is an extremely pleasant town. It was granted the status of a city in the 13th century. It still retains its medieval plan, which is based around three long parallel streets.

Maximilianstraße, the main street in Lindau

⊞ Maximilianstraße

The town's main street, Maximilianstraße, is also its widest. Like the parallel streets of In der Grub and Ludwigstraße, it contains houses dating from the 15th to 19th centuries.

The small, compact houses with gables facing the street have windows that are often divided by columns, while the façades are broken up by oriels. The arcades and the old hoisting devices of the warehouses in the garrets bear witness to the town's character as a centre of trade.

⊞ Altes Rathaus

Bismarckplatz 4.
The old town hall, built in 1422–36, was remodelled several times during the 16th century, and again in 1724 and 1865. The programme of rebuilding that took place in 1885–7 was undertaken by Friedrich von Thiersch, who restored the stepped gable that had been removed in 1865 and reconstructed the exterior staircase. The façade was also painted by Joseph Widmann.

⊞ Neues Rathaus

Bismarckplatz 3.
The new town hall, built in 1706–17, was also remodelled by Friedrich von Thiersch in 1885. A two-storey building crowned by a tall shaped gable decorated with vases and obelisks, it now houses the police headquarters.

⊞ Haus zum Cavazzen

Marktplatz 6. **Städtisches Museum**
[(08382) 94 40 73.
🔾 Easter–Oct: 11am–5pm Tue–Fri, Sun, 2–5pm Sat.
This elegant patrician building is named after the de Cavazzo

family, in whose ownership it was from 1540 to 1617.

The present Baroque house was built for the von Seutter family in 1729–30. It has a tall mansard roof and the façade is covered with paintings of herms, atlantes, sphinxes and garlands of fruit. The house now accommodates the **Städtisches Museum** (local history museum), which among other exhibits contains an interesting collection of artisans' tools.

🔒 Stephanskirche

Marktplatz 8. [(08382) 33 44.
Originally a Catholic church, it became a Protestant church in 1528. The original 12th-century Romanesque building was refurbished several times during the 14th, 15th and 16th centuries. Its present-day form – a three-nave, barrel-vaulted basilica – dates from 1781–3, when it was remodelled.

🔒 Stiftskirche

Stiftplatz 1. [(08382) 58 50.
The church originally belonged to the Benedictine monks who settled here in about 800. Vestiges of the pre-Romanesque church, which was built after 948, are preserved in the west wall. In about 1100 a Romanesque basilica with a transept and a west tower was built.

After the fire that devastated the town in 1728, the church was rebuilt to its Romanesque plan. The present airy Baroque church, lavishly decorated with mouldings and wall paintings, resulted from work carried out in 1748–55 under the direction of Johann Caspar Bagnato.

Baroque epitaph in the Haus zum Cavazzen

A lion and a lighthouse framing the harbour entrance against the Alps

VISITORS' CHECKLIST

Road map A5. 🏠 *25,000.*
📧 📞 *(08382) 94 44 16.*
ℹ️ *Ludwigstr. 68, (08382)
26 00 30.*
🌐 *www.Lindau.de; www. lindau-tourismus.de*
@ *tourist-information.lindau@t-online.de*

🚢 The Harbour

The harbour that was built at the southern end of the island in 1811 was modernized in 1856. A marble Lion of Bavaria set on a pedestal 6 m (20 ft) high was added to the tip of the mole at the harbour entrance. A new lighthouse, 33 m (108 ft) high was built on the tip of the opposite mole. These two structures came to symbolize Lindau.

The promenade beside the harbour, where the former lighthouse, known as the **Mangturm**, stands, is popular with tourists. Built in about 1200, the old lighthouse has a projecting upper storey with a pointed steeple covered in 19th-century glazed tiles. It was originally part of the city's fortifications.

🔒 Peterskirche

Oberer Schrannenplatz 5/7.

This is the oldest church in the entire Bodensee region. The presbytery and eastern section date from about 1180. The western part was added in the late 15th century. The five-storey tower that stands near the apse, and that was originally in the Romanesque style, was rebuilt in 1425. The interior walls are decorated with frescoes dating from the 13th to 16th centuries. They include works ascribed to Hans Holbein the Elder. Since 1928 the church has functioned as a memorial to war heroes.

Beside the church stands the **Diebsturm** (Thieves' Tower), a circular watchtower built in 1370–80, which was used in conjunction with the Pulverturm (Powder Tower), Ludwigsbastion and Maximilianschanze (Maximilian's Redoubt).

The Mangturm, formerly a lighthouse and watchtower

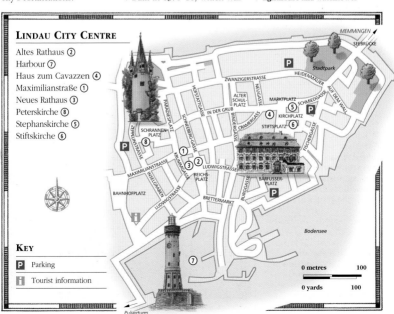

LINDAU CITY CENTRE

Altes Rathaus ②
Harbour ⑦
Haus zum Cavazzen ④
Maximilianstraße ①
Neues Rathaus ③
Peterskirche ⑧
Stephanskirche ⑤
Stiftskirche ⑥

MEMMINGEN
SEEBRÜCKE

Stadtpark

ZWANZIGERSTRASSE
HEIDENMAUER
AUF DEM WALL
HOFSTATTGASSE
NEUGASSE
ALTER SCHUL-PLATZ
MARKTPLATZ
IN DER GRUB
SCHMIEDGASSE
BINDERGASSE
CRAMERGASSE
KIRCHPLATZ
SCHNEEBERGGASSE
PARADIESPLATZ
STIFTSPLATZ
FISCHERGASSE
SCHRANNEN-PLATZ
ZEPPELINSTRASSE
KRUMMGASSE
LUDWIGSTRASSE
MAXIMILIANSTRASSE
INSELGRABEN
REICHS-PLATZ
BURGGASSE
BÄRFÜSSER-PLATZ
BAHNHOFPLATZ
LUDWIGSTRASSE
BRETTERMARKT

Bodensee

KEY

P Parking

ℹ️ Tourist information

0 metres   100

0 yards   100

Pulverturm

Kempten ⑰

Coat of arms on the town hall

ORIGINALLY a Roman town, Kempten was divided into a monastic and a secular district in the Middle Ages. The monastic district was centred around a Benedictine abbey, and in 1712 the monks were granted city rights. The secular district of Burghalde, which grew at the foot of the hill, was a Free City of the Empire from 1289 and accepted the Reformation in 1527. In 1802 the two districts were combined into a single entity and incorporated into Bavaria. Today Kempten is the Allgäu's thriving capital.

The late Gothic façade of St Mang Kirche, with its tall tower

Façade of the town hall, featuring Kempten's coats of arms

🏛 Rathaus
Rathausplatz.
The late Gothic town hall, built in 1474, has a stepped gable crowned by a small tower. The wooden ceilings of the interior date from about 1460 and originally came from the house of the weavers' guild. Before the town hall stands a copy of a Mannerist fountain of 1601.

🏛 Rathausplatz
The square on which the town hall stands is lined with patrician palaces and merchants' and guildsmens' houses, which were either remodelled or newly built in the Baroque and Neo-Classical periods. The three-storey Londonerhof at No. 2 has a Rococo façade lavishly covered with stuccowork and featuring a Neo-Baroque doorway of 1899. The Hotel Fürstenhof at No. 8 was built in about 1600. The Ponickau-haus at Nos. 10 and 12 was

created in 1740 when two 16th-century houses were knocked together, the first floor being converted into a lavishly decorated Festsaal.

🏛 St Mang-Kirche
St.-Mang-Platz 6.
The original church dedicated to St Mang was built in 869. The present church dates from 1426–40, when it was built as the parish church of the Free Imperial City. In 1525 it became a Protestant church, and was remodelled as a three-nave basilica with a tall tower. It was most recently rebuilt in 1767–8, when the vaulting and late Rococo mouldings were added.

🏛 The Residence
Residenzplatz. **Prunkräume der Residenz** 🔲 (0831) 25 62 51.
⬜ Apr–Sep: 9am–4pm Tue–Sun; Oct: 10am–4pm Tue–Sun; Nov–Dec: 10am–4pm. ⬤ Jan–Mar. 🎫
In 1651–74 a group of 11th-century buildings, which were destroyed in 1632, were replaced by a new Baroque monastery. It was also a

residence. The monastery consists of buildings grouped around two courtyards. The elegant apartments on the second floor, which were decorated in 1730–35, echo those of the Residenz in Munich (see pp74–7). The mouldings were executed by stuccoists from Wessobrunn, while the vaulting is by Franz Georg Hermann. The Throne Hall is the one of the finest examples of Bavarian and Swabian Rococo interiors.

🏛 The Orangery
The garden once adjoined the Residence on its southern side. The orangery that was built here in 1780 now houses the municipal library.

🏛 Alpinmuseum and Alpenländische Galerie
Landwehrstr. 2–4. 🔲 (0831) 54 01 80. ⬜ 10am–4pm Tue–Sun. 🎫
The Alpine Museum, housed in the Residence's former stables, is dedicated primarily to skiing and mountaineering. It also encompasses topography and the natural environment, and poetry and

One of the fine apartments in the Residence

painting relating to the mountains. There is also a gallery of regional art.

Lorenzkirche

Landwehrstr. 3.

The church is a three-nave basilica with two pairs of domed side chapels and an octagonal presbytery that is also crowned by a dome. This arrangement created two separate areas: one for the faithful and one for the friars. The interior is breathtaking. The stuccowork in the nave, aisles and presbytery was executed by Johann Zucalli in 1660–70, and the ceilings were painted by Andreas Asper. A comparatively modest twin-towered façade is fronted by a grand staircase. To the east of the presbytery stands the Residence.

The prominent towers and dome of the Lorenzkirche

Kornhaus

Großer Kornhausplatz 1. **Allgäu-Museum** (0831) 54 02 120.
10am–4pm Tue–Sun.

This former grain warehouse was built in 1700. Today it houses a museum dedicated to the history, culture and art of the town and the region.

VISITORS' CHECKLIST

Road map B5.
62,000.
Bahnhofplatz.
Rathausplatz 24, (0831) 25 25 237. www.kempten.de
Allgäuer Festwoche (Aug).

Burghalde

Burgstr.

In 1488 a castle was built on a hill beside the River Iller, where a Roman fort once stood. The castle was incorporated into the town's fortifications and was then demolished in 1705. Part of the town walls, together with the northern tower and its wooden gatehouse of 1883 survive. A romantic walkway runs round the town walls.

Archäologischer Park Cambodunum

Cambodunumweg 3.
(0831) 57 42 50. May–Oct: 10am–5pm Tue–Sun; Nov–Apr: 10am–4:30pm Tue–Sun. Jan–Feb.

Kempten was once the Roman settlement of Cambodunum. Excavations have uncovered a forum, a basilica and baths. The finds from the site are displayed in the Zumsteinhaus, a Neo-Classical building of 1802.

Remains of Roman baths in the settlement of Cambodunum

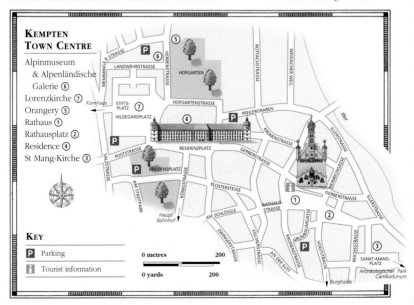

KEMPTEN TOWN CENTRE

Alpinmuseum & Alpenländische Galerie ⑥
Lorenzkirche ⑦
Orangery ⑤
Rathaus ①
Rathausplatz ②
Residence ④
St Mang-Kirche ③

KEY

🅿 Parking

ℹ Tourist information

0 metres 200

0 yards 200

NORTHERN SWABIA

*N*ORTHERN SWABIA *constitutes that part of historical Swabia that now belongs to Bavaria, hence its name – Bayerisches Schwaben (Bavarian Swabia). In terms of its politics and its culture as well as its scenery, it is the most diverse region of southern Bavaria. Its main attractions for tourists are its historic towns, notably Augsburg, the great Ries Basin and its scenic river valleys.*

Throughout the course of history, this region was divided into numerous ducal and monastic possessions and Imperial Cities (Reichsstädte). This served to promote the development of art, which can be seen in the region's castles and palaces and particularly in its churches and monasteries. Until 1806 Swabia formed part of Bavaria, and was subjected to assimilation. However, in this transitional area between the German states of Bavaria and Baden-Württemberg, significant differences in attitude, language and customs survive to this day among Swabians.

The historical need for differentiation, self-definition and individuality has made Swabia a country of small towns each with their own character and history. This is particularly apparent during local festivals.

The scenery is equally diverse and varied. The north consists of the rolling wooded hills of the western Schwäbische Alb massif. Beside them lies the Ries. This area, renowned for its microclimate and its rich soil, has been inhabited since Palaeolithic times.

The Danube cuts through the northern part of Swabian Bavaria. The extensive moors of the Donauried (the Danube valley) bear witness to frequent river flooding in the past. Lying almost parallel from south to north are the great moraine valleys of the Iller, the Günz and the Lech.

Augsburg, almost in the centre of the region and founded in Roman times, was an early centre of the Reformation and of goldsmiths. West of Augsburg is the Westliche Wälder, a vast forest reserve whose unspoiled scenery makes it popular with hikers.

A flower shop in Augsburg, with its displays spilling onto the pavement

◁ Golden Hall of the Town Hall in Augsburg

Exploring Northern Swabia

NORTHERN SWABIA'S principal city is Augsburg. The third-largest city in Bavaria after Munich and Nuremberg, Augsburg demands several days' exploration, as it has much to offer of architectural interest. The city is also a useful starting point for various excursions. Within easy reach to the north are the Ries Basin, a huge crater nestling the town of Nördlingen, and the impressive Harburg Castle, as well as towns on the Danube such as Donauwörth, Dillingen and Günzburg. In the southwest are the castles belonging to the Fugger family. With their varied architecture and scenic settings, all of the region's towns have much to interest visitors.

Christ on a donkey, from the former Augustinian monastery at Wettenhausen

SIGHTS AT A GLANCE

GETTING AROUND

Two motorways run through Swabia. The A8, running along an east–west axis, connects Munich and Stuttgart via Augsburg and Günzburg. The A7 runs in a north–south direction, following the course of the River Iller. Parallel to it is the Romantische Straße (Romantic Route), which passes through towns such as Nördlingen, Harburg, Donauwörth and Augsburg. The good road network makes the other towns of the region easily accessible by car or by bus. The larger cities also have rail links. Situated near to Munich, Augsburg has its own airport.

Harburg Castle in its picturesque location

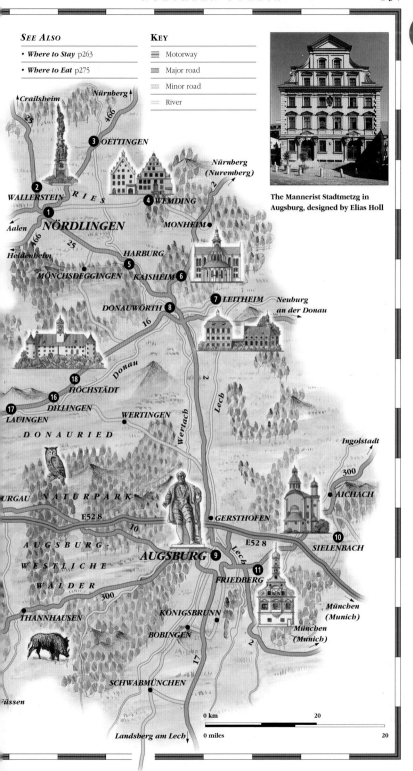

KEY

▬▬	Motorway
▬▬	Major road
▭▭	Minor road
▬▬	River

The Mannerist Stadtmetzg in Augsburg, designed by Elias Holl

Crailsheim

Nürnberg

466

25

3 OÉTTINGEN

Nürnberg (Nuremberg)

2

2

WALLERSTEIN   R I E S

4 WEMDING

1

Aalen   **NÖRDLINGEN**

MONHEIM

466

25

Heidenheim

HARBURG

5

MÖNCHSDEGGINGEN   KAISHEIM **6**

7 LEITHEIM   *Neuburg an der Donau*

DONAUWÖRTH **8**

16

Donau

2

Lech

Ingolstadt

18

HÖCHSTÄDT

16

17   DILLINGEN   *WERTINGEN*

LAUINGEN

D O N A U R I E D

300

Wertach

AICHACH

URGAU   N A T U R P A R K

E52 8

10

A U G S B U R G -

GERSTHOFEN

W E S T L I C H E

E52 8

W Ä L D E R

10

SIELENBACH

300

Lech

AUGSBURG 9

11

FRIEDBERG

THANNHAUSEN

KÖNIGSBRUNN

München (Munich)

BOBINGEN

München (Munich)

2

17

SCHWABMÜNCHEN

0 km   20

üssen

0 miles   20

Landsberg am Lech

Nördlingen ➊

Coat of arms in Baldingerstraße

Nördlingen, encircled by defensive walls, is the "capital" of the Ries Basin and one of the most picturesque towns in Swabia. Several hours can be spent wandering along its streets and alleys, where the Gothic and the Renaissance periods have left their mark. In the 14th century the town almost doubled in size and was surrounded by walls. The streets that run from the five town gates merge on Marktplatz, at the heart of the town. A good time to visit is in July, when the Scharlachrennen, a horse race and parade dating back to the 15th century, is held.

Exploring Nördlingen

The most attractive aspect of Nördlingen is its houses, most of which are half-timbered, with colourful, cascading window boxes. Many of the houses are several storeys high, with attic storerooms. In the Gergerviertel, the tanners' quarter, the houses on the River Eger are well preserved. Two of the town's most interesting houses are that at Paradiesstraße 4, dating from 1350 and the town's oldest half-timbered house, and the 1678 Wintersches Haus at Braugasse 2, the best-preserved private house in Nördlingen.

Bas-relief of a fool on the town hall

🏛 Rathaus
Marktplatz 1.

The town hall was built in the 14th century and rebuilt after 1500, acquiring its present form at the beginning of the 17th century. Its most noteworthy feature is the external stone stairway, built by Wolfgang Waldberger. Beside the doors beneath the stairway is a bas-relief depicting a fool, with the ironic inscription "*Nun sind unser zwey*" ("Now it is the two of us") addressing the reader. The wall of the grand Federal Room on the second floor has a painting of the heroic feats of the biblical Judith by Hans Schäufelein.

⛪ Georgskirche
Am Obstmarkt.

Georgskirche, built in 1427–1505, stands in the centre of the town. Like many other buildings in the region, it was built with suevite from the Ries Basin *(see p240)*. The interior features finely carved late Gothic stalls and a pulpit, a sacrarium of 1522–5 and numerous epitaphs and tombs. The tower, 90 m (295 ft) high, known as the Daniel Tower, can be seen from far away. A flight of 331 stairs leads to the top. The effort of climbing them is rewarded by a panoramic view of the Ries Basin. For 300

Organ loft in the Gothic Georgskirche

years a night watchman has called from the top of the tower, sometimes every half hour. Today this occurs only between 10pm and midnight.

🏛 Tanzhaus
Marktplatz 15.

This Gothic half-timbered hall dating from 1442–4 was built for official dances and receptions. The ground floor contained bakers' shops, which is why the building was also known as the Brothaus (Bread House). On a console on the eastern façade stands a Gothic statue of 1513. Known as *The Last Knight*, it depicts Maximilian I as a knight in armour. Maximilian was a frequent visitor to Nördlingen, which he greatly admired.

The richly decorated Mannerist doorway of the Klösterle

⛪ Klösterle
Beim Klösterle 1.

The monastery church known as the Barfüßerkirche, built in 1422, was converted into a Renaissance-style grain warehouse by Wolfgang Waldberger in 1584–6. The southern façade has a fine doorway dating from 1586, crowned with the town's coat of arms and decorated with figures of tradesmen.

🏛 Hohes Haus
Marktplatz 16.

This tall, nine-storey house, which stands next to the Tanzhaus, is the oldest brick building in Nördlingen. It is mentioned as early as 1304, and for many years it was used as a warehouse.

⛪ Spital

Vordere Gerbergasse 1. **Stadtmuseum** 🗐 *(09081) 27 38 23 10.*
⏲ *1 Mar–4 Nov: 1:30–4:30pm
Tue–Sun.* 🎟 Eugene-Shoemaker-
Platz 1. **Rieskrater-Museum**
🗐 *(09081) 27 38 220.*
⏲ *May–Oct:10am–4:30pm
Tue–Sun; Nov–Apr:
10am–noon & 1:30–4:30pm.* 🎟

The town's former hospital
complex is the largest in
Germany. The buildings of
the Spitalkrankenhaus and
Holzhofstadel that form part
of it are now used as museums.

The **Stadtmuseum**,
founded in 1960, has a
collection of paintings on
panel by late Gothic and
Renaissance artists including
Friedrich Herlin, Hans
Schäufelein and Sebastian
Daig, and a model of the
Battle of Nördlingen of 1634
with 6,000 tin soldiers. The
Rieskrater-Museum features
among its exhibits Moon
rocks donated by NASA.

⛪ Hallgebäude

Weinmarkt 1.
On the south side of the Wine
Market stands a fine building
of 1543 with four attic storeys.
A corner has polygonal oriels,
one of them decorated with a
cartouche containing the civic
coat of arms. The building

**The domed Löpsinger Tor, one
of Nördlingen's five town gates**

was once used for storing
wine and salt, for currency
offices and the town weights.

⛪ Alte Schranne

Schrannenplatz.
This storehouse, built in 1602,
has a total of five storeys,
three of which are in the attic

VISITORS' CHECKLIST

Road map B2 🏘 *21,000.*
🚉 🛈 *Marktplatz 2, (09081)
43 80/84 11 67.*
🌐 *www.noerdlingen.de
verkehrsamt@noerdlingen.de*
🎭 *Stabenfest (second Mon in
May); Scharlachrennen (Jul).*

area. The southern façade
features a sundial and an Art
Nouveau fountain is in the
square before the building.

⛪ Löpsinger Tor
and Town Walls

Stadtmauermuseum 🗐 *(09081)
91 80.* ⏲ *15 Jan–15 Nov: 3–6pm
Tue–Sun.*

The walls encircling Nördlingen were begun in 1327.
The walkway around the
fortifications provides a
variety of views over the
town. The walls are pierced
by five gates, 12 towers and a
bastion. All the gates except
the Baldinger Tor have towers.
They are the Reimlinger Tor,
the oldest and largest gate, on
the road from Augsburg; the
Berger Tor; the Löpsinger
Tor, which houses the
Stadtmauermuseum, whose
domed circular tower dates
from 1593–4, and the taller
and narrower Dieninger Tor.

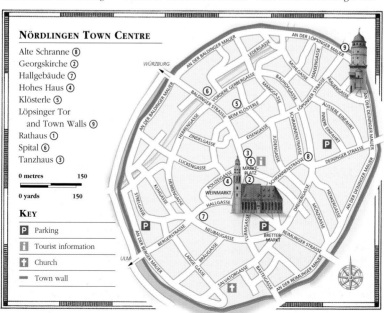

NÖRDLINGEN TOWN CENTRE

Alte Schranne ⑧
Georgskirche ②
Hallgebäude ⑦
Hohes Haus ④
Klösterle ⑤
Löpsinger Tor
and Town Walls ⑨
Rathaus ①
Spital ⑥
Tanzhaus ③

0 metres   150
0 yards   150

KEY

🅿 Parking

🛈 Tourist information

✝ Church

— Town wall

Wallerstein **❷**

Road map B2. 🏘 *3,200.* 🚌 🚉
ℹ️ *Weinstr. 19, (09081) 27 60 18.*

W ALLERSTEIN is a small town at the foot of a hill on which stands a castle that commands a fine view of the Ries Basin. On the hilltop are the remains of 12th-century fortifications, which were destroyed in 1648, as well as a **ducal brewery** and restaurant.

The **Neues Schloss** opposite the castle hill is surrounded by a park and contains a porcelain museum. **Albanskirche** was built in 1612–13 in the Gothic style. The **plague column** that stands nearby, commemorating the Marseilles plague of 1720–21, has figures of saints and is crowned with figures of St Mary and the Holy Trinity.

Plague column in Wallerstein

♣ **Neues Schloss**
Herrenstr. 78. 📞 *(09081) 78 23 00.*
🕐 *1–4pm Tue–Sun; 10am–5pm Fri–Sun.*

Oettingen **❸**

Road map B2. 🏘 *5,200.* 🚌
🚉 ℹ️ *Schlossstr. 36, (09082) 70 951.*
🌐 *www.oettingen.de*

T HIS TOWN, with an oval outline, was surrounded by a wall in the late 13th century. The town gates on the south side – the **Unteres Tor** and the **Königstor**, which was built in the 16th century – still stand.

Schlossstraße, the main street, is lined with half-timbered town houses built between the 15th and 18th centuries. The 15th-century Gothic **town hall** contains the local history museum. Despite their elegance, the **town houses** pale in comparison to **Neues Schloss**, the resplendent Baroque residence of the Dukes of Oettingen-Spielberg, built in 1679–83. To the west the palace looks out over landscaped gardens, which are peopled with statues of dwarfs and a Hercules of 1678 based on the statue on the fountain in Augsburg by Adriaen de Vries.

The palace, whose interior is decorated with stuccowork and mural paintings, is now the **Museum Residenzschloss**. Visitors can see the apartments and reception rooms and admire the collections of 18th-century pewter, porcelain and faience. The palace courtyard is surrounded by outbuildings and has a fountain dating from 1720–28 in the centre.

The **Jakobskirche** which stands nearby was remodelled in the Baroque style after 1680 and decorated with stuccowork by Matthias Schmuzer the Younger. Inside is an interesting pulpit and baptismal font from the last quarter of the 17th century, and numerous tombstones and plaques from the 15th to 18th centuries.

🏛 **Museum Residenzschloss**
Schlossstr. 1. 📞 *(09082) 96 94 24.*
📷 *1 May–Oct: 2pm Tue–Sat, 11am, 2pm, 3pm, 4pm Sun & public holidays; Jul–Sep: also 11am Tue–Sun.*

Wemding **❹**

Road map B2. 🏘 *5,600.* 🚌
🚉 ℹ️ *Marktplatz 3, (09092) 96 90 35.* 🌐 *www.wemding.de*

S ET ON THE rim of the Ries Basin, this charming little town retains its medieval character. The main square, lined with Renaissance and Baroque houses with typically Bavarian decorated gables, has often been used as a location by filmmakers.

Prominent among these houses is the Renaissance **town hall** of 1551–2. On Wallfahrtstraße, near the gate tower, is a typical mid-16th-century house with a corner oriel, now the **Gasthaus zum Weißen Hahn** inn. The tower of **Emmeramskirche** dominates the skyline. The church dates from the 11th

Renaissance tombstone in Jakobskirche, Oettingen

RIES BASIN

This crater, 25 km (15 miles) across, was made when a meteorite hit the Earth 15 million years ago. The impact melted the rocks, creating suevite, or Swabian rock, which the local people used as a building material. NASA carried

Suevite on the edge of the Ries Basin

out scientific studies on the crater and used it for astronauts who were to be sent to the Moon. They later found rock identical to suevite on the Moon. A suevite moon rock donated by NASA can be seen in the Rieskrater-Museum *(see p239).*

century, but its current Baroque form is the result of rebuilding carried out in the 17th century.

It is worth taking a walk along the **defensive walls**, built in the first half of the 16th century and particularly well preserved on the north side of the town.

On the road leading out towards Oettingen the small pilgrimage chapel of **Maria Brünnlein** can be seen in the distance. The interior is decorated with Rococo mouldings and frescoes by Johann Baptist Zimmermann.

The Baroque palace and palace chapel at Leitheim

One of the courtyards in Harburg Castle

Harburg ➎

Road map B2. 👥 5,900. 🚌
🚉 ℹ️ *Schlossstr. 1, (09080) 96 99 24.*

T HE LARGE **castle** was built by the Hohenstaufens before 1150. It was later acquired by the counts of Oettingen, and since 1731 has been in the possession of the Oettingen-Wallerstein family. It is one of the oldest, largest and best-preserved castles in southern Germany.

Dramatically situated on a high rocky hill overlooking the Wörmitz river valley, Harburg castle dominates the entire area. In the 14th and 15th centuries it was surrounded by walls set with towers. It has two entrance gates on the northwestern side, with a picturesque gatehouse dating from 1703. Within the walls stands

Michaelskirche, the castle church. At the bottom of the castle hill nestles the small town of Harburg. It is worth a visit for a walk around the charming and diminutive market square and along the winding streets, which are lined with picturesque old houses.

🏛 Burg Harburg
Burgstr. 1. 📞 *(09080) 96 860.*
⬭ *24 Mar–Oct:10am–5pm Tue–Sun.*

Kaisheim ➏

Road map C2. 👥 4,000. 🚌
🚉 ℹ️ *Münsterplatz 5, (09099) 96 600.*

T HE EXTENSIVE complex of the former Cistercian monastery consists of the 14th-century Gothic **Mariä Himmelfahrtskirche** as well as the monastery itself, which has two cloisters dating from 1716–21. The monastery was converted into a prison in the 19th century. The exquisite Kaisersaal (Imperial Hall), with ornate stuccowork, was completed in about 1720.

Notable features of the church include the Baroque organ loft of 1677, whose carvings are ascribed to Andreas Thamasch. In the nave is a sarcophagus of 1434 with a statue of the founder of the original Romanesque church, who died in 1142, showing him holding a model of the church in his hands.

Crest in the Kaisersaal, Kaisheim

Leitheim ➐

Road map C2. 🚌 🚉 *Donauwörth.*
ℹ️ *Rathausgasse 1, Donauwörth, (0906) 78 91 51.*

S ET HIGH on a bank of the Danube, **Schloss Leitheim** and a **chapel** were built in 1685 to designs by Wölfl as a summer residence for Cistercian monks from the monastery at Kaisheim. For centuries the monks tended vineyards on the sunny slopes around the residence. Indeed, Leitheim was one of the centres of wine-making in the Danube region, and the quality of the wine produced here rivalled that of the Rhine wines.

The chapel was decorated in the late 17th century by artists from Wessobrunn. In the mid-18th century an additional storey and a mansard roof were added to the palace. The fine stucco-work and painting in the state rooms on the second floor are among the finest examples of Bavarian-Swabian Rococo.

After 1835 the palace passed into the hands of the Tucher von Simmeldorf family. The owners organize highly popular chamber concerts here.

⚓ Schloss Leitheim
Schlossstr. 1. 📞 *(09097) 10 16.*
⬭ *May–Sep: by prior arrangement only.*

Donauwörth ❽

Road map C2. 🏛 *18,000.* 🚌
🚉 ℹ️ *Rathausgasse 1, (0906) 78 91
51.* 🅦 *www.donauwoerth.de*
🎭 *Schwäbischwerder Kindertag (first
Sun in Jul), Reichsstraßenfest (Jul,
every two years, the next in 2003),
Donauwörther Kulturtage (Oct).*

DONAUWÖRTH is one of the
largest towns in Swabian
Bavaria. It is located at the
confluence of the Wörnitz
and the Danube, and its
development was shaped
largely by its position at the
point where major trade
routes crossed the Danube.

Reichsstraße, the main
street, is lined with colourful
gabled houses and is one of
the finest streets in southern
Germany. It stretches from **Zu
Unserer Lieben Frau**, the
church built in 1444–67 and
decorated with 15th- and
16th-century frescoes, to the
town hall, remodelled in the
Neo-Gothic style in 1853.

The west end of the town is
dominated by a former Bene-

**The picturesque Reichsstraße
in Donauwörth**

dictine monastery, of which
the **Kreuzkirche**, built by
Josef Schmuzer in 1717–22,
formed a part.

Not to be missed is a walk
along the **town walls**, which
run parallel to an arm of the
Wörnitz. The **Riedertor**, one
of the two town gates, houses
a museum dedicated to the
town's history. Also worth
visiting are the **Heimatmuseum** of local history and
the **Käthe-Kruse-Puppen-
Museum**, with a collection of
dolls made by Käthe Kruse.

🏛 **Käthe-Kruse-Puppen-
Museum**
Pflegstr. 21a. 📞 *(0906) 78 91 85.*
⏰ *Apr and Oct: 2–5pm Tue–Sun;
May–Sep: 11am–5pm Tue–Sun;
Nov–Mar: 2–5pm Wed, Sat–Sun &
public holidays.*
🏛 **Heimatmuseum**
Hindenburgstr. 15. 📞 *(0906) 78 91
85.* ⏰ *May–Sep: 10am–noon
& 2–5pm first Sat in the month,
2–7pm Wed.*

Augsburg ❾

See pp244–9.

Sielenbach ❿

Road map C3. 🏛 *1,500.* 🚌
🚉 *Weissenhorn.* ℹ️ *Schweigstr. 16,
(08258) 91 40.*
🅦 *www.meinestadt.de/Sielenbach*

THE PILGRIMAGE church of
Maria Birnbaum ("Mary
in the Pear Tree") is located
at the southern end of the
town, which it dominates. It

is an exceptional work of
17th-century Bavarian
architecture. It was built in
1661–8 by Konstantin Bader
to a design by Jakob von
Kaltenthal, a Commander of
the Teutonic Knights. It
consists of five circular, semi-
circular and oval rooms. In
particular the towers and
onion domes are unique,
and are reminiscent of an
Eastern church.

The interior, which is lit by
large windows in the shape
of upright ovals and decorated with stuccowork by
Matthias Schmuzer the
Younger, is far more unified.

The object of worship is a
late Gothic Pietà dating from
the early 16th century, to
which miraculous powers are
ascribed. It stands on the high
altar in a pear tree. The tree
and the name of the church
commemorate the miraculous
survival of the figure in 1632,
during the Thirty Years' War
when in the course of the
Swedish invasion the figure
survived thanks to its being
hidden in a pear tree.

**Maria Birnbaum, the Eastern-style
church in Sielenbach**

Friedberg ⓫

Road map C3. 🏛 *29,000.* 🚌
🚉 ℹ️ *Marienplatz 5, (0821) 60 02
125.* 🅦 *www.stadt-friedberg.de*
🎭 *Friedberger Zeit (every three years
in Jul, the next in 2004).*

DURING THE Middle Ages
this town was a fortress,
its purpose being to protect
the region from attacks by the
inhabitants of Augsburg. In
about 1490 defensive walls
set with semicircular towers

ROMANTISCHE STRASSE

**Information signpost at
Neuschwanstein**

The Romantic Route
follows the course of the
Roman Via Claudia.
Beginning in Franconian
Würzburg, it passes
through the towns of
Nördlingen, Donauwörth,
Augsburg, Landsberg,
Schongau, Steingaden and
Füssen, in southern
Bavaria, and ends at
Neuschwanstein, Ludwig
II's famous castle. The
best known and most
frequented of the tourist
routes in Germany, it is
particularly popular with
American and Japanese
tourists. Directions are
even given in Japanese.

The Baroque town hall in Friedberg's main square

were added. The medieval **castle** in the north of the town was destroyed during the Thirty Years' War and re-built in 1652–6. It now houses a local history museum, the **Museum der Stadt Friedberg**.

The streets are lined with outstanding houses dating from the 17th and 18th centuries. In the centre of the main square stands the **town hall**, built in 1680 and decorated in the style of Elias Holl. **Jakobskirche**, which has an unusual design, was built in 1871–3 in imitation of the Romanesque cathedral of St Zeno in Verona.

The finest building in Friedberg is **Herrgottsruh**, a pilgrimage church located in the east of the town. In the Middle Ages it was built as a rotunda resembling the Church of the Holy Sepulchre in Jerusalem. Fragments of the building were uncovered beneath the presbytery of the present church.

The latter, built in 1731–51 by Johann Benedikt Ettl, has a tall tower and imposing domed rotunda. The paintings in the presbytery and the dome are by Cosmas Damian Asam, while those in the nave are by Matthäus Günther. The Rococo mouldings are by Franz Xaver the Elder and Johann Michael Feichtmayr.

The silver antependium of the high altar was made by Johann Georg Herkomer of Augsburg. The altar in the south aisle contains a 15th-century group of figures of the Sorrowing Christ to which miraculous powers are ascribed. Votive images fill the aisles.

🏛 **Museum der Stadt Friedberg im Schloss**
Schlossstr. 21. ☎ *(0821) 60 56 51.*
🕐 *2–4pm Wed, 10am–noon & 2–5pm Sun and public holidays. Other days (except Mon and Feb) by arrangement.*

Roggenburg ⑫

Road map B3. 👥 *2,500.* 🚌
🚉 *Vohringen. Klosterstr. 5.*
☎ *(07300) 96 960.*
ⓦ *www.roggenburg.de*

THE TOWERS of the town's former Premonstratensian monastery can be seen from a distance and rightly suggest that this is an exceptional building. Despite its monumentality, the cavernous interior of **Mariä Himmelfahrtskirche**, which was built in the late 18th century, produces an impression of levity, and it is light even though the windows, which are concealed behind the columns, cannot be seen. The organ loft is one of the finest in Germany. However, the real rarities here are the two

Interior of the church in Roggenburg

reliquaries with painted images of the bodies of St Severinus and St Laurentius, in fine costume of the period. The monastery, built from 1732 to 1766, houses local government offices, although parts are open to the public.

Painting from Oberes Tor, one of Weißenhorn's town gates

Weißenhorn ⑬

Road map A3. 👥 *12,300.* 🚌
🚉 *Vohringen. Kirchplatz 2/4.*
☎ *(07309) 840.*
ⓦ *www.weissenhorn.de*

NEAT, QUAINT and tidy, Weißenhorn is the quintessential small Swabian town. Its historic character is preserved virtually intact. The main thoroughfare is the Hauptstraße, running from a large, irregular square where the church and palace stand, to the **Unteres Tor** (Lower Gate). The 15th-century **Oberes Tor** (Upper Gate), flanked by circular towers, opens on to the square. Adjoining the gate is the former **weighhouse**, dating from the 16th century, and the **Neues Rathaus**, built in the 18th century, which together form a harmonious group.

The **Altes Schloss**, dating from 1460–70, and **Neues Schloss**, built by the Fuggers *(see p249)* in the 16th century, are interconnected. The dominant building in the town is **Mariä Himmelfahrtskirche**, built in 1864–71, one of the finest examples of the revivalist trend in Swabia's religious architecture.

Street-by-Street: Augsburg ❾

Goldsmith statue on the fountain

BAVARIA'S THIRD-LARGEST city, Augsburg has a population of a quarter of a million and is the main university town of Bavarian Swabia. Founded by the Emperor Augustus on the final stretch of the trans-Alpine Via Claudia, it was a bridgehead for Italian culture. It stands at the confluence of the rivers Lech and Wertach, and because of its system of canals it has been called the Venice of the North. Tourists are drawn by the city's history and magic. It is the city of the Protestant Confession of Augsburg and a centre of the goldsmith's art. It is also the birthplace of Bertolt Brecht, Rudolf Diesel and the ancestors of Mozart.

Period houses on Steingasse were destroyed by World War II air raids in 1941, but were rebuilt in the 1960s.

Dom

RATHA
PLAT

PHILIPPINE–WELSER–STR.

Augustusbrunnen
This statue of the Emperor Augustus on the fountain on Rathausplatz is a copy. The original, cast in bronze in 1588, is in the Maximilian-museum.

ANNASTR.

BGM–FISCHER–

★ Annakirche
The chapel of the Fugger family (1509–12) is an architectural jewel. It is the earliest Renaissance building in Germany.

★ Zeughaus
The old arsenal, begun in 1607 by Elias Holl, is widely held to be one of the finest achievements of Mannerist architecture. The building's façade has come to stand as the symbol of Augsburg.

KÖNIGS–
PLATZ

ZEUGGA

★ Maximilianmuseum
The museum is located in one of the city's finest patrician palaces, built in 1543–6. Exhibits include a large collection of artifacts by local goldsmiths.

KEY

– – – Suggested route

The Perlachturm is a tower 70 m (230 ft) on the west front of Peterskirche. Its height was increased through the centuries, and in 1616 Elias Holl added the steeple.

VISITORS' CHECKLIST

Road map C3. 🔢 *265,000.*
✈ *5 km (3 miles) north.*
🚉 🚌 *Bahnhofstraße 7, (0821)
50 20 70.*
Ⓦ *www.regio-augsburg.de*
@ *augsburg@augsburg.de*
🎭 *Frühjahrsplärrer (week after
Easter), Herbstplärrer (Aug/Sep),
Friedensfest (8 Aug),
Mozartsommer (Aug).*

★ **Rathaus**
*Built in 1615–20
by Elias Holl,
Augsburg's town
hall is the finest
secular Mannerist
building in
Europe. The
famous Golden
Hall is on the
second floor.*

Merkurbrunnen
*The sculpture on this
fountain was cast by
Wolfgang Neidhart in
1599 after a model by
Adriaen de Vries. It is
crowned by a statue of
Mercury, god of trade.*

Fuggerhäuser
*The two adjacent palaces
at Maximilianstraße 36
each have elegant, airy
Renaissance courtyards.*

Maximilianstraße
*Augsburg's main street, with its
Mercury fountain by Adriaen
de Vries, is one the finest in
southern Germany.*

MAXIMILIANSTR.

WINTERGASSE

MAXIMILIANSTR.

KLEINES KATHARINENGÄSSCHEN

St Ulrich- und
St Afrakirche

Moritzkirche, a Gothic-Baroque church, was modernized several times over the centuries. Destroyed by bombing in 1944, it was rebuilt in 1946–51.

0 metres 50
0 yards 50

STAR SIGHTS

★ **Annakirche**

★ **Maximilianmuseum**

★ **Rathaus**

★ **Zeughaus**

Exploring Augsburg

Coat of arms on the town hall

AUGSBURG is known for its secular buildings. Although many of them were destroyed by air raids in 1944, they were rebuilt after World War II. The city's appearance was largely defined in the early 17th century by Elias Holl, the architect of many of the buildings here, most notably the Mannerist town hall. The surrounding countryside, with its forests and the Kuhsee, provides the inhabitants with ideal places for weekend outings.

The entrance to the Baroque Residenz am Fronhof

The Gothic Dom St Maria

🔒 Dom St Maria
Frauentorstr. 1.

The cathedral, whose origins go back to the 9th century, retains the twin towers on the west front that were built in 1150, and two Romanesque crypts. It was remodelled in the Gothic style in the 14th and 15th centuries.

Among the cathedral's many notable features is the world's oldest Romanesque stained-glass window, dating from 1140 and depicting figures of the Prophets. Its 11th-century Romanesque bronze doors, with scenes from the Old Testament, are now on display in the Diocesan Museum.

🏛 Residenz am Fronhof
Fronhof 10.

The former bishop's residence was given its present appearance in 1740–52. Since 1817 it has housed the government offices of Bavarian Swabia.

It was in the ornate Festsaal in the west wing that the Emperor Karl V received the historic Confession of Augsburg in 1530. The park

adjoining the residence contains a fountain and 18th-century gnomes.

🏛 Stadtmetzg
Metzgplatz 1.

This Mannerist building was built by Elias Holl in 1606–09 for the butchers' guild. A technological innovation of the time was routing one of the town's canals beneath the cellars of the Stadtmetzg so that they would be kept cool for the effective storage of perishable food.

🏛 Fountains

Augsburg is renowned for its beautiful fountains, of which there are ten. The most famous are the Mannerist Augustus, Mercury and Hercules fountains, made in the late 16th century to mark the city's 1,600th anniversary. The two latter, located on Maximilianstraße, were designed

by Adriaen de Vries (although they are copies, the originals now being in the Maximilianmuseum). Also noteworthy are the Neptunbrunnen of 1536, the Georgsbrunnen of 1563–5, and the Art Nouveau Goldschmiedebrunnen of 1913.

♣ Schaezlerpalais
Maximilianstr. 46. **Staatsgalerie**
☎ (0821) 32 44 102.
◯ 10am–5pm Wed–Sun. 🖼

The palace, the finest Rococo building in Augsburg, was built in 1765–70. The famous Festsaal features fine stuccowork, paintings, carvings, chandeliers and candelabras.

The palace's two art galleries – the Altdeutsche Galerie and the Deutsche Barockgalerie – contain works by such masters as Dürer, Hans Holbein the Elder, van Dyck and Tiepolo.

TOWN HALL

This, Europe's largest and finest Mannerist town hall, was built by Elias Holl in 1615–20. The building's showpiece is the Golden Hall. Its exquisite ornate ceiling is attached to the roof beams by means of 27 chains.

Destroyed during air raids in 1944, the town hall was meticulously restored, and the ceiling of the Golden Hall was reconstructed in 1985 to commemmorate the 2,000th anniversary of the foundation of the city in 15 BC.

Onion-domed flanking towers

Gable with painted coat of arms

Windows of the Golden Hall on the second floor

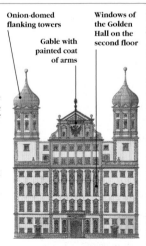

♣ Fuggerhäuser
Maximilianstr. 36/38.

These two neighbouring early 16th-century Renaissance palaces of the Fugger family were rebuilt after being destroyed in 1944. The splendour of the original buildings with their inner courtyards can be seen in the arcaded marble Damenhof. The palace was inhabited by the family of Jakob II der Reiche Fugger and his descendant Anton.

🏛 Zeughaus
Zeugplatz 6.

The arsenal, Elias Holl's first project and also one of his finest works, was built in 1602–07. The façade is decorated with a bronze sculpture by Hans Reichle depicting St Michael overcoming Satan.

🏛 Annakirche
Im Annahof 2.

The former Carmelite church of St Anne, now Protestant, was built in the 14th century, at the same time as the monastery. It was rebuilt in the 16th century and the tower, designed by Elias Holl, was added in 1602. In the mid-18th century the interior was remodelled in the Rococo style. It contains one of the earliest organ lofts in Europe, dating from 1512.

An exceptional example of Renaissance art is the burial chapel of the Fuggers (1509–12), with epitaphs by Albrecht Dürer, a sculpted *Lamentation* by Hans Daucher, and figures of putti on the balustrade.

🏛 Römisches Museum
Dominikanergasse 15.
📞 (0821) 32 44 131. ⏱ 10am–5pm Tue–Sun.

The Roman Museum is housed in the former Dominican monastery, built in 1513–15. The two-naved hall, which is divided by a row of columns, was rebuilt in the Baroque style in 1716–24. The ceiling, which dates from that time, is decorated with religious stuccowork and paintings. The museum has interesting exhibits from

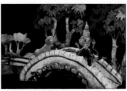
the Roman and as well as the early Medieval periods, including a gilded horse's head that once formed part of a Roman equestrian statue.

🏛 St Ulrich- und St Afrakirche
Ulrichplatz 23.

This late Gothic triple-nave basilica is the most recent in a succession of churches built for the Benedictine monastery that has stood here since about 1000, but that was dissolved in the early 19th century. Work on the basilica began in 1474 and continued for almost 140 years. Although two towers were planned, only the northern one was built, in 1594. Rising a height of 93 m (305 ft) high, it is visible from a great distance.

Putto in the burial chapel in Annakirche

The Mannerist furnishings were added in 1604–08. The exquisitely designed and crafted altar, pulpit, organ loft and stalls harmonize well with the late Gothic architecture of the interior. The nave and aisles are separated by a delicate grille of 1712.

🏛 Rotes Tor and City Walls

The Rotes Tor (Red Gate) was built by Elias Holl in 1622, replacing the medieval gate. Leading in from the road that followed the old Roman Via Claudia, it was the main gate into the city. The Rotes Tor, together with the Wallanlage and the Heilig-Geist-Spital, are the finest group of buildings designed by Elias Holl.

Large sections of the city walls still stand to the north and east, as do the walls surrounding the Jakobervorstadt, with two bastions of about 1540, and the Gothic Jakobertor. There is a landing stage for canoes at the tower of the Oblatterwall bastion.

✡ Synagogue
Halderstr. 8. **Jüdisches Kulturmuseum** 📞 (0821) 51 36 58. ⏱ 9am–4pm Tue–Fri , 10am–5pm Sun. ♿

Built in 1914–17, the synagogue is one of the finest to be built in Europe at the time. The exquisite interior is crowned by a tall dome decorated in the Byzantine style. The Jüdisches Kulturmuseum (Jewish Culture Museum) is laid out in one of the wings of the synagogue.

Baroque grille, St Ulrich- und St Afrakirche

The Fuggerei of Augsburg

Bell-pull on a house

AMONG Augsburg's main tourist attractions is one of the world's oldest public housing projects. It was established by Jakob II Fugger, "the Rich", together with the friars, for the people of Augsburg who had fallen on hard times. Built by Thomas Krebs in 1514–23, it was called the Fuggerei in honour of its founder. Situated east of Rathausplatz, in the Jakobervorstadt, this walled "town within a town" has retained its medieval atmosphere. This can best be savoured outside the tourist season, when it is less crowded. The Fuggerei is entered through gates that bear the original dedication, the date 1519 and the Fuggers' armorials.

VISITORS' CHECKLIST

The settlement is located east of Maximilianstr. ⏰ 5am–10pm.
No vehicular access.
Fuggereimuseum, Mittlere Gasse 13. 📞 (0821) 31 98 810.
🌐 *www.fugger.de*
⏰ Mar–Dec: 9am–6pm daily. 🎫

★ Fuggereimuseum
At Mittlere Gasse 13 visitors can see an apartment (a bedroom and a kitchen) furnished in the style of the period.

★ Markuskirche
The church was built in 1581 by Johannes Holl, father of the renowned Elias Holl. Destroyed in 1944, it was subsequently rebuilt.

| 0 metres | 20 |
| 0 yards | 20 |

Fountain
At the point where Herrengasse and Mittlere Gasse meet, forming a small square, stands a modest fountain. The focal point of the Fuggerei, it is also the favourite meeting place both of the local residents and of tourists.

STAR SIGHTS

★ **Fuggereimuseum**

★ **Markuskirche**

KEY

— — — Suggested route

Gardens at the rear of the houses in the Fuggerei

Exploring the Fuggerei

The estate originally comprised 53 buildings designed to house 106 families. Partly forming a continuous, symmetrical ensemble, they stand on an uneven plot of land and are surrounded by a wall with five gates.

The houses have modest façades and steep roofs with stepped gables. Each front door still has its bell-pull and iron handle, and the exterior walls still have sandstone plaques with the old house numbers inscribed on them.

The Fuggerei was badly damaged by the air raids of 1944. During the painstaking process of reconstruction, which was carried out in 1947–55 and was financed by the Fugger estate, 14 additional houses were built.

Today about 200 people live in the Fuggerei. All the houses have been modernized and have electricity, heating and other modern conveniences. The estate of the Fugger family decides who can live in the Fuggerei. Originally housing families with children, it has recently been designated for needy people, who must be Catholic and must have lived in Augsburg for at least two

years. Residents pay a nominal annual rent equal to 1 Rhenish guilder (€86), in return for which they undertake to say a daily prayer for the founders. There is also supplement of €45 per month to finance communal services.

Herrengasse, the main street in the Fuggerei

An interesting feature of the Fuggerei is the fine late Gothic oriel of 1504–07 on the corner of the Seigniory House by the gate on Jakoberstraße. It was transferred from the bombed ruins of a house belonging to the Höchstetter family, contemporaries of the Fuggers. The **Seigniory House**, which was rebuilt after 1954, contains on its ground floor a Gothic chapel that was transferred here in 1962 from the ruined house of the Welsers.

Markuskirche, in Herrengasse, is decorated with a tall shaped gable and has an Angelus bell. It is furnished with items from various other churches. A *Crucifixion* by Jacopo Palma the Younger of about 1600 can be seen on the Mannerist high altar. Ulrich Fugger's epitaph, depicting the deceased wrapped in a shroud, was designed by Albrecht Dürer and made by Adolf Daucher in 1512–15.

The resident of the house at Mittlere Gasse 14 was Franz Mozart, great-grandfather of the composer Wolfgang Amadeus. He made himself unpopular with his clients by carrying out burials for the executioner, which was considered to be a disgraceful deed. As a result he lost business and became so impoverished that he had to go and live in the Fuggerei.

Memorial plaque to Franz Mozart, one-time resident of the Fuggerei

THE FUGGERS

The career of the Fuggers began in 1367, when Hans Fugger, a native of Graben, came to Augsburg. Jakob I (who died in 1459) founded the family of merchants and bankers that still exists today. His sons Ulrich, Georg and particularly Jakob II, "the Rich", acquired unheard-of wealth, ensuring a life of opulence for the entire family. Jakob II was banker to emperors, kings and popes. He funded the election of Karl V as German Emperor. He was also known as a patron of the arts, and thanks partly to him Renaissance art took root in Germany. He also founded social institutions. Once the owners of 100 villages, the Fuggers still own several castles in Bavaria.

Monument to Hans Jakob Fugger, Augsburg

The Imperial Hall of the former Augustine monastery in Wettenhausen

Wettenhausen ⑭

Road map B3. 🚌 🚉 *Günzburg.*
Abbey *Kammeltal, Dossenberger-
str. 55.* 📞 *(08223) 40 040.*

STANDING LIKE a fortress, the old Augustinian monastery in Wettenhausen dominates the surrounding landscape. **Mariä Himmelfahrtskirche**, originally a Romanesque church, was rebuilt in the late Gothic style in the early 16th century and remodelled in the Baroque style in 1670. The frescoes, of about 1685, and the highly decorative altars and pulpit, dating from the same period, create a unified interior. The altar in the south chapel features a fine late Gothic Coronation of the Virgin carved in 1524.

Part of the **abbey**, including the Imperial Hall and the cloistered courtyard, are open to the public. The rooms in the cloister are visible through a decorative wrought-iron grille. One of them contains a figure of Christ seated on a donkey made in 1456, probably in the workshop of Hans Multscher of Ulm.

Günzburg ⑮

Road map B3. 🚶 *20,000.* 🚌
🚉 ℹ️ *Jahnstraße 2, (08221)*
36 630. 🌐 *www.guenzburg.de*

THE ORIGINS of this sizeable town at the confluence of the rivers Günz and Danube go back to Roman times. Much of it has been pedestrianized, and it invites leisurely strolls through its

attractive streets. **Münzgasse**, lined with 17th- and 18th-century houses with projecting upper storeys, is especially picturesque.

The main square, closed off by the 14th-century **Unteres Tor** (Lower Gate), is surrounded by Baroque houses with typically Swabian gables. These houses recall the days when the town was at its height. Notable is **Brentanohaus** at No. 8, built in 1747 with a tiled mansard roof and Rococo mouldings on its elegant façade.

Beside the old Franciscan monastery stands the **Frauenkirche**, built in 1736–41 by Dominikus Zimmermann. Substantial fragments of the 15th-century town walls, defensive towers and gateways survive.

Houses in Münzgasse, one of Günzburg's picturesque streets

Dillingen ⑯

Road map B3. 🚶 *18,000.* 🚌
🚉 ℹ️ *Königstr. 37, (09071)*
54 108, 54 109. 🌐 *www.dillingen-donau.de*

FOR CENTURIES Dillingen, the spiritual capital of Swabia and a town dubbed the "Rome of Swabia", was the seat of the bishops of Augsburg and a major university town. The main street, Königstraße, lined with patrician town houses, defines the town's character. Königstraße leads into Kardinal von Waldburgstraße, on which the elongated Baroque façade of the **Jesuit University** rises. It was built in 1688–9 to a design by Michael Thumb and visitors can admire the Rococo Golden Hall within. The former **college** beside the university has a fine Baroque library, which occupies two floors and has furnishings carved by Georg Bschorer.

Lion outside the castle in Dillingen

The highlight of the town is the formerly Jesuit **Mariä Himmelfahrtskirche**, built in the early 17th century by Johann Alberthal. The early Baroque architecture of the building and its Rococo stuccowork, painting and furnishings combine to produce a splendid ensemble. The high altar still has its *Theatrum Sacrum*, where the tradition of performing Passion plays at Easter was recently revived.

The early Rococo **Franciscan monastery** and **church** were designed by Johann Georg Fischer. The stately 13th-century **castle**, which before the secularization of the state was the seat of the capital and of the bishops of Augsburg, has preserved its defensive character despite rebuilding on numerous occasions over the centuries. Fragments of the town walls, set with towers and pierced by the **Mittleres Tor** (Middle Gate), can still be seen today.

Roman ruins in Faimingen, a suburb of Lauingen

Lauingen ⑰

Road map B3. 🏛 *10,500.* 🚌
🚉 🅸 *Herzog-Georg-Str. 17, (09072) 99 81 13.*
ⓦ *www.lauingen.de*

Sᴇᴛ ᴏɴ a high bank over-looking the Danube, this town has largely preserved its medieval character. It has an oval outline and was once surrounded by walls, the surviving parts of which are a **gate** and two bastions.

The slender outlines of two tall towers that dominate the town can be seen from a distance. The more distinctive of the two is the former watchtower that stands in the main square. Exceptionally tall and narrow, it was built in 1457–78 together with the adjacent arcades containing market stalls, and was extended in 1571. It is known as the **Schimmelturm** (Grey Mare Tower) because of the image of the horse near the bottom, which has been renewed and repainted several times.

The **town hall**, built in 1783–91 to a Neo-Classical design by Lorenz J Quaglio, was erected on the orders of the Elector Karl Theodor despite strong opposition from the townspeople.

Martinskirche, the parish church built in 1516, is one of the last Gothic hall-churches to have been built in southern Germany. Its triple-nave interior with web vaulting is unparalleled in height and the walls and ceilings are decorated with frescoes painted in 1521.

Among the many tombs and epitaphs is a fine cenotaph that is the symbolic tomb of Elisabeth, wife of the Palatine, who died in 1563.

The tomb is surrounded by a wrought-iron grille and on it lies a white marble figure of the deceased supported by four lions. The tall free-standing **belfry** is, with the Schimmelturm, a defining feature of the town's skyline.

Eɴᴠɪʀᴏɴꜱ: In the suburb of Faimingen, on the road to Günzburg, the remains of Roman buildings can be seen. The partially reconstructed **Temple of Apollo Grannus**, the Roman deity who also came to be worshipped by the Celts, bears witness to Lauingen's long history.

The Schimmelturm, the tallest tower in Lauingen

Höchstädt ⑱

Road map B3. 🏛 *6,800.* 🚌
🚉 🅸 *Herzog Philipp-Ludwig-Str. 10, (09074) 44 12.*
ⓦ *www.hoechstaedt.de*

Tʜɪꜱ ʟɪᴛᴛʟᴇ town on the banks of the Danube is flanked by its church and its castle. On the west side are the church and the town hall, on a square located between two streets that lead to the castle.

The late Gothic **Mariä Himmelfahrtskirche**, which was completed in about 1520, is decorated with frescoes in the same style, painted in 1520–30 and also with Mannerist frescoes in a contrastingly florid style dating from about 1600.

The town's finest historic building is the turret-shaped Gothic sacristy, built in attractive sandstone in 1480–90. The Baroque altar was added in 1695.

The polygonal **chapel** beside the church was built in 1664. It features a deep niche containing a Pietà dating from the first quarter of the 18th century. Above the statue is a theatrical scene depicting Christ and the Apostles on the Mount of Olives. The scene, consisting of figures set against a painted background, was created by Johann Michael Fischer in 1760.

The **Heimatmuseum** has numerous collections of objects relating to local history, including a display of 9,000 tin soldiers re-creating the Battle of Höchstädt that took place in 1760.

On a hill overlooking the town stands the Renaissance **castle**, built in about 1589 to replace the medieval seat of Duke Philip Ludwig, the Palatine of Neuburg. Well restored, it is now used as the museum's headquarters. The castle complex has an almost square plan with a central courtyard, four circular corner towers and a chapel in the west wing. The main entrance is a doorway flanked by pairs of columns, with coats of arms in the tympanum and a barrel-vaulted archway with coffered ceiling.

🏛 **Heimatmuseum**
Marktplatz 7. 🅲 *(09074) 49 56.*
⭕ *10am–noon first Sun in the month and by arrangement.*

The doorway of the castle in Höchstädt

TRAVELLERS' NEEDS

WHERE TO STAY 254-263

WHERE TO EAT 264-277

SHOPS AND MARKETS 278-281

WHERE TO STAY

MUNICH AND THE Bavarian Alps are the most popular tourist destinations in Germany. The region offers a wide variety of hotels with different levels of service. Finding somewhere to stay, either in Munich itself or throughout the Bavarian Alps, presents no problem, whatever price and standard of accommodation are required. As well as luxury hotels, which are often converted

Logo of Munich's Eden-Wolff hotel

stately palaces or romantic castles, and international chains such as Marriott, Hilton or Sheraton, travellers in the Bavarian Alps have a choice of many small hotels and guesthouses. Accommodation, particularly in Munich, is harder to find during the Oktoberfest and when trade fairs take place in the city, and during festivals and public holidays, when tourist resorts become more crowded.

The Kempinski Hotel Vier Jahreszeiten in Munich *(see p258)*

FINDING ACCOMMODATION

IN TOWNS AND CITIES hotels are usually located in or near the historic centre or near tourist attractions. When choosing somewhere to stay it is advisable to ensure that it is not on or near a noisy street, or near a night-spot or a church, as the ringing of church bells can awaken the deepest sleeper.

If you decide on a hotel in central Munich, you may need to enquire about parking facilities. Organizations such as the **Bayerischer Tourismusverband** can be a great help here. If you choose a hotel further away from the centre, make sure that it is near public transport links. Most hotels, including de luxe hotels, are located on the periphery of the Old Town and in Schwabing. There are also hotels around Munich's

main railway station, although these are not of the highest standard. Hotels belonging to major groups such as Marriott and Sheraton can be found near main highways.

THE RANGE OF HOTELS

MANY HOTELS are marked with stars indicating the quality (and therefore the cost) of the accommodation

and services that they provide. Top-class hotels usually have their own high-quality restaurants, as well as banqueting suites, swimming pool, gyms, saunas and laundry facilities. Those outside cities may also have tennis courts and golf links.

There is also a network of more modern bed-and-breakfast hotels that offer fewer supplementary services. On motorways and major roads, you can find motels or *Rasthäuser*, which are basically restaurants with single-night accommodation.

In tourist towns a common type of accommodation is *Halbpension* (half-board lodgings), where a hot meal is offered in addition to breakfast, or *Vollpension*, (lodging with full board).

All hotels and other types of accommodation are extremely clean. Toilet and bathroom facilities, even when shared, are of a high standard. Regardless of the category of the establishment, guests are often offered many extras.

Guests checking into a small hotel

The bar in the Königshof hotel in Munich *(see p260)*

HOTEL PRICES

HOTEL PRICES vary greatly. A single room can range from €40–75 in a tourist-class hotel to €150 in a top-class hotel, and up to €360 in a luxury establishment. Prices in Munich are naturally higher than those elsewhere, and at their highest during the Oktoberfest.

At holiday and spa resorts a three-tier price system operates – high season, mid-season and low season. Prices at high season can be double those of low season.

Many hotels offer reductions at weekends and even if you turn up without having made a reservation, you may be able to negotiate a discount. If you are planning a longer stay, you may also be able to negotiate a discount, especially at times of year when business is slack.

HOW TO BOOK

HOTEL ACCOMMODATION can be booked direct by telephone, letter or fax, as well as by e-mail or through the Internet. Travellers already in Bavaria can obtain brochures and lists of addresses at tourist offices and health resort offices *(Kurverwaltung)*.

When making a reservation, you will need to confirm the method of payment. An advance payment or credit card details will sometimes be requested. Those who make their reservation well in advance will usually receive written confirmation, often with a bank deposit form attached for the advance payment. Some hotels offer insurance against cancellation due to unforeseen circumstances.

On arrival guests are asked to complete a registration form and may be requested to show their passport. Full payment is made when checking out and, especially in the case of small provincial hotels, it is always worth making sure in advance that cards or travellers' cheques are accepted. In health spas an additional charge known as a *Kurtaxe* is payable. In top-class and luxury hotels,

The ornate courtyard of the Opera garni hotel in Munich *(see p259)*

tips are expected for additional services. It is also customary, even in more modest hotels, to leave a few Euros for the chambermaid.

DISABLED TRAVELLERS

AN INCREASING number of hotels and youth hostels cater for disabled travellers. Most have ramp access and a few rooms with bathrooms and toilets adapted for use by disabled people. Facilities are, however, likely to be better in hotels of a higher standard than in budget hotels.

Handicapped-Reisen Deutschland is a guide that lists hotels in Germany with facilities for disabled people. Information can also be obtained from BAGH and CBF *(see p257)*.

Tables on the terrace restaurant at the Parkhotel in Donauwörth

TRAVELLING WITH CHILDREN

TRAVELLING WITH children in the Bavarian Alps should not present any problems. Most hotels will provide an additional bed or cot, often at no extra charge. Many hotels have children's corners – play areas equipped with children's furniture as well as games and toys – and some of the better hotels have babysitting facilities. If a child is sick, the hotel's reception will call a paediatrician.

Standard equipment in every restaurant includes a high chair for toddlers, while menus almost always include the option of smaller portions for children.

Tourist resorts offer special programmes of supervised activities for children.

Alpenrose guesthouse, Alpsee *(see p227)*

ROOMS IN PRIVATE HOUSES

BED-AND-BREAKFAST accommodation is not widespread in cities. However, in popular tourist areas and most smaller towns, you will often come across houses with a sign saying *"Zimmer"* (rooms). The sign will be accompanied by another saying either *"frei"* (vacancies) or *"belegt"* (no vacancies).

Prices for such rooms are relatively low – from €10 per person. Other benefits are a homely atmosphere and a lavish breakfast. Toilets and bathrooms are usually shared, but the rooms have washbasins and telephones.

HOLIDAY APARTMENTS

FOR VISITORS spending their holiday in one particular place, holiday apartments *(Ferienwohnung)* are the best and cheapest type of accommodation. They are available in all holiday resorts, and brochures can be obtained at tourist information centres.

The size, standard and price of the apartments vary. Most have a kitchen, plus a television, vacuum cleaner, iron, bookshelves and cupboard with glasses and tablecloths.

Holiday apartments are found mainly in private houses and apartment blocks, and in some larger hotels. They are rented for at least a week. The tenant is responsible for cleaning, and pays an additional charge for final cleaning *(Endreinigung)*.

AGROTOURISM

STAYING ON a farm *(Bauernhof)* is a popular and inexpensive way of spending a holiday. It is particularly suitable for families with children. Rooms in large farmhouses or separate apartments are provided, and they range in standard from modest to luxurious.

Guests have the opportunity to help with the daily work on the farm, and children can feed the animals. Another advantage is the delicious food, with fresh dairy products, that is served to guests staying on the farm.

Another type of holiday is a riding holiday. Guests stay on horse or pony farms *(Reiterhöfe* and *Ponyhöfe)*, and go horse-riding or pony-trekking.

YOUTH HOSTELS

ALMOST EVERY sizeable town in Bavaria has a youth hostel *(Jugendherberge)*. Youth hostels are divided into four categories according to their location and the standard of accommodation they offer. Many are relatively comfortable, although there is always the possibility that the only beds available will be in a dormitory. Toilets and bathrooms are usually communal. Almost all youth hostels have dining rooms

Logo of the German Youth Hostel Association

where breakfast and hot meals are served. Many hostels have their own sports facilities. The cost of accommodation is about €12 per night. In popular tourist resorts early booking is recommended. Information can be obtained from the **Landesverband Bayern des DJH**.

Bavarian youth hostels are open to members of the IYHF, people up to the age of 26 and families with children who have family membership. The age limit does not apply to people in charge of youth groups. Besides youth hostels, young tourists in Germany can also use student hotels and unaffiliated shelters.

MOUNTAIN SHELTERS

MOUNTAIN SHELTERS offering food, rest and sometimes accommodation to skiers and hikers are to be found in many places in the Bavarian Alps. The German Alpine Association (**Deutscher Alpenverein**) alone has some 100 shelters. Members may use them at a discount and have priority in renting accommodation. As well as individual rooms, the shelters also have bunk beds in communal rooms.

Shelters are usually open during the summer months, from May to October or from June to September. Shelters near skiing pistes and along the most popular hiking trails are also open in winter.

A mountain shelter for hikers and skiers near Zugspitze

CAMPING

SOUTHERN BAVARIA'S many camp sites are usually situated in picturesque locations and are ideal for peaceful holidays. Although they vary in size and standard, most have good toilet and washing facilities, and may also have a shop and a café. Many also offer cultural programmes.

Most camp sites are open from April to October, although some are also suitable for use in winter.

GASTHÖFE

FOR TRAVELLERS looking for unpretentious accommodation, the roadside inns known as *Gasthöfe* that are found throughout Bavaria are an attractive and convenient option. The sign *"Gasthof"* will probably be accompanied by another saying *"Zimmer"* (rooms).

Prices are very affordable – usually between €20 and €35 for a double room.

A well-kept *Gasthof*, one of the many roadside inns in Bavaria

Drinking beer and eating simple homemade fare is one of the greatest pleasures of staying in a *Gasthof.*

SPA RESORTS

THE BRACING mountain air, as well as the many mineral springs and curative mud found in the region of the Bavarian Alps, have led to the growth of large numbers of spa resorts. Most can be identified by the word *"Bad"* (bath) before the name of the town.

In these resorts, a spa tax *(Kurtaxe)* is added to the charge of the room. This small additional charge also gives a reduction on the entry charge to many cultural and sporting events, and various kinds of therapy on offer.

Bavarian spas specialize mostly in respiratory and circulatory disorders and rheumatic ailments. Visitors to the spas have at their disposal excellent rest and recuperation facilities, with doctors and convalescence specialists to monitor their health.

DIRECTORY

INFORMATION ON ACCOMMODATION & RESERVATIONS

Bayern Tourismus Marketing Gmbh
Leopoldstr. 146, Munich.
📞 *(089) 21 23 97 30.*

Fremdenverkehrs-amt München
Neues Rathaus, Marienplatz.
📞 *(089) 23 30 300.*
FAX *(089) 23 33 02 33.*
⏰ *10am–8pm Mon–Fri, 10am–4pm Sat.* Hauptbahnhof, Bahnhofplatz 2.
⏰ *9am–8pm Mon–Sat, 10am–6pm Sun.*
W *www.muenchen-tourist.de*

BED & BREAKFAST

Bed & Breakfast Mitwohnzentrale
Schulstr. 31, Munich.
📞 *(089) 16 88 781.*
FAX *(089) 16 88 791.*

City Mitwohnzentrale
Lämmerstr. 4, Munich.
📞 *(089) 19 430.*
FAX *(089) 59 45 64.*

AGROTOURISM

"Urlaub auf dem Bauernhof"
Kaiser-Ludwig-Platz 2, Munich.
📞 *(089) 53 43 12.*
W *www.bauernhof-urlaub.com*

YOUTH HOSTELS

DJH-Gästehaus
Miesingstr. 4, Munich.
📞 *(089) 72 36 550/560.*
FAX *(089) 72 42 567.*

DJH München
Wendl-Dietrich-Str. 20, Munich.
📞 *(089) 13 11 56.*
FAX *(089) 16 78 745.*

Haus International
Elisabethstr. 87, Munich.
Map 1 A1.
📞 *(089) 12 00 60.*
FAX *(089) 12 00 62 51.*

Landesverband Bayern des DJH
Mauerkircherstr. 5, Munich.
📞 *(089) 92 20 980.*
W *www.djh.de*

MOUNTAIN SHELTERS

Deutscher Alpenverein (DAV)
Von-Kahr-Str. 2–4, Munich.
📞 *(089) 14 00 30.*

CAMPING SITES

ADAC- Camping-Referat
Am Westpark 8, Munich.
📞 *(089) 76 760.*

Deutscher Camping Club
Mandlstr. 28, Munich.
Map 2 F2.
📞 *(089) 38 01 420.*

Langwieder See
Eschenrieder Str. 119, Munich.
📞 *(089) 86 41 566.*

München-Obermenzing
Lochhausener Str. 59.
📞 *(089) 81 12 235.*

München-Tahlkirchen
Zentralländstraße 49
📞 *(089) 72 31 707.*

DISABLED TRAVELLERS

Bundesarbeits gemenschaft Hilfe für Behinderte (BAGH)
Kirchfeldstr. 149, Düsseldorf.
📞 *(0211) 31 00 60.*

Club Behinderter und ihrer Freunde (CBF)
Eupener Str. 5, Mainz.
📞 *(06131) 22 55 14.*
Knorrstr. 25, Munich.
📞 *(089) 35 68 808.*

Choosing a Hotel

THE HOTELS IN THIS GUIDE have been chosen on the basis of good value, attractive location and amenities offered. Entries are listed by price category within each town or region, with colour-coded thumb tabs to indicate the area covered on each page. Map references in Munich refer to pages 140–149; outside Munich they refer to the inside back cover.

	NUMBER OF ROOMS	PARKING OR GARAGE	SWIMMING POOL	RESTAURANT	GARDEN OR TERRACE

MUNICH

OLD TOWN (SOUTH): *Schlicker* €€
Tal 8, D-80 331. **Map** 3 C2 (6 D4). (*(089) 24 28 870.* FAX *(089) 29 60 59.*
@ Schlicker-munich@t-online.de
Located in a convenient part of the city, just beside Marienplatz, in a historic building that also houses the Churrasco restaurant. 1 🛏 🔃 🌿

	72	●			

OLD TOWN (SOUTH): *Daniel garni* €€
Sonnenstr. 5, D-80 331. **Map** 3 A2 (5 A3). (*(089) 54 82 40.* FAX *(089) 55 34 20.*
@ info@Hotel-Daniel.de
Recommended for families with children, who are well catered for here. Sonnenstraße is a busy shopping street. 1 🛏 🔃 🌿 🐟 🕴 🝙 🌿

	77				

OLD TOWN (SOUTH): *Deutsche Eiche* €€
Reichenbachstr. 13, D-80 469. **Map** 3 C3 (6 D5). (*(089) 23 11 660.*
FAX *(089) 23 11 66 93.* @ info@deutsche-eiche.com
Located beside the Viktualienmarkt. Rooms are furnished in a modern and functional style. The breakfast buffet is in the winter garden.
1 🛏 🔃 🌿

	46	●		●	■

OLD TOWN (SOUTH): *Torbräu* €€€€
Im Tal 41, D-80 331. **Map** 3 C3 (6 E4). (*(089) 24 23 40.* FAX *(089) 23 23 42 34.*
@ info@torbraeu.de
A luxury hotel in the heart of Munich, with origins going back to the 15th century. The rooms have comfortable modern furnishings. The hotel restaurant offers Italian cuisine. 1 🛏 🔃 🌿 🐟 🌿

	86	●		●	■

OLD TOWN (NORTH) : *Concorde* €€€
Herrnstr. 38–40, D-80 539. **Map** 3 C3 (6 E3).
(*(089) 22 45 15.* FAX *(089) 22 83 282.*
Located in a quiet side street right beside the most attractive part of the city. The hotel, near foreign consulates, is frequented by diplomats. The rooms have modern furnishings. 1 🛏 🔃 🐟 🌿

	71	●		●	■

OLD TOWN (NORTH): *Platzl Hotel* €€€€
Sparkassenstr. 10, D-80 331. **Map** 3 C2 (6 E3). (*(089) 23 70 30.* FAX *(089) 23 70 38 00.*
@ info@platzl.de. W www.platzl.de
Located in the heart of historic Munich, opposite the famous Hofbräuhaus. The rooms are furnished in old Bavarian style, and the restaurant offers Bavarian specialities. 🛏 🔃 🌿 🐟 🝙 🝓 🌿

	167	●		●	■

OLD TOWN (NORTH): *Bayerischer Hof* €€€€€
Promenadeplatz 2–6, D-80 333. **Map** 3 B2 (5 C2). (*(089) 21 200.*
FAX *(089) 21 20 906.* @ hbh@compuserve.com
Tastefully fitted out with French and English furniture. There is a swimming pool and sauna on the roof. The hotel has three restaurants, shops and a theatre. 1 🛏 🔃 🌿 🐟 🌿

	405	●	■	●	■

OLD TOWN (NORTH): *Kempinski Hotel Vier Jahreszeiten* €€€€€
Maximilianstr. 17, D-80 539. **Map** 3 C2 (6 E3). (*(089) 21 25 270.*
FAX *(089) 21 25 27 77.* @ reservation.vierjahreszeiten@kempinski.com
This hotel has presidential apartments, where royalty and heads of state have slept. Its rooms are decorated in 1970s style. The restaurant is one of the best in the city. 1 🛏 🔃 🌿 🐟 🌿

	266	●	■	●	

OLD TOWN (NORTH): *Mandarin Oriental* €€€€€
Neuturmstr. 1, D-80 331. **Map** 3 C2 (6 E3). (*(089) 29 09 80.* FAX *(089) 22 25 39.*
@ info-momuc@mohg.com.
The interior of this Neo-Renaissance building is considered to be one of the finest in Germany. The rooms are hung with works of art, and there is a roof terrace with a pool (open in summer). The hotel has a high-quality restaurant. 1 🔃 🐟 🕴 ☰ 🌿

	73	●	■	●	■

<table>
<tr><td colspan="3">

Price categories for a standard double room per night including breakfast, service and tax (in euros):

€ up to 77 euros
€€ from 77 to 128 euros
€€€ from 128 to 179 euros
€€€€ from 179 to 230 euros
€€€€€ over 230 euros

</td></tr>
</table>

PARKING OR GARAGE
The hotel has its own car park or garage. Some hotels have an additional charge for this.

SWIMMING POOL
The hotel has a swimming pool, which may be indoor or outdoor.

RESTAURANT
The hotel has a restaurant that is open to non-residents as well as to hotel guests.

GARDEN OR TERRACE
The hotel has a garden, courtyard or terrace, often with tables for eating outside.

	NUMBER OF ROOMS	PARKING OR GARAGE	SWIMMING POOL	RESTAURANT	GARDEN OR TERRACE
AROUND THE ISAR: *Domus* €€€ St.-Anna-Str. 31 D-80 538. **Map** 4 D1. ((089) 22 17 04. FAX (089) 22 85 359. w www.domus-hotel.de The hotel is conveniently located for the Englischer Garten. The building looks more like a private house than a hotel. Rooms are tastefully furnished, with interesting colour schemes.	45	●			
AROUND THE ISAR: *Adria München* €€€ Liebigstr. 8a, D-80 538. **Map** 4 E1. ((089) 29 30 81. FAX (089) 22 70 15. @ reception@adria-münchen.de Located within easy reach of both the Englischer Garten and the museums on Prinzregentenstraße, this hotel has a hospitable atmosphere, with comfortable rooms. Parking is available nearby.	46				
AROUND THE ISAR: *Advocat garni* €€€ Baaderstr. 1, D-80 469. **Map** 3 C3 (6 E5). ((089) 21 63 10. FAX (089) 21 63 190. @ info@hotel-advocat.de This hotel, located close to Isartor, has functional rooms furnished with aristocratic simplicity. Two-room apartments are also available on the seventh floor, which has stunning views.	50				■
AROUND THE ISAR: *Opera garni* €€€€ St.-Anna-Str. 10, D-80 538. **Map** 4 D2. ((089) 21 04 340. FAX (089) 21 04 34 77. @ reception@hotel-opera.de Located next to the opera house, this hotel is frequented by actors. It has a pretty courtyard filled with flowers. The rooms are decorated in various styles ranging from Bavarian to Japanese and Empire.	25				■
AROUND THE ISAR: *Hilton München City* €€€€€ Rosenheimer Str. 15, D-81 667. **Map** 4 D4. ((089) 48 040. FAX (089) 48 04 48 04. @ fom_munich-city@hilton.com This modern 15-storey hotel is ideally suited to the requirements of travelling businesspeople.	481	●	■	●	■
THE UNIVERSITY DISTRICT: *Am Siegestor* € Akademiestr. 5, D-80 799. **Map** 2 E4. ((089) 39 95 50/51. FAX (089) 34 30 50. @ sigiestor@t-online.de This budget hotel and boarding house has a convenient location near Siegestor and the main university building.	20				
THE UNIVERSITY DISTRICT: *Carolin garni* € Kaulbachstr. 42, D-80 538. **Map** 2 E4. ((089) 34 57 57. FAX (089) 33 44 51. This small, guesthouse-type hotel is located near the university and the State Library.	6	●			
THE UNIVERSITY DISTRICT: *Cosmopolitan garni* €€ Hohenzollernstr. 5, D-80 801. **Map** 2 E2. ((089) 38 38 10. FAX (089) 38 38 11 11. @ cosmopolitan-hotel@cosmopolitan.de Recently restored, this hotel has well-appointed rooms. The bar is a popular meeting-place in the evenings.	71	●			
THE UNIVERSITY DISTRICT: *Hauser* €€€ Schellingstr. 11, D-80 799. **Map** 2 D4. ((089) 2 86 67 50. FAX (089) 28 66 75 99. @ Hotel-Hauser@Munich-info.de Located right beside the university, this hotel has a range of facilities for young children as well as a sauna, steam bath and cycle hire.	34	●			
THE MUSEUMS DISTRICT: *Lex garni* € Brienner Str. 48, D-80 333. **Map** 1 A5. ((089) 54 27 260. FAX (089) 52 32 423. @ mail@hotel-lex.de Located near Lenbachhaus and the Palaeontology Museum, this guesthouse-type, budget hotel offers a high standard of service.	16	●			

Price categories for a standard double room per night including breakfast, service and tax (in euros):

€ up to 77 euros
€€ from 77 to 128 euros
€€€ from 128 to 179 euros
€€€€ from 179 to 230 euros
€€€€€ over 230 euros

PARKING OR GARAGE
The hotel has its own car park or garage. Some hotels have an additional charge for this.

SWIMMING POOL
The hotel has a swimming pool, which may be indoor or outdoor.

RESTAURANT
The hotel has a restaurant that is open to non-residents as well as to hotel guests.

GARDEN OR TERRACE
The hotel has a garden, courtyard or terrace, often with tables for eating outside.

	Price	NUMBER OF ROOMS	PARKING OR GARAGE	SWIMMING POOL	RESTAURANT	GARDEN OR TERRACE
THE MUSEUMS DISTRICT: *Theresia garni* Luisenstr. 51, D-80 333. **Map** 1 B4. 📞 *(089) 52 12 50.* **FAX** *(089) 54 20 633.* @ hoteltheresia@yahoo.de Located near the Alte Pinakothek and Neue Pinakothek, this budget hotel offers a standard of service that reflects the price 1	€	28	●			
THE MUSEUMS DISTRICT: *Stefanie garni* Türkenstr. 35, D-80 799. **Map** 2 D4. 📞 *(089) 28 81 400.* **FAX** *(089) 28 81 40 49.* @ reservierung@hotel-stefanie.de This small, modest hotel located on one of Munich's most colourful streets is within easy reach of the Alte Pinakothek and Neue Pinakothek and Schwabing. A lavish breakfast buffet is offered. 1	€€	32	●			
THE MUSEUMS DISTRICT: *Königshof* Karlsplatz 25, D-80 335. **Map** 3 A2 (5 A2). 📞 *(089) 55 13 60.* **FAX** *(089) 55 13 61 13.* @ reservat.koenigshof@tgeisel-hotels.de Established in 1862 and located beside the famous Stachus, this hotel offers traditional comfort combined with all modern conveniences. It also has a restaurant. 1	€€€€€	87	●		●	
FURTHER AFIELD: *Golden Leave Hotel Altmünchen* Mariahilfplatz 4, D-81 541. **Map** 4 D5. 📞 *(089) 45 84 40.* **FAX** *(089) 45 84 44 00.* @ ham@blattl.de Furnished in traditional Bavarian style, this hotel offers a lavish buffet breakfast. 1	€€€€	31	●		●	■
FURTHER AFIELD: *Englischer Garten* Liebergesellstr. 8, D-80 802. 📞 *(089) 38 39 410.* **FAX** *(089) 38 39 41 33.* In a villa overgrown with ivy on the edge of the Englischer Garten, this small hotel is an oasis of peace. Advance booking is required. 1	€€	35	●			■
FURTHER AFIELD: *Jedermann* Bayerstr. 95, D-80 335. 📞 *(089) 54 32 40.* **FAX** *(089) 54 32 41 11.* @ info@hotel-jedermann.de Although it is near Schloss Nymphenburg and Theresienwiese, where the Oktoberfest takes place, this is nevertheless a quiet hotel, furnished in traditional Bavarian style Delicious buffet breakfast. 1	€€	55	●			
FURTHER AFIELD: *Kriembild garni* Guntherstr. 16, D-80 639. 📞 *(089) 17 11 17-0.* **FAX** *(089) 17 11 17 55.* @ hotel@kriemhild.de This hotel is located near Schloss Nymphenburg and its park. The standard of the rooms is superior for the price category. 1	€€	18	●			
FURTHER AFIELD: *Eden-Hotel-Wolff* Arnulfstr. 4–8, D-80 335. 📞 *(089) 55 11 50.* **FAX** *(089) 55 11 55 55.* @ sales@ehw.de Located near the railway station, this hotel combines Bavarian tradition with elegance and modernity. Some of the lounges and rooms have the theme of famous people or historic cities. 1	€€€€	216	●		●	
FURTHER AFIELD: *Forum* Hochstr. 3, D-81 669. **Map** 4 E4. 📞 *(089) 48 030.* **FAX** *(089) 44 88 277.* @ muchb@intercontinti.com This 11-storey hotel by the River Isar is popular with businesspeople. It has three restaurants, a sauna and a solarium. 1	€€€€	582	●	■	●	■
FURTHER AFIELD: *Hilton München Park* Am Tucherpark 7, D-80 538. 📞 *(089) 38 450.* **FAX** *(089) 38 45 25 88.* @ hiltonmunichpark@hotmail.com This is a hotel with functional, modern rooms located near the Englischer Garten. Services offered include a beauty salon, sauna and solarium. 1	€€€€	480	●	■	●	

UPPER BAVARIA (NORTH)

DACHAU: *Fischer* €€€ 26
Bahnhofstr. 4, D-85 221. **Road map** D4. ((08131) 78205. FAX (08 131) 78 508.
Comfortable hotel located opposite the InterCity Express station. The rooms have modern furnishings. 1 ⊟ ⊡ ⩓ ⊛

EICHSTÄTT: *Adler garni* €€ 36
Marktplatz 22–24, D-84 076. **Road map** C2. ((08421) 67 67. FAX (08421) 82 83.
Located in a restored 17th-century building, with rooms furnished in a homely and stylish manner. 1 ⊟ ⊛

FREISING: *Bayerischer Hof* € 70
Untere Hauptstr. 3, D-85 354. **Road map** D3.
((08161) 53 83 00. FAX (08161) 53 83 39.
Located in a historic building at the foot of the cathedral hill. The rooms are equipped with all modern facilities and the rustic restaurant serves Bavarian dishes. 1 ⊟ ⊛

INGOLSTADT: *Ara Hotel* €€ 95
Schollstr. 10, D-85 055. **Road map** D2. ((0841) 95 430.
FAX (0841) 95 43 444.
Newly built hotel furnished in the Italian style. There is a pleasant terrace cafeteria. 1 ⊟ ⊡ ⊛

NEUBURG: *Zum Klosterbräu* €€ 24
Kirchplatz 1, D-86 633. **Road map** C2. ((08431) 67 750. FAX (08421) 41 120.
@ klosterbraeu@flairhotel.de
This modern hotel in the old Bavarian style has a peaceful ambience. The restaurant specializes in fish and game dishes. 1 ⊟ ⊡ ⩓ ⊡ ⩔ ⊛

LOWER BAVARIA

DEGGENDORF: *Parkhotel Astron* €€ 124
Edlmaistr. 4, D-94 469. **Road map** F2. ((0991) 34 460. FAX (0991) 34 46 423.
Large modern hotel set amid greenery between the promenade by the Danube and the old town. It has an impressive gym, as well as a sauna, solarium and baths. There is also a restaurant. 1 ⊟ ⊡ ⊡ ⊛

LANDSHUT: *Romantik Hotel Fürstenhof* €€ 24
Stethaimer Str. 3, D-84 034. **Road map** E3. ((0871) 92 550. FAX (0871) 92 55 44.
Hotel located in a fine villa near the town centre. It is well equipped for tennis and golf enthusiasts and has two restaurants. 1 ⊟ ⊡ ⊛

PASSAU: *Wilder Mann* € 43
Schrottgasse 1, D-94 032. **Road map** C3. ((0851) 35 071. FAX (0851) 31 712.
Despite its good location, this hotel, in an old building, is reasonably priced. It has a long history, and its guests have included the Empress Elizabeth (Sissi), wife of Franz Joseph. 1 ⊟ ⊡ ⊡ ⩔ ⊛

STRAUBING: *Römerhof Hotel* €€ 26
Ittlinger Str. 136, D-94 315. **Road map** E2. ((09421) 99 820.
FAX (09421) 99 82 29. @ hotel@troemerhof-straubing.de
Pleasant hotel of average size, suitable both for families and for businesspeople. It has an interesting restaurant, and drinks and meals can be served on the terrace. 1 ⊟ ⊡ ⩔ ⊡ ⊛

UPPER BAVARIA (EAST)

ALTÖTTING: *Zur Post* €€ 102
Kapellplatz 2, D-84 503. **Road map** F4. ((08671) 50 40. FAX (08671) 62 14.
This highly regarded hotel offers a good standard of service and comfort. It has an excellent restaurant with a beer garden on the terrace. It also offers cycle hire and a swimming pool. 1 ⊟ ⊡ ⩓ ⊡ ⊛

BAD REICHENHALL: *Steigenberger Axelmannstein* €€€€€€ 151
Salzburger Str. 2–6, D-83 435. **Road map** F5. ((08651) 77 74 84.
FAX (08651) 59 32.
This renowned hotel, recently refurbished, is located in a splendid historic palace set in parkland with ancient trees and a pond. 1 ⊟ ⊛

BERCHTESGADEN: *Fischer* €€ 54
Königsseer Str. 51, D-83 471. **Road map** F5. ((08652) 95 50. FAX (08652) 64 873.
Built in traditional Bavarian style. The comfortable rooms, with balconies, are themed by region. The hotel also has a sauna and solarium. 1 ⊟ ⊛

For key to symbols *see back flap*

<table>
<tr><td colspan="2">

Price categories for a standard double room per night including breakfast, service and tax (in euros):

€ up to 77 euros
€€ from 77 to 128 euros
€€€ from 128 to 179 euros
€€€€ from 179 to 230 euros
€€€€€ over 230 euros

</td>
<td colspan="6">

PARKING OR GARAGE
The hotel has its own car park or garage. Some hotels have an additional charge for this.

SWIMMING POOL
The hotel has a swimming pool, which may be indoor or outdoor.

RESTAURANT
The hotel has a restaurant that is open to non-residents as well as to hotel guests.

GARDEN OR TERRACE
The hotel has a garden, courtyard or terrace, often with tables for eating outside.

</td></tr>
</table>

		NUMBER OF ROOMS	PARKING OR GARAGE	SWIMMING POOL	RESTAURANT	GARDEN OR TERRACE
BURGHAUSEN: *Reisingers Bayerische Alm* €€ Robert-Kochstr. 211, D-84 498. **Road map** F4. (*(08677) 98 20.* FAX *(08677) 98 22 00.* A hotel in fine Bavarian style set in verdant surroundings on the River Salzach. It has comfortable rooms. [1] 🚗 📶 🚫 🛏 🕴 ❄ 🌳		30	●		●	▪
REIT IM WINKL: *Unterwirt* € Kirchplatz 2, D-83 242. **Road map** E5. (*(08640) 80 10.* FAX *(08640) 80 11 50.* This hotel, built in the local Alpine style, is located right in the centre of this pretty mountain town. The spacious rooms are furnished in rustic style and have balconies. [1] 🚗 📶 🛏 🌳		71	●			▪
ROSENHEIM: *Panorama* €€ Brixstr. 3, D-83 022. **Road map** E4. (*(08031) 30 60.* FAX *(08031) 30 64 15.* This modern hotel in the heart of Rosenheim cleverly blends into the town's architecture. The rooms are small but functionally designed. Prices are lower on Fridays and Saturdays. [1] 🚗 📶 🚫 🛏 🌳		89	●			

UPPER BAVARIA (SOUTH)

		NUMBER OF ROOMS	PARKING OR GARAGE	SWIMMING POOL	RESTAURANT	GARDEN OR TERRACE
BAD TÖLZ: *Jodquellen Alpamare* €€ Ludwigstr. 13–15, D-83 646. **Road map** D5. (*(08041) 50 90.* FAX *(08041) 50 95 55.* The interior of this hotel, built in 1860, has been thoroughly modernized. It is located beside the Alpamare water park, free use of which can be made by the hotel guests. Pleasantly appointed rooms with balconies. [1] 🚗 📶 🕴 🌳		75				▪
DIESSEN: *Strandhotel* €€ Jahnstr. 10, D-86 911. **Road map** C4. (*(08807) 92 220.* FAX *(08807) 89 58.* Located directly on the shore of Ammersee, with rooms opening onto gardens. The hotel has its own swimming pool and beach. The fine restaurant with a terrace serves fresh fish from the lake as well as Bavarian delicacies. [1] 🚗 📶 🚫 🛏 🕴 🌳		17	▪	●	▪	
GARMISCH-PARTENKIRCHEN: *Grand Hotel Sonnenbichl* €€€ Burgstr. 97, D-82 467. **Road map** C5. (*(08821) 70 20.* FAX *(08821) 70 21 31.* The finest hotel in the region. The Jugendstil building, dating from 1898, offers a view of the Wetterstein mountain range and the Zugspitze. It has two smart restaurants, the Blauer Salon and the Zirbelstube, which serves Bavarian specialities. [1] 📶 🚫 🛏 🕴 🍴 ❄ 🌳		93	●	▪	●	▪
KOCHEL AM SEE: *Seehotel Grauer Bär* € Mittenwalder Str. 82, D-82 431. **Road map** C5. (*(08851) 92 500.* FAX *(08851) 92 50 15.* Located on the lakeshore, with a breathtaking view of the mountains. Comfortable rooms with balconies and an excellent restaurant. Swimming pool and bicycle and boat hire. [1] 🚗 📶 🚫 🛏 🕴 🍴 ▤ 🌳		30	●	▪	●	▪
LANDSBERG AM LECH: *Goggl garni* €€ Hubert-von-Herkomer-Str. 19–20, D-86 899. **Road map** C4. (*(08191) 32 40.* FAX *(08191) 32 41 00.* The Goggl garni is located in a late 17th-century building in the heart of Landsberg next to the historic town hall. The hotel offers a wide range of sports and recreation, such as tennis, golf and cycling. [1] 🚗 📶 🛏 🕴 🍴 🌳		59	●			
MITTENWALD: *Hotel Post* €€ Obermarkt 9, D-82 481. **Road map** C5. (*(08823) 93 82 333.* FAX *(08823) 93 82 999.* A Renaissance hotel whose origins go back to 1632, when it was a roadside inn for travellers crossing the Alps. Comfortable rooms and breakfast served on a sunny terrace. A distinguishing feature of the bar is its fireplace. [1] 📶 🚫 🛏 🕴 🌳		81	●			▪

OBERAMMERGAU: *Böld Landhotel* €€ 57
König-Ludwig-Str. 10, D-82 487. **Road map** C5. **(** *(08822) 91 20.*
FAX *(08822) 71 02.*
Comfortable, well-appointed rooms, most of them with a balcony. The restaurant serves both international and regional cuisine. 1 ⊟ ⊠ ⊟ ⊠

THE ALLGÄU

FÜSSEN: *Alpenblick* €€ 62
Uferstr. 10, D-87 629. **Road map** B5. **(** *(08362) 50 570.* FAX *(08362) 50 57 73.*
A hotel with pleasant rooms and luxury apartments with views of the lakes and the Alps. It has a sauna, solarium and a bar. 1 ⊟ ⊠ ⊠

KEMPTEN: *Hotel Fürstenhof* € 54
Rathausplatz 8, D-87 435. **Road map** B5. **(** *(0831) 25 360.* FAX *25 36 120.*
Located in a historic patrician's palace that was rebuilt in about 1600, it has been frequented by the crowned heads of the Stauffer and Habsburg families. Rooms furnished in Old English style. Peace and quiet guaranteed. 1 ⊟ ⊠ ⊠ ⊟ ⊠ ⊠

LINDAU: *Bayerischer Hof* €€€ 100
Seepromenade, D-88 131. **Road map** A5. **(** *(08382) 91 50.* FAX *(08382) 91 55 91.*
Located on the town's main promenade, with incomparable views of the lake and the Austrian and Swiss Alps. Guests can also make use of the swimming pool, sauna and solarium, and hire bicycles. 1 ⊟ ⊠ ⊠ ⊠

MEMMINGEN: *Parkhotel* €€ 90
Ulmer Str. 7, D-87 700. **Road map** B4. **(** *(08331) 93 20.* FAX *(08331) 48 439.*
A hotel in the city centre with cosy, traditionally furnished rooms. An appetizing breakfast is served, and there is a beer garden, sauna and solarium. 1 ⊟ ⊠ ⊟ ⊠ ⊠ ⊠

OBERSTDORF: *Exquisit* €€ 35
Prinzenstr. 17, D-87 561. **Road map** B6. **(** *(08322) 96 330.* FAX *(08322) 96 33 60.*
Nicely located on the edge of the town. Elegant rooms furnished in a rustic style. Sports and recreation activities. 1 ⊟ ⊠ ⊠ ⊟ ⊠ ⊠ ⊠

NORTHERN SWABIA

AUGSBURG: *Romantik Hotel Augsburger Hof* €€ 36
Auf dem Kreuz 2, D-86 152. **Road map** C3. **(** *(0821) 34 30 50.*
FAX *(0821) 34 30 555.*
Part of an international chain of hotels located in fine historic buildings. The exterior of the building and the furnishings within create a romantic atmosphere. 1 ⊟ ⊠ ⊠

AUGSBURG: *Steigenberger Drei Mohren* €€€ 107
Maximilianstr 40, D-86 150. **Road map** C3. **(** *(0821) 50 360.*
FAX *(0821) 15 78 64.* @ augsburg@steigenberger.de
Located in the town's main thoroughfare, though well protected from street noise. The hotel has several restaurants and cafeterias and a ballroom. 1 ⊟ ⊠ ⊠ ⊟ ⊠

DILLINGEN: *Dillinger Hof* € 49
Rudolf-Diesel-Str. 8, D-89 407. **Road map** B3. **(** *(09071) 58 740.* FAX *(09071) 83 23.*
A modern hotel with small, conventionally furnished rooms. Reasonably good restaurant, and sauna and solarium. 1 ⊟ ⊠ ⊠ ⊠ ⊠

DONAUWÖRTH: *Euroring Posthotel Traube* €€ 40
Kapellstr. 14, D-86 609. **Road map** C2. **(** *(0906) 70 64 40.* FAX *(0906) 23 390.*
A hotel steeped in history – Mozart and Goethe slept here. It specializes in conferences and in accommodating tour groups.
1 ⊟ ⊠ ⊠ ⊟ ⊠ ⊠

HARBURG: *Gasthof zum Straußen* € 15
Marktplatz 2, D-86 655. **Road map** B2. **(** *(09080) 13 98.* FAX *(09080) 43 24.*
Surprisingly inexpensive accommodation. The restaurant serves excellent Swabian dishes in generous portions. 1 ⊟ ⊠

NÖRDLINGEN: *Astron Hotel Klösterle* €€ 98
Beim Klösterle 1, D-86 720. **Road map** B2. **(** *(09081) 87 080.*
FAX *(09081) 87 08 100.*
Located in a former Franciscan monastery, with comfortable rooms and elegant suites. From the gym on the fourth floor there is a fine view of the old town. 1 ⊟ ⊠ ⊠ ⊟ ⊠ ⊠ ⊟ ⊠

For key to symbols *see back flap*

WHERE TO EAT

ALTHOUGH THE food that is normally served in the Bavarian Alps is rather basic fare, it is however always tasty and satisfying. Grilled knuckle of pork, sausage, dumplings and the indispensable litre mugs of beer are enjoyed everywhere from village inns to renowned Munich pubs. Consumed against a background of heated conversation, laughter and singing, they constitute a kind of culinary experience in themselves. The beer garden *(Biergärten)* is one of Bavaria's trademarks. The best-known beer gardens, usually attached to monastic breweries, are popular gathering places for local people and tourists alike. Those looking for a little more sophistication will find a variety of restaurants in towns and holiday resorts, where Italian, Turkish and Greek restaurants enjoy the greatest popularity.

A chef at the Leopold restaurant in Munich

The Palm Garden of the Café Luitpold in Munich (*see p277*)

TYPES OF RESTAURANTS

THE GREAT variety of restaurants that can be found in the Bavarian Alps reflects the fact that the region is orientated towards tourism. Genuine Bavarian meals are served primarily in *Gasthaus*-type establishments. In central Munich and in tourist resorts, restaurants tend towards the kitsch, and some leave something to be desired. It is vastly preferable to eat in an inn frequented by local people, where prices are lower and where dishes, although they are served with less ceremony, usually taste much better. However, visitors should be prepared for a little local colour: some local inns are filled with cigarette smoke or may reverberate to the sound of loud conversations between drinkers who have over-indulged.

A good place eating place is usually the *Ratskeller*, a pub in the cellar of the town hall, where regional specialities are served. There are also wine bars *(Weinstuben)*, which in addition to fine wines also serve good food, although usually charging relatively high prices.

Other options for sampling good regional food along with local beer are the *Bierstuben* and *Bierkeller*, pubs usually belonging to a local brewery. They are often noisy, and seating is on long benches where you soon fall into conversation with your fellow-diners and drinkers.

Attractive features of Bavarian beer-drinking rituals are the gigantic beer tents *(Bierzelte)* that are put up during local holidays, as well as the charming little beer gardens *(Biergärten)*, where customers order their drinks from the bar. It is even permissible to bring your own food to some of them.

There are also Italian pizzerias, Greek tavernas, steak houses, and Chinese, Turkish and Balkan restaurants as well as the ubiquitous international fast-food outlets and snack bars.

At the other end of the scale, particularly in Munich, there are elegant, discerning restaurants with elevated standards of service, décor and cuisine, with high prices to match.

The Hunsingers Pacific restaurant in Munich (*see p271*)

WHAT AND WHEN TO EAT

BREAKFAST IS USUALLY a hearty affair with various types of bread accompanied by cheese, sausages and marmalade. On Sundays brunch is served in

A sunny beer garden near the Viktualienmarkt, Munich

The Tivoli Restaurant in the Hilton München Park Hotel

most places until 2pm: this is a combination of breakfast and lunch, in the form of a Swedish buffet. During the lunch period (noon to 2pm) most establishments serve excellent salads or bowls of filling soup, while many restaurants offer a fixed-price menu. Restaurants start to fill up in the evenings between 6 and 7pm, although dinner is usually eaten after 8pm.

OPENING HOURS

Most cafeterias and fast-food chains open at 9am. Other establishments open at noon and usually close after the lunchtime period until about 6pm. Many restaurants close on one day of the week, known as *Ruhetag*. Beer gardens in towns usually close at 11pm. Most restaurants stay open right up until midnight or 1am.

MENU

Most restaurants post their menu, together with their prices, at the door. Attached to the main menu may be an additional sheet listing seasonal dishes, such as fresh mussels, or indicating the dish of the day, such as fresh fish, roast meat or homemade pies. Desserts and soft and alcoholic drinks are usually listed on a separate menu.

In many good restaurants the menu is written in German and English, and sometimes also in French. In cafés and less expensive restaurants, the menu may be handwritten, in which case staff may be able to help with a translation.

RESERVATIONS

Making a prior reservation is essential in all the best restaurants. In most good and medium-standard restaurants it is advisable to do so, particularly on a Friday or Saturday night or on public holidays. If you have not made a reservation, you may be asked to wait or to return later.

Many inns and restaurants in Bavaria have a *Stammtisch*, a table set aside for regular local people and groups at certain times on certain days.

PRICES AND TIPS

Prices charged in Bavarian restaurants are diverse, those in Munich's top restaurants being the highest. A meal consisting of roast meat with dumplings and salad served in a country inn is almost half the price that is charged in the most popular tourist areas.

The cost of a main meal in an inn or restaurant ranges from €5–6 in the cheapest places to €13–18 in superior establishments. The average cost of a three-course meal

including salad and beer is about €25. This includes tax and service, but it is customary to leave a 10 per cent tip. If paying by card, this can be added to the bill.

VEGETARIAN FOOD

Vegetarian food has become increasingly popular in Germany in recent years. The number of vegetarian restaurants is increasing, and snack bars offering vegetarian meals are enjoying considerable popularity. More inns and restaurants now include meat-free meals on their main menus, while vegetarian pizzas are a standard item in Italian restaurants.

The Bratwurst Glöckl am Dom restaurant in Munich (see p270)

DISABLED VISITORS

Many inns and restaurants are unfortunately without access facilities for disabled people. Often doorways are too narrow for wheelchairs and tables are too closely placed, and there may be no specially adapted toilets. When making the reservation, it is advisable to enquire what the conditions are in a particular establishment.

The main room of the Munich Ratskeller

What to Eat

MANY BAVARIAN specialities are unique to the region and are not found anywhere else. One of the most famous is *Weißwurst*, boiled white sausage that is eaten with sweet mustard. Another popular dish is *Leberkäse*, literally "liver cheese", which has nothing to do with liver sausage or with cheese, but is a type of sausage meat eaten warm. A Swabian dish is *Käsespätzle*, flat dumplings covered with grated cheese, and *Maultaschen*, pasties filled with meat and vegetables.

Radishes

Krautschupfnudeln
Appetising, elongated fried dumplings are served with boiled cabbage and fried bacon.

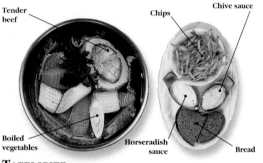

Tender beef

Chips

Chive sauce

Boiled vegetables

Horseradish sauce

Bread

TAFELSPITZ

Tender beef cooked in stock and usually served with potatoes, bread and horseradish or chive sauce, and vegetables boiled in stock.

Käsespätzle
This is a dish of noodles covered with grated cheese and chopped onions.

Wurstsalat
Sliced pork sausage with onion is usually served with a marinade sauce.

Kartoffelsalat
Potato salad is a popular dish that is often enjoyed with beer.

Krautsalat
Light salad with raw cabbage is served with a vinegar sauce dressing.

Presssack
The white variety is similar to brawn and the dark similar to black pudding.

WEIßWURST MIT SÜSSEM SENF

Boiled white sausage with sweet mustard is the most renowned Bavarian food. Gourmets do not cut it up, but noisily suck it from its skin. Traditionally it is served simply with bread.

Sweet mustard

Pretzel

Weißwurst (white sausage)

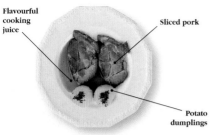

Flavourful cooking juice

Sliced pork

Potato dumplings

Schweinebraten
This method of cooking pork chops demands certain culinary skills. The meat should have a little fat and should be served with its own juice.

Schweinshaxe
This dish of grilled knuckle of pork is very filling. It has an unusual flavour and is at its best when served with beer.

Leberkäse mit Spiegelei
This unusual roast, which has the flavour of sausage, is topped with a fried egg.

Pork sausage

Brown and black pudding

Horseradish (Rettich)

Blue cheese

Cold roast pork

Cooked ham

Pickled gherkins

Paté

Salami

BROTZEITTELLER
This popular accompaniment to beer is often served to a group of people on a single platter. It includes smoked and cooked meats, sausage, cheeses and vegetables.

Maultaschensuppe
This vegetable stock is served with shaped dumplings stuffed with meat and vegetables.

Leberknödelsuppe
A large dumpling of chopped liver, breadcrumbs and eggs is served with this clear soup.

Leberspätzlesuppe
Flat dumplings are added to this clear soup and served with chopped liver.

Zwetschgenstrudel
Often served hot, this dessert is a kind of strudel made with sliced plums.

Bayerische Creme
The creamy consistency of this dessert is produced by slowly adding egg to hot milk.

Dampfnudel
These steamed dumplings of leavened dough are served with vanilla sauce and fruit.

Beer in Bavaria

Hop flower

BAVARIA IS famous the world over for its excellent beer, which is exported to over 140 countries. As part of their cultural tradition, Bavarians scrupulously observe the *Reinheitsgebot*, a law of 1516 accord-ing to which the only ingredients brewers may use are barley, hops and water. The Bavarians even made accession to the Weimar Republic in 1919 conditional on the acknowledg-ment of this law. The annual Oktoberfest is the high point of Bavaria's brewing tradition.

The Oktoberfest – a beer festival that is cheerfully celebrated by the Bavarians

Logo of one of Bavaria's best-known breweries

The famous Löwenbräu beer

A beer mat

BAVARIAN BREWERIES

IN 1040 the monks of Weihenstephan monastery, which is now in the outskirts of modern Freising, were granted a licence to brew beer by the city's bishop. The brewery, which still produces beer to this day, is the oldest in the world. One out of every two breweries in the European Union is located in Bavaria. Many Bavarian breweries have centuries of tradition behind them. The best-known are the main Munich breweries – Löwenbräu, Hofbräu, Paulanerbräu, Augustinerbräu, Spatenbräu and Hacker-Pschorrbräu.

Many smaller breweries can also be found throughout the region, usually with their own inns *(Wirtschaft)* or pubs with beer gardens. Many of them are the object of special "pilgrimages" made both by Bavarians and by tourists. The most highly esteemed of these inns include the Klosterbrauerei Andechs, the Weltenburg and Irsee breweries, which continue the time-honoured tradition of monastic brewing, and Schlossbrauerei Kaltenberg, which belongs to Duke Luitpold of Bavaria. The long-standing debate over who brews the best beer will, quite obviously, never be resolved.

TRADITIONAL DARK AND LIGHT BEERS

UNTIL THE 19th century, the only beer drunk in Bavaria was the sweeter dark beer *(Dunkel)*. Some breweries continue to specialize in *Dunkel* today; the best known of these are the Weltenburg monastery brewery (which makes Barock Dunkel) and the Schlossbrauerei Kaltenberg (König Ludwig Dunkel).

In the 20th century dark beer was replaced by lighter lager-type beer *(Helles)*, which is clear, a little more potent and with a less bitter taste. *Naturtrüb*, an unfiltered beer with an excellent taste, is slightly cloudy because of its yeast content.

Good beer is served cold and should have a thick head that does not settle quickly. It is served in a litre (2-pint) mug *(eine Maß)*, as a half litre (1 pint) *(eine Halbe)* and more rarely as a quarter litre (half a pint) *(eine Kleines)*. It tastes best when served from the barrel (as *Fassbier*). Beer served from a keg under pressure is sacrilege to a Bavarian. On hot days, people may drink *Radler*, which is *Helles* mixed with lemonade.

Berchtesgaden lager

König Ludwig dark beer

Paulanerbräu lager

MÄRZENBIER

B EFORE THE invention of refrigeration systems, beer was brewed in winter, when the heat would not disrupt the fermentation process. The last brewing was in March and the beer had a higher alcohol content, which helped to prevent it going off. If the brewers' stocks lasted until autumn, before the new season's beer was brewed the cellars were opened and a beer festival was held. The brewing of *Märzenbier* (March beer) continues to this day, even though modern technology has rendered the process obsolete.

At the big autumn beer festivals millions of litres of this strong-tasting light-brown beer are consumed. Beer brewed by the major Munich brewers specially for the Oktoberfest is called *Oktoberfestbier* or *Wiesenbier*. In the autumn it is on offer in many pubs and is sold bottled in shops.

The most widely used type of beer mug

Oktoberfestbier from the Paulanerbräu

BOCK AND DOPPELBOCK

T HIS FAMOUS beer gets its name from the town of Einbeck in Lower Saxony. The word "Einbeck" was transmuted by the Bavarian brogue into "Oanbock", which was abbreviated to "Bock". *Bockbier* was first brewed by the court brewery *(Hofbräu)*, founded in 1589. The Pauline monks were later renowned for making this type of beer. A more potent variety called *Doppelbock* was produced under the name Salvator. This beer, which the monks used to help them through the rigours of Lent, was brewed to celebrate 19 March, the feast day of St Joseph, the order's patron saint. To this day Joseftag marks the beginning of Munich's *Starkbierfest* (strong beer festival), which takes place in the Paulaner brewery's pub. Salvator inaugurated the production of several other *Doppelbock* beers. The beer is an amber colour and has a strong, slightly bitter taste and a 7 per cent alcohol content.

Salvator Doppelbock

Bretzels – an ideal snack to enjoy with beer

WEIZENBIER

T HIS TYPE of beer is extremely popular in southern Germany, particularly in summer as it is a very refreshing drink. During the brewing process, twice the amount of malted wheat is added to the malted barley, which is why it is known as *Weizenbier* (wheat beer).

Weizenbier has a 5 per cent alcohol content and is a *Vollbier* (full beer). To enhance the flavour it is often drunk with a sliver of lemon. There are many kinds of wheat beer: the light and dark *Weizen-Bockbier* and the yeasty *Hefeweizen* beer. The frothy *Weizen* is slowly poured into a glass which broadens at the top. Mixed with lemonade, it is called *Russ*.

Franziskaner Hefe-Weißbier

Paulanerbräu wheat beer

WHERE TO DRINK

B EER, THE Bavarian national drink, is also called "liquid nourishment". It is drunk anywhere and everywhere throughout the region – from the most exclusive restaurants down to the smallest food stalls. However, beer is best enjoyed in beer gardens or at the inns of breweries.

A certain amount of ceremony is attached to the drinking of beer: it is drunk sitting down, in large groups, with songs, laughter and flirting. Almost every town in Bavaria holds a beer festival at least once a year.

A beer garden is the best place to enjoy a glass of beer

Choosing a Restaurant

THE RESTAURANTS in this guide have been selected because of their good food and interesting location, or because of the good value that they offer. The colour-coded thumb tabs on the side of the page correspond to the relevant pages in the book. Map references in Munich refer to pages 140–149; outside Munich they refer to the inside back cover.

	CREDIT CARDS ACCEPTED	TABLES OUTDOORS	VEGETARIAN DISHES	REGIONAL CUISINE	GOOD WINE LIST

MUNICH

OLD TOWN (SOUTH): *Tankstelle Buena Vista* €
Am Einlaß 2a. **Map** 3 B3 (5 C5). [(089) 26 02 28 11.
Located in a former service station, this restaurant has a Cuban theme and is decorated with musical motifs. The menu offers a variety of Latin American food. Recommended are the Buena Vista fish soup and the platter of appetisers for two. ♫ ○ *6pm–1am Sun–Thu, 6pm–3am Fri–Sat.*
| | ● | | | | ● |

OLD TOWN (SOUTH): *Bratwurstherzl* €€
Dreifaltigkeitsplatz 1. **Map** 3 B1 (5 B2). [(089) 29 51 13.
W www.bratwurstherzl.de
A comprehensive range of Nuremberg sausages, grilled meats and typical Munich food is served in two halls with seating for up to 160.
○ *10am–11:30pm Mon–Fri, 9am–4pm Sat.* ● *Sun and public holidays.*
| | ● | ■ | | ■ | |

OLD TOWN (SOUTH): *Glockenspiel* €€€
Marienplatz 28. **Map** 3 B2 (6 D3). [(089) 26 42 56.
This restaurant's pleasant atmosphere is enhanced by the interplay of light and dark colours in a classical interior. In autumn, the roof terrace is covered to make a winter garden. The cuisine has a Mediterranean flavour, with Asian influences. ♿ ○ *10–1am daily.*
| | ● | ■ | ● | | ● |

OLD TOWN (SOUTH): *Kay's Bistro* €€€
Utzschneiderstr. 1. **Map** 3 B3 (6 D4). [(089) 26 03 584.
This fashionable cult bistro is frequented by actors and singers. The walls are hung with portraits of such stars as Sophia Loren and Tina Turner. The cuisine is French and international. ○ *7pm–3am daily.*
| | ● | | | | |

OLD TOWN (SOUTH): *Master's Home* €€€€€
Frauenstr. 11. **Map** 3 C3 (6 D4). [(089) 22 99 09.
The doors and entrance hall, with marble walls and intricate gilt details, hint at the luxury within. The armchairs and sofas are of teak, with safari trophies hung on the walls. This and the excellent Italian food combine to create a truly sumptuous atmosphere. ○ *6pm–3am daily.*
| | ● | | | | ● |

OLD TOWN (NORTH): *Nürnberger Bratwurst Glöckl am Dom* €€
Frauenplatz 9. **Map** 3 B2 (5 C3). [(089) 22 03 85.
A traditional inn near the cathedral offering numerous Bavarian specialities. The sausages, of all varieties, are especially tempting.
○ *10am–1am daily.*
| | ● | ■ | ● | ■ | |

OLD TOWN (NORTH): *Dukatz* €€€
Salvatorplatz 1. **Map** 3 B1 (5 C1). [(089) 29 19 600.
Cuisine distinguished by tempting starters and main dishes, ranging from fine macaroni and risotto to lamb tripe in champagne sauce with vegetables. The benches, plates and cups are inscribed with aphorisms by Oskar Maria Graf. ○ *10am–1pm Mon–Sat, 10am–6pm Sun.*
| | ● | ■ | | | |

OLD TOWN (NORTH): *Roma* €€€
Maximilianstr. 31. **Map** 4 D2 (6 F3). [(089) 22 74 35.
This restaurant's clientele has included Friedrich Dürrenmatt, Boris Becker and Mario Adorf. The décor features a copy of the Capitoline Wolf in Rome, given by Steven Spielberg to the actress Iris Berben, who owns the restaurant. It serves international cuisine with a marked Italian influence, particularly in the vegetarian menu. ○ *8pm–3am daily.*
| | ● | ■ | ● | | |

OLD TOWN (NORTH): *Bogenhauser Hof* €€€€
Ismaninger Str. 85. **Map** 4 F2. [(089) 98 55 86. ☎ (089) 28 10 221.
A restaurant with a warm, intimate atmosphere, where guests can enjoy both Bavarian and international cuisine, from lobster soup to Franconian-style black pudding. The wine list features over 100 wines.
○ *noon–2:30pm and 6–10:30pm Mon–Sat.* ● *Sun and public holidays.*
| | ● | ■ | | ■ | ● |

Price categories are for a three-course meal for one with half a bottle of wine and including service and taxes (in euros):

€ up to 23 euros
€€ from 23–33 euros
€€€ from 33–43 euros
€€€€ from 43–53 euros
€€€€€ over 53 euros

CREDIT CARDS ACCEPTED
The following credit cards are accepted: American Express, Diners Club, Eurocard, MasterCard, Visa.
TABLES OUTDOORS
Food is served on the terrace or in the garden.
VEGETARIAN DISHES
A good choice of vegetarian dishes is available.
REGIONAL CUISINE
Restaurant offers traditional Bavarian food.
GOOD WINE LIST
A wide choice of different wines is available.

	CREDIT CARDS ACCEPTED	TABLES OUTDOORS	VEGETARIAN DISHES	REGIONAL CUISINE	GOOD WINE LIST
OLD TOWN (NORTH): *Am Marstall* €€€€€	●				
AROUND THE ISAR: *Kytaro* €		■			
AROUND THE ISAR: *Akasaka* €€	●	■			
AROUND THE ISAR: *Islay* €€	●				
AROUND THE ISAR: *Pacific Times* €€	●	■			
THE MUSEUMS DISTRICT: *Taverna Robinson* €			●		
THE MUSEUMS DISTRICT: *Hunsingers Pacific* €€€	●		●		●
THE MUSEUMS DISTRICT: *Königshof* €€€€€	●		●		●
THE UNIVERSITY DISTRICT: *Cohen's* €					

OLD TOWN (NORTH): *Am Marstall* €€€€€
Maximilianstr. 16. **Map 3 C2 (6 E2).** (*(089) 29 16 55 11.* FAX *(089) 29 16 55 12.*
Bernhard Diers, the chef here, belongs to the German culinary elite. The food is imaginative, such as cold seafood soup with lobster and melon.
○ *noon–2pm and 6–10pm Tue–Sat.* ● *Sun and Mon.*

AROUND THE ISAR: *Kytaro* €
Innere Wiener Str. 36. **Map 4 E3.** (*(089) 48 01 176.*
This old taverna run by Greek staff serves hot and cold mezes, octopus with accompaniments, roast lamb and duck in orange sauce.
♫ ○ *5pm–1am daily.*

AROUND THE ISAR: *Akasaka* €€
Thierschstr. 35. **Map 4 D2.** (*(089) 29 31 00.* FAX *(089) 22 83 427.*
@ kenji-makita@classic.msn.com
The impeccably courteous kimonoed staff and the Japanese airline posters on the walls create a unique atmosphere in which the regional specialities of Japan are served. ○ *6–10:30pm Mon–Sat.*

AROUND THE ISAR: *Islay* €€
Thierschstr. 14. **Map 4 D3 (6 F4).** (*(089) 29 16 37 00.* W www.islaywhisky.de
In an ambience of subdued lighting a variety of dishes are served – from chicken in marinade with chilli sauce and ginger, to potato dumplings with wild mushrooms. The choice of different whiskies at the bar is one of the widest in Munich. ○ *5pm–1am Mon–Sat.* ● *Sun.*

AROUND THE ISAR: *Pacific Times* €€
Baaderstr. 28. **Map 3 C3 (6 E5).** (*(089) 20 23 94 70.*
This American bar won *Playboy* magazine's Best Bar of the Year award in 1999. Original side dishes and steaks predominate. Drinks – chosen from a 64-page list – are artfully served by the bar staff.
○ *5pm–1am Sun–Thu, 5pm–3am Fri–Sat.*

THE MUSEUMS DISTRICT: *Taverna Robinson* €
Gabelsbergerstr. 50. **Map 1 B5.** (*(089) 52 23 31.*
One of the best Turkish restaurants in Munich, serving mainly Anatolian specialities and fish. It is also the venue for concerts and shows, to which members of the audience can contribute with a song of their own.
♫ & ○ *5:30pm–1am Mon–Thu, 5:30pm–3am Fri–Sun.*

THE MUSEUMS DISTRICT: *Hunsingers Pacific* €€€
Maximiliansplatz 5. **Map 3 B1 (5 C1).** (*(089) 55 02 97 41.*
FAX *(089) 55 02 97 42.*
The chef at this renowned establishment is Werner Hunsinger, who cleverly blends Mediterranean and Pacific cuisine. There is a wide variety of fish dishes and an exquisite couscous with shellfish and prawns.○ *noon–2:30pm and 6–10:30pm Mon–Fri, 6–10:30pm Sat.*
● *Sun.*

THE MUSEUMS DISTRICT: *Königshof* €€€€€
Karlsplatz 25. **Map 3 A2 (5 A2).** (*(089) 55 13 60.* FAX *(089) 55 13 61 62.*
This restaurant, in the hotel of the same name, has a regular, wealthy clientele. The food is exquisitely prepared and elegantly served. The fish dishes in particular are highly recommended.
♫ & ○ *noon–2:30pm and 6:30–10pm daily.*

THE UNIVERSITY DISTRICT: *Cohen's* €
Theresienstr. 31. **Map 2 D5.** (*(089) 28 09 545.*
This restaurant is frequented by actors, students, models and artists. The varied cuisine offers food from all over the world, along with Jewish specialities such as gefilte fish (minced fish balls) and cholent (meat and bean stew). ♫ ○ *12:30pm–1am daily.*

For key to symbols *see back flap*

Price categories are for a three-course meal for one with half a bottle of wine and including service and taxes (in euros):

€ up to 23 euros
€€ from 23–33 euros
€€€ from 33–43 euros
€€€€ from 43–53 euros
€€€€€ over 53 euros

CREDIT CARDS ACCEPTED
The following credit cards are accepted: American Express, Diners Club, Eurocard, MasterCard, Visa.
TABLES OUDOORS
Food is served on the terrace or in the garden.
VEGETARIAN DISHES
A good choice of vegetarian dishes is available.
REGIONAL CUISINE
Restaurant offers traditional Bavarian food.
GOOD WINE LIST
A wide choice of different wines is available.

	CREDIT CARDS ACCEPTED	TABLES OUTDOORS	VEGETARIAN DISHES	REGIONAL CUISINE	GOOD WINE LIST

UNIVERSITY DISTRICT: *Le Caribeau*   €

Königinstr. 34. **Map** 2 E5. (089) 33 04 01 50.
Highly imaginative Caribbean cuisine. Worth mentioning is *callalco* – a soup with prawns, coconut milk and spinach – and chicken calypso – chicken breast with prawns, vegetables, garlic and sweet potatoes.
5pm–1am Sun–Thu, 5pm–3am Fri–Sat.

Tables Outdoors: ■

UNIVERSITY DISTRICT: *Bistro Terrine*   €€€

Amalienstr. 89. **Map** 2 D4. (089) 28 17 80. **FAX** (089) 28 09 316.
The Art Deco interior gives this restaurant a Parisian flavour. Immaculate service and the fine cooking of chef Werner Licht ensure that the restaurant maintains its good name. Excellent fillet of rabbit with mushrooms and salad, as well as lamb with beans and potato puree.
noon–3pm and 6:30pm–1am Mon–Sat. Sun and public holidays.

Credit Cards Accepted: ● Tables Outdoors: ■

UNIVERSITY DISTRICT: *Halali*   €€€

Schönfeldstr. 22. **Map** 2 E5. (089) 28 59 09.
This restaurant specializes in game, as the hunting weapons displayed on the walls suggest. The appetisers in the form of home-made black pudding on a ragout of apples in truffle sauce are notable. noon–3pm and 6pm–midnight Mon–Fri, 6pm–1am Sat. Sun.

Credit Cards Accepted: ● Regional Cuisine: ■ Good Wine List: ●

UNIVERSITY DISTRICT: *Leopold*   €€€

Leopoldstr. 50. **Map** 2 E3. (089) 38 38 680. **FAX** (089) 38 38 68 22.
Furnished in 1920s style, this restaurant offers Bavarian specialities, such as tender beef served in bouillon in a copper bowl. 10am–1pm Fri–Sat, 10am–midnight Sun–Thu.

Credit Cards Accepted: ● Tables Outdoors: ■ Vegetarian Dishes: ● Regional Cuisine: ■

FURTHER AFIELD: *Don Quijote*   €€

Biedersteinerstr. 6. (089) 34 23 18.
The oldest Spanish restaurant in Munich is tucked away in a quiet and simply arranged cellar, not easily noticeable from the street. Among the wide variety of dishes on offer, the fish dishes are particularly good.
6:30pm–1am daily.

Tables Outdoors: ■

FURTHER AFIELD: *Georgios*   €€

Schleißheimerstr. 188. (089) 30 89 396.
The chefs here prepare delicious Greek food in front of guests in the middle of the restaurant. The sirloin steak in red wine sauce is highly recommended. 5:30pm–1am daily.

Credit Cards Accepted: ●

FURTHER AFIELD: *Spago*   €€

Neureutherstr. 15. (089) 27 12 406. **FAX** (089) 27 80 448.
A truly astonishing variety and quantity of Venetian fish and meat dishes are on offer here. This restaurant is widely regarded as the finest open-air dining in Schwabing, with seating for 80 people.
noon–2:30pm and 6:30–11:30pm Mon–Sat. Sun.

Credit Cards Accepted: ● Tables Outdoors: ■ Good Wine List: ●

FURTHER AFIELD: *Tantris*   €€€€€

Johann-Fichte-Str. 7. (089) 36 19 590. **FAX** (089) 36 19 522.
W www.tantris.de @ tantris@t-online.de
This cult restaurant is one of the finest in the whole of Germany. The distinguished cuisine, combined with luxurious furnishing in 1970s style and prompt, professional service account for its great popularity.
noon–3pm and 6:30pm–1am Tue–Sat. Sun and Mon.

Credit Cards Accepted: ● Tables Outdoors: ■ Good Wine List: ●

UPPER BAVARIA (NORTH)

DACHAU: *Aurora*   €€€

Roßwachstr. 1. **Road Map** D4. (08131) 51 530. **FAX** (08131) 51 53 32.
The hotel of the same name has a small gourmet restaurant with a terrace and a winter garden. Recommended dishes are the vegetables with lamb and the sirloin steak. noon–2pm and 6:30pm–1am daily.

Credit Cards Accepted: ● Tables Outdoors: ■ Good Wine List: ●

EICHSTÄTT: *Domherrnhof* €€€
Domplatz 5. **Road map** C2. 🕻 *(08421) 61 26.* FAX *(08421) 80 849.*
Located in an elegant former canons' palace, the restaurant serves
exquisite dishes such as salad with grilled prawns or duck breast in
lentils. ⬜ *11:30am–2:30pm and 6pm–midnight Tue–Sun.* ⬤ *Mon.*

FREISING: *Gasthaus Landbrecht* €
Freisinger Str. 1, Freising-Handlfing. **Road map** D3. 🕻 *(08167) 89 26.*
FAX *(08167) 86 47.*
This moderate-sized restaurant is renowned for its excellent Bavarian
cuisine, consisting of a wide variety of fine dishes. The celery and herb
soup and the roast pork are recommended. ⬜ *6–10:30pm Wed–Fri,*
11:30am–3pm and 6–10:30pm Sat–Sun. ⬤ *Mon–Tue.*

INGOLSTADT: *Restaurant im Stadttheater* €€€
Schloßlände 1. **Road map** D2. 🕻 *(0841) 93 51 50.* FAX *(0841) 93 51 520.*
This is the best restaurant in Ingolstadt. It offers fine European cuisine,
including French, as well as excellent Bavarian dishes.
⬜ *11am–1am Tue–Sat, 11am–3pm Sun.*

NEUBURG AN DER DONAU: *Zum Klosterbräu* €€
Kirchplatz 1., Neuburg-Bergen. **Road map** C2. 🕻 *(08431) 67 750.*
FAX *(08431) 41 120.* 🔲 www.zum-klosterbraeu.de
📧 boehm@zum-klosterbraeu.de
A hotel restaurant specializing in local cuisine. The game and fish dishes
are recommended. ⬜ *from 10am Tue–Sun, until 5pm Sun.* ⬤ *Mon.*

LOWER BAVARIA

DEGGENDORF: *Grauer Hase* €€€€
Untere Vorstadt 12. **Road map** F2. 🕻 *(0991) 37 12 70.*
FAX *(0991) 37 12 720.* 🔲 www.grauer-hase.de 📧 info@grauer-hase.de
The refined interior perfectly complements the superbly appetizing
European dishes. ⬜ *from 10am Mon–Sat, 11:30am–2:30pm Sun.*

GRAFENAU: *Säumerhof* €€
Steinberg 32. **Road map** G2. 🕻 *(08552) 40 89 90.* FAX *(08552) 40 89 950.*
🔲 www.saeumerhof.de 📧 saeumerhof@t-online.de
A recommended dish at this hotel restaurant is stuffed cabbage in red
wine sauce, which is perfectly complemented by celery and green peas.
⬜ *6–9:30pm Tue–Fri, noon–2pm Fri–Sun.*

LANDSHUT: *Fürstenhof* €€€
Stethaimerstr. 3. **Road map** E3. 🕻 *(0871) 92 550.* FAX *(0871) 92 55 44.*
🔲 www.romantikhotels.com/landshut 📧 fuerstenhof@romantik.de
This restaurant, with highly distinguished décor, is part of the hotel of the
same name. The regional cuisine is manifested in many ingenious dishes.
⬜ *noon–2pm and 6:30–9:30pm Mon–Sat.*

PASSAU: *Passauer Wolf* €€€
Rindermarkt 6. **Road map** G2. 🕻 *(0851) 93 15 110.* FAX *(0851) 93 15 150.*
This restaurant has a scenic location overlooking the Danube. Of the
exquisite regional dishes, the roast zander (pike-perch) is highly
recommended. ⬜ *noon–2pm and 6–10pm Mon–Fri, 6pm–10pm Sat.* ⬤ *Sun.*

STRAUBING: *Seethaler* €€
Theresienplatz 25. **Road map** E2. 🕻 *(09421) 93 950.* FAX *(09421) 93 95 50.*
This restaurant is run by the Seethaler family, who specialize in exquisite
regional dishes. ⬜ *10am–midnight Tue–Sat.*

UPPER BAVARIA (EAST)

ALTÖTTING: *Weißbräu Graming* €€
Graming 79. **Road map** F4. 🕻 *(08671) 96 140.* FAX *(08671) 96 14 44.*
This inn with a beer garden shaded by trees serves Bavarian delicacies
such as offal with dumplings. The beer is brewed on the premises. The
dark beer is recommended. ⬜ *8am–midnight Fri–Wed.*

BAD REICHENHALL: *Kirchbergschlössel* €€€
Thumseestr. 11. **Road map** F5. 🕻 *(08651) 27 60.* FAX *(08651) 25 24.*
Located in a small Baroque palace, this restaurant has a festive ambience.
The menu – featuring dishes such as chicken stuffed with chanterelles –
is excellent. On cool evenings warm shawls are offered to guests dining
on the balcony. ⬜ *11am–3pm and 6pm–1am Tue–Sun.*

For key to symbols *see back flap*

		CREDIT CARDS ACCEPTED	TABLES OUTDOORS	VEGETARIAN DISHES	REGIONAL CUISINE	GOOD WINE LIST

Price categories are for a three-course meal for one with half a bottle of wine and including service and taxes (in euros):

€ up to 23 euros
€€ from 23–33 euros
€€€ from 33–43 euros
€€€€ from 43–53 euros
€€€€€ over 53 euros

CREDIT CARDS ACCEPTED
The following credit cards are accepted: American Express, Diners Club, Eurocard, MasterCard, Visa.
TABLES OUTDOORS
Food is served on the terrace or in the garden.
VEGETARIAN DISHES
A good choice of vegetarian dishes is available.
REGIONAL CUISINE
Restaurant offers traditional Bavarian food.
GOOD WINE LIST
A wide choice of different wines is available.

SEEON: *Klostergaststätte Seeon*   €€   ● ■
Klosterweg 2. **Road map** E4. ((08624) 30 85. FAX (08624) 47 96.
This monastery restaurant on the lake serves European cuisine, and fish dishes in particular. The pike-perch fillet in horseradish and cabbage sauce is especially recommended. ◯ 8:30am–midnight daily. ● Nov–Easter

TRAUNSTEIN: *Schnitzlbaumer*   €€   ● ■   ●
Taubenmarkt 11a–13. **Road map** E4. ((0861) 98 66 50. FAX (0861) 98 66 520.
This restaurant, in the heart of the town, serves good Bavarian seasonal dishes, such as boletus mushrooms with dumplings. ◯ 9–1am daily.

WAGING AM SEE: *Wirtshaus am See*   €€€   ● ■   ●
Am See 1. **Road map** F4. ((08681) 40 09 12.
Overlooking the lake, this restaurant serves good Bavarian food. The menu also includes some Mediterranean dishes.
♫ ◯ 10am–11pm Wed–Sun. ● Mon–Tue.

WASSERBURG AM INN: *Herrenhaus*   €€€   ●   ●
Herrengasse 17. **Road map** E4. ((08071) 28 00.
The cuisine here consists of classic Bavarian dishes, freshly prepared with seasonal products. The French dishes are similarly excellent.
◯ 11:30am–2pm and 6pm–1am Tue–Sat.

UPPER BAVARIA (SOUTH)

ANDECHS: *Klostergasthof Andechs*   €   ● ■   ■
Bergstr. 2. **Road map** C4. ((08152) 93 090. FAX (08152) 93 09 11.
w www.klostergasthof.de @ KlostergasthofAndechs@t-online.de
Located in the monastery, this restaurant serves beer brewed on the premises. The recommended accompaniment is knuckle of pork with sauerkraut. ◯ 10am–11pm daily.

BAD TÖLZ: *Altes Fährhaus*   €€€   ● ■
An der Isarlust 1. **Road map** D5. ((08041) 60 30. FAX (08041) 72 270.
Probably the finest food in the region is served here. In summer, diners can sit by the riverside eating lobster or venison with dumplings.
◯ 11:30–2pm and 6pm–midnight Wed–Sun. ● Mon–Tue.

BENEDIKTBEUERN: *Kloster-Bräustüberl*   €€   ■   ■
Zeiler Weg 2. **Road map** C5. ((08857) 94 07.
The beer garden here has a captivating view of the monastery and the lake. Recommended side dishes to enjoy with the beer are fine Bavarian-style knuckle of pork or smoked mackerel. ◯ 9am–midnight daily.

FELDAFING: *Kaiserin Elisabeth*   €€€   ● ■ ● ■ ●
Tutzingerstr. 2–6. **Road map** C4. ((08157) 93 090. FAX (08157) 49 39.
w www.kaiserin-elisabeth.de @ info@kaiserin-elisabeth.de
Located in the hotel of the same name, this restaurant serves fine international and Bavarian cuisine. Many of the dishes are made with fish caught in Starnberger See. ◯ 7:30am–11pm daily.

GARMISCH-PARTENKIRCHEN: *Reindl's Restaurant*   €€€   ● ■   ●
Bahnhofstr. 15. **Road map** C5. ((08821) 94 38 70. FAX (08821) 94 38 72 50.
@ Reindl@Oberland.net
Some exceedingly fine dishes, such as jellied trotters in vinaigrette sauce and roast venison with apple, mushroom and celery mousse are on the menu of this hotel restaurant. ◯ noon–2:30pm & 6:30–11pm daily.

MITTENWALD: *Arnspitze*   €€€   ● ■
Innsbruckerstr. 68. **Road map** C5. ((08823) 24 25.
This hotel restaurant serves the finest food in Mittenwald. The sole with home-made dumplings and the wiener schnitzel in cream sauce are recommended. ◯ noon–2pm and 6–11pm Thu–Mon. ● Tue–Wed after 6pm.

TEGERNSEE: *Berggasthof Lieberhof* €€
Neureuthstr. 52. **Road map** D5. 【 *(08022) 41 63.*
This inn has a terrace with seating for 200 and a view of the lake and the surrounding area. Dishes on offer include Bavarian specialities such as duck with red cabbage and steamed dumplings. ☐ *9am–10pm daily.*

THE ALLGÄU

FÜSSEN: *Geiger* €€
Uferstr. 18, Füssen-Hopfen am See. **Road map** B5. 【 *(08362) 70 74.*
FAX *(08362) 38 838.*
Located in the hotel of the same name, the restaurant offers fine cuisine and a panorama of the lake. ☐ *noon–1:45pm and 6pm–midnight daily.*

KEMPTEN: *M & M* €€€
Mozartstr. 8. **Road map** B5. 【 *(0831) 26 369.*
With simple ingredients, the chef creates flavoursome dishes such as veal ragout with potato dumplings. The menu features dishes from Syria, the chef's country of origin. ☐ *6pm–1am Tue–Sat.*

LINDAU: *Bayerischer Hof* €€€€
Seepromenade. **Road map** A5. 【 *(08382) 91 50.* **FAX** *(08382) 91 55 91.*
@ Bayerischerhof-Lindau@t-online.de
Located in the hotel of the same name, this restaurant stands on the shore of Bodensee. Among the many recommended dishes is the trout, served in various ways. ☐ *11:30am–1:45pm and 7–9:45pm daily.*

OBERSTDORF: *Maximilians* €€€€
Freibergstr. 21. **Road map** B6. 【 *(08322) 96 780.* **FAX** *(08322) 96 78 43.*
@ info@maximilians-restaurant.de
A superb restaurant furnished with elegant simplicity. The contemporary cuisine includes lobsters in truffle sauce. Reservations required.
☐ *from 6pm Mon–Sat.*

OTTOBEUREN: *Mohren* €
Markplatz 1. **Road map** B4. 【 *(08332) 92 130.* **FAX** *(08332) 92 13 49.*
In a 17th-century building located opposite the town hall, this restaurant serves authentic cuisine, including regional dishes. ☐ *11am–11pm daily.*

NORTHERN SWABIA

AUGSBURG: *Die Ecke* €€€€
Elias-Holl-Platz 2. **Road map** C3. 【 *(0821) 51 06 00.*
FAX *(0821) 31 19 92.*
Located opposite the town hall, this restaurant is one of the finest, and also one of the most expensive, in Augsburg. Traditionally furnished, it has plenty of atmosphere. ☐ *11am–2pm and 5:30–10pm daily.*

DILLINGEN: *Storchennest* €€€
Demleitnerstr 6, OT Fristingen. **Road map** B3. 【 *(09071) 45 69.*
FAX *(09071) 61 80.*
Regional cooking with Mediterranean accents, and wines from the Bodensee and Franconia regions. ☐ *11:30am–3pm and 6pm–midnight Wed–Sun.*

DONAUWÖRTH: *Tanzhaus* €€
Reichsstr. 34. **Road map** C2. 【 *(0906) 50 01.* **FAX** *(0906) 24 50 01.*
This restaurant, in a historic building in the town centre, offers Swabian and Bavarian dishes in a congenial atmosphere.
☐ *10:30am–2:30pm and 5:30–11pm Tue–Sun.*

FRIEDBERG: *Herzog Ludwig* €€
Bauernbräustr. 15. **Road map** C3. 【 *(0821) 60 71 27.* **FAX** *(0821) 60 71 26.*
W www.herzog-ludwig.de @ gasthaus@herzog-ludwig.de
A small gourmet restaurant with a quiet, romantic courtyard. The speciality here is Mediterranean cuisine. ☐ *Jan–Apr: 11am–2pm and 6pm–midnight Wed–Sat; May–Dec: 11am–2pm and 6pm–midnight Tue–Sat.*

NÖRDLINGEN: *Meyers Keller* €€€
Marienhöhe 8. **Road map** B2. 【 *(09081) 44 93.* **FAX** *(09081) 24 931.*
W www.meyerskeller.de @ meyers.keller@t-online.de
An elegant and tastefully appointed restaurant. The cream of chicken soup, brisol of veal, loin steak and veal tripe in Riesling are recommended. ☐ *6pm–midnight Tue, 11:30am–2pm and 6pm–midnight Wed–Sun.*

For key to symbols *see back flap*

Pubs, Cafés and Bars in Munich

Munich abounds with bars, cafés, clubs and, of course, hugely popular pubs and beer gardens. There is something for every taste. Places where people go to drink coffee or beer, to have a snack or simply to socialize informally are mostly concentrated in the city centre and in Schwabing. Even in the more outlying districts an abundance of pleasant cafés and bars can be found. Many food shops also set aside a corner for eaters and drinkers.

PUBS AND BEER GARDENS

The features most typical of Munich, and seen everywhere in the city, are spacious pubs often fronted by gardens shaded by chestnut or linden trees. These pubs serve beer from the local breweries as well as generous helpings of good Bavarian food. Waitresses dressed in the traditional *Dirndl* wind their way among the tables and there is often an oompah band playing a repertoire of folk melodies.

Munich's most famous pub is the **Hofbräuhaus**, which today is filled with more American and Japanese tourists than local drinkers. Seated on wooden benches at large tables arranged in spacious rooms, garrulous crowds of guests enjoy their favourite drink as they sing along with and sway in time to the Bavarian music.

Almost equally renowned is the **Augustiner Gaststätte**, which also has a restaurant. The interior is decorated in late 19th-century style, and has a very pleasant courtyard surrounded by arcades, which induce the desire to linger for as long as possible.

Munich's next most famous pubs are the **Löwenbräu-keller** and the **Donisl**. In the latter, with its old-style furnishings, authentic Bavarian folk music is also played. The city's finest beer garden is the **Chinesicher Turm** in the Englische Garten, where there are a total of 6,000 seats for its international clientele.

Many pubs and beer gardens allow drinkers to bring their own food. Beer is best served straight from the barrel. A popular type of beer is *Helles*, a light lager beer. Also widely drunk is *Radler*, beer to which lemonade is added *(see p268)*.

CAFÉS, BARS AND BISTROS

A great variety of different establishments come under the name of "café". They include traditional coffee shops, where people go for *Kaffee und Kuchen*, (coffee and cake), the coffee helping to wash down a large pastry or slice of cake. Two such coffee shops are the old-world **Café Kreutzkamm**, which moved here from Dresden after World War II (it is known for its chocolates, *Dresdner Stollen* and pyramidal cakes), and the **Café Luitpold**, which tempts with its equally excellent cakes and chocolates.

A real oasis of peace – a commodity highly valued by the citizens of Munich – is the **Café am Beethovenplatz**. Time passes more slowly here, and the gentle classical music seems to make the coffee smell and taste better than elsewhere. The atmosphere of the **Kaffeehaus Altschwabing** takes you back to the turn of the 19th and 20th centuries. Thomas Mann and other writers once enjoyed the strong coffee that is served here.

Another type of café is a place offering hot and cold food and a range of soft and alcoholic drinks. The atmosphere is more like that of a bar or bistro. These bar-type cafés are the centre of the social life of Munich. They range from somewhere to go to grab a sandwich or drop in for a coffee or beer, to pretentious places where high society meets. There are also gay and lesbian bars, such as **Café Glück** and **Iwan**, and bars for businessmen, as well as bars for connoisseurs of tobacco, wine or whisky and for pool players.

Many bars serve large and delicious breakfasts and lunches. Others specialize in ice cream. Many, including the **Nachtcafé** or **Roxy**, are open until late at night.

A feature unique to Munich is **Kunstpark Ost**, an extensive leisure park near the Eastern Station. There is nothing quite like it anywhere else. It has clubs, discos (such as the hugely popular Babylon) and bars (such as the much-frequented Bongo Bar) where many Munich people as well as visitors go for entertainment.

TAKE-AWAYS (TAKE-OUTS)

Numerous booths and stalls selling take-away food are to be seen in the streets of Munich, particularly in the main shopping areas of the Old Town and Schwabing, as well as in pedestrian subways and at railway stations.

The traditional take-aways are those of the well-known international fast-food chains. There are also many take-away pizza, sausage, baguette and kebab houses. The **Nordsee** restaurant offers delicious freshly made sandwiches with herring, fried fish or crab salad, and the **Wienerwald** restaurants sell chicken cooked in every possible way.

There are also take-away stands in almost all butcher's shops, where pre-packaged lunch dishes in aluminium trays are sold. The food sold in Munich's most renowned delicatessens, the **Dallmayr** and **Käfer**, is excellent, although the prices can seem a little high *(see p279)*. A good alternative are the hot food stalls to be found in **Viktualienmarkt**.

DIRECTORY

PUBS

Andechser am Dom
Weinstr. 7.
Map 3 B2, 6 D3.
29 84 81.

Augustiner Gaststätte
Neuhauser Str. 27.
Map 3 A2, 5 B3.
23 18 32 57.

Augustiner Keller
Arnulfstr. 52.
59 43 93.

Chinesischer Turm
Englischer Garten 3.
Map 2 F4.
38 38 730.

Donisl
Weinstr. 1.
Map 3 B2, 6 D3.
22 01 84.

Franziskaner Garten
Friedenspromenade 45.
43 00 996.

Grüntal
Grüntal 15.
98 09 84.

Hofbräuhaus
Am Platzl 9.
Map 3 C2, 6 E3.
22 16 76.

Hofbräukeller
Innere Wiener Strasse.
45 99 250.

Kaisergarten
Kaiserstr. 34.
34 02 02 03.

Löwenbräukeller
Nymphenburgerstr. 2.
52 60 21.

Paulaner Bräuhaus
Kapuzinerplatz 5.
54 46 110.

Seehaus
Kleinhesselohe 3.
38 16 130.

Tassilogarten
Auerfeldstr. 18.
44 80 022.

Wintergarten
Elisabethplatz 4B.
Map 2 D3.
27 13 899.

CAFÉS AND BARS

Aficionado
Leopoldstr. 25.
Map 2 E3.
33 08 92 92.

Atzinger
Schellingstr. 9.
Map 2 D4.
28 28 80.

Café am Beethovenplatz
Goethestr. 35.
54 40 43 48.

Café d'Accord
Nordendstr. 62.
Map 2 D2.
27 14 506.

Café Glück
Palmstr. 4.
Map 3 A5.
20 11 673.

Café Glyptothek
Königsplatz 3.
Map 1 B5.
28 61 00.

Café Kreutzkamm
Maffeistr. 4.
Map 3 B2.
29 32 77.

Café im Lenbachhaus
Luisenstr. 33.
Map 1 B5.
52 37 214.

Café Luitpold
Brienner Str. 11.
Map 6 D1.
24 28 750.

Café Munich
Leopoldstr. 9.
Map 2 E3.
34 38 38.

Café Puck
Türkenstr. 33.
Map 2 D4.
28 02 280.

Café Schwabing
Belgradstr. 1.
Map 2 D2.
30 88 856.

Charivari
Türkenstr. 92.
Map 2 D4.
28 28 32.

Interview
Klenzestr. 33.
Map 3 C3, 6 D5.
20 21 649.

Iwan
Josephspitalstr. 15.
Map 3 A2.
55 49 33

Kaffeehaus Altschwabing
Schellingstr. 56.
Map 1 C4.
27 31 022.

Königsquelle
Baaderplatz 2.
Map 3 C3, 6 E5.
22 00 71.

Kunstpark Ost
Grafingerstr. 6.
49 00 27 94.

Münchner Freiheit
Münchner Freiheit 20.
34 90 80.

Nachtcafé
Maximiliansplatz 5.
Map 3 B1, 5 C1.
59 59 00.

Ododo
Buttermelcherstr. 6.
Map 3 C3, 6 D5.
26 07 741.

Pacific Times
Baaderstr. 28.
Map 3 C3, 6 E5.
20 23 84 70.

Pusser's
Falkenturmstr. 9.
22 05 00.

Roxy
Leopoldstr. 48.
Map 2 E3.
34 92 92.

Schumann's
Maximilianstr. 36.
Map 4 D2, 6 F3.
22 90 60.

Skebe Social Room & Bar
Theresienstr. 70.
Map 1 C5.
28 80 83 93.

Speisecafé West
Tulbeckstr. 9.
50 54 00.

Stadtcafé im Stadtmuseum
St-Jakobs-Platz 1.
Map 3 B2, 5 C4.
26 69 49.

Tambosi
Odeonsplatz 18.
Map 3 C1, 6 D1.
29 83 22.

TiefenRausch
Schellingstr. 91.
Map 1 C4.
27 27 20 10.

Tresznjewski
Theresienstr. 72.
Map 1 C5.
28 34 49.

Wiener's
Maximilianstr. 13
Map 3 C2.
29 25 69.

Zum Zum
Türkenstr. 51.
Map 2 D4.
27 24 097.

TAKE-AWAYS

Adria
Leopoldstr. 19.
Map 2 E3.
39 65 29.

Nordsee
Viktualienmarkt 10.
Map 3 B3.
Leopoldstr. 82
Map 2 E3.

Thai Magic
Frauenstr. 2.
Map 3 C3, 6 D4.

Wienerwald
Amalienstr. 23
Map 2 D4.

SHOPS AND MARKETS

RETAILERS IN the Bavarian Alps who cater both to the tourist trade and to the more affluent Bavarians offer for sale virtually everything from the finest luxury goods to local arts and crafts. A particularly ubiquitous Bavarian speciality is sports, hiking and mountaineering equipment, which is displayed for sale in many outlets.

Logo of the Loden Frey shop

There is also a large market for anything in traditional Bavarian style, from beer steins to *Lederhosen* to fine glass and porcelain. An enjoyable way of spending a few hours is to stroll among the stalls in the spa towns selling locally made items. In complete contrast, Munich, one of the most sophisticated European cities, has some very exclusive shops.

The greengrocer's counter in one of Munich's elegant delicatessens

WHERE TO SHOP

SHOPS RANGING from department stores to boutiques to souvenir shops can be found in Munich. All larger towns in the Bavarian Alps have a shopping district, usually pedestrianized.

Also popular are the out-of-town superstores, which attract large numbers of shoppers because of their competitive prices and ease of parking for drivers.

SHOPPING IN MUNICH

MUNICH'S MAIN shopping district is the pedestrianized area of the Old Town around Neuhauser Straße, Kaufinger Straße and the Marienplatz area, where stores and shops of major European retailers are located. This whole area probably has the largest daily turnover in the whole of Germany, and one of the best stores is Ludwig Beck am Rathauseck on Marienplatz. Around Theatinerstraße, Maximilianstraße and Brienner Straße are exclusive

clothes shops such as Versace, Gucci, Escada and Donna Karan, whose prices are out of the reach of most tourists. Maximilianstraße is also the home of the eccentric Munich couturier Rudolf Moshammer.

In the famous Schwabing district, particularly in the area between Amalienstraße, Schellingstraße and Türkenstraße, exclusive boutiques and tasteful second-hand shops can be found, as well as many bookshops (selling both new and second-hand books) and antique shops.

OPENING HOURS

SHOPS ARE legally permitted to open from 6am to 8pm from Monday to Friday, and from 8:30am to 4pm on Saturdays. In practice, most food shops are open between 7am and 9am (bakeries opening the earliest), and close at 8pm. Other shops, including supermarkets, are usually open from 9am to 8pm.

Small shops, particularly in more out-of-the-way places, often close for lunch then stay open until 6pm. At railway stations in large towns it is possible to buy food and beverages until 11pm, even on Sunday. Petrol (gas) stations that also sell food and drink are often open until late at night; some open 24 hours.

PAYING

TRAVELLERS' CHEQUES AND credit cards are accepted in department stores and in larger shops. In Germany the most widely accepted credit card is Euro-card. Somewhat less popular is VISA. In smaller shops cash is preferred.

The showroom of a shop specializing in Nymphenburg porcelain

Advertisement for an exclusive designer fashion shop in Ruhpolding

FOOD AND DRINK

AS ELSEWHERE in Europe, food shops have largely been taken over by retail chains. The exceptions are small butcher's shops, bakeries and confectioners. Fruit and vegetables are still sold in markets, with the most famous being the Viktualienmarkt *(see p64)*. A visit to the delicatessens **Dallmayr** and **Käfer** will be memorable.

The decorative entrance to one of Munich's delicatessens

GIFTS AND SOUVENIRS

IT IS virtually impossible to leave the Bavarian Alps without a souvenir beer mug or a decorative bottle of beer. Particularly suitable as presents are bottles of the local spirits and drinks presented in stoneware bottles, often bearing the portrait of the legendary king Ludwig II.

Tourist resorts are full of souvenir shops. Besides the folksy kitsch there is some good-quality woodcarving, pottery, painted glass and porcelain. Stylized Bavarian costume and accessories made of natural materials are ubiquitous. Conforming to the latest fashion, they are often quite attractive. The best place in Munich for gifts of this type are the **Wallach Haus** and **Loden Frey**.

SPECIALIST SHOPS

MUNICH BOASTS several specialist shops of renown. **Sport Scheck** is an outstanding sports shop. The best bookshops include **Geobuch**, which specializes in maps and guidebooks, **Hugendubel** and **Werner**, which sell books on art, architecture and design. **Hieber am Dom** specializes in musical instruments and literature, while **WOM** and **Zauberflöte** sell CDs and cassettes. Lovers of fine antique furniture and paintings should visit the famous antique shop **Bernheimer Fine Old Masters**.

A shop in Augsburg selling pottery and basketware

What to Buy in the Bavarian Alps

Bavarian felt hat with a *Gamsbart*, or feather

BESIDES A vast range of German and European goods, the visitor to the Bavarian Alps can also purchase local products that make perfect gifts and souvenirs. They are usually inspired by folk traditions, and their artistic merit varies greatly. The sheer quantity of gift-shop kitsch is quite overwhelming, particularly items related to beer-drinking ceremonies and devotional art. However, it is also perfecly possible to find good-quality, tasteful and authentic examples of the arts and crafts of the Bavarian Alps.

Porcelain
Dolls dressed in Bavarian costume make good presents for girls or collectors.

FOLK ART

Many shops selling folk art can be found in the Bavarian Alps. As well as wood carvings, for which Oberammergau is particularly renowned, good-quality paintings and antique items of often striking simplicity are available.

Copy of a Baroque statue

A 19th-century votive painting

Painting on Glass
Painting on glass is a widespread craft in the region, with the main centre being Murnau. Subjects are usually images of saints or religious scenes depicted in a naïve style.

Flat tin figure painted in enamels

GLASS AND CERAMICS

Workshops in the Bavarian Forest region are famous for their glassware *(Waldglass)*. They produce both classic functional items, as well as modern art glass in a range of novel shapes and colours. Folk ceramics include painted pottery and stoneware that characteristically has the colour of grey granite. One of the most prominent centres of ceramic production is Dießen.

Stoneware snuff box

Plate with the Bavarian coat of arms

Bavarian Waldglass

Nymphenburg Porcelain
Usually of a high artistic quality and relatively expensive, hand-painted figurines like this are produced by the famous Nymphenburg porcelain factory.

REGIONAL COSTUME

Bavarian folk costume is attractive and practical in its modern-day form. Usually made of high-quality wool, linen or leather, it gives protection from cold or heat. Recommended for children are the famous Bavarian *Lederhosen*, which are practically dirt-proof but also machine washable should the need arise.

A soft woollen *Janker*

The famous Bavarian
Lederhosen

A decorated leather belt

Leather Goods

Bavaria is renowned for its high-quality leather goods. The material is surprisingly soft, and the items often have a crude but deliberate old-worldliness about them.

Knitted woollen
socks

Decorated
hunter's bag

Leather shoes in Bavarian
folk style

Silver necklace with
colourful pendants

Embroidered
tasselled shawl

DRINKING ACCESSORIES

Among the articles most widely produced by the souvenir industry are beer mugs of all descriptions, ranging from simple stoneware vessels to highly colourful mugs decorated with paintings or reliefs and fitted with pewter lids. They are characteristic of Bavaria and make good gifts.

A finely decorated
beer bottle

Collectors' Items

Both beer-related artifacts as well as antique beer mugs and lids are valued items that are bought and sold by international antiques collectors.

Beer mug with the coat
of arms of Bavaria

Antique beer mug lids

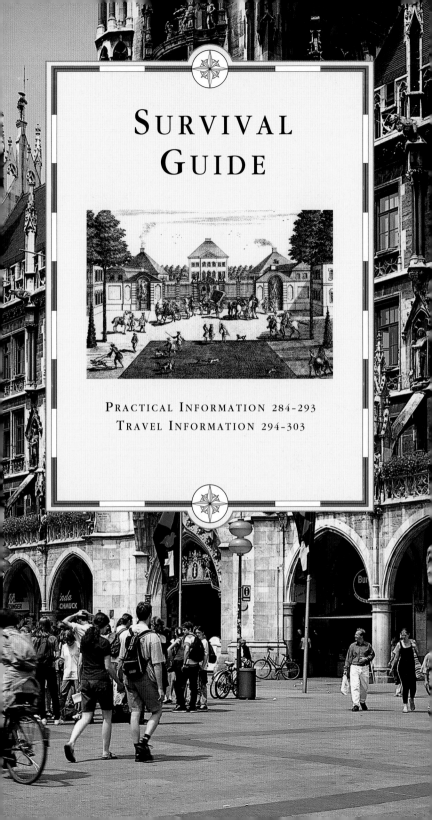

SURVIVAL
GUIDE

PRACTICAL INFORMATION

Tourist information logo

FAMOUS FOR their breathtaking scenery and historic monuments, the Bavarian Alps are the most popular destination for visitors to Germany. Like Munich, the regional capital, this alpine region is well prepared to receive tourists from all over the world. Hotels and catering facilities and an excellent road, rail and public transport network makes travelling in the area a pleasure. The Bavarians are generally friendly and hospitable, although communication may be difficult in smaller towns and villages unless you speak German. This, however, is not a problem in cosmopolitan Munich. The best time to come to the Bavarian Alps is in summer, when the weather is most likely to be good, although out of the high season prices tend to be lower and crowds fewer.

Information plaques on historic buildings

MUSEUMS AND HISTORIC MONUMENTS

ALMOST EVERY TOWN, city and tourist resort in the Bavarian Alps has its own local history museum (*Heimatmuseum*) where local art and artifacts relating to local history are displayed. Even the more out-of-the-way places can reveal private collections of unexpected quality and interest. Bavaria's finest museums are, of course, in Munich.

Most museums in Bavaria are open to the public from 10am to 5pm or 6pm, usually from Tuesday to Sunday. Details of precise opening hours are given on the relevant pages of this guide.

Many reductions on the price of admission to museums and historic monuments are available, and information on these can be obtained at tourist offices or hotel reception desks. A *Verbundeintrittskarte*, available at museum admission desks, costs €15 and gives admission to 30 state museums and residences in Munich for a 14-day period.

Of equally good value is the *München Welcome Card*, valid for one, two or three days for one person, or for three days for two people. This allows travel on all urban public transport in the Blue Zone (*Blaue Zone*), and also gives a 50 per cent reduction on admission to 35 of the city's attractions, which are listed in

A one-day München Welcome Card

a brochure attached to the card. The card can be bought at tourist information offices, in many hotels, and wherever the *München Welcome Card* sign is displayed.

Many churches are open to visitors from 8am until the evening service. However, sightseeing is prohibited during religious services.

TOURIST INFORMATION

TOURIST INFORMATION bureaux are generally found in town centres, in main squares and near railway stations. In towns where there is no tourist information bureau, visitors can obtain information at the town hall (*Rathaus*) or civic centre (*Gemeindehaus*). In spa resorts, information is available from the Resort Administration (*Kurverwaltung*). The general rule at information bureaux is: the fewer the tourists, the friendlier and more exhaustive the service.

In addition to free town maps, tourist information bureaux provide a range of brochures on principal local attractions and programmes for local shows and cultural events. They also assist tourists who are seeking accommodation, help to organize guided tours, and provide information on travel and admission reductions.

St-Jakobs-Platz, one of the most popular tourist spots in Munich

STUDENT AND YOUTH TRAVEL

Tourist resorts in the Bavarian Alps take considerable trouble to ensure that young people are offered interesting entertainment programmes. Information is available at hotel receptions and information points, where programmes of events are usually available.

Young people with an International Student Identity Card (ISIC) are entitled to reductions in many cultural institutions and on urban public transport. "GO 25" and "Euro<26" cards provide similar benefits. In the larger towns and cities there are special information bureaux for young people, where legal advice and support on such issues as education and employment is also available.

The Olympiapark, offering plenty of activities for children

GUIDED TOURS

Tourist information bureaux can arrange specialized tours conducted by guides who are experts in their field. Many tourist agencies offer coach, walking and cycling tours around Munich and the Bavarian Alps, with transport for walkers and cyclists provided where necessary. Guides can be hired for tailor-made excursions or as part of a regular organized tour. In Munich guides who between them speak up to 20 languages are available.

Schloss Neuschwanstein, one of the most popular tourist sites

EVENTS

All year round, the Bavarian calendar is packed with a variety of lively cultural and sporting events, as well as religious and secular celebrations and festivals. Free programmes of such events are available in all towns, cities and tourist resorts. Information on local entertainment can be found in local newspapers, including free newspapers.

For events in Munich, the monthly *In München* and the magazine *Prinz*, which are available at newspaper kiosks and in bookshops, pubs and cinemas, carry information on all important events as does the yellow monthly programme of events that is available at tourist information bureaux.

DISABLED VISITORS

Almost all modern public buildings have access facilities for disabled visitors, and parking spaces reserved for people with disabilities are increasingly common. Institutions that are unable to provide wheelchair access give assistance in other ways.

Munich's Association for the Disabled has issued a guide that makes a stay in the city much easier, giving information on using the underground and on hotel and restaurant facilities. The guide is available from the Association's main office, located at Schelling straße 29/31 in Munich.

DIRECTORY

TOURIST INFORMATION BUREAUX

Bayerntouristik Marketing Gmbh
Leopoldstr. 146, Munich.
Map 4 D1. [(089) 21 23 97 30. FAX (089) 29 35 82.
W www.btl.de; www.bayern.by

Fremdenverkehrsamt München, Rathaus
Marienplatz 8, Munich.
Map 3 B2, 6 D3.
[(089) 23 30 300.
FAX (089) 23 33 02 33.

Hauptbahnhof
Bahnhofplatz 2, Munich.

Fremdenverkehrsverband Allgäu/ Bayerisches Schwaben
Fuggerstr. 9, Augsburg.
[(0821) 33 335.
FAX (0821) 38 331.

Tourismusverband München-Oberbayern
Bodenseestr. 113, Munich.
[(089) 82 92 180.
FAX (089) 82 92 18 28
W www.blt.de/oberbayern; www.oberbayern-tourismus.de

Tourismusverband Ostbayern
Luitpoldstr. 20, Regensburg.
[(0941) 58 53 90.
FAX (0941) 58 53 939.

INFORMATION FOR YOUNG PEOPLE

Jugendinformations- zentrum
Paul-Heyse-Str. 22, Munich.
[(089) 51 41 06 60.

Stadtjugendamt
Paul-Heyse-Str. 20, Munich.
[(089) 23 33 43 56.

GUIDED TOURS

München Stadt- rundfahrten oHG
[(089) 55 02 89 95.

Stattreisen München
[(089) 54 40 42 30.

DISABLED VISITORS

Sozialverband Vdk
Schellingstr. 29/31, Munich.
Map 2 D4. [(089) 21 170.

A typical newspaper kiosk in Munich

CUSTOMS AND VISA REGULATIONS

THE BORDER between Bavaria and Austria is practically non-existent, the only indication of its presence being road signs and some deserted customs buildings. However, travellers crossing the border will need to take their passport with them.

Citizens of countries belonging to the European Union, the US, Canada, Australia, and New Zealand do not require a visa to visit Germany, so long as their stay does not exceed three months' duration. Visitors from South Africa will need a visa. In addition, citizens of many EU countries do not require a passport to enter Germany, although a national ID card with photograph is necessary.

German regulations totally prohibit the importation of firearms, drugs, animals and exotic plants that are under special protection.

Customs limits for travellers from countries outside the EU are 200 cigarettes, or 250g (9oz) of tobacco or 50 cigars, one litre of spirits or two litres of wine. Items for personal use, provided they are not in quantities intended for trade, are not subject to customs duty. Commercial imports must be cleared by Customs.

TAX REFUNDS

ALL GOODS sold in Germany are subject to 16 per cent tax *(Mehrwertsteuer)*. Except for citizens of other EU countries, visitors to Germany are entitled to a tax refund on the price of any non-edible goods that are bought in German shops.

Shops with the Tax Free sign will always issue a tax certificate or Tax-Free cheque when the value of the items purchased exceeds a specified total, which is usually around €50.

A passport must be shown before a certificate or cheque can be issued. When going through Customs on leaving Germany, the certificate must be stamped. Visitors may be asked to show the goods, which must still be in their original packaging, unopened and unused. The tax is either refunded at the border or will be sent to the address on the envelope containing the cheque.

Tax-free shopping sign

TIME

GERMANY IS on Central European Time (GMT plus one hour). Clocks move forward one hour on the last Sunday in March and back on the last Sunday in October.

TELEVISION AND RADIO

DOMINATION OF the national television broadcasters ARD and ZDF and of the local network – the so-called "third channels" *(Dritte Programme)* – has been broken by cable and satellite television. The Bavarian third channel (BR), which provides local news, is largely linked to the local authorities.

Popular new channels are RTL, SAT1, VOX and Pro Sieben, RTL plus, RTL 2 Arte. Their headquarters are in Munich, which after Cologne is Germany's second most important producer of television programmes.

Most televisions receive at least one English-language channel (CNN or BBC World), as well as the French channel TV5. Bavarian radio stations are Antenne Bayern (101.3 & 102.7 FM), with modern music and news, Bayerischer Rundfunk (91.3 & 93.7 FM), with music and local news, and Klassik Radio Bayern (102.3 & 103.2 FM), with classical music. Traffic news (with reports of delays on motorways and railways at border-crossing points.) is broadcast mainly on Bayern 3. Larger towns in Bavaria have several local radio stations.

Tourists in the formal gardens at Schloss Nymphenburg in Munich

Consulates and Embassies

MANY FOREIGN countries have consulates in Munich, although many of them, including the American Consulate, do not issue visas. Visitors who lose their passport or experience any serious problems should turn to their country's consulate for help. The British Embassy and the United States Embassy, together with the embassies of other countries, are located in Berlin.

Newspapers

MAINSTREAM international newspapers such as the *International Herald Tribune*, *The Guardian*, *Le Monde*, *El País*, *Neue Zürcher Zeitung* and *Corriere della Sera* are usually available at kiosks on

Poster advertising one of Munich's major galleries

the day they are published, while others appear a little later.

The main German daily newspapers are the centre-right *Frankfurter Allgemeine Zeitung*, the centre-left *Süddeutsche Zeitung* and the weekly *Die Zeit* and *Der Spiegel*. *Süddeutsche Zeitung*, which is published in Munich, is issued with a large local supplement.

Newspapers also widely read in Munich are the tabloids *Abendzeitung* and *tz*. These are available from automatic vending machines in the street. In the evenings, papers are distributed in bars and restaurants by news vendors.

Of special interest to tourists are the magazines *Prinz* and *Münchner* (this is offered free of charge) which carry information about events and exhibitions. Throughout the Bavarian Alps local illustrated magazines such as *Allgäu* and *Kempten* are available.

Electricity

THE ELECTRICAL system in Germany provides 220-volt, 50 Hz AC, except in some hotel bathrooms, where a lower current is provided as

A newspaper vending machine

a standard safety measure. Electric plugs are of the two-pin European type. UK 220-volt appliances can be plugged into German sockets with an adaptor. US 110-volt appliances will have to be used with a transformer. All hotels in Germany have 220-volt sockets for razors and hair-dryers. Certain appliances work on both 110-volt and 220-volt current.

Public Conveniences

IN BAVARIA'S larger towns and cities, public conveniences can be found without much difficulty and are kept in a good state of cleanliness. They are marked with male and female silhouettes or with the letter D *(Damen)* for Ladies and H *(Herren)* for Gentlemen. Busy parts of cities are well provided with public toilets, although a small payment is usually required. Toilets are also provided in shopping centres, public institutions, hotels and restaurants. In the case of restaurants, if you are not having a meal there, it is courteous to ask permission. For people travelling by car, there are toilets in car parks and at petrol (gas) stations.

Security and Health

Logo of the Munich police

Like the rest of Germany, Munich and the Bavarian Alps benefit from a rigorous public safety policy, and are safe areas for travellers. However, police presence is discreet here and the general public fairly conservative. Stations and trains are patrolled by officers of the Border Police (*Bundesgrenzschutz*). Munich is safer than other large German cities, although, as in all large urban areas, vigilance must be exercised against pickpockets. Tourists who experience problems of any kind should go to the police for help.

Policeman and policewoman

POLICE AND FIRE BRIGADE

THE POLICE and fire brigade are state-run services. Police officers wear green uniforms and police vehicles are green and white. Traffic police (*Verkehrspolizei*), who look after safety on the streets, roads and motorways, are distinguished by their white caps. Urban police in navy-blue uniforms are responsible for catching motorists who have parked illegally or who have failed to pay the correct parking fee. The *Kriminal-polizei* are generally dressed in plain clothes. They will produce their identification and insignia as necessary.

For assistance in an emergency, dial 110 for the police or 112 for the fire brigade. You will be asked to give your name, the reason for the call and your location. The fire brigade can also be called by operating special alarms.

PERSONAL PROPERTY

ALTHOUGH THEFT is not a major problem in Munich, special care should be taken in crowded trains and U-Bahn and S-Bahn stations, in and around the central railway station and around large beer-halls, all of them places where pickpockets operate. The station area is not somewhere to linger, as it is frequented by drug addicts and a few harmless albeit annoying drunks and tramps.

Tourists should take basic safety precautions, such as not carrying large sums of money with them and keeping cameras safe. Most hotels have secure lockers or safes where documents and valuable items can be left. For owners of expensive cars, the extra cost of a guarded car park is worth the peace of mind. Never leave valuables in view when you park your car.

It is advisable to take out comprehensive insurance cover before travelling. Victims of theft should immediately report the crime to the police, who will issue a certificate enabling a claim to be made.

SAFETY IN THE MOUNTAINS

ONE OF THE greatest attractions of the Bavarian Alps is the scope that they offer for hiking, skiing and snow-boarding. However, personal safety depends on awareness and preparation. Hikers can easily be misled by fine weather, so that possible dangers are forgotten. For hiking in the mountains, it is essential to take proper hiking-boots and a rucksack with warm clothes and something to eat and drink, and to carry a detailed map, a first-aid kit and a form of identity.

Hikers should plan their route in advance, match its level of difficulty with their own physical condition, and keep to the marked routes. Skiers and snowboarders should beware of avalanches and never use pistes that are closed. For more difficult routes, it is advisable to hire a guide. (Consult the local **Deutscher Alpenverein** office or tourist information bureau.)

The most common type of police car in Munich

Police vans – widely used in Bavarian towns

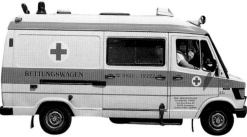

Ambulance of the paramedic rescue services

In the Bavarian Alps there are many mountain shelters where hikers and skiers can rest and eat, and even sleep.

In an emergency, help can be summoned by repeating a sound or light signal six times per minute at one-minute intervals. The response is a signal three times per minute. Mountain rescue teams or emergency services can also be called by telephone.

LOST PROPERTY

IF PROPERTY has been lost, it is worth asking at the local police station or lost property office (**Städtisches Fund-büro**). Lost property offices in smaller towns and spa resorts are often located in the town hall or spa adminis-tration building. For items found on trains, there are the **Deutsche Bahn AG Fund-büro** (for Munich) and the **Deutsche Bahn AG Fund-büro Bundesweit** (for all of Germany). The **Regional-verkehr Oberbayern** deals with items found on buses. The central post office has a lost property office for items left in post offices.

INSURANCE

CITIZENS OF COUNTRIES within the European Union do not have to take out medical insurance in order to obtain free medical care in Germany, although for this they must obtain form E111 from a main post office before leaving home. However, it is still advisable to take out some form of health insurance, and visitors from other countries should take out insurance. If plans include hiking, skiing

or other sporting activities, make sure that the policy covers the costs of rescue services. Insurance against loss of luggage and holiday cancellation is also advisable.

MEDICAL ASSISTANCE

GERMANY HAS one of the best health services in the world. When called, ambulances arrive promptly. Those able to reach a hospital themselves should enter by the entrance marked **Notaufnahme** (Accident and Emergency). Less serious cases can be dealt with in one of the many private clinics. Advice can also be obtained in a pharmacy (**Apotheke**). Most pharmacies are open until 6pm (some until 8pm), and every area has one all-night pharmacy. The address of the nearest all-night pharmacy is given on the door of each pharmacy. In Munich you can also find the nearest all-night pharmacy by telephoning 55 17 71.

Pharmacy logo

The window display of a pharmacy in the Bavarian Alps

DIRECTORY

EMERGENCY SERVICES

Police
℡ 110.

Fire brigade
℡ 112.

Ambulance
℡ 19 222.

Emergency Poison Help Line
℡ (089) 19 240.

Confidential Help Line
℡ (089) 56 79 00.

Duty Doctor and Pharmacy Information
℡ (089) 55 17 71.

LOST PROPERTY

Städtisches Fundbüro
Oetztaler Str. 17, Munich.
℡ (089) 23 300.
⏱ 8:30am–noon Mon–Fri, 2–6:30pm Tue.

Bundespost – Fundbüro
℡ (01802) 33 33.

Deutsche Bahn AG Fundbüro
Hauptbahnhof, Munich.
℡ (089) 13 08 66 64.
⏱ 6:30am–11pm Mon–Fri, 7:30am–10:45pm Sat–Sun.

Deutsche Bahn AG Fundbüro Bundesweit
℡ (01805) 99 05 99.

Regionalverkehr Oberbayern (RVO)
Truderingerstr. 2, Munich.
℡ (089) 41 41 94 60.
⏱ 7:30am–4pm Mon–Fri.

CREDIT CARDS

American Express
℡ (069) 97 97 10 00.

Diner's Club
℡ (05921) 86 12 34.

EuroCard
℡ (069) 74 09 87.

EuroCard & MasterCard
℡ (069) 79 220.

VISA
℡ (0800) 81 49 100.

Banks and Local Currency

Logo of the ReiseBank

ALTHOUGH THERE is no limit to the amount of currency that can be brought in or taken out of Germany, for large amounts of cash a statement of import (or export) may be required by the customs department. Travellers' cheques and credit cards are widely accepted, both of which minimize problems in case of loss or theft. Cash will be needed for small purchases. Foreign currency can be exchanged in banks, at exchange bureaux and at currency exchange machines.

A currency exchange machine on Marienplatz in Munich

CHANGING CURRENCY

BANKS IN Germany are generally open from 8:30am to 4pm Monday to Friday, but many close early on Wednesdays. Currency can be changed at the larger branches of major banks as well as at bureaux de change, which are located throughout Munich and in larger towns throughout the Bavarian Alps.

Cash can easily be obtained with a cash withdrawal card at an automatic cash machine (ATM). All major banks have automatic cash machines at almost all their branches. The machines are usually located in the lobby, which can be entered after closing time by swiping a cash card. Automatic cash machines are also found in all large shopping centres throughout the Bavarian Alps.

Automatic cash machine

German banks usually charge foreign card-users between €2 and €4 per withdrawal, and card withdrawals are usually the cheapest way of obtaining cash. Changing currency will usually incur higher charges. While the best currency exchange rates are generally found at branches of Sparkasse, the least favourable are usually those offered at airports, in city centres and in most major hotels.

Currency can also be exchanged at automatic currency exchange machines, although these are relatively few. They also only accept banknotes in the most common currencies.

CREDIT CARDS AND TRAVELLERS' CHEQUES

CREDIT CARDS can be used to pay bills in most hotels and restaurants, in all depart-

ment stores and in most shops. Credit cards are not accepted in many smaller shops and restaurants, and usually not for amounts of less than €25.

Travellers' cheques can be used to pay for goods and services, and to settle hotel bills, although it is very often best to pay in cash. Travellers' cheques can be cashed in banks and currency exchange bureaux. It is a best to purchase travellers' cheques in Euro denominations.

Head office of the Bank of Bavaria, now Hypovereinsbank, in Munich

CURRENCY

O**N** 1 **JANUARY** 2002 the Euro, the common unit of currency of the European Union, was introduced into general circulation, replacing the former Deutschmark in Germany. The notes and coins are legal tender in Germany as well as in other countries that have signed up to the Euro. In an initial move over to the common currency, the Euro has been introduced in 11 other countries: Austria, Belgium, Finland, France, Greece, Holland, Ireland, Italy, Luxembourg, Portugal and Spain. Although the value of the Euro fluctuates, it is worth approximately US$1 or 62 UK pence.

Euro Banknotes

Euro banknotes are distinguished from each other by colour and size – which reflects their value. The smallest is a note worth 5 Euros (grey) and the largest 500 Euros (purple). All banknotes bear the stars of the European Union and various architectural details.

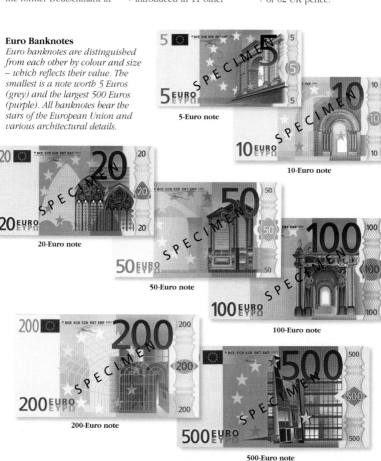

5-Euro note

10-Euro note

20-Euro note

50-Euro note

100-Euro note

200-Euro note

500-Euro note

2-Euro coin 1 Euro 50 Eurocent 20 Eurocent 10 Eurocent

Coins

Euro coins are issued in the following denominations: 1 and 2 Euro, and 1, 2, 5, 10, 20 and 50 Eurocents. The 1 and 2 Euro coins are dual-coloured, silver-gold, while the 1, 2 and 5 Eurocent coins are bronze. The 10, 20 and 50 Eurocent coins are a gold colour.

5 Eurocent 2 Eurocent 1 Eurocent

Communications

Deutsche Telekom sigh

THE POSTAL and telecommunications services in Germany are very efficient. Although it may be necessary to queue for a while in the post office, letters and postcards are usually delivered within the country in 24 hours. Telephone boxes can be found on street corners, in stations, and in restaurants and cafés. Mail boxes (once yellow, but now often grey and pink) are found everywhere, even in the most out-of-the-way corners of the Bavarian Alps.

Colourful chip telephone card (back and front)

USING THE TELEPHONE

AS EVERYWHERE else in Europe, the market for telephone services in Germany has changed fundamentally in recent times. The introduction of mobile phones has brought about a revolution in telephone usage. Visitors wishing to use their mobile phone in Germany should contact their service provider for information.

  Much has also changed in traditional landline phone services, although the principal provider continues to be Deutsche Telekom, which is responsible for all public telephones in Germany. The number of payphones taking coins,

Card-operated telephone sign

rather than cards, is constantly dwindling. If a user inserts too many coins into a payphone, the unused coins will be returned after the call, although change will not be given. A telephone card (costing €6 or €25) gives better value for money. The cards can be bought at post offices and most newsagents. Alternatively, travellers can purchase an international phone card before leaving home. While a phonecard is being used in a public phone, an illuminated display shows the amount of credit remaining on the card.

  In many busy areas of towns and cities and at railway stations and in airports public telephones operated

by credit cards can be found. In order to use them it is necessary to dial in a PIN number. Many public phones have their own telephone number. These can receive incoming calls, so that you can be called back if your money or card runs out.

  Every public telephone should be equipped with a set of local telephone directories, although these are often missing. Most post offices have telephone directories for the whole country. Deutsche Telekom recommends the use of its national information service, although at about €1 per enquiry, using it is expensive.

  Charges for local, national and international calls depend on the time of day. The cost of calls made from hotel rooms is considerably greater than from public telephones.

USING A COIN-OPERATED TELEPHONE

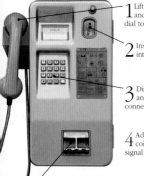

1 Lift the handset and wait for the dial tone.

2 Insert coins into the slot.

3 Dial number and wait to be connected.

4 Add more coins when signal is given.

5 When you have finished your call, or have not been connected, replace the handset. For the return of unused coins, press the button above the slot where you inserted the coins.

USING A CARD-OPERATED TELEPHONE

1 Lift the handset and wait for the dial tone.

2 Choose the appropriate language.

3 Insert the card as instructed. The illuminated display will show the amount of credit remaining.

4 Dial the number and wait to be connected.

5 After finishing the call replace the handset. Withdraw the card by pressing on the green button.

POSTAL SERVICES

POST OFFICES are indicated by the word *"Post"* while mail boxes and the Deutsche Post logo are a distinctive yellow. In large towns post offices are usually open from 8am to 6pm on weekdays and from 8am until noon on Saturdays. Branches with service on Sundays or with longer opening hours can be found at most airports and large railway stations.

Stamps for letters and postcards can be bought at post offices and from automatic stamp machines, and are sometimes sold along with postcards. Some mailboxes have two slots – for local post and for all other destinations. Collection times are also shown on the mailbox.

Letters sent *Poste Restante* are usually issued from post offices near railway stations. Such correspondence should be marked with the words *"Postlagernde Briefe/ Sendungen"*. In order to collect mail, a passport or other form of identification must be produced.

Just as in other countries, registered mail, telegrams and parcels can be sent from post

Post Office No. 32, at the Central Station in Munich

offices. Besides stamps, post offices sell phone cards, postcards, envelopes and cartons in which to send items by post.

Many former post offices have been converted into service centres offering such facilities as a fax and photocopying service. They also sell books and stationery.

THE INTERNET AND E-MAIL

THE INTERNET and e-mail have become increasingly popular and essential as a means of communication, and

they can be especially useful for people who are abroad on holiday or business. As a result, many hotels now offer their guests access to the Internet as well as e-mail facilities. Internet cafés, where online access can be obtained for a small fee, can be found in most towns and cities throughout southern Bavaria, while computers can often be hired by the hour in commercial centres.

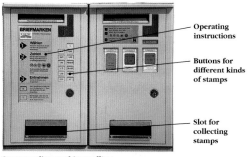

Operating instructions

Buttons for different kinds of stamps

Slot for collecting stamps

Street vending machines selling postage stamps and telephone cards

Collection times

Slot for local letters

Slot for long-distance mail

USEFUL TELEPHONE NUMBERS

- National directory enquiries: 11 833.
- International directory enquiries: 11 834.
- To make an international call: dial 00, wait for the dialling tone, then dial country code, area code + number, omitting the first 0.
- Country codes: UK 44; Eire 353; Canada and USA 1; Australia 61; South Africa 27; New Zealand 64.
- Country and area code for Munich: 49 89.

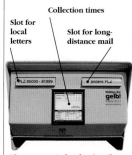

The most typical style of mail-box seen in Germany

TRAVEL INFORMATION

THE BAVARIAN ALPS are situated in the heart of Europe. Thanks to Bavaria's excellent road and rail network, and to Munich's large, modern international airport, reaching the Bavarian Alps – Germany's most popular tourist destination – from anywhere in Europe is fairly straightforward. Buses are comfortable and effi-

Lufthansa plane

cient and are particularly useful in rural areas not served by rail. In Munich – the heart of Bavaria – trams, buses and the U-Bahn and S-Bahn network provide a swift and convenient way of moving around the city. The Bavarian Alps are also a gateway on the route into Italy: roads can become congested at peak holiday times.

ARRIVING BY AIR

MUNICH'S Franz-Josef-Strauß international airport is Germany's second-busiest after that at Frankfurt am Main. Flying to Munich takes you to the heart of Bavaria. The main airlines providing links between the UK and Bavaria are British Airways and Lufthansa, Germany's national airline. Both operate regular flights from London direct to Munich. The low-cost airline Go also serves Munich from London's Stansted airport, with two flights daily.

Direct flights to Germany are usually available from major US cities, including New York (JFK), Washington DC, Boston, Chicago, San Francisco and Los Angeles. Most arrive at Berlin or Frankfurt. Although Canada does not have have many direct flights to Germany,

Air Canada operates regular flights from Toronto to Frankfurt and from Vancouver to Frankfurt.

Deutsche BA (a subsidiary of British Airways) serves Munich with direct flights from Berlin, Bonn/Cologne, Düsseldorf and Hamburg.

AIR FARES

SCHEDULED AIR FARES can vary considerably, with possible reductions for children, students, people under the age of 26, elderly people, and groups. The cheapest scheduled ticket is an APEX, to which certain conditions apply. The cheapest fares are often those offered by the new low-cost airlines or by discount agents. Apart from over the Christmas period, some of the cheapest fares are available from November to March, coinciding with the best Alpine skiing conditions.

Flight information board in Munich's airport

GETTING TO MUNICH AIRPORT

FRANZ-JOSEF-STRAUSS International Airport, which opened in 1992, is one of the most modern and important airports in Europe. It is located 28 km (17 miles) from central Munich, and thanks to efficient connections you can get to the city centre in about 45 minutes, although delays can occur on the motorway, especially during the rush hour.

The quickest and most reliable way of getting to and from the airport is by the S-Bahn, whose lines S1 and S8 run from about 4am to 1am (with a service every 20 minutes after 5am). Travellers taking the S1 to the airport should board one of the rear carriages marked "*Flughafen*" (airport), as the train's front carriages are uncoupled at Neufahrn and continue to Freising.

The railway station is situated beneath the airport, and all directions are clearly

Arriving by bus or train, two ways of getting to Munich airport

One of the lounges at Munich's Franz-Josef-Strauß International Airport

signposted. Rail tickets from Munich to the airport cost €8, but if you buy a *Streifenkarte*, for €9 , you need to punch only eight of the 10 sections. Children (aged 6–15) pay €.80 and €.65 respectively (for one red section of a child *Streifenkarte*). Groups of up to five people can buy a group ticket *(Gruppenkarte)* for €14.

Taxi fares from Munich to the airport are relatively high – around €50. An *Airport-Bus* runs between Munich's Central Station and the airport every 20 minutes: the cost is €9 for adults and €4.50 for children. The first bus leaves Central Station at 5:10am, and the last at 7:50pm. There are also bus links between the airport and other towns and cities in Bavaria.

The use of luggage trolleys is free in the arrivals lounge, but in the departure lounge the cost is €1 .

MUNICH AIRPORT

Passengers waiting for their flights have a wide variety of bars and restaurants to choose from. In addition to fast-food outlets, the airport has a good-quality restaurant, as well as cafés and self-service snack bars.

There is also a range of shops selling Bavarian delicacies, as well as clothes, toys and various souvenirs. There is also a perfumery, a pharmacy and bookshops,where foreign newspapers are available. All shops in the airport accept the main credit cards, although for small purchases and in snack bars cash payment is required.

Additional facilities include a health centre with a 24-hour service. Some airlines, such as British Airways and Lufthansa, have special check-in desks for passengers arriving late for their flights. The desks are to be found in the central area of the airport.

Munich airport is designed in the shape of an elongated rectangle, and travellers should bear in mind that there are substantial distances between its individual sections, although travelators help passengers cover long distances between them with the minimum of effort.

The shape of the airport's buildings and the design of its interior reflect the high-tech style of the early 1990s. Its individual sections contain various artistic installations, and the entire complex conveys a monolithic and unified impression.

A major attraction is the Besucherpark (visitors' centre), which can be reached from car park P51, or by a two-minute S-Bahn journey (alight at Besucherpark).

In addition to its own restaurant and playground, the centre has a special simulator for visitors to experience the sensations of flight, an information point about the latest air-travel technology and a viewing platform where planes can be seen taking off and landing at close quarters.

Travellers needing to spend the night near the airport can stay at one of the modern hotels nearby, such as the Kempinski Hotel Airport München.

Control tower at Munich airport

Munich's central railway station

ARRIVING BY TRAIN

THE BAVARIAN ALPS are well served by a relatively extensive railway network. Trains are very frequent and delays are a rarity.

Munich has direct connect-ions with most major European cities. Main routes from the United Kingdom are via Dover to Ostend or Harwich to the Hook of Holland. An alternative is to travel to Brussels by Eurostar and pick up an onward connection to Germany from there.

GERMAN TRAINS

GERMAN TRAINS, which are operated by **Deutsche Bahn AG**, are comfortable and only crowd-ed during the peak holiday season. The fastest trains, the high-speed InterCity Express (ICE), have air-conditioning and airline-style seats, a bistro and restaurant, card-operated payphones and newspapers and earphones on sale. Somewhat slower and less expensive are the InterCity (IC) trains and EuroCity (EC), on which a small supplement is payable regardless of the distance travelled. The network also runs Interregio (IR) trains and slow trains (D). Short-distance links between towns are made by Regional-Express (RE), StadtExpress (SE) and the suburban S-Bahn trains.

TRAIN TICKETS

TRAIN TICKETS can be purchased at the ticket offices of railway stations, or at station ticket machines for shorter journeys. Although long queues are rare, it is wise to allow 10–15 minutes for buying a ticket. Tickets for journeys of less than 100 km (62 miles) are valid only on the day of purchase. Others are valid for four days, and return tickets are valid for one month. It is also possible to buy tickets in advance and to reserve seats.

Deutsche Bahn railway workers

Train fares in Germany are quite expensive. How-ever, a wide range of discounts is available, particularly during the summer season. One way to travel more cheaply is to buy a *Bahn-Card*, which gives a 50 per cent discount. An InterRail card, available to all European citizens, is economical for extensive or frequent rail travel.

For rail travel in Bavaria, the *Bayern-Ticket* offers good value. A one-day ticket, cost-ing €20, can be used by up to five people from Monday to Friday, or by parents with any number of their own children up to the age of 17. These tickets are valid only on RE, RB and S-Bahn trains and time restrictions apply. The *Schönes-Wochenend-Ticket* (SWT), costing ™18, also for use only on RE, RB and S-Bahn trains, is valid all day and most of the night on either a Saturday or a Sunday. Both tickets also give free travel on urban transport in Munich.

ARRIVING BY COACH

MUNICH AND other cities in the Bavarian Alps can be reached by coach (long-distance bus). For tourists already in Austria, Switzerland or Italy who want to visit Bavaria, coaches from Vienna, Zurich or Bozen (Bolzano) terminate at Munich's central station. Routes from the UK are operated by Eurolines.

TRAVELLING BY BUS

ALMOST ALL Bavarian towns and villages are connected by a local bus network, particularly in places where there is no railway station. Bus timetables are devised mainly to suit commuters, so that the service is very frequent at peak hours and relatively sparse at weekends and on public holidays.

Most towns have a *Zentraler Omnibus Bahnhof* (ZOB) close to the train station and it is here that most bus services originate and where service timetables and other information can be obtained and tickets purchased.

In rural areas there are many request stops. Here every bus stop has a time-table, and tickets can also be bought from the driver.

Comfortable, long-distance, double-decker coach

A popular way of seeing Bavaria is on a coach tour. Information is available from any tourist information office, hotel or travel agent. A wide range of tours is on offer – from sightseeing tours of Munich to special-interest tours and skiing trips.

BOAT TRIPS

BAVARIA'S MANY rivers and lakes make boat trips a great attraction. The most scenic of these are on the region's largest lakes – the Starnberger See, Ammersee, Tegernsee, Chiemsee and Königssee – and on rivers such as the Danube and the Altmühl. Their confluence is the start of canals linking the Rhine and the Main. On many of the smaller lakes, small privately run boats operate, and it is also possible to hire boats there. Rafting is possible on the River Salzach near Burghausen, and particularly on the River Isar. The Isar route covers the stretch of river from Wolfratshausen to Thalkirchen, a southern district of Munich. Longer cruises are available on the Danube from Passau to Vienna. This can be pleasantly combined with visits to the historic sights of the Danube valley.

Boats moored at the jetty at Stock am Chiemsee

DIRECTORY

Deutsche Bahn AG
[Information and reservations
0180 59 96 633.
W www.bahn.de
W www.deutsche-bahn.de

RAILWAY STATIONS

Hauptbahnhof
[Information 01 80 59 96 633.

DB-Touristik
[(089) 13 08 54 07.

TRAVEL AGENT

Deutsches Reisebüro (DER)
Landshuter Allee 38,
D- 82515 Munich.
[(089) 12 04 237.
W www.dertravel.co.uk

RAFTING ON THE ISAR

Josef Seitner Floßfahrten
Lindenweg 1,
D- 82637 Wolfratshausen.
[(08171) 78 518.

TRAIN ROUTES IN SOUTHERN BAVARIA

Southern Bavaria has an extensive rail network providing convenient links between all larger towns and cities in the region.

KEY
— Railway line
= S-Bahn

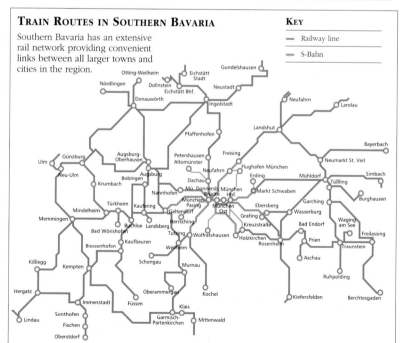

Munich's Buses, Trams, U-Bahn and S-Bahn

I N ADDITION TO its eight underground (U-Bahn) lines, Munich has an extensive network of bus and tram routes. The environs of Munich are connected to the city by the fast suburban overground (S-Bahn) trains, which also serve Munich itself. The city's S-Bahn stations are linked to over 200 bus routes, so that the whole region is well connected by public transport. As all four networks are part of the Münchner Verkehrs- und Tarifverbund (MVV), uniform regulations and fares apply.

One of Munich's trams, bearing the city's coat of arms

TRAVELLING BY BUS AND TRAM

W ITH 82 bus routes and 23 tram routes (seven of them served by night trams), overground travel in Munich is easy. For tourists in particular, buses and trams are an attractive alternative to the U-Bahn and S-Bahn networks as they are less crowded and allow passengers to see the city as they travel.

Buses and trams are frequent and punctual. Each stop has a route map giving details of timetables, connections and multiple tickets. Tickets can be purchased at machines situated beside the stops as well as on the buses and trams themselves. To buy a ticket at a machine, press the button to select the appropriate ticket, insert the payment into the slot (accepted coins and notes are listed) and take the ticket, together with any change. When you board the tram or bus, you must validate the ticket by stamping it at the franking machine located just inside the doors. However, in the new-style trams, tickets are sold ready-stamped.

Each bus or tram stop is either announced by a recorded voice (or the driver), or is displayed on a screen. If

in doubt, ask the driver or other passengers.

The city and its environs are divided into four zones, each of which is indicated on maps by a different colour. For tourists, Zone 1 (the blue zone) is the most important, because it covers the city centre. Single tickets cost €1.94 for travel within Zone 1, €4 for Zone 2, €6 for Zone 3 and €8 for Zone 4. If you intend to make several journeys, it is cheaper to buy a *Streifenkarte* (strip card), which costs €9. The card is divided into 10 sections; you will need two sections for each zone you travel through. The ticket should be folded at the appropriate place and inserted into the franking machine. The last stamp cancels all previous ones. For short journeys (of up to four stops), a *Kurzstrecke* ticket costing €1 can be bought. Alternatively, you can frank just one section of a *Streifenkarte*.

For tourists, the best type of ticket is the one-day *Tageskarte*, or the three-day *3-Tageskarte*. Both are available in two forms – for a single person *(Single)* or for

Typical bus stop in Munich

groups of up to five people *(Partner)*. Two children aged 6–14 count as one person. A *Tageskarte* costs €4.60 *(Single)* or €7 *(Partner)*, while a *3-Tageskarte* costs €11 *(Single)* or €18 *(Partner)*. These tickets are available at tourist information offices, in most hotel receptions, and in travel agents, newsagents and stationers. They are valid from the time they are stamped until 6am the following day.

For visitors staying in Munich for an extended period, a weekly, monthly or even annual *Isarcard* may be more advantageous. The cost depends on the number of "rings", or zones, which will be used. The maximum number of rings is 16, four of which are in the centre of Munich. A weekly four-ring *Isarcard*, for example, costs €13. All *Isarcards* allow any number of the holder's children plus three other children to travel free. They are valid

A long Munich bus, serving one of 82 bus routes in the city

**Information panel in one of
Munich's U-Bahn stations**

after 9am Monday to Friday, and all days Saturday, Sunday and on public holidays.

Children under the age of six travel free. Single tickets for children aged 6–15 cost €.82, and a 5-section child's *Streifenkarte* €3.30 (only one section needs to be franked for travel over any distance). A one-day child's *Tageskarte* valid for the whole public transport network costs €1.60. Young people aged 15–20 need to stamp only one section of their *Streifenkarte* per zone, in effect travelling half-price.

All passengers with valid tickets are entitled to carry one dog free of charge. A child fare must be paid for each additional dog. This does not apply to animals in baskets or carriers.

The Münchner Verkehrs-und Tarifverbund (MVV) also offers various combination tickets, such as the *München Welcome Card (see p284)* and the *Weißblaue Kombikarte*, which includes boat travel on Starnberger See and

Ammersee. Full details regarding combination tickets are available at tourist information offices.

THE U-BAHN AND S-BAHN NETWORKS

MUNICH'S UNDERGROUND rail network – the U-Bahn – is a relatively new development in the city's transport system. The first section opened in 1971 and some stretches are still not completed. The S-Bahn, which is a fast suburban train network, coincides in some places with the U-Bahn, which emerges above ground outside the city centre.

Many U-Bahn and S-Bahn stations are decorated with motifs that have some connection with the relevant area of the city above the station. In the U-Bahn station at Königsplatz, for example, the decoration is based on some of the exhibits displayed in the museums on the square.

The fare system on the U-Bahn and S-Bahn is the same as that which applies on Munich's trams and buses. Tickets can be bought at machines or at ticket offices in most stations. Before boarding the

Logo of the S-Bahn suburban network

FRANKING MACHINE

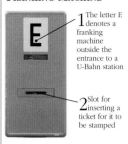

1 The letter E denotes a franking machine outside the entrance to a U-Bahn station

2 Slot for inserting a ticket for it to be stamped

train, tickets must be stamped in a franking machine, which is often located at the top of the stairs leading down to the platform. If you are not travelling yourself but only accompanying someone who holds a valid ticket, you need to buy a platform ticket (*Bahnsteigkarte*).

Tickets for events such as concerts or football matches often include the price of the fare to the venue on the U-Bahn or S-Bahn. This is stated on the ticket for the event.

The U-Bahn and S-Bahn trains are frequent and reliable, although they are likely to become quite crowded during the morning and evening rush hours. Before boarding an S-Bahn train, check the destination given on the electronic information boards. On the U-Bahn, boarding the wrong train is easy to do because trains travelling in opposite directions come in on either side of one platform. Check the *Richtung* (direction) panel as well as the destination to ensure that you board the correct train.

TICKET MACHINE

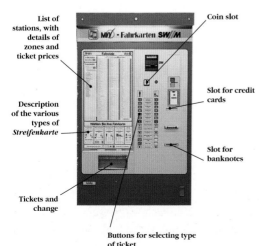

List of stations, with details of zones and ticket prices

Description of the various types of *Streifenkarte*

Tickets and change

Coin slot

Slot for credit cards

Slot for banknotes

Buttons for selecting type of ticket

One of the U-Bahn's green trains at underground station

Getting around Munich on Foot, by Bicycle, Taxi and Car

MOST OF Munich's tourist attractions and historic monuments are located in the city centre and distances between them are not far, making it easy to see Munich on foot. The numerous cafés, squares and parks provide ample opportunity to rest in pleasant surroundings. Because of traffic congestion and parking problems, driving in Munich is a less inviting prospect. Cycling, by contrast, is very popular and bicycles can be hired at one of the many cycle hire points.

A typical Munich street sign

AROUND MUNICH ON FOOT

EXPLORING MUNICH on foot is especially interesting and rewarding. Much of the Old Town has been closed to traffic, and only in the main shopping streets do you have to struggle through crowds.

Most of the tourist attractions in the Old Town are within less than 20 minutes' walk of each other and, when venturing further afield, strolling through the city's various districts can be a pleasant experience in itself.

Drivers in Munich are courteous to pedestrians, even though not all pedestrians obey the rules. A basic rule is that pedestrians do not cross the road when a red pedestrian light shows, even if the road is clear. Pedestrian crossings often have a sign saying "Set an example to children". The many cyclists that circulate in the city can be a danger to careless pedestrians. Cyclists using the special cycle lanes can gather considerable speed and pedestrians who stray on to these lanes often receive a severe reprimand or may even find themselves in an unpleasant collision.

Locating a particular address in Munich is straightforward. Street names are posted at junctions and buildings are clearly numbered, with odd and even numbers on opposite sides of the street.

Munich's many parks make walking in the city very attractive. To escape the urban bustle, it is pleasant to walk in the delightful Englischer Garten or the green spaces of Maximilian-anlagen on the river bank, or take a trip to Nymphenburg park or the Botanical Gardens. A cold beer in a beer garden is an excellent reward for the exercise.

BY BICYCLE

MUNICH IS A city of cyclists. Cycle lanes are marked off on pavements (sidewalks) and on the edges of roads. Special bicycle stands can also be found throughout the city and large numbers of bicycles can be seen parked at railway and S-Bahn stations. However, before leaving their bicycle, owners should lock it securely.

Bicycles can be taken on the U-Bahn and S-Bahn, but not on trams or buses.

Sign for a pedestrian zone

Travellers taking their bicycle onto a U-Bahn or S-Bahn train should board at the appropriate door and stand their cycle in the appropriate place (no more than two bicycles are allowed). Bicycles cannot be taken on the U-Bahn or S-Bahn between 6 and 9am and 4 and 6pm Monday to Friday, although this restriction is suspended during school holidays. Taking a bicycle on the U-Bahn or S-Bahn costs €2 or two sections of a *Streifenkarte (see p298)*. The cheapest way is to buy a one-day cycle card for €2.30.

There are bicycle hire points *(Fahrradverleih)* at various places in the city centre as well as at MVV stations and at major tourist spots. Bicycle hire is quite cheap, and cycling in the city is a great pleasure.

Tourist information offices provide cycle maps of Munich and brochures showing the routes of the best cycling tours around the city. MVV also publishes a guide entitled *Radeln mit dem MVV (Cycling with MVV)*, showing 52 cycle routes around the most scenic parts of Munich.

BY TAXI

TAXIS IN MUNICH, as else-where in Germany, are invariably large cream-coloured cars with a "TAXI" sign on the roof; this is illuminated when the taxi is

Cycling – a quick and popular way of getting around Munich

A taxi in Munich, identifiable by its cream colour and "Taxi" sign

available. Taxis can be hailed on the street or booked by telephone. They can also be picked up at a taxi rank, although these are rare. If the rank is empty, a cab can be called from the telephone there. Taxi ranks together with their telephone numbers are also listed under *"Taxi München AG"* in Yellow Pages *(Gelbe Seiten)*.

The fare is calculated by an illuminated meter on the dashboard. The lowest rates apply during the week, for journeys within the city limits. At night and at weekends the rates are higher. It is customary to give a small tip.

DRIVING IN MUNICH

MUNICH IS at the hub of a network of motorways radiating in many directions. To the south are motorways A8 to Salzburg and A95 to Garmisch Partenkirchen, to the southwest is motorway A96 to Lindau, to the west is motorway A8 to Stuttgart, to the north motorway A9 to Nuremberg, and to the east motorway A95 to Passau.

There is a ring road *(Auto-bahnring)* around the city, although this is often congested. Munich also has two smaller ring roads, the *Mittlerer Ring* and the *Altstadtring*, which relieve some of the congestion but are themselves often filled to capacity with traffic.

One of the biggest problems for motorists in Munich is finding a parking space. Although there are many multi-storey car parks *(Parkhäuser)*, they are expensive and often full. (The word *"Frei"* indicates that parking spaces are available.) Most on-street parking must be paid for, either by inserting coins into a meter or by buying a pay-and-display ticket. Another problem is that there is a strict time limit for parking in

Parking sign with information

the city centre, one hour often being the maximum time allowed. Parking attendants *(Politessen)* patrol the streets, issuing tickets when cars are illegally parked or parking is unpaid.

Parking rules in Germany are much stricter than in most other European countries. Cars can only be parked in the same direction as the flow of traffic. Parking is forbidden even slightly on the kerb (unless there is a sign or markings allowing this). Some of the strictest penalties are for the unauthorized use of parking spaces reserved for disabled drivers.

For those who are not familiar with the city, driving in Munich can be quite a harrowing experience. The traffic is relatively heavy and although drivers obey regulatons, their driving style is quick and decisive. Visitors are advised to leave their car at their hotel or in the outskirts of the city, and use the excellent public transport system instead.

Pay-and-Display Ticket Machine
Automatic parking-ticket machines like this issue receipts that are placed inside the car windscreen.

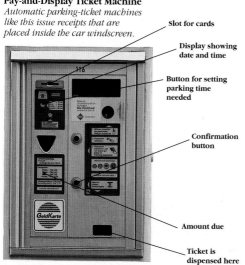

Slot for cards

Display showing date and time

Button for setting parking time needed

Confirmation button

Amount due

Ticket is dispensed here

Travelling by Car

BY FAR THE fastest and most comfortable way of travelling around Bavaria is to use the motorways. However, during the holiday season, the Bavarian Alps become a transit route for motorists from northern Europe travelling south to Austria and Italy. To avoid long delays check the holiday calendar in advance, or avoid the motorways altogether. Although it is a little slower, travelling on the well maintained network of main roads allows visitors to reach interesting places and see the country at a more intimate level.

GETTING TO THE BAVARIAN ALPS

GETTING TO the Bavarian Alps by car is quite easy. The only problem is that, in the summer months and over public holidays, considerable queues can build up at border crossings into Germany, especially on the frontier with Poland and the Czech Republic. However, under normal circumstances, providing that you carry the necessary documents and your car does not look disreputable, you should experience a minimum of delay and formalities at border crossings.

Non-EU citizens do not have to make a Customs declaration on arrival but there are limits on the amount of duty-free goods that can be brought in to the country (*see p286*).

Road signs to the motorway

WHAT TO TAKE

VISITORS travelling by car in Germany must carry a valid driving licence as well as their vehicle's registration document and insurance policy. Before leaving home check with your insurance company whether your policy will cover you while you are in Germany. It may be necessary to obtain a Green Card to extend the cover for the duration of your stay.

The car must carry a plate indicating country of origin and it must also be equipped with a first-aid kit and a red warning triangle for use in case of breakdown.

ROADS AND MOTORWAYS

MOTORWAYS (*Autobahn*) in Germany are toll-free and have regularly spaced petrol stations and facilities with toilets, restaurants and motels. An *Autobahn* is indicated by the letter "A" followed by a number. Some motorway signs also have the letter "E" and a number, indicating that the road crosses the German border. A *Bundesstraße* (main road) is indicated by the letter "B" and a number.

ROAD SIGNS

IN ADDITION to internationally understood road signs, on German roads there are words that clarify the meaning of the sign above. On mountain roads, for example, a warning sign showing a car tyre wrapped in a chain is accompanied by the word *"Schnee"*, which warns about driving without chains when there is snow.

CAR RENTAL

MAJOR INTERNATIONAL car rental companies such as **Hertz** and **Avis** have offices in the Bavarian Alps, particularly near railway stations and at airports. They are, however, rivalled, both with regard to price and class of car, by the Munich-based car hire company **Sixt**.

It is sometimes advantageous to rent a car from a smaller agency, particularly after comparing the prices of various companies. Telephone numbers of car rental companies can be found under *"Autovermietung"* in Yellow Pages (*Gelbe Seiten*).

Airlines and railway companies offer a variety of combined tickets that include car rental. This is usually slightly cheaper than booking each separately.

Rates for car rental vary greatly, depending primarily on the model of car chosen. For holidaymakers another option is to rent a camper van (*Wohnmobile*), which outside

One of the many picturesque roads with a view of the Alps

the holiday season can be rented for the price of a medium-sized car and offers a great deal of freedom.

Parking

Most towns and cities in the Bavarian Alps are crowded during office hours and parking is quite a problem. Town centres are less congested at weekends, when parking is usually free. Tickets issued for illegally parked vehicles usually involve complex procedures that are often more strictly followed in small towns than in cities. Drivers should take special care not to exceed the parking time paid for, as a few minutes' excess can result in a costly fine. Drivers whose car has been towed away should approach the police, who will give instructions on how to proceed.

Sign for a pay-and-display machine

Roadside Assistance

Germany has an efficient roadside assistance infrastructure. On motorways, emergency telephones *(Notrufsäulen)* are situated at intervals of 1 km (0.62 mile). ADAC, the German motoring association, is the main provider of roadside assistance. Calling for help from a roadside telephone is simple for tourists, as the location is automatically transmitted. ADAC repairmen will try to fix the car by the roadside (this is free for ADAC members), or will tow it to a garage.

When a road accident occurs, the police and an ambulance always attend, with the fire brigade or air ambulance if necessary.

On the approach roads to the motorways to Salzburg and Stuttgart are "pilot stations" *(Lotsenstationen)* where drivers can obtain information and directions. You can also hire a car with driver to show you the way.

An ARAL petrol (gas) station, one of the most widely seen in Bavaria

Petrol (Gas) Stations

Petrol and diesel stations on motorways are most often located at junctions or at *Rasthöfe* – rest areas with car parks, restaurants, bars, shops and toilets with showers.

The cost of fuel provided by the main petroleum companies (Shell, BP, Aral and DEA) is usually fairly uniform. The cheapest fuel is that sold at petrol stations in shopping centres.

Petrol stations are open until late at night, many of them 24 hours. They also sell motoring accessories, as well as newspapers and refreshments. On lesser roads and in remote or rural areas, petrol stations are likely to be few and far between.

Motorway telephone

Rules of the Road

Speed limits in Germany are 50 km/h (30 mph) in built-up areas and 100 km/h (62 mph) elsewhere. On motorways there is no speed limit unless this is indicated. When travelling with a caravan or camping trailer outside built-up areas it is 70 km/h (44 mph) and on motorways 100 km/h (62 mph). Speed traps are frequent and fines high. The maximum limit for alcohol in the blood is 0.5 per cent. Seat belts must be worn at all times, children under 12 must travel in the back seats and small children be secured in child seats. The use of mobile phones while driving is restricted to hands-free sets.

General Index

Acknowledgments

DORLING KINDERSLEY would like to thank the following people for their help in preparing this guide:

ADDITIONAL PHOTOGRAPHY
Horst Höfler, Katarzyna and Sergiusz Michalscy, Tomasz Myśluk, Werner Nikolai, Gregor M. Schmid, Oda Sternberg, Paweł Wójcik

PUBLISHING MANAGERS
Kate Poole
Helen Townsend

DTP DESIGNERS
Jason Little
Conrad Van Dyke

PRODUCTION
Sarah Dodd

CONSULTANT
Gerhard Bruschke

FACT CHECKER
Barabara Sobek

PROOFREADER
Stewart Wild

INDEXER
Hilary Bird

DIRECTOR OF PUBLISHING
Gillian Allan

EDITORIAL AND DESIGN ASSISTANCE
Arwen Burnett, Jo Cowen, Marcus Hardy, Casper Morris, Marianne Petrou and Dave Pugh.

SPECIAL ASSISTANCE
The publisher would also like to thank the following for their assistance on the guide:

Anette Alwast, Ingrid Baudrexl-Czuraj, Prof. Dr Adrianowi von Buttlarowi, Tamarze and Jackowi Draberom, Iris and Wolfgangowi Hermannom, Barbarze Januszkiewicz, Irenie Hiemeyer, Aleksandrze Markiewicz German Book Information Centre, Goethe-Institut in Warsaw, Ulliemu Nerdingerowi, Wilhelminie and Wernerowi Nikolai, Dr Elisabeth Pfaud, Margarete Roeck, Dr Thomasowi Weidnerowi and Kartographie Huber (Gerhild Kemper-Wildtraut), Käthe-Kruse-Puppen-Museum in Donauwörth, Kultur- und Fremdenverkehrsamt der Stadt Landsberg am Lech (Ulla Kurz), Kur- und Ferienland Garmisch-Partenkirchen, Kurverwaltung Schwangau, Meteorologisches Institut der Universität München (Heinz Lösslein), Presse-und Öffentlichkeitsarbeit der Stadt Pfaffenhofen an der Ilm Sr. (Elisabeth Benen), Rieskrater-Museum in Nördlingen (Dr Michael Schieber, Monika Spörl), Stadt Donauwörth (Bernhard Kunz, Gudrun Reißer), Steigenberger Drei Mohren (Robert Strohe), Theresienthaler Krystallglasmanufaktur GmbH (Ralph A.W. Wenzel), Tourismus Straubing (Bettina Schauer), Tourist Info Kochel am See (Sabine Rauscher), Touristinformation Stadt Freising (Barabara Sibinger), Verkehrsverband Laufen, Verkehrsverein Lindau (Hans Stübner), Wittelsbacher Ausgleichsfonds, Inventarverwaltung (Andreas von Majewski, Sibille Herz)

PHOTOGRAPHY PERMISSIONS
The publisher would also like to thank all the people and institutions who allowed photographs belonging to them to be reproduced, as well as granting permission to use photographs from their archives:

AB PhotoDesign in Kellberg (Dionys Asenkerschbaumer), Alois Dallmayr in Munich (Patricia Massmann), Alpines Museum in Munich (Ulrike Gehrig), Amt für Tourismus Straubing (Frau Baumhof), Archäologische Staatssammlung in Munich (Dr Dorothea van Endert) Artothek (Jürgen Hinrichs), Augsburger Puppenkiste, Bavaria Filmstadt in Munich, Bayerische Staatsgemäldesammlungen (Prof. Dr Christian Lenz, Christina Schwill, D. Cornelia Syre), Bayerische Verwaltung der Staatlichen Schlösser, Gärten und Seen (Eva Gerum, Michael Teichmann), Bayerisches Nationalmuseum in Munich (Dr Nina Gockerell, Dr Sgoff) Benediktinerabtei Ottobeuren, Bildvorlagen Römerschatz – Gäubodenmuseum in Straubing (Dr Prammer), Bischöfliches Ordinariat Augsburg (Monsignore Josef Heigl), Bischöfliches Ordinariat Passau (Franz Sr. Gabriel) BMW Group Mobile Tradition and.V. (Nikola von Ondarza), Britstock-Ifa in London, Café Luitpold in Munich (Carmen Brenner), Deutsche Bahn (Hans-Joachim Kirsche), Deutsche Press Agentur (Tanja Teichmann), Deutsches Museum in Munich (Marlene Schwarz), Diözesanbauamt Eichstätt (Dr Claudia Grund), Erzbischöfliches Ordinariat München (Dr Norbert Jocher, Dr Hans Ramisch, Hans Rohrmann, Gabriele Skornia), Flash Press Media (Sylwia Wilgocka), Flughafen München GmbH (Wilhelm Hennies, Fr. Kiener), Foto-Production in Gilching (Gregor M. Schmid), Fremdenverkehrsamt in Altötting, Fremdenverkehrsamt in Mühldorf (Peter-Alexander Berger), Galerie im Lenbachhaus in Munich (Daniela Müller), Haus der Bayerischen Geschichte-Bildarchiv in Augsburg (Dr Rudolf Wildmoser), Haus der Kunst in Munich (Claus Vogel), Heimatmuseum der Stadt Bad Tölz, Hilton München Park (Katharina Rösel), Hotel Königshof in Munich (Frieder Lempp), Hotel Residenz Passau (Dieter Austen), Hunsingers Pacific in Munich (M. Hunsinger), Institut für Kunst Geschichte TU in Brunswick 36b, 37c, 37br, 37bl, 39c, 44c, 45c, 49cl, Jura-Museum in Eichstätt (Jutta Streit), Alter Simpl Café in Munich, Kristall Museum Riedenburg, Kurdirektion des Berchtesgadener Land (Vroni Aigner, Birgit Tica), Landeshauptstadt München, Referat für Arbeit und Wirtschaft Fremdenverkehrsamt (Stefan Böttcher), Leopold restaurant in Munich, Marionettebühne in Munich, Minaralogische Staatssammlung in Munich (Dr G Simon), Münchner Stadtmuseum (Dr Götz), Museum "Reich der Kristalle" in Munich, Neue Messe München GmbH (Julia Spiegelhalder), Nürnberger Bratwurst Glöckl am Dom in Munich (Nadja Beck), Paläontologisches Museum in Munich (Dr H. Mayr), Parkhotel in Donauwörth (Eugen Schuler), Passauer Glasmuseum (Birgitte Holles), Ratskeller München (Renate Werner), SiemensForum in Munich (Dr Marie Schlund), Shop with devotional figures C. Huber in Augsburg, Staatliche Antikensammlungen und Glyptothek (Dr Martin Schulz, Vincent Brickmann), Staatliche Sammlung Ägyptischer Kunst in Munich, Stadt Kempten (Elli Cascio, Marlene Köhler), Stadtarchiv München (Dr Graf), Stadtbildstelle Augsburg, Stadtmuseum in Munich, Ursulinenkloster Straubing (Sr. Judith Reis, Oberin), Verkehrsamt der Stadt Nördlingen (Katja Jaumann), Villa Stuck in Munich, ZEFA (Ewa Kozłowska), Zentrum für Aussergewöhnliche Museen in Munich (Frau Klauda)

PICTURE CREDITS
t = top; tl = top left; tc = top centre; tr = top right; c= centre; cb = centre below; ca = centre above; cl = centre left; clb = centre left below; cla = centre left above; cr = centre right; crb = centre right below; cra = centre right above; b = bottom; bl = bottom left; bc = bottom centre; br = bottom right; bra = bottom right above; tla = top left above; tlb = top left below; trb = top right below

Alois Dallmayr (Munich) 278cl
Alpines Museum (Munich) 89b, 91c
Amt für Tourismus Straubing 31t
Archäologische Staatssammlung (Munich) 36b, 107c
Artothek 27tr, 52tr, 119tc, 125t
W. Bahnmüller 43c, 43bl

Bayer & Mitko 119b, 124b
Joachim Blauel 42tr, 43tc, 43tc, 43tp, 43cl, 43bl, 113c, 118ca, 118cb, 119tc, 119c, 120b, 121c, 121b, 122tr, 122ca, 123tl, 123crb, 123bl, 124tr, 124cl, 125cl, 125br
Blauel & Gnamm 43bl, 117b, 118tl, 118b, 119tr, 120t, 120c, 121t, 122cb, 123trb, 123cla,
Sophie-R. Gnamm 92t
Toni Ott 42bl, 42br
Augsburger Puppenkiste 247tr
Bayerische Staatsgemäldesammlungen (Munich) 115t
Bayerische Verwaltung der Staatlichen Schlösser, Gärten und Seen 8–9, 38t, 40t, 46 cl, 47tl, 47tr, 75tl, 132br, 133crb
Bayerisches Nationalmuseum (Munich) 53śca, 108tl, 108tr, 108tla, 108tlb, 108b, 109t, 109ca, 109cb, 109b
Bildvorlagen Römerschatz – Gäubodenmuseum (Straubing) 35b, 180tl
Bischöfliches Ordinariat Passau 23t, 26tp, 41cl, 184tl, 184tc, 184br, 189tl
BMW Group Mobile Tradition & V. (Munich) 19t, 134tr
Britstock-Ifa
Rolf Zscharnack 70
Café Luitpold (Munich) 264cla
Deutsche Bahn (Berlin)
Mann 296tl
Deutsche Presse Agentur (dpa) 19b, 21tl, 28t, 28b, 29t, 29b, 33t, 33b, 49bra, 268tr
Deutsches Historisches Museum (Berlin) 39b, 48c, 49bl
Deutsches Museum (Munich) 10, 94t, 94ca, 94cb, 94b, 95t, 95ca, 95b, 96t, 96c, 96b, 97t, 97c, 97b, 166br
Erzbischöfliches Ordinariat München 60b, 61t, 61c, 61bl, 61bc, 61br, 63t
Flash Press Media 48bl
Flughafen München GmbH 294cr, 294bl, 295tl, 295bc
Fremdenverkehrsamt (Altötting) 20tl, 30tr, 191b
Fremdenverkehrsamt (Mühldorf) 28c
Galerie im Lenbachhaus (Munich) 105cla, 105crb, 112cla, 211cr, 214cr
Haus der Bayerischen Geschichte Bildarchiv 45t, 48t
Haus der Kunst (Munich) 107t
Hilton München Park 265tl
Horst Höfler 256bl
Hotel Königshof (Munich) 255tl
Hotel Residenz Passau 254bl
Hunsingers Pacific (Munich) 264crb
Jura-Museum (Eichstätt) 160b
Kristall Museum Riedenburg 179trb

Kurdirektion des Berchtesgadener Land 48br, 197bc
Landeshauptstadt München, Referat für Arbeit und Wirtschaft Fremdenverkehrsamt
Bjarne Geiges 269bl
W. Hausmann 50–51
Robert Hetz 49tl
Rudolf Sterlinger 2–3
Marionettenbühne (Munich) 136tl
Katarzyna and Sergiusz Michalscy 17t, 217clb, 240bl
Münchner Stadtmuseum 4t, 5cl, 26cl, 26bl, 65b
Dorothee Jordens-Meintker 34, 44b
Museum "Reich der Kristalle" (Munich) 117t
Neue Messe München GmbH
Loske 139tr
Werner Nikolai 30b
Nürnberger Bratwurst Glöckl am Dom (Munich) 265cr
Paläontologisches Museum (Munich) 112tr
Parkhotel in Donauwörth 255cl
Passauer Glasmuseum 187c
Ratskeller München 265br
Gregor M. Schmid half-title, 86, 154
SiemensForum (Munich)
Bernd Müller 81t
Staatliche Antikensammlungen und Glyptothek (Munich) 52ca, 114c, 116b
Staatliche Sammlung Ägyptischer Kunst (Munich) 77cl
Stadt Kempten 233tc, 233bl
Stadtarchiv München 102b
Oda Sternberg 84b
Tomasz Myśluk 222tr, 222cl, 223bc
Verkehrsamt der Stadt Nördlingen 11
Villa Stuck (Munich) 15b
Paweł Wójcik 20tl, 23b, 23bl, 29c, 31c, 45bl, 49br, 57clb, 62c, 65t, 68tl, 68tr, 72br, 73tl, 78b, 80c, 80b, 82t, 83c, 84t, 85c, 100t, 101t, 103c, 104t, 112cb, 114t, 138tl, 161bl, 178t, 201tr, 201br, 222br, 229tr, 229c, 232tl, 232tr, 232cl, 232br, 254tc, 256c, 278tc, 280tr, 280cla, 280clb, 280cra, 280crb, 280cb, 280bl, 280cb, 281tl, 281tc, 281tr, 281cl, 281c, 281cra, 281crb, 281cr, 281bl, 281bc, 281bca, 281bc, 286c, 288tl, 289bl, 293tc, 298tr, 298clb, 298b, 302c, 303tl, 303dcb
ZEFA 62t, 220
Damm 218
Rossenbach 153tl
Zentrum für Aussergewöhnliche Museen (Munich) 64c

All other images ©Dorling Kindersley.
For further information see: www.dkimages.com

Phrase Book

IN AN EMERGENCY

Where is the telephone?	Wo ist das Telefon?	voh ist duss tel-e-fone?
Help!	Hilfe!	**hilf**-uh
Please call a doctor	Bitte rufen Sie einen Arzt	**bitt**-uh **roof**'n zee ine-en artst
Please call the police	Bitte rufen Sie die Polizei	**bitt**-uh **roof**'n zee dee poli-**tsy**
Please call the fire brigade	Bitte rufen Sie die Feuerwehr	**bitt**-uh **roof**'n zee dee **foyer**-vayr
Stop!	Halt!	**hult**

COMMUNICATION ESSENTIALS

Yes	Ja	**yah**
No	Nein	**nine**
Please	Bitte	**bitt**-uh
Thank you	Danke	dunk-uh
Excuse me	Verzeihung	fair-**tsy**-hoong
Hello (good day)	Guten Tag	**goot**-en tahk
Hello	Grüß Gott	**grooss** got
Goodbye	Auf Wiedersehen	owf-**veed**-er-zay-ern
Good evening	Guten Abend	goot'n **ahb**'nt
Good night	Gute Nacht	goot-uh **nukht**
Until tomorrow	Bis morgen	biss **morg**'n
See you	Tschüss	**chooss**
See you	Servus	sayr **voos**
What is that?	Was ist das?	voss ist duss
Why?	Warum?	var-**room**
Where?	Wo?	**voh**
When?	Wann?	**vunn**
today	heute	**hoyt**-uh
tomorrow	morgen	**morg**'n
month	Monat	**mohn**-aht
night	Nacht	**nukht**
afternoon	Nachmittag	**nahkh**-mit-tahk
morning	Morgen	**morg**'n
year	Jahr	yar
there	dort	**dort**
here	hier	**hear**
week	Woche	**vokh**-uh
yesterday	gestern	**gest**'n
evening	Abend	**ahb**'nt

USEFUL PHRASES

How are you? (informal)	Wie geht's?	vee gayts
Fine, thanks	Danke, es geht mir gut	dunk-uh, es gayt meer goot
Until later	Bis später	biss **shpay**-ter
Where is/are?	Wo ist/sind...?	voh ist/sind
How far is it to...?	Wie weit ist es...?	vee **vite** ist ess
Do you speak English?	Sprechen Sie Englisch?	shpresh'n zee **eng**-glish
I don't understand	Ich verstehe nicht	ish fair-**shtay**-uh nisht
Could you speak more slowly?	Könnten Sie langsamer sprechen?	**kurnt**-en zee **lung**-zam-er **shpresh**'n

USEFUL WORDS

large	groß	**grohss**
small	klein	**kline**
hot	heiß	**hyce**
cold	kalt	**kult**
good	gut	**goot**
bad	böse/schlecht	**burss**-uh/**shlesht**
open	geöffnet	g'**urff**-nett
closed	geschlossen	g'**shloss**'n
left	links	**links**
right	rechts	**reshts**
straight ahead	geradeaus	g'**rah**-der-**owss**

MAKING A TELEPHONE CALL

I would like to make a phone call	Ich möchte telefonieren	ish mer-**shtuh** tel-e-fon-**eer**'n
I'll try again later	Ich versuche es später noch einmal	ish fair-zookh-uh es **shpay**-ter nokh ine-mull
Can I leave a message?	Kann ich eine Nachricht hinterlassen?	kan ish **ine**-uh nakh-risht hint-er-**lahss**-en
answer phone	Anrufbeantworter	an-roof-be-**ahnt**-vort-er
telephone card	Telefonkarte	tel-e-**fohn**-kart-uh
receiver	Hörer	**hur**-er
mobile	Handy	han-dee
engaged (busy)	besetzt	b'zetst
wrong number	Falsche Verbindung	falsh-uh fair-**bin**-doong

SIGHTSEEING

entrance ticket	Eintrittskarte	ine-tritz-**kart**-uh
cemetery	Friedhof	**freed**-hofe
train station	Bahnhof	**barn**-hofe
gallery	Galerie	**gall**-er-ree
information	Auskunft	**owss**-koonft
church	Kirche	**keersh**-uh
garden	Garten	**gart**'n
palace/castle	Palast/Schloss	pallast/shloss
place (square)	Platz	**plats**
bus stop	Haltestelle	**hal**-te-shtel-uh
free admission	Eintritt frei	ine-tritt fry

SHOPPING

Do you have/ Is there...?	Gibt es...?	geept ess
How much does it cost?	Was kostet das?	voss **kost**'t duss?
When do you open/ close?	Wann öffnen Sie? schließen Sie?	vunn **off**'n zee? **shlees**'n zee?
this	das	duss
expensive	teuer	**toy**-er
cheap	preiswert	**price**-vurt
size	Größe	**gruhs**-uh
number	Nummer	**noom**-er
colour	Farbe	**farb**-uh
brown	braun	brown
black	schwarz	**shvarts**
red	rot	**roht**
blue	blau	**blau**
green	grün	**groon**
yellow	gelb	**gelp**

TYPES OF SHOP

chemist (pharmacy)	Apotheke	appo-**tay**-kuh
bank	Bank	**bunk**
market	Markt	**markt**
travel agency	Reisebüro	**rye**-zer-boo-roe
department store	Warenhaus	**vahr**'n-hows
chemist's, drugstore	Drogerie	droog-er-**ree**
hairdresser	Friseur	freezz-**er**
newspaper kiosk	Zeitungskiosk	tsytoongs-kee-osk
bookshop	Buchhandlung	**bookh**-hant-loong
bakery	Bäckerei	beck-er-**eye**
butcher	Metzgerei	mets-ger-**eye**
post office	Post	**posst**
shop/store	Geschäft/Laden	gush-**eft/lard**'n
film processing shop	Photogeschäft	fo-to-gush-**eft**
clothes shop	Kleiderladen, Boutique	klyder-lard'n boo-**teek**-uh

STAYING IN A HOTEL

Do you have any vacancies?	Haben Sie noch Zimmer frei?	harb'n zee nokh tsimm-er-fry
with twin beds?	mit zwei Betten?	mitt tsvy bett'n
with a double bed?	mit einem Doppelbett?	mitt ine'm dopp'l-bet
with a bath?	mit Bad?	mitt bart
with a shower?	mit Dusche?	mitt doosh-uh
I have a reservation	Ich habe eine Reservierung	ish harb-uh ine-uh rez-er-veer-oong
key	Schlüssel	shlooss'l
porter	Pförtner	pfert-ner

EATING OUT

Do you have a table for...?	Haben Sie einen Tisch für...?	harb'n zee tish foor
I would like to reserve a table	Ich möchte eine Reservierung machen	ish mer-shtuh ine-uh rezer-veer-oong makh'n
I'm a vegetarian	Ich bin Vegetarier	ish bin vegg-er-tah-ree-er
Waiter!	Herr Ober!	hair oh-bare!
The bill (check), please	Die Rechnung, bitte	dee resh-noong bitt-uh
breakfast	Frühstück	froo-shtock
lunch	Mittagessen	mit-targ-ess'n
dinner	Abendessen	arb'nt-ess'n
bottle	Flasche	flush-uh
dish of the day	Tagesgericht	tahg-es-gur-isht
main dish	Hauptgericht	howpt-gur-isht
dessert	Nachtisch	nahkh-tish
cup	Tasse	tass-uh
wine list	Weinkarte	vine-kart-uh
glass	Glas	glars
spoon	Löffel	lerff'l
fork	Gabel	gahb'l
teaspoon	Teelöffel	tay-lerff'l
knife	Messer	mess-er
starter (appetizer)	Vorspeise	for-shpize-uh
the bill	Rechnung	resh-noong
tip	Trinkgeld	trink-gelt
plate	Teller	tell-er

MENU DECODER

Apfel	upf'l	apple
Apfelsine	upf'l-seen-uh	orange
Aprikose	upri-kawz-uh	apricot
Artischocke	arti-shokh-uh-	artichoke
Aubergine	or-ber-jeen-uh	aubergine (eggplant)
Banane	bar-narn-uh	banana
Beefsteak	beef-stayk	steak
Bier	beer	beer
Bohnensuppe	burn-en-zoop-uh	bean soup
Bratkartoffeln	brat-kar-toff'ln	fried potatoes
Bratwurst	brat-voorst	fried sausage
Brezel	bret-sell	pretzel
Brot	brot	bread
Brühe	bruh-uh	broth
Butter	boot-ter	butter
Champignon	shum-pin-yong	mushroom
Currywurst	kha-ree-voorst	sausage with curry sauce
Ei	eye	egg
Eis	ice	ice/ ice cream
Ente	ent-uh	duck
Erdbeeren	ayrt-beer'n	strawberries
Fisch	fish	fish
Fleisch	flaysh	meat
Forelle	for-ell-uh	trout
Gans	ganns	goose
gebraten	g'braat'n	fried
gegrillt	g'grilt	grilled
gekocht	g'kokht	boiled
geräuchert	g'rowk-ert	smoked
Geflügel	g'floog'l	poultry

Gemüse	g'mooz-uh	vegetables
Gulasch	goo-lush	goulash
Hähnchen (Hendl)	haynsh'n	chicken
Hering	hair-ing	herring
Himbeeren	him-beer'n	raspberries
Kaffee	kaf-fay	coffee
Kalbfleisch	kalp-flysh	veal
Kaninchen	ka-neensh'n	rabbit
Karotte	car-ott-uh	carrot
Kartoffelpüree	kar-toff'l-poor-ay	mashed potatoes
Käse	kayz-uh	cheese
Knoblauch	k'nob-lowkh	garlic
Knödel	k'nerd'l	dumpling
Kuchen	kookh'n	cake
Lachs	lahkhs	salmon
Leber	lay-ber	liver
Marmelade	marmer-lard-uh	marmalade, jam
Milch	milsh	milk
Mineralwasser	minn-er-arl-vuss-er	mineral water
Nuss	nooss	nut
Öl	erl	oil
Olive	o-leev-uh	olive
Pfeffer	pfeff-er	pepper
Pfirsich	pfir-zish	peach
Pflaume	pflow-me	plum
Pommes frites	pomm-fritt	chips/ French fries
Rindfleisch	rint-flysh	beef
Rührei	rhoo-er-eye	scrambled eggs
Saft	zuft	juice
Salat	zal-aat	salad
Salz	zults	salt
Sauerkirschen	zow-er-keersh'n	cherries
Sauerkraut	zow-er-krowt	sauerkraut
Sekt	zekt	sparkling wine
Senf	zenf	mustard
scharf	sharf	spicy
Schlagsahne	shlahgg-zarn-uh	whipped cream
Schnitzel	shnitz'l	veal or pork cutlet
Schweinefleisch	shvine-flysh	pork
Semmel	tsem-mel	bread roll
Spargel	shparg'l	asparagus
Spiegelei	shpeeg'l-eye	fried egg
Spinat	shpin-art	spinach
Tee	tay	tea
Tomate	tom-art-uh	tomato
Wassermelone	vuss-er-me-lohn-uh	watermelon
Wein	vine	wine
Weintrauben	vine-trowb'n	grapes
Wiener Würstchen	veen-er voorst-sh'n	frankfurter
Zitrone	tsi-trohn-uh	lemon
Zucker	tsook-er	sugar
Zwiebel	tsveeb'l	onion

NUMBERS

0	null	nool
1	eins	eye'ns
2	zwei	tsvy
3	drei	dry
4	vier	feer
5	fünf	foonf
6	sechs	zex
7	sieben	zeeb'n
8	acht	uhkht
9	neun	noyn
10	zehn	tsayn
11	elf	elf
12	zwölf	tserlf
13	dreizehn	dry-tsayn
14	vierzehn	feer-tsayn
15	fünfzehn	foonf-tsayn
16	sechzehn	zex-tsayn
17	siebzehn	zeep-tsayn
18	achtzehn	uhkht-tsayn
19	neunzehn	noyn-tsayn
20	zwanzig	tsvunn-tsig

EYEWITNESS *TRAVEL GUIDES*

COUNTRY GUIDES

AUSTRALIA • CANADA • CRUISE GUIDE TO EUROPE AND THE
MEDITERRANEAN • CUBA • EGYPT • FRANCE • GERMANY
GREAT BRITAIN • GREECE: ATHENS & THE MAINLAND
THE GREEK ISLANDS • IRELAND • ITALY • JAPAN
MEXICO • POLAND • PORTUGAL • SCOTLAND
SINGAPORE • SOUTH AFRICA • SPAIN
THAILAND • GREAT PLACES TO STAY
IN EUROPE • A TASTE OF SCOTLAND

REGIONAL GUIDES

BALI & LOMBOK • BARCELONA & CATALONIA • CALIFORNIA
EUROPE • FLORENCE & TUSCANY • FLORIDA • HAWAII
JERUSALEM & THE HOLY LAND • LOIRE VALLEY
MILAN & THE LAKES • MUNICH & THE BAVARIAN ALPS • NAPLES WITH
POMPEII & THE AMALFI COAST • NEW ENGLAND • NEW ZEALAND
PROVENCE & THE COTE d'AZUR • SARDINIA
SEVILLE & ANDALUSIA • SICILY • SOUTHWEST USA & LAS VEGAS
A TASTE OF TUSCANY • VENICE & THE VENETO

CITY GUIDES

AMSTERDAM • BERLIN • BOSTON • BRUSSELS • BUDAPEST
CHICAGO • CRACOW • DELHI, AGRA & JAIPUR • DUBLIN
ISTANBUL • LISBON • LONDON • MADRID
MOSCOW • NEW YORK • PARIS • PRAGUE • ROME
SAN FRANCISCO • STOCKHOLM • ST. PETERSBURG
SYDNEY • VIENNA • WARSAW • WASHINGTON, DC

NEW FOR AUTUMN 2002

INDIA • MOROCCO • NEW ORLEANS • TURKEY

FOR INFORMATION ON OUR NEW EYEWITNESS TOP TEN POCKET SERIES
AND ON
TRAVEL PLANNERS, CITY MAPS, &
PHRASEBOOKS

VISIT US AT
www.dk.com

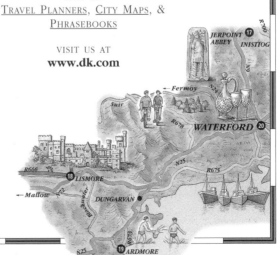

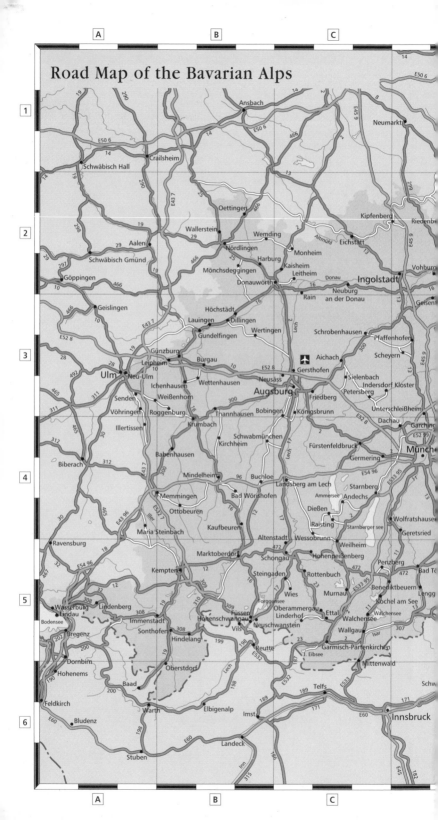